Entrepreneurship in Africa

# African Dynamics

VOLUME 15

The titles published in this series are listed at *brill.com/ad*

# Entrepreneurship in Africa

*Edited by*

Akinyinka Akinyoade
Ton Dietz
Chibuike Uche

BRILL

LEIDEN | BOSTON

This research is part of a wider project on increasing the value of Dutch multinationals for national economies: a comparative study of Kenya and Nigeria. The above project is part of the research agenda of the Knowledge Platform on Inclusive Development Policies, which is funded by the Dutch Ministry of Foreign Affairs through NWO-WOTRO (2014–2017).

Names: Akinyoade, Akinyinka, editor, author. | Dietz, Ton, editor. | Uche, Chibuike U., editor, author.
Title: Entrepreneurship in Africa / edited by Akinyinka Akinyoade, Ton Dietz, Chibuike Uche.
Description: Boston : Brill, 2017. | Series: African dynamics ; V. 15 | Includes bibliographical references and index.
Identifiers: LCCN 2017027679 (print) | LCCN 2017028540 (ebook) | ISBN 9789004351615 (E-book) | ISBN 9789004349773 (pbk : alk. paper)
Subjects: LCSH: Entrepreneurship--Africa, Sub-Saharan. | Businesspeople--Africa, Sub-Saharan. | Africa, Sub-Saharan--Economic conditions--21st century.
Classification: LCC HC800 (ebook) | LCC HC800 .E567 2017 (print) | DDC 338.040967--dc23
LC record available at https://lccn.loc.gov/2017027679

Typeface for the Latin, Greek, and Cyrillic scripts: "Brill". See and download: brill.com/brill-typeface.

ISSN 1568-1777
ISBN 978-90-04-34977-3 (paperback)
ISBN 978-90-04-35161-5 (e-book)



This book is printed on acid-free paper and produced in a sustainable manner.

# Contents

# List of Illustrations

## Figures



## Tables

# Notes on Contributors

*Kenneth Amaeshi*
Ph.D. (2007), University of Warwick, is a Professor of Business and Sustainable Development at the University of Edinburgh, United Kingdom. He has published many articles on sustainability strategy, leadership, international management, ethics and governance in developing economies.

*Akinyinka Akinyoade*
Ph.D. (2007) International Institute of Social Studies Den Haag, is Senior Researcher at the African Studies Centre, Leiden University. He has published articles and books on Africa, including *African Roads to Prosperity: People en Route to Socio-cultural and Economic Transformations* (Brill 2015).

*Crescence Marie France Okah Atenga*
Ph.D. student in criminal law, University of Lorraine (France), is a Temporary Lecturer and Research Assistant at Haute Alsace University, Institute of technology. She has published many articles and a book titled *Sanction Pénale et Règlementation Bancaire: cas de la Zone CEMAC*, (EUE, 2012).

*Ton Dietz*
(Ph.D. 1987, University of Amsterdam) was director of the African Studies Centre, Leiden University, and Professor African development at the Leiden University, as well as guest professor Human Geography at the University of Amsterdam. He has published many monographs, edited books, journal articles and other publications, many of those about Africa. Recent example (together with others): *African Engagements. Africa Negotiating an Emerging Multipolar World* (Brill 2011).

*Françoise Okah Efogo*
Ph.D. (2016), University of Yaounde II- Cameroon is Lecturer and Researcher at that university. She has published a book and some articles including *Female Entrepreneurship and Growth in Cameroon* (2015) and *The Role of Entrepreneurship Motivations on Microfinance Institutions Performance* (2016).

*Emiel L. Eijdenberg*
Ph.D. (2016, University of Amsterdam), University Hohenheim in Stuttgart (Germany), is a Postdoctoral Researcher on sustainable entrepreneurship at the Bottom of the Pyramid at that university. He has published much of his

research in books and many scientific journals, including the International Journal of Entrepreneurial Behavior and Research, the Journal of Enterprising Culture, and the Journal of Entrepreneurship in Emerging Economies.

*Abel Ebeh Ezeoha*

Ph.D. (2008), University of Nigeria, is a Senior Lecturer at Ebonyi State University. He has published articles on Africa, including *Corporate Finance in Africa: The Interactive Impact of Firm Nationality and Characteristics* (Review of Development Economics, 2016).

*Yagoub Ali Gangi*

Ph.D. (1999), Manchester Metropolitan University, U.K. is Associate Professor of Economics at Ahmed Bin Mohamed Military College, Qatar. He was Associate Professor of Economics at University of Khartoum. His research interest are FDI and Entrepreneurship. He has published many articles in these fields.

*Miguel Heilbron*

MSc (2008), works as an independent consultant at Social Innovation Works and lectures at Nyenrode New Business School, Amsterdam. He works on social innovation and development. He contributed to the Venture Finance in Africa research project (VC4A, 2015).

*Uwafiokun Idemudia*

Ph.D. (2007), Lancaster University, is Associate Professor of Development Studies and African Studies at York university, Toronto Canada. He has published monographs, and many articles on Natural resources, development, corporate social responsibility and conflict in Africa.

*Nsubili Isaga*

Ph.D. (2012), VU University, Amsterdam, is a lecturer of business studies at Mzumbe University Tanzania. She has published monograph and articles on Tanzania, including *Owner-manager motives and the growth of SMEs in developing countries: Evidence from furniture industry in Tanzania* (2015).

*Afam Ituma*

Ph.D. (2005), Brunel University (UK), is an Associate Professor of Entrepreneurship and Management Studies at Federal University Ndufu-Alike, Ikwo (FUNAI) Nigeria. He has published widely cited research on a broad range of people management issues in developing economies, in a number of top-tier journals.

*Jane N.O. Khayesi*
Ph.D (2010), University of Lausanne, is a Lecturer in Management at Essex Business School. She has published on social capital and entrepreneurship in Africa in top tier journals.

*Rebecca I. Kiconco*
Ph.D. Candidate, Eindhoven University of Technology. Faculty staff at Makerere University Business School. She has carried out research on Mobile technology adoption, Taxation, and Entrepreneurship in Uganda.

*Peter Knorringa*
Ph.D. (1995), ISS/ Erasmus University Rotterdam, is Professor of Private Sector & Development at that university, and Director of the Centre for Frugal Innovation in Africa. His research focuses on the developmental implications of business activities.

*Jerry Kolo*
is Professor of Urban Planning, and Coordinator of the Master of Urban Planning program at the American University of Sharjah in the United Arab Emirates. He specializes in political ecology; public policy planning; and sustainable community planning. Jerry has extensive consulting and public service experience with municipal and non-profit agencies.

*Addisu Lashitew*
is a post-doctoral researcher at Rotterdam School of Management of Erasmus University. He holds a PhD (2014) in economics from the University of Groningen. His area of research includes firm innovation, productivity and sustainability issues in emerging and developing countries.

*André Leliveld*
Ph.D. (1994), is senior researcher at the African Studies Centre, Leiden University, and Associate Director of the Centre for Frugal Innovation in Africa. He works on innovation and development in Africa. He co-edited *Transforming Innovations in Africa* (Brill, 2012).

*Marta Lindvert*
Mid Sweden University is a Ph.D. candidate within business. Her research focus on financing for women entrepreneurs in developing countries, with the latest publication *Perceptions of financial sources among women entrepreneurs in Tanzania,* AJEMS 2015.

*Nnamdi O. Madichie*

is Director of the Centre for Research & Enterprise at the London School of Business and Management. He specialises in marketing and entrepreneurship in developing countries. He is author of *A Preliminary Assessment of Middle East Investments in Sub-Saharan Africa: Insights from the Mobile Telecom Sector.*

*Hesham E. Mohamed*

Ph.D. (2000), University of Khartoum, Sudan. Former Associate Professor of Management, University of Khartoum. Currently Associate Professor at Ahmed Bin Mohamed MC, Doha. His research interests are in organization structure & context and service quality. He published many articles in these fields in international journals.

*Knowledge C. Mpofu*

is HND Course Leader at the London School of Business and Management. He specialises in Organisational leadership/ Change, SMEs and ICT development. He is co-author of an award-winning paper *Understanding ICT adoption in the small firm sector in Southern Africa.*

*Albogast Kilangi Musabila*

Ph.D. (2012), VU University, Amsterdam, is a Lecturer in Business Management, Procurement and Logistics Management, as well as Information System and Technology. He is a holder of PhD in Information Technology Management from VU University, Amsterdam.

*Ayodeji Olukoju*

(Ph.D., Ibadan, 1991) is Professor of History, University of Lagos, Nigeria. His publications on maritime, social and economic history include *The Liverpool of West Africa* (2004) *and Culture and Customs of Liberia* (2006).

*Eunice Abbam Quaye*

Bachelor of Arts (Geography and Sociology) with First Class Honours at the University of Cape Coast, Ghana (2014). She has professional experience as a Business Development Officer, an Executive Administrator, as well as a tutor of Geography and Social Studies in Ghana. Honours include: Dean's Award for Academic Excellence (2011/2012 and 2012/2013).

*Miriam Siun*

research master's student in African Studies in Leiden. Her current research activity is on gender dynamics within networks in market places in Nigeria.

*Arthur Sserwanga*
Ph.D. (2010), Makerere University, is Professor of Entrepreneurship and Vice Chancellor at Muteesa I Royal University. He has published a number of articles and book chapters on entrepreneurship in Uganda. He is a founder of Prison Education Project-Uganda.

*Rob van Tulder*
is a professor of international business-society management at Rotterdam School of Management, Erasmus University (RSM). His research has been published extensively on the topics of European business, multinationals, high-tech industries, corporate social responsibility, network strategies and other topics.

*Chibuike Uche*
Ph.D. (1997) London School of Economics, is the Stephen Ellis Professor of the Governance of Finance and Integrity in Africa at the African Studies Centre, Leiden University. His current research interests include, corporate governance and ethics, financial regulation and business history.

*Jaap Voeten*
Ph.D. is a Research Fellow at the Tilburg School of Economics and Management (TiSEM) Tilburg University.

CHAPTER 1

# Introduction

*Akinyinka Akinyoade, Ton Dietz and Chibuike Uche*

The term "entrepreneur" was first used in 1755 to describe "someone who exercises business judgement in the face of uncertainty" (Bull and Willard 1993). It involves strategic planning and risk taking (Cf: Nijkamp 2003; Shimizu 2012; Luchsinger and Bagby 1987). One of the earliest definitions of entrepreneurship describes it as the combination of resources in new ways (Tsai and Ghoshal 1998; Schumpeter 1976). Entrepreneurship is therefore more than simply starting or inheriting a business. It "is a process through which individuals identify opportunities, allocate resources, and create value. This creation of value is often through the identification of unmet needs or [...] of opportunities for change." Generally, "entrepreneurs see 'problems' as 'opportunities,' then take action to identify the solutions to those problems and the customers who will pay to have those problems solved." Entrepreneurial success is thus "simply a function of the ability of an entrepreneur to see these opportunities in the marketplace, initiate change (or take advantage of change) and create value through solutions." (Cf. Foriwaa and Akuamoah-Boateng 2013; this definition can be found in Watson 2011: 1).

It is the duty of entrepreneurs to consistently seek out opportunities from their environment. Such opportunities can be in the form of the creation of new products and services or the use of existing products and services in new ways. Such opportunities therefore depend on the specificities of the local environment. In other words, entrepreneurial opportunities are context specific. What constitutes an opportunity in one country may not constitute an opportunity in another country (Venkataraman and Sarasvathy 2001).

From the above, it is clear that the understanding of one's environment is critical to identifying and exploiting entrepreneurial opportunities. Embedded in entrepreneurship are the concepts of strategy and risk (Ogbor 2009). With respect to the importance of strategy in entrepreneurship, it has been noted that firms generally have to make strategic choices if they are to survive. Such choices include: the selection of goals; deciding on the products and services to offer; deciding on the design and configuration of policies that determine how the firm positions itself to compete in product markets; determining the appropriate level of scope and diversity of the firm's operations; and, deciding on the design of the organisational structure, administrative system and policy

 | DOI 10.1163/9789004351615_002

that would be used to define and coordinate work. It is the integration and combination of the above choices that culminates in an organisational strategy (Rumelt et al. 1991). Such strategies allow firms to be innovative, creative and responsible for the decisions they take (Ireland et al. 2009).

Although strategy may improve the chances of entrepreneurial success, it does not eliminate the risks associated with entrepreneurship. In fact, it is generally believed that engaging in new ventures or adopting new strategies are normally riskier than maintaining the status quo (Sarasvathy et al. 1998). This is mainly because of the lack of organisational experience and cohesion on the part of the entrepreneur in operationalising such new ventures or strategies (Nijkamp 2003). After all, "entrepreneurship is to a great extent, a form of art, a practice oriented endeavor that requires a sensitive and committed engagement with a range of phenomena in the surrounding world" (Berglund 2007: 75). The success of an entrepreneur is therefore not dependent on the absence of risks, but rather on the way such risks are perceived and managed.

An in-depth knowledge and understanding of a business's socio-political and economic environment is critical to the effective management of business risks. Such knowledge enables businesses to: reduce operational surprises and their associated costs or losses; identify and proactively optimise opportunities; improve the deployment and allocation of capital on the basis of risk perception; identify and develop an integrated response to multiple and cross-enterprise risks; enhance the ability of the enterprise to identify and select from among alternative risk responses – risk avoidance, reduction, sharing and acceptance – and, integrate the risk appetite of the business in the evaluation of strategic opportunities (COSO 2004).

From the above, it is clear that good planning and analytical skills as well as good reading and understanding of one's environment are essential characteristics of entrepreneurship. Understanding the administrative and political structure of nation states and the dynamics of governance in specific contexts are important strands of entrepreneurship. An appreciation of the dynamics of states and their *modus operandi* could help entrepreneurs take calculated risks. At another level, understanding the needs, goals and aspirations of host governments (central and local) are important for the formulation of effective organisational strategies.

Although the subject of entrepreneurship in Africa is increasingly attracting attention, Africa, which is currently the poorest and economically most backward continent in the world, still remains better known for its numerous social and economic vices than for its entrepreneurship prowess. While the continent's economic underdevelopment can create immense opportunities for entrepreneurship, the poor governance structure in several of the countries in the continent has greatly impeded such development. Such governance structures have simply helped to encourage the development of a corrupt and inept environment that encourages rent-seeking and racketeering to the detriment of entrepreneurial development. This results in the suboptimal exploitation of economic and entrepreneurial opportunities in many African countries. Despite the abundance of natural resources and/or economic opportunities in the continent, the above social and economic ills have, in part, been responsible for the paucity of basic infrastructure that could aid entrepreneurship and business development in the continent. Such infrastructure include roads, security, electricity and also the educational system. The essence of this book of readings is to contribute to the growing literature on the structure, theory and practice of current African entrepreneurship.

## Entrepreneurs in Africa

Historically, entrepreneurs have always played a central role in the development of nation states (Marsden 1990, 1992). Aside from rentier states, which depend extensively on the availability of mineral resource rents, most economically prosperous nations in the world have strong, innovative and competitive business enterprises and entrepreneurs as the bedrock of their economic development and prosperity. In other words, there is a positive correlation between the presence of strong and competitive business enterprises and the economic development of nations. This is not surprising, especially given the definition and characteristics of entrepreneurship, which has been highlighted above. It is therefore logical to expect countries that have a dearth of entrepreneurial skills to exhibit plenty of missed opportunities for economic enterprise and thus curtailed economic development.

Based on the above, it is not surprising that competitive and innovative business enterprises are not widespread in Africa. Although foreign multinationals have successful operations across the African landscape, this has not changed the fact that entrepreneurial skills remain thinly spread across the continent. There is thus a dearth of successful indigenous business enterprises in the continent. It is such characteristics that have also led some to conclude that "the development of large-scale industrialisation in Africa appears to be a remote possibility at least in the short to intermediate run" (Cader and Norman 2006).

Reasons that have been adduced for the entrepreneurial deficiency in Africa include the dearth of finance and management skills. Along the above lines, it has been argued that "African entrepreneurs experience serious difficulties in developing and sustaining effective organiszational arrangements"

(Kiggundu 2002). Iliffe also argued that "capital was more easily available than competent entrepreneurs" and that "the quality of management was the most important reason for [...] [African business] failure" (1983: 68–70). Several other studies have also raised similar concerns about African entrepreneurship (Cf: Harris and Rowe 1966; Steele 1975: 18; Heilman and Lucas 1997: 141). The above entrepreneurial deficiencies are responsible for the relatively short lifespans of many of the businesses started by African entrepreneurs (Cf. Forrest 1994: 328; Leap Africa 2014).

The above dynamics have no doubt negatively affected the balance of the entrepreneurship discourse in the continent. Few, for instance, dispute the old conclusion that "much that has been written about entrepreneurship in Africa makes gloomy reading" (Elkan 1988: 171). The above scenario simply suggests that Africans have, at least in general terms, been unable to understand and exploit the abundant economic opportunities in their local environment. Specifically, it was the dearth of entrepreneurial skills and the resultant enormous economic and business opportunities in Africa that encouraged foreign adventurers, explorers and entrepreneurs to push for the colonisation of the continent. In this regard, it has been rightly noted that the whole idea of colonial rule, at least in British Africa, was promoted by British commercial interests in the continent (Cain and Hopkins 1980; Tignor 1987; Hopkins 1968). This explains the close relationship between foreign businesses and the state throughout the colonial era.

The above relationship also explains why foreign entrepreneurs were not trusted by Africans during the decolonisation era, African countries were thus almost unanimous in concluding that political independence without economic independence was nothing but an empty shell (Cf. Tignor 1998). This also explains the post-independence rush by many African states to nationalise foreign business interests. The result was that, between 1960 and 1974, the African continent witnessed more expropriations of foreign business interests than any other region in the world (Uche 2012; Rood 1976; Akinsanya 1981). Since most Africans at the time neither had the finance, nor entrepreneurial skills to run such nationalised foreign businesses, African governments had no choice but to play a major role in the nationalisation process. State ownership of nationalised foreign firms was therefore rampant. State investments in diverse economic sectors also blossomed during the period.

Over time, however, the inefficiencies of the above system became apparent. Racketeering, corruption and rent seeking blossomed. The subsequent economic crisis faced by many African countries in the 1980s forced many of them to jettison the idea of state-led industrialisation and economic growth. Most of the concerned states approached the World Bank and the International

Monetary Fund (IMF) for financial assistance. Both organisations demanded the adoption of structural adjustment policies by such African countries. This essentially meant reducing state involvement and intervention in economic activities and allowing market forces to reign in all spheres of economic activity.

It was on the basis of the above philosophy that a 1989 World Bank Report declared that entrepreneurs will play a central role in transforming African economies (World Bank 1989). The report went on to argue that achieving sustainable growth in the continent "will depend on the capacity of people from all levels of African society to respond flexibly as new market and technical opportunities emerge." The report also predicted that since the African population was bound to increase by over 100 per cent by 2020. "Africa's entrepreneurs must create these jobs. Only their initiative can ensure that the long-term demand for low-cost products and services will be met" (World Bank 1989: 155, quoted in Cader and Norman 2006: 279). More recently, a report published by the Harvard Business Review has also expressed similar optimism (Cf. Ekekwe 2016).

So what is the situation in the mid-2010s? Who are the leading African entrepreneurs? The US-based business intelligence company Forbes makes lists of the most wealthy entrepreneurs on earth, and they have a specific list for Africa:[1] "Africa's 50 richest". For the year 2015, they presented these 50 richest African entrepreneurs, with some personal information and some information about their sources of wealth. We will summarise this information based on countries, gender and racial background (as this still matters a lot in debates about colonialism and postcolonialism) See: www.forbes.com/africa-billionaires.

Among the 50 wealthiest entrepreneurs there are two (black) women (Isabel dos Santos from Angola, and Folorunsho Alakija from Nigeria), and it is interesting to note that in racial categories there are now as many "black" entrepreneurs as there are "white" entrepreneurs (if we exclude the category of North Africans). It is also clear that four countries dominate the list. South Africa is still number one in numbers, but close to losing the number one position in total accumulated wealth of its richest entrepreneurs, a total of US$28.6 billion in 2015. Nigeria follows with ten entrepreneurs and an accumulated total wealth of those ten of US$27.4 billion. Egypt and Morocco are number three and four, with seven entrepreneurs and US$16 billion for Egypt and eight entrepreneurs and US$12.8 billion for Morocco. In total, Forbes gives an accumulated wealth of close to US$100 billion for Africa's top-50 wealthiest entrepreneurs, and the entrepreneurs in the four leading countries share 85 per cent of that wealth.

1 http://www.forbes.com/africa-billionaires/list/2/#tab:overall.

TABLE 1.1 *Forbes' list of most wealthy African entrepreneurs in 2015*

| Country | White (all men) | North-African (all men) | Afro-asiatic (all men) | Black African male and female |
|---|---|---|---|---|
| South Africa | Oppenheimer 2 | | Saad 20 | Motsepe 14(m) |
| 16x | Wiese 3 | | | Ramaphosa 42(m) |
| | Rupert 4 | | | |
| | Bekker 14 | | | |
| | Mouton 24 | | | |
| | Dippenaar 35 | | | |
| | Le Roux 38 | | | |
| | Akkerman 39 | | | |
| | Gore 41 | | | |
| | Ferreira 44 | | | |
| | Attridge 45 | | | |
| | Jooste 46 | | | |
| | Ravazzotti 49 | | | |
| Nigeria | | | | Dangote 1 (m) |
| 10x | | | | Adenuga 7 (m) |
| | | | | Alakija 13 (f) |
| | | | | Otedola 16 (m) |
| | | | | Rabiu 23 (m) |
| | | | | Danjuma 30 (m) |
| | | | | Elumelu 31 (m) |
| | | | | Ovia 37 (m) |
| | | | | Indimi 40 (m) |
| | | | | Kalu 50 (m) |
| Morocco | | MohammedVI 5 | | |
| 8x | | Benjellom 12 | | |
| | | Akhannouch 18 | | |
| | | Bensalah 27 | | |
| | | Chaabi 28 | | |
| | | Sefrioui 33 | | |
| | | Elalamy 34 | | |
| | | Wakrim 43 | | |

| Country | White (all men) | North-African (all men) | Afro-asiatic (all men) | Black African male and female |
|---|---|---|---|---|
| Egypt 7x | | Nassef Sawiris 6<br>Naguib Sawiris 10<br>M. Mansour 11<br>Yousuf Mansour 15<br>Onsi Sawiris 17<br>Yasseen Mansour 19<br>Samih Sawiris 26 | | |
| Kenya 3x | | | Shah 32<br>Raval 47<br>Merali 48 | |
| Tanzania 3x | | | Dewji 21<br>Azizi 25<br>Bakhresa 36 | |
| Algeria 1x | | Rebrab 9 | | |
| Angola 1x | | | | Dos Santos 8 (f) |
| Uganda 1x | | | Ruparelia 29 | |
| Total 50x | 13 | 16 | 8 | 13 |

The wealthiest African entrepreneur (Aliko Dangote from Nigeria, see elsewhere in this book) had an estimated wealth of US$16.7 billion and was supposed to be the 67th richest person on earth. Twenty-four of the 50 richest African entrepreneurs had an accumulated estimated wealth of more than a billion US dollars. Number 50 on the list still had a respectable US$300 million. Forbes also gives information about the economic sectors in which the most wealthy Africans are engaged. Banking and financial services are mentioned most (8 times), followed by oil and gas (7), telecom (4), cement (3), real estate (3), and insurance (3), although 11 people had a "diversified portfolio", or just did "investments". In larger categories, among the 50 leading entrepreneurs, nine are mostly active in mining, ten in manufacturing, five mainly in trade, and the others either have a diversified portfolio or are mostly active in the service sector (banking, insurance, media, real estate). Not on the list yet are the most wealthy religious entrepreneurs. According to an interesting website about the most wealthy religious leaders in the world,[2] two in the top ten are from Nigeria, David Oyedepo (the world's number three and worth US$150 million) and Chris Oyakhilome (the world's number 10, with US$50 million).[3] But also in the entertainment industry people can earn fortunes. The best paid African sportsman is Cameroonian soccer player Samuel Eto'o, worth US$98 million.[4] And it can also help to be a successful political entrepreneur.[5] The list of richest African Presidents has Angola's President Dos Santos on top with an estimated wealth of US$20 billion (which is more than Africa's richest economic businessman), followed by King Mohammed VI of Morocco (who has been included in Forbes' list of Africa's top 50 of economic entrepreneurs with an accumulated wealth of US$5.7 billion in 2015). Other African Presidents have not made it to the list of billionaires in US dollars, but are on their way: Equatorial Guinea's Nguema (600 million), Kenya's Kenyatta (500 million), Cameroon's Biya (200 million), Swaziland's King Mswati (100 million), Chad's Deby (50 million) and Zimbabwe's Mugabe (10 million).

The Forbes list of wealthiest African entrepreneurs also allows us to look at the geographical distribution of the economic activities of these businessmen and women, thanks to the brief profiles of their economic biographies. Let us look at the top ten entrepreneurs. Africa's leading businessman, Aliko Dangote (again: see later in this book), can truly be seen now as a pan-African entrepreneur, with activities in 15 different African countries, from a strong base in Nigeria. Nicky Oppenheimer, number 2 on the Forbes list, and (although he recently sold his De Beers shares to multinational mining giant Anglo American) active in the diamond trade. He was/is mainly active in Botswana, Namibia

2 http://dustoffthebible.com/Blog-archive/2015/10/28/15-religious-leaders-that-make-more-money-getting-out-of-bed-than-youll-make-all-year/.

3 http://www.factsuniversity.com/religion/45-list-of-world-s-richest-pastors-2015.html even gives these two religious leaders places 1 and 2 on the list of most wealthy pastors in the world. And they add that among the ten wealthiest pastors, five are currently from Nigeria. In addition to David Oyedepo and Chris Oyakhilome, these are T.B. Joshua, Matthew Ashimolowo, and Chris Okotie.

4 http://www.africaranking.com/top-10-richest-african-footballers/.

5 http://www.africaranking.com/richest-presidents-in-africa/4/.

and South Africa and has a link with an investment firm in Singapore. Number 3 on the list, Christopher Wiese is one of the continent's leading retailers, with stakes in Shoprite, a supermarket chain active in 15 African countries now. But he clearly connects his African business empire with many activities in Europe. Tobacco and luxury goods giant Johann Rupert (number 4 on the list), although based in South Africa, mainly has a European portfolio. King Mohammed VI's (number 5) wealth is primarily in Morocco. Egypt's leading businessman, Nassef Sawiris (number 6), is mainly active in Egypt itself, but spreads his fortune by also investing in shares in multinational companies like Adidas and through a connection with the Euronext stock market in Amsterdam. He also connects to Abu Dhabi and Dubai. Mike Adenuga (number 7) combines oil wealth in his homeland Nigeria, with growing telecom activities in Nigeria, but also in Ghana and Benin. Isabel dos Santos (number 8 and the only woman among the top ten) made her fortune in Angola and Portugal, and combines activities in oil, telecom, banking and electricity. Algerian Issad Rebrab (number 9) owns a big company active in food production in Algeria, but has also become active in France as an investor. And finally, number 10, Egyptian Naguib Sawiris, is mainly active in Egypt's telecom business, but also in Lebanon, Pakistan, and (interestingly) North Korea, and he recently started investing in Europe. So if we look at this top ten, the two Nigerians and one of the South Africans can be seen as becoming "pan-African" entrepreneurs, but the others mainly connect their activities in their home country with investment activities in Europe, and/or the Middle East. It would be good, though, to keep a sharp eye on the emergence of "multinational companies", originating from Africa (Kaynak 2014, focusing on Ghana), and on the interesting issue of African companies going global or African entrepreneurs investing outside the continent, which already seems to be the rule, and not the exception.

Of course, we should not only focus on the most wealthy entrepreneurs. Numerous less wealthy entrepreneurs are active in Africa, and it is probably good to say that many poor and middle-class Africans would never have survived without an entrepreneurial spirit, often in dire circumstances; but, between 2000 and 2015 there was a chance to use the opportunities of an expanding economy and a more liberal political environment. The flip-side of the success stories are the enormous inequalities in opportunities, and in income and wealth levels. Half of Africa's population can still be regarded as being part of or close to the "bottom billion" in the world (Collier 2008), and Africa can now be regarded as the continent with the most severe economic disparities between the haves and the have-nots. The measure for economic inequality that is often used, the Gini coefficient, is really extreme in countries like South

Africa (63.4 in 2012[6]). Many small-scale (or micro) entrepreneurs are feeling blocked by political, economic, and sometimes also cultural barriers and are not able to expand. Policies meant to "upscale" successful enterprises are often failing, despite the attention for micro-credit or micro-finance programmes (e.g. Buckley 1997; Akoten et al. 2006) for "frugal innovation" (e.g. Peša 2015; Knorringa et al. 2016), "social entrepreneurship" (Urban 2008) and "black empowerment" (Tangri and Southal 2008).

A focus on successful entrepreneurship in Africa needs a focus on institutional arrangements. Frequently, the first thing that comes to mind is the role of the state. In comparative studies about the success of emerging economies in, for instance, East and Southeast Asia and Africa (often described as 'lagging behind') a lot of emphasis is given to a combination of sound and dependable macro-economic policies, and dedicated policy implementation by the state for poverty alleviation, and economic support to small-scale entrepreneurs (e.g. in the Tracking Development project, see Berendsen et al. 2013, and Henley 2015), or the Developmental Regimes in Africa project (Booth et al. 2015). However, it is probably wise not to focus too much on the state, and to look at institutional arrangements beyond the state, or where the state agencies are only one of the partners (Booth and Unsworth 2014; McDade & Spring 2005; Rogerson 2001). This was also a strong suggestion in an earlier edition of *African Dynamics* (Akinyoade et al. 2014) with an emphasis on agricultural 'pockets of effectiveness' in Africa, and the need to study private and public support institutions, and the way these interact with entrepreneurs. These institutions deal with self-organisation, like Chambers of Commerce, or Associations of Manufacturers, but also with transport and other physical infrastructure (and its maintenance), credit facilities, innovation incubators, training, education and research agencies, and so many other things that can make or break an entrepreneur (e.g. Robson et al. 2009). This book puts African entrepreneurs centre stage, and tries to look at their perspectives and networks. It is a pioneering book due to the fact that little is known about this subject in academic circles. A lot of information has recently become available through journalistic media and think tanks, like http://africabusiness.com/, venturesafrica.com, africanbusinessmagazine.com, africanbusinesscentral.com, http://ayeonline.org/, http://allafrica.com/business/, and the daily memoranda published by Fernando Matos Rosa (linked to the European Business Council for Africa and the Mediterranean; www.ebcam.eu; also see www.nabc.nl for its member in the Netherlands, the Netherlands-African Business Council[7]).

6 https://en.wikipedia.org/wiki/List_of_countries_by_income_equality.

7 In 2012, 2014 and 2016 the African Studies Centre in Leiden co-organised Africa Works conferences with the NABC, with the major aim to connect the worlds of business, academia,

Various authors of the chapters in this book have made important contributions that will help enhance our understanding of the theory, structure and practice of entrepreneurship in Africa from an academic perspective.

## Summary of Contributions

Following the introductory chapter, contributions in this book are in three broad sections. The first section is an examination of related theories and innovations. Firstly, is Emiel Eijdenberg's examination of methodological challenges of entrepreneurship research in East African Least Developed Countries. This is based on the contention that "an underestimation has been observed concerning the influence of the individual's external factors, like those from the small business owner, and an overestimation on important internal factors of the individual." And as there is a growing interest to involve the context in which economic behaviour, like starting a small business as a form of entrepreneurship, occurs, it is imperative to answer the important question of "How to contextualise entrepreneurship?" by focusing on situational and temporal boundaries. Using extensive qualitative and quantitative data collections among entrepreneurship experts, and small business owners in the formal and informal economies in a number of East African observations, it is observed in Uganda that push- and pull factors are not mutually exclusive in understanding entrepreneurial motivation. However, pull factors dominate the push factors as the small business owners' entrepreneurial motivation. In Rwanda, small business growth is primarily predicted by two groups of entrepreneurial motivations: one group with a mix of motivations, and one group with predominantly opportunity motivation. In Burundi, while effectuation-oriented small business owners perceive more uncertainty, both effectuation and causation orientations have more or less no effect on the growth of the small businesses. And in Tanzania, entrepreneurial motivation and entrepreneurial orientation do not play an important role as predictors for small business growth. The development of personal wealth is partly determined by the subsistence entrepreneur's age. Eijdenberg concluded that future research should go beyond the sample limitations of the studies in East Africa, because the collection of data at a different time or for other types of businesses might produce different findings.

---

policymakers and NGOs, and to connect African and European entrepreneurs and academics interested in African entrepreneurship development.

Kenneth Amaeshi and Uwafiokun Idemudia systematically explore the concept of Africapitalism as a management idea for business in Africa. This term, coined by a Nigerian banker and economist – Mr Tony Elumelu (31st richest person in Africa)[8] – is an economic philosophy that embodies private sector's commitment to the economic transformation of Africa through investments that generate both economic prosperity and social wealth. Amaeshi and Idemudia linked Africapitalism to the broader literature on business and society, and critically interrogated the concept as a possible management idea for business in Africa in response to the onslaught of global capitalism. It is noted that the literature on the role of business in society often takes context for granted (as Eijdenberg earlier pointed out). This chapter first provides enlightenment on the prospects, problems and paradoxes of global capitalism, and thereafter looks at Africapitalism as an imaginative moral-linguistic project. It is concluded that Africapitalism, as "capitalism by Africa-oriented entrepreneurs for Africa, allows for a space to re-appropriate the discourse of capitalism in a manner that puts Africa, its culture and people front and centre of any possibility of capitalist development in the region." It is a creative way of unmasking the good face of capitalism, a novel way of domesticating and unleashing the power of capitalism, and a concept that can easily unbridle the emotive imagination of Africans and refocus their minds on what it means to be African entrepreneurs in Africa. While the concept is a creative push back on the disadvantages of globalisation, the authors caution that "Africapitalism without a strong philosophy behind it runs the risk of being hollow and ungrounded." Despite being an expression of economic patriotism continentally, Africapitalism can only thrive in a politically stable and environmentally sustainable Africa.

Addisu Lashitew and Rob van Tulder interrogate the priorities, strategies and challenges of Inclusive Business in Africa. Inclusive business strategies exemplify how the private sector could contribute to inclusive and sustainable development. Little is known about inclusive businesses in Africa, specifically regarding the social issues private organisations prioritise, the strategies they use, and the challenges they encounter. Using primary data obtained in six East African countries on African and Dutch private organisations operating therein, the authors discovered that the level of emphasis given to inclusive business practices is generally high, although NGOs give greater weight to inclusiveness than businesses do. Notable differences are revealed across organisations in the extent to which inclusiveness is integrated with their core

8 Forbes 2016, #31 Tony Elumelu 2015 Africa's 50 Richest, http://www.forbes.com/profile/tony-elumelu/?list=africa-billionaires.

operations, and the most important strategies of inclusiveness include providing affordable products for low-income customers and value chain development. The chapter concludes with a reflection on potential policy interventions for addressing internal and external challenges to inclusiveness.

Miguel Heilbron, André Leliveld and Peter Knorringa's chapter on innovation as a key to success was studied in a backdrop of the impression that African economies have been lagging behind when it comes to innovation, bolstered by indices such as the Global Innovation Index in which the majority of African countries can be found at the lower end of the ranking. But these authors argue that African economies have always been sources of creativity and innovation, manifested mostly from the informal sector and have remained largely "below the radar" in official statistics and reports. And that the innovation landscape is changing dramatically in many African countries, as it is changing worldwide. Moreover, new developments in ICT have been picked up rapidly by innovative entrepreneurs in many African economies, for example in countries like Kenya, Nigeria, South Africa, Tunisia, Senegal and Morocco, the ICT sector contributes more than 10 per cent to respective GDP. This chapter contributes a more nuanced picture on innovation and (successful) entrepreneurship in Africa by systematically examining some cases of innovative entrepreneurs, particularly innovative start-ups in Kenya and Nigeria, which are exemplary for a new generation of companies started and managed by African entrepreneurs. Determinants of success of the presented firms in which innovation has played a major role were presented.

Jaap Voeten based his examination of innovation in manufacturing SMEs in Kenya, Ghana and Tanzania on a grounded view of research and policy issues. In this chapter, a selection of three concrete (typical) successful examples of innovation in manufacturing SMEs, which are initiated and owned by African entrepreneurs are examined, on the basis of three overall research questions: what and how do innovations materialise within manufacturing SMEs? What are the firms' strong and weak internal capabilities? How does the external business and institutional context play a supporting or hampering role in the innovation process? Systematic analyses of these cases confirm the picture that SMEs, the "missing middle", are weak in both Ghana and Kenya because of challenging business conditions: poor infrastructure, inefficient legal systems, inadequate financial systems and unattractive tax regimes. The companies see promising market opportunities on the one hand, but a harsh institutional context on the other, which makes business operations, innovation and development problematic. Before considering explicit innovation policies, addressing this hostile institutional environment as a first step could already bring significant benefit.

The second broad section of this book focuses on country studies of entrepreneurship development. Here, Abel Ezeoha and Afam Ituma employ Institutional Theory to discuss some key factors that shape and constrain entrepreneurship development in Nigeria. Their chapter highlights the context-specific nature of entrepreneurship and attempts to reveal the influence of various factors and variables on entrepreneurship development. Institutional influence on entrepreneurship development in Nigeria is examined in three ways: firstly, the regulative institutional pillar, followed by the normative (social) context, and then the Cognitive (cultural) pillar. The authors argue conclusively that individuals and firms do not always take rational decisions, rather decisions and behaviour are framed by certain presupposed expectations. Thus, entrepreneurship development should not be thought of as primarily driven by individual free choice, but wider contextual factors that create opportunities and barriers for individual career development need to be considered. Importantly, scholars are scientifically persuaded to give greater attention to the interactions among the institutional pillars and the simultaneous influence of these pillars on aggregate entrepreneurship.

Nnamdi Madichie, Knowledge Mpofu and Jerry Kolo use insights from Nigeria and Zimbabwe's telecom companies to appraise the challenges and opportunities for entrepreneurship development in the aforementioned countries. Drawing from institutional theory, this cross national comparative analysis provides insights on the diverse and unique configuration of institutional logics that promote or constrain entrepreneurship development in these two sub-Saharan African (SSA) economies. The telecommunication sector is used to highlight the issues that shape current trends and implications for the future of entrepreneurship development championed by a "new generation of African entrepreneurs". Both case studies provide critical analyses of emerging issues through compelling success stories of entrepreneurship initiatives despite infrastructure challenges and unstable economic and political landscapes experienced in the two SSA countries in recent years.

Entrepreneurship development in Sudan is evaluated by Yagoub Ali Gangi and Hesham Mohammed. It is noted that studies on entrepreneurship development are rare, and at the international level, Sudan is not even covered by the Global Entrepreneurship Monitor (GEM) reports. Available studies tend to indicate that Sudan is entrepreneurially underdeveloped, hence the current study into the role of national factors on shaping and constraining the entrepreneurship state in Sudan. In the author's examination of the state of entrepreneurship in Sudan, it is observed that while the Central Bureau of Statistics (CBS) in Sudan does not publish data on entrepreneurial activities, indirect sources of information can be sourced from "data on new business registered which was published by the Companies Registration Authority of the Ministry of Justice as an indicator for entrepreneurial activities." The limitation of this source is that a considerable number of registered new firms might not have started-up their businesses. However, the registration of any new firm can be taken as an indicator for the procession of a new business idea. In addition, it is a useful indicator for the intention of the firm's owner to transfer a business idea into actual business. Contextual factors for shaping entrepreneurship in Sudan examined by the authors include the mixed economic environment (macroeconomic stability, per capita income levels, and factors of production), financial systems and operations, political environment (including legal landscape – taxation policy, employment law, competition policy, patent law and regulation of financial markets), as well as cultural factors (power distance, individualism, uncertainty avoidance, and long-term orientation) all of which influence a Sudanese entrepreneur's decision making.

Nsubili Isaga and Albogast Musabila's chapter focuses on entrepreneurship development in Tanzania. This chapter is a qualitative investigation that relies on three case studies of Tanzanian SMEs. Findings indicate that motivation for owner-managers to start a business varied from need for independence, to make a living, to increasing personal income. Other success factors include the desire to fulfill family responsibilities, having more customers and trust. But, self-determination, creativity, passion and respect for business were least mentioned by all owner-managers interviewed as major driver for their success. For wood furniture enterprises in particular, lack of access to finance, international competition and cheap imports, poor power supply and inadequate infrastructure appear to be the major constraints to performance. And while some NGOs have strived to promote SMEs, it was discovered that many of them are rather weak, and concentrated in urban areas, which leads to a call for linkages of the institutions supporting SMEs.

Françoise Okah-Efogo and Crescence Marie-France Okah-Atenga throw their searchlight on institutional and contextual factors that may constitute constraints to entrepreneurship in Cameroon, with a special focus on the country's transport services sector. Documentary analysis of laws and regulations governing entrepreneurship in Cameroon's transport sector was conducted and a case study of two companies is used to validate or challenge some theoretical assumptions. Their analyses yielded three results: firstly, regulatory institutions governing entrepreneurship in Cameroon is sufficiently dynamic to promote entrepreneurship in the nation's transport sector; secondly, in order to encourage investors in the transport services sector there is a need to address contextual constraints. Therefore, thirdly, rehabilitation of roads and creation of new roads are important catalysts for the creation of new opportunities and expansion of the sector.

In the third main section of this book, where the focus is on entrepreneurship and sectoral considerations or determinants, Akinyinka Akinyoade and Chibuike Uche explore the expansion of Dangote Cement into other African countries. Their chapter shows that although both ECOWAS and the African Union are supposed to help promote such intra- continental business expansion, the reality is more complex as diverse forces have affected the investment of Dangote in some of these African countries. On one hand, the advent of Dangote Cement into other African countries has helped promote competition; on the other hand, the company's investments and business strategies in some of these African countries have been questioned. This chapter also further demonstrates that adverse economic developments in Dangote Cement's home country is now beginning to affect the company's Pan African expansionist bid.

Dwelling more on the cultural (cognitive) pillar angle, Jane Khayesi, Arthur Sserwanga and Rebecca Kiconco use available evidence to critically examine how cultural factors facilitate and/or constrain entrepreneurship development in Uganda. This is in view of the fact that "there remains ambivalence about the contribution of culture to entrepreneurship development in African countries. While on the one hand there are stories of successful entrepreneurial efforts, on the other hand, there are tales of failure attributed to cultural factors." This chapter is based on case studies of culture-related opportunities and difficulties encountered by Ugandan entrepreneurs in the development of their businesses.

Miriam Siun's, Akinyinka Akinyoade's and Ewurabena Quaye's chapter on African women large-scale entrepreneurs in Angola, Ghana and Nigeria is a critical examination of the road to prosperity for three African women entrepreneurs of large-scale businesses within male-dominated fields of portfolio-investments, oil production and construction. The three women are Angolan Isabel Dos Santos, Nigeria's Folorunsho Alakija and Ghana's Theresa Oppong-Beeko, who are highly ranked among the wealthiest women in Africa. The first two are positioned number 8 and number 13, respectively, in the African section of Forbes annual list of the world's billionaires, in terms of personal wealth on the continent irrespective of gender (see above). Along with Ghana's Dr. Theresa Oppong-Beeko, they have firmly established themselves and their companies in their respective industries, despite the challenges women face to enter these spheres. In some quarters, their individual trajectories to wealth calls meritocracy (for women) into question, as claims of patrimonialism and corruption is sometimes used to taint their accomplishments. This necessitates further studies on the obstacles for African women to becoming large-scale entrepreneurs without personal connections to influential people/high profile leadership. The chapter cautions against uncritical praise of success stories on the basis of gender.

Maria Lindvert's chapter on financial barriers and how female entrepreneurs can overcome them in Tanzania focuses on resource acquisition among women entrepreneurs in a country where potential female entrepreneurs have almost no access to formal capital from the commercial bank sector. To a large extent, women entrepreneurs still rely on informal sources of capital, such as loans from family and friends. This study draws on institutional theory and qualitative data to discuss how formal and informal institutions create barriers and opportunities for women, and presents how women in Tanzania act in order to overcome financial barriers, as they start or develop their ventures.

The penultimate chapter by Ayodeji Olukoju "Gentlemanly capitalism and entrepreneurial management: Formation and rise of Nigeria's Guaranty Trust Bank, 1990–2002", provides perspectives on transformations in Nigerian capitalism. This chapter reflects on a major problematique – the challenge of building credible and competitive financial institutions in colonial and post-independence Nigeria. The chapter draws upon an extensive collection of documentary evidence – previously inaccessible private papers and minutes of meetings of GTBank's board of directors, and newspaper reports – and interviews with the promoters and foundation staff of the bank. Key to the bank's success is the managerial entrepreneurship of its co-founders, whose duumvirate leadership model epitomised the innovativeness of their enterprise. The formation and rise of GTBank exemplify three connected aspects of entrepreneurship as identified by Stevenson and Jarillo (1990): "what happens when entrepreneurs act: why they act; and how they act."

The final chapter of this book, by Chibuike Uche, critiques the rise of Nigerian multinational banks. This development is traced to 2004 when a dramatic increase in the minimum share capital requirement forced Nigerian banks to begin to aggressively explore the provision of cross border banking services. Arguably, that regulation has been the major factor in the emergence of Nigerian multinational banks. A related explanatory factor is the pursuit of business opportunities in host countries especially in Africa. The findings in this chapter appear to contradict a conventional hypothesis that multinational banks normally follow their customers abroad from home countries.

## References

Akinsanya, A. (1981). "Host Government Responses to Foreign Economic Control: The Experience of Selected African Countries", *International and Comparative Law Quarterly* 30: 769–770.

Akinyoade, A., Dietz, T. & A. Leliveld (2014). "Agricultural Pockets of Effectiveness: A Comparative Inventory of Nigeria, Kenya, Tanzania and Uganda since 2000". In: A. Akinyoade, W. Klaver, S. Soeters & D. Foeken. *Digging Deeper: Inside Africa's Agricultural, Food and Nutrition Dynamics*. Leiden/Boston: Brill.

Akoten, J.E., Sawada, Y, & K. Otsuka (2006). "The Determinants of Credit Access and its Impacts on Micro and Small Enterprises: The Case of Garment Producers in Kenya". *Economic development and cultural change*, 54(4): 927–944.

Berendsen, B., Dietz, T., Schulte Nordholt, H. & R. van der Veen (2013). *Asian Tigers, African Lions: Comparing the Development Performance of Southeast Asia and Africa.* Leiden/Boston: Brill.

Berglund H. (2007). "Researching Entrepreneurship as Lived Experience". In: H. Neergaard & J.P. Ulhøi (eds) *Handbook of Qualitative Research Methods in Entrepreneurship*. Cheltenham: Edward Elgar.

Booth, D. & S. Unsworth (2014). *Politically Smart, Locally-Led Development*. London: ODI.

Booth, D., Dietz, A.J., Golooba-Mutebi, F., Fuady, A.H., Henley, D., Kelsall, T., Leliveld, A.H.M. and J.K. van Donge (2015). *Developmental Regimes in Africa Synthesis Report*. London: ODI.

Buckley, G. (1997). "Microfinance in Africa: Is it Either the Problem or the Solution?" *World Development*, 25(7): 1081–1093.

Bull, I. & G. Willard (1993). "Towards a Theory of Entrepreneurship", *Journal of Business Venturing* 8: 183–195.

Cader, H.A. & D.W. Norman (2006). "Entrepreneurship Education for the African Informal Sector". In: A. Fayolle & H. Klandt (eds), *International Entrepreneurship Education.* Cheltenham: Edward Elgar: 277–296.

Cain, P. & A. Hopkins (1980). "The Political Economy of British Expansion Overseas, 1750–1914". *The Economic History Review* 33: 4, 463–490.

Collier, P. (2008). *The Bottom Billion: Why the Poorest Countries are Failing and What Can be Done About It.* Oxford: Oxford University Press.

Committee on Sponsoring Organizations of the Treadway Commission (COSO) (2004) (2004) Enterprise Risk Management – *Integrated Framework* (New York, AICPA).

Ekekwe, N. (2016). "Why African Entrepreneurship is Booming", *Harvard Business Review* (11 July 2016) downloaded from <https://hbr.org/2016/07/why-african-entrepreneurship-is-booming> on 20 July 2016.

Elkan, W. (1988). "Entrepreneurs and Entrepreneurship in Africa", *World Bank Research Observer* 3: 171–188.

Foriwaa, K. & I. Akuamoah-Boateng (2013). "Entrepreneurship in Adentan-Dodowa Localities-Challenges", *American Journal of Industrial and Business Management*, 3: 121–125.

Forrest, T. (1994). *The Advance of African Capital: The Growth of Nigerian Private Enterprise.* Edinburgh: Edinburgh University Press.

Harris, J. & M. Rowe (1966). "Entrepreneurial Patterns in the Nigerian Sawmilling Industry", *Nigerian Journal of Economic and Social Sciences* 8: 67–95.

Heilman, B. & J. Lucas. (1997). "A Social Movement for African Capitalism? A Comparison of Business Associations in Two African Cities", *African Studies Review* 40: 141–171.

Henley, D. (2015). *Asia-Africa Development Divergence. A Question of Intent.* London: Zed Press.

Hopkins, A. (1968). "Economic Imperialism in West Africa: Lagos, 1880–92", *The Economic History Review* 21: 580–606.

Iliffe, J. (1983). *The Emergence of African Capitalism.* London: Macmillan.

Ireland, R.D., Covin, J.G. & D.F. Kuratko (2009). "Conceptualizing Corporate Entrepreneurship Strategy". *Entrepreneurship Theory and Practice*, 33: 19–46.

Kaynak, E. (2014). *Internationalization of Companies from Developing Countries.* London: Routledge.

Kiggundu, M. (2002). "Entrepreneurs and Entrepreneurship in Africa: What Is Known and What Needs to Be Done", *Journal of Developmental Entrepreneurship* 7: 239–258.

Knorringa, P., Peša, I., Leliveld, A. & C. van Beers (2016). "Frugal Innovation and Development: Aides or Adversaries?" *The European Journal of Development Research*, 28(2), 143–153.

Leap Africa (2014). *Defying the Odds: Case Studies of Nigerian Organizations that have survived Generations.* Lagos: Leap Africa.

Luchsinger, V. & D. Bagby (1987). "Entrepreneurship and Intrapreneurship", *SAM Advanced Management Journal* 52:10–13.

Marsden, K. (1990). "African Entrepreneurs: Pioneers of Development", *International Finance Corporation Discussion Paper* Number 9. Washington D.C.: The World Bank and International Finance Corporation.

Marsden, K. (1992). "African Entrepreneurs: Pioneers of Development", *Small Enterprise Development*, 3(2): 15–25.

McDade, B.E. & A. Spring (2005). "The 'New Generation of African Entrepreneurs': Networking to Change the Climate for Business and Private Sector-led Development", *Entrepreneurship & Regional Development*, 17(1): 17–42.

Nijkamp, P. (2003). "Entrepreneurship in a Modern Network Economy". *Regional Studies*, 37: 395–405.

Ogbor, J. (2009). *Entrepreneurship in Sub-Saharan Africa: A Strategic Management Perspective*. Bloomington, IN: Authorhouse.

Peša, I. (2015). "Homegrown or Imported? Frugal Innovation and Local Economic Development in Zambia". *Southern African Journal of Policy and Development*, 2, 15.

Robson, P.J.A., Haugh, H.M. & B.A. Obeng (2009). "Entrepreneurship and Innovation in Ghana: Enterprising Africa". *Small Business Economics* 32 (3): 331–350.

Rogerson, C.M. (2001). "In Search of the African Miracle: Debates on Successful Small Enterprise Development in Africa". *Habitat International* 25 (1): 115–142.

Rood L. (1976). "Nationalisation and Indigenisation in Africa", *Journal of Modern African Studies* 14: 427–428.

Rumelt, R., Schendel, D. & D. Teece (1991). "Strategic Management and Economics", *Strategic Management Journal* 12: 5–30.

Sarasvathy, D., Simon, H. & L. Lave (1998). "Perceiving and Managing Business Risks: Differences between Entrepreneurs and Bankers". *Journal of Economic Behavior and Organization*, 33: 207–225.

Schumpeter, J. (1976). *Capitalism, Socialism and Democracy*. New York: Harper Collins.

Shimizu, K. (2012). "Risks of Corporate Entrepreneurship: Autonomy and Agency Issues". *Organization Science*, *23*: 194–206.

Steele, D. (1975). "The Theory of the Dual Economy and African Entrepreneurship in Kenya", *The Journal of Development Studies* 12: 18–38.

Stevenson, H.H. & J.C. Jarillo (1990). "A Paradigm of Entrepreneurship: Entrepreneurial Management", *Strategic Management Journal, 11, Special Issue: Corporate Entrepreneurship* (Summer), 17–27.

Tangri, R. & R. Southall (2008). "The Politics of Black Economic Empowerment in South Africa". *Journal of Southern African Studies*, 34(3): 699–716.

Tignor, R. (1998). *Capitalism and Nationalism at the End of Empire: State and Business in Decolonizing Egypt, Nigeria and Kenya, 1945–1963*. Princeton, NJ: Princeton University Press.

Tignor, R. (1987). "Decolonizing and Business: The Case of Egypt". *The Journal of Modern History* 59: 479–505.

Tsai, W. & S. Ghoshal (1998). "Social Capital and Value Creation: The Role of Intrafirm Networks". *Academy of Management Journal*, 41: 464–478.

Uche, C. (2012). "British Government, British Businesses and the Indigenization Exercise in Post-Independence Nigeria", *Business History Review* 86: 745–771.

Urban, B. (2008). "Social Entrepreneurship in South Africa: Delineating the Construct with Associated Skills". *International Journal of Entrepreneurial Behavior & Research*, 14(5), 346–364.

Venkataraman, S. & S. Sarasvathy (2001). "Strategy and entrepreneurship: Outlines of an Untold Story", Darden Graduate School of Business Administration Working Paper No. 01–06.

Watson, G. (2011). "Definition of entrepreneurship". www.gregwatson.com/entrepreneurship-definition.

World Bank (1989). *Sub-Saharan Africa. From Crisis to Sustainable Growth.* Washington, D.C.: World Bank.

# PART 1

## *Examination of Related Theories and Innovations*

CHAPTER 2

# Methodological Challenges of Entrepreneurship Research in the Least Developed East African Countries

*Emiel L. Eijdenberg*

## Introduction

The word "context" is derived from the Latin *contexere*, *con* stemming from "com", which means "together", and "text" from *texere*, which means "to weave". Hence, context means "to weave together": it simultaneously affects business, and it comes in many shapes and forms (Van Gelderen and Masurel 2012: 2).

Context is important: it helps us to explain why certain individuals, like entrepreneurs (hereafter referred to as *small business owners*) recognize opportunities and others do not, and why the outcomes of entrepreneurial activities, such as starting a small business, vary across different countries, regions, and other contexts (Baker et al. 2005). Recently, there is a growing interest in the context in which economic behaviour, like starting a small business as a form of entrepreneurship, occurs (Hjorth et al. 2008; Welter 2011; Welter and Xheneti 2013; Zahra and Wright 2011; Zahra et al. 2014).

Context has been discussed in terms of who, where, and when (Whetten 1989). The "where" and the "when" are of particular interest for entrepreneurship research (Welter 2011), because these influence the "who", i.e. the individual. In regard to the "where" and the "when", the context has been set out in different levels of analyses, such as the business level (i.e. industry, market), the social level (i.e. network, household, family), the spatial level (i.e. geographical environments), and the institutional level (i.e. culture and society) (Johns 2006; Welter 2011). However, an important unanswered question remains on the research agenda: Is it possible to contextualize entrepreneurship by focusing on situational and temporal boundaries? "Contextualisation" is "linking observations to a set of relevant facts, events, or points of view that make possible research and theory that form part of a larger whole" (Rousseau and Fried 2001: 1). In doing so, we could more adequately tackle important challenges, as discussed by Welter (2011) in terms of developing research designs. In this

 | DOI 10.1163/9789004351615_003

regard, this chapter[1] discusses a number of methodological challenges that are observed in studies based on data collection in five of the world's poorest countries on the African continent: the Least Developed Countries (LDCs) in East Africa. To illustrate the girth of the LDCs: more than one billion people on our planet live in absolute poverty. This group of people is referred to as "the bottom billion" (Collier 2007) and many of "the bottom billion" live in the LDCs. Based on United Nations (UN) criteria, 34 of the world's 48 LDCs are on the African continent. For many small business owners in East African LDCs, it is this context that allows them to use situational cues that are instrumental for making decisions and implementing – what they perceive to be – an innovation (Rooks et al. 2014). Many of these innovations are called "frugal innovations": products with a "design innovation process in which the needs and context of citizens in the developing world are put first in order to develop appropriate, adaptable, affordable, and accessible services and products for emerging markets" (Basu et al. 2013: 64). The features of frugal innovations are beneficial to the end-consumer: generally, frugal innovations are cheap, easy to use, easy to access/purchase, portable, and both economically and socially sustainable (Basu et al. 2013; Rao 2013). Typical frugal innovations in Africa include recycled car tyre sandals (the so-called *lugabire*) (New Vision 2007); self-made mosquito nets; home-built water purifiers; and a large variety of self-made utensils, games, and practical applications (e.g. bottle openers, chessboards, footballs, and batteries). The "typical" picture of African small businesses is that these frugal innovations, together with a large variety of other small consumer goods, are sold in kiosks, mini-markets and shops that are owned by one or two persons who employ a small number of workers who are either friends, family or relatives.

## Point of Departure

In this chapter, I rely on personal observations from extensive qualitative and quantitative data collection among entrepreneurship experts and small business owners in the formal and informal economies in the East African LDCs. During five years, I collected data for studies in Uganda, Rwanda, Burundi and

1 This book chapter is inspired by Emiel Eijdenberg's PhD dissertation entitled "Small business growth in East African Least Developed Countries – Unravelling the role of the small business owners" (Eijdenberg 2016a). On the basis of textual adjustments, some parts from the Introduction and Conclusions chapters of the PhD dissertation are used to enhance the fit in this book.

Tanzania. Each of these research projects are published in scientific journals. Each study is summarised as follows:

1) The study in Uganda investigates entrepreneurial motivation by answering the research question: *Which entrepreneurial motivation is more important for people in a Least Developed Country to start a business: Push factors or pull factors?*. On the basis of 11 expert interviews and 106 questionnaires completed by kiosk-owners in Kampala, the answer to the research question is that push factors and pull factors are not mutually exclusive. Here, pull factors dominate the push factors as the small business owners' entrepreneurial motivation (Eijdenberg 2016a: 185; also see Eijdenberg and Masurel 2013).
2) Subsequently, the study in Rwanda investigates entrepreneurial motivation as a determinant for small business growth by answering the research question: *To what extent is small business growth in a Least Developed Country determined by the small business owner's entrepreneurial motivation?*. On the basis of a pre-study with 25 experts and a main study of 133 owners of handicraft shops in Kigali and Gisenyi, the answer is that small business growth is primarily predicted by two groups of entrepreneurial motivations: one group with a mix of motivations, and one group with predominantly opportunity motivation (Eijdenberg 2016a: 185; see also Eijdenberg et al. 2015).
3) The study in Burundi investigates how small business owners' decision-making, in terms of effectuation and causation orientations, can determine the growth of their small business. The following research question is answered: *To what extent is the growth of small businesses in an uncertain environment determined by the owners' effectuation and causation orientation?* on the basis of 29 expert interviews and 154 questionnaires completed by mini-market owners. The results show that while effectuation-oriented small business owners perceive more uncertainty, both effectuation and causation orientations have little effect on the growth of the small businesses (see Eijdenberg 2016a: 185–186; see also Eijdenberg et al. 2017).
4) Finally, the study in Tanzania investigates how entrepreneurial motivation and entrepreneurial orientation determine the development of personal wealth of subsistence entrepreneurs in the informal economy. On the basis of a pre-study with 27 experts and a main study of 152 questionnaires from informal food vendors in Iringa, the answer to the research question: *To what extent is the development of the personal wealth of subsistence entrepreneurs in the informal economy associated with entrepreneurial motivation and entrepreneurial orientation?* is that

> entrepreneurial motivation and entrepreneurial orientation do not play an important role as predictors for small business growth. The development of personal wealth is partly determined by the subsistence entrepreneur's age (see Eijdenberg 2016a, 2016b).

Research on geographical contexts such as the above-mentioned East African LDCs are referred to as "non-traditional contexts" (Kriauciunas et al. 2011), and are different from the "traditional" contexts, i.e. the United States and Western Europe. These "non-traditional contexts" often involve major difficulties with data collection (Kolk and Van Tulder 2010). The observations are based on studies that aim to explain small business growth as an important significant driver of economic development. I have looked at how small business owners engage with their immediate context (Van Gelderen and Masurel 2012), in terms of their entrepreneurial motivation, effectuation and causation orientations (Sarasvathy 1998, 2001) and entrepreneurial orientation (Hughes and Morgan 2007). As a result, my epistemological position is one of "positivism": "collecting data about an observable reality and search for regularities and causal relationships" (Saunders et al. 2012: 134). This implies making use of existing theories to develop and test hypotheses. The main reason for this is that the theoretical subjects in the studies are in the "mature" phase of the literature (Edmonson and McManus 2007); that is to say, they are significantly developed and empirical evidence has been produced from Western countries, such as Germany, and non-Western countries, such as South Africa (see, for example, Brettel et al. 2012; Krauss et al. 2005).

Each study in one of the East African LDCs (I–IV) contained one or more of the aforementioned theoretical subjects that could possibly explain small business growth. The items in the surveys in each country were marginally adjusted on the basis of: (a) an ongoing literature review prior to the data collection; (b) pre-studies of expert interviews prior to the quantitative data collection among the small business owners; and (c) the confirmation from a pilot group of (generally) 10 respondents and local assistance on the spot while completing the surveys.

The next section briefly reflects on the relevant literature of entrepreneurship and the East African LDCs.

## Reflections Based on Existing Scientific Literature

### *Entrepreneur(ship)*

Entrepreneurship literature incorporates many perspectives on "the entrepreneur". For example, the Austrian school sees the entrepreneur as an economic actor of *Schöpferische Zerstörung*, i.e. creative destruction, who drives economic development (Kirzner 1997; Schumpeter 1934). In the context of East African LDCs, the most applicable term for "the entrepreneur" is the "small business owner", which could mean "a person (or group of people) who creates a new business (for profit) and employs at least one other paid employee" (Kirkwood 2009: 350). Small business owners in East African LDCs are becoming increasingly important, and they represent one of the important drivers of a country's economic development (Audretsch et al. 2006; Baumol et al. 2007; Powell 2008), and when they are perceived as the means for poverty alleviation (Naudé 2011). Fighting poverty is important country-wide, but it is particularly relevant for the most vulnerable people at the bottom of the pyramid (BoP). Many of these vulnerable small business owners in the BoPs of East African LDCs are active in the informal economy. In the context of East African LDCs, informal business ownership particularly concerns the role of "informal institutions in facilitating, organizing and transacting" (Webb et al. 2014: 8). Entrepreneurial activity outside the formal institutional boundaries but within the informal institutional boundaries entails "how entrepreneurs operate informal institutional voids by drawing upon informal institutions as providing complementary, substitute mechanisms for organizing and transacting" (Webb et al. 2014: 8). Schneider (2005: 600) describes business in the informal economy as "all market-based legal production of goods and services that are deliberately concealed from public authorities for reasons of taxation, employment, and administrative regulation." Many of the small business owners in East African LDCs organise themselves in micro- and small-sized enterprises (MSEs) (Kiggundu 2002). MSEs are generally one-person operations; they are poorly managed, sometimes temporary, usually not very productive and they are often undercapitalised. Among various types of businesses in the informal economy, such as undocumented workers, unregistered businesses and trader-tourism, the skirting of different sorts of institutional regulations is common among MSEs: the "*mama lishe*" in Tanzania, a Kiswahili term for informal food vendors. "*Mama lishe*" mainly sell local dishes and beverages. In many cases, the owners of such businesses have other, additional jobs. These jobs are unrelated to their "*mama lishe*" and are usually done outside of the peak hours, such as being a taxi driver or a cell phone card vendor. The majority of "*mama lishe*" can be found in the city centres or along important, often congested roads and railways, where many people pass by to stop and have a quick bite, lunch or dinner. Many "*mama lishe*" prepare food and sell from little, often self-built premises, but they also operate with mobile food carts on the street. "Street-vending is a key element of this informal economy and important to surviving poverty and to the escape from poverty in developing countries" (Lyons et al. 2014: 4).

### *East African* LDC*s*

A common distinction, concerning context, is made between the narrow (micro), and the wider setting (meso and macro). The narrow setting involves the "life-space", or close environment, of the individual or the group. For example, the immediate social setting and the individual circumstances, such as one's preferences and intentions (Van Gelderen and Masurel 2012). Before the micro context is discussed, the wider setting, which is the institutional context in terms of, for example, the economic and cultural society, is discussed. Subsequently, the third section deals with the methodological concerns from the narrow setting, i.e. the micro context: "one's circumstances".

### *Institutional Context: The Economy in East African* LDC*s*

In the wider setting, "Africa is a diverse continent with distinct historic, economic, and social traditions" (Khavul et al. 2009: 1221). The continent has approximately one-seventh of the world's population, divided into 54 independent states on about 20.3% of the world's surface. Furthermore, "low population density means that the cost of economic integration in terms of transportation is high. When the land is sparsely settled, groups come together less, and thus have less in common, which, in turn, undermines economic integration, knowledge transfer, and trade based on comparative advantage" (Ibid.). Liberalisation policies of the governments in East Africa have resulted in an expanding free market and international trade, which have favoured the development of economies (Kristiansen 2002). From the 34 African LDCs, Burundi, Rwanda, Tanzania and Uganda form an economic community with Kenya, a non-LDC: the East African Community (East African Community 2014), in the "Great Lakes" region of Africa (Edmonds et al. 2009; Eijdenberg 2016a: 4–5). Burundi, Rwanda, Tanzania and Uganda are discussed briefly below.

Bujumbura is Burundi's capital. The country has approximately 10.4 million people living on the country's surface of almost 28,000 square kilometres. The median age is 17 years. While the gross domestic product (GDP) growth rate in 2013 was an estimated 4.5%, the GDP per capita was an estimated $600 in 2013. The economy is largely dependent on agriculture and the primary exports are coffee and tea (Central Intelligence Agency 2015a). Kigali is the capital of Rwanda, a country of approximately 12.3 million people living on a surface of roughly 26,000 square kilometres. The median age is 18.7 years. While the GDP growth rate in 2013 was an estimated 7.5%, the GDP per capita was $1500 in 2013. Agriculture accounts for Rwanda's largest economic sector and tourism, minerals, coffee and tea are the main exports (Central Intelligence Agency 2015b). Concerning Tanzania: while Dodoma is the legislative seat, Dar Es Salaam is the largest, commercial city and capital. The country counts approximately 50 million people living on a surface of a little more than 947,000 square kilometres. The median age is 17.4 years. While the GDP growth rate was an estimated 7% in 2013, the GDP per capita was approximately $1700 in 2013. Tanzania's economy mainly depends on agriculture, which also accounts for the majority of the country's exports (Central Intelligence Agency 2015c). Finally, Kampala is the capital of Uganda. This country is home to almost 36 million people living on approximately 241,000 square kilometres. The median age is 15.7 years. While the GDP growth rate was an estimated 5.6% in 2013, the GPD per capita was $1500 in 2013. Like the previously mentioned countries, agriculture is Uganda's largest sector. Coffee accounts for the majority of the country's exports (Central Intelligence Agency 2015d).

#### *Institutional Context: Culture of East African LDCs*

The information about East African culture and society in entrepreneurship literature is scarce. East African LDCs host many different ethnic groups: Burundi and Rwanda has three large ethnic groups, which are the Hutu, Tutsi, and the Twa; Uganda has more than ten substantial ethnic groups, the largest of which is the Baganda; and Tanzania is home to more than 130 ethnic groups (Central Intelligence Agency 2015a, 2015b, 2015c, 2015d). While ethnic diversity is generally a "positive aspect of society when accompanied by democracy" (Khavul et al. 2009: 1221), autocracy and concentration of power generally prevail in East African countries. Notwithstanding the autocracy and concentration of power, particularly within and across the ethnic groups, the traditional East African culture is largely collectivist. However, times are changing. The contrast between rural and urban regions have become larger. In the large cities, such as the capitals, the traditional African collective culture has increasingly changed into a more individualistic culture (Rooks et al. 2014). This change happens due to reasons such as modernisation and internationalisation, and a growing population with an increasing number of different, interacting ethnic goups (Vaunne and Schoeneman 1997).

For centuries, the extended family, which can be explained as a large group of family members with differing degrees of relativeness, has represented a sanctuary for many people in East Africa (Dau 2003). Therefore, the social ties within a specific group in East Africa, for example an extended family, are strong (Khavul et al. 2009). Due to a lack of easily accessible resources in the vicinity or an inability to optimally exploit resources, the majority strongly rely on their social networks in order to bring about an economic transaction, such as the exchange of a product or a service. Mutually beneficial cooperation is typical for extended families in African society (Otite 1978). Traditional East African culture has norms and values with a clear "gender divide" (Hagos

2000). Women are responsible for the household tasks and they take care of the children. More recently, an increasing number of women have begun an MSE in parallel to the work of their husbands: "hundreds of millions of poor people in developing countries make their living as micro-entrepreneurs: as farmers, street-vendors and home workers, and in a range of other occupations, a large share of them women" (World Bank 2004: 33), because starting a business has become increasingly important amongst women to make a living (Hanson 2009; Minniti and Naudé 2010; Strier 2010). Despite the positive effects of some women's activism (Snyder 2000), many female small business owners face gender disparities, not least because when starting a business they enter a work domain dominated by men (Langevang and Gough 2012; Overå 2007). Therefore, women have to deal with even more business-related challenges compared to their male counterparts, such as access to capital and overcoming bureaucratic hurdles.

More information about East African culture and society, in relation to management and business, can be found in other social science disciplines, such as cultural and anthropological literature. A quick glance at some literature from cultural studies shows that "whereas Western management thought advocates Euro-centrism, individualism and modernity; African management thought emphasizes ethnocentrism, traditionalism, communalism and cooperative teamwork" (Nzelibe 1986: 11). While there is no "one African culture", there are some other examples beyond the previously described "presence" of collectivist culture in Africa. Particularly in the larger organisations or the public sector, people can live by diverging values and beliefs, as typified by Jackson (2004: 20–21): "post-colonial", "post-instrumental", "African renaissance" (which mostly relates to collectivism), and "East Asian/Japanese". According to some older sources, many of the previously mentioned African culture types in the large organisations and the public sector imply very centralised and hierarchical structures, with the management often overworking, but adopting an authoritarian and paternalistic decision style (Kiggundu 1989). The organisations are too large, very bureaucratic and they are reluctant to change (Blunt and Jones 1992). These organisations lack clear results and objectives orientation; they lack a clear mission statement (Kiggundu 1989); they are often over-staffed, but have very few job descriptions, job evaluations and incentive systems; and they have a poor internal infrastructure (Joergensen 1990). As a result, people with a paid job at such organisations are often very risk averse, demotivated, unwilling to take independent action, often absent, have poor morale, and are unproductive (Kiggundu 1989). While some employees might lose their job because of one or more of the aforementioned factors, and are therefore pushed to start a small business for themselves, others "voluntarily" quit their paid job because they experience a mismatch between the institutional culture and their own values and beliefs. However, whether people are employed by an organisation, or whether they are a small business owner, many Africans do not perceive work as a central aspect of life; rather, they demonstrate an instrumental attitude towards work (Mufene 2003). That is to say, work is perceived purely as a means to a salary at the end of every four weeks (Blunt and Jones 1992).

Concerning the collectivist culture, as previously discussed using an example from the entrepreneurship literature (i.e. Rooks et al. 2014), many Africans live by the concept of *Ubuntu* (Mufene 2003). This concept involves tolerance and kindness and it emphasises helping others as a way of helping oneself: there is a collective well-being and activity as opposed to individualism; there is a unification as opposed to division; and there is respect for elders and sharing (Saule 1998). With regard to *Ubuntu*, there is an overlap with other, comparative studies on (East) African culture. For example, Noorderhaven and Tidjani (2001), who find that the most important African values are human goodness, rules and hierarchy, importance of religion, traditional wisdom, sharing, collectivism, and social responsibility. Furthermore, African scholars (for example, Akong'a 1995; Ahiazu 1995) suggest that there are African values and beliefs that influence everyday behaviour, including making decisions about starting and running a business (Onwuejeogwu 1995). These values and beliefs are (quoted from Munene et al. 2000: 342):

1. View the world as an integrated whole in which all events are traceable to one source.
2. Ground practical/common-sense thinking in proverbs.
3. Root theoretical thinking in mysticism.
4. View truth as depending on one's relationship with or the status of its source.
5. Fully trust relatives but not strangers.
6. Maintain order in life by avoiding unnecessary risks.
7. View wisdom as thought and behavior in harmony with one's ancestors.
8. Define wisdom as making the best of available opportunities.
9. See success as dependent on help or hindrance by powerful others.
10. See advancement as dependent on allegiance to powerful groups or individuals.

In particular, point four "View truth as depending on one's relationship with or the status of its source" and point five "Fully trust relatives but not strangers," are related to the previously discussed value of the extended family in Africa

(Khavul et al. 2009). On the basis of personal experiences and in regard to what is known from the literature, the next section discusses the methodological concerns regarding the world's poorest countries in East Africa, observed within a narrow setting.

## Methodological Concerns of Conducting Research in the World's Poorest Countries

In this section, the methodological concerns are discussed regarding the literature reflections and the personal observations from the studies in Uganda, Rwanda, Burundi and Tanzania. The concerns are mainly to do with the aforementioned narrow setting: the micro context, i.e. the personal circumstances of the respondents and the researcher at the time of the data collection. Although researching context is interesting, the methodologies are challenging (Van Gelderen and Masurel 2012). While qualitative studies have included context factors in their work of understanding a certain phenomenon (for example, Gartner and Birley 2002; Steyaert 1997), quantitative studies of context are also highly valuable, for example when it concerns comparative methods and replication research (Van Gelderen and Masurel 2012): hence, the positivist position of the studies in Uganda, Rwanda, Burundi and Tanzania (Saunders et al. 2012). Comparative methods allow the comparison of a phenomenon in multiple settings (Rousseau and Fried 2001). Replicated studies are useful to test whether, for example, widely known theories from one context also hold in other, often substantially different contexts (Van Gelderen and Masurel 2012). Concerning replication studies, the remainder of this chapter discusses the methodological challenges that are observed from replicating theoretical subjects that are widely discussed in the entrepreneurship literature: entrepreneurial motivation (the studies in Uganda, Rwanda and Tanzania), effectuation and causation orientations (the study in Burundi), entrepreneurial orientation (the study in Tanzania), and the growth measurement of a small business (the studies in Rwanda, Burundi and Tanzania).

Many studies of (East) African LDCs in the entrepreneurship literature refer to different types of methodological shortcomings in terms of, for example: a limited number of regions that were included (Rooks et al. 2014); the use of only a cross-sectional research design (Frese et al. 2007; Frese et al. 2002; Krauss et al. 2005); difficulties with the use of certain (in)dependent variables in a study to capture a subject, particularly the subject of business performance (Frese et al. 2002, 2007; Krauss et al. 2005); difficulties with obtaining reliable data from the businesses that are dealt with (Kuzilwa 2005); and shortcomings in terms of the choice of a certain type of sample (Krauss et al. 2005). However, culture has featured too little in entrepreneurship studies (Rooks et al. 2014) and, therefore, pushes entrepreneurship researchers in East African LDCs to "step back, stop, and ask critical questions, using qualitative methods" (Khavul and Bruton 2013: 297), and invite colleagues from other social sciences disciplines, such as development economics, anthropology or human geography, to help the scientific community explain the methodological concerns and shortcomings. Before the concerns about qualitative and quantitative data collection are discussed more in-depth, Table 2.1 presents a brief overview of the quantitative studies discussed. In Table 2.1, column one presents the details of the data collection and the theoretical subject of interest, and column two presents the methodological concerns.

The common denominator in the studies in Table 2.1 is that, on the one hand, the theoretical subjects under study are all established among the respondents, i.e. they can be measured and they do exist. On the other hand, the causal relationships that are studied (e.g. entrepreneurial motivation, effectuation and causation orientations, and entrepreneurial orientation *on* small business growth) are either absent or do not have sufficient explanatory power. On the basis of Table 2.1, the next sections discuss the challenges observed in relation to the collection of qualitative data and quantitative data in East African LDCs. In these sections, the letters [a] to [m] in the third column of "Methodological concerns" are further explained.

### *Qualitative Data Collection in East African LDCs*

The studies in the East African LDCs followed a "qual → QUAN" mixed methods approach (Molina-Azorin et al. 2012: 442). The purpose of a qualitative prestudy is: (1) to obtain a general overview of the subject in the local context and to shape the questionnaire in the main study according to the local context; and (2) to specify who would be the most appropriate respondents. In the qualitative pre-studies, so-called experts are used to gain "in-depth knowledge of specific industry, and local and regional contexts" and "to inform the design of survey questions for structured interviewing" (Molina-Azorin et al. 2012: 435). In general, the pre-studies were finished after 20 to 30 interviews, at which the point of minimal incremental learning was reached and phenomena were reported repetitively (Eisenhardt 1989; Glaser and Strauss 1967). The experts were, for example, representatives and policymakers from the Chamber of Commerce; representatives from business incubators; local small business owners who were recognised as "successful" by the representatives of local authorities, such as the Chamber of Commerce; representatives from governmental institutions (for example, ministries); managers from the financial

TABLE 2.1 *Overview of methodological concerns*

| **Study number. Country. City. Methodology. Sector of the quantitative sample. Size of business in terms of number of employees.** *Theoretical subject*[2] | **Methodological concerns** |
|---|---|
| I. Uganda, Kampala. A qualitative pre-study (11 interviews), and a quantitative main study (106 questionnaires). Kiosks. Only owners employing less than five (unregistered) persons. *Entrepreneurial motivation (see Eijdenberg and Masurel 2013).*<br>II. Rwanda, Kigali and Gisenyi. A qualitative pre-study (25 interviews) and a quantitative main study (133 questionnaires). Handicrafts shops. Mainly less than 10 employees. *Entrepreneurial motivation, and small business growth (see Eijdenberg et al. 2015).*<br>III. Burundi, Bujumbura. A qualitative pre-study (29 interviews), and a quantitative main study (154 questionnaires). Mini-markets. Generally less than 10 employees. *Effectuation and causation orientations, and small business growth (see Eijdenberg 2016a; Eijdenberg et al. 2017).*<br>IV. Tanzania, Iringa. A qualitative pre-study (27 interviews) and a quantitative main study (152 questionnaires). Informal food vendors: "*mama lishe*". Mostly, less than five unregistered persons working with a single owner. *Entrepreneurial orientation, and small business growth (see Eijdenberg 2016a,b).* | [a] Language difficulties: the respondents face a ("lost in") translation bias.<br>[b] There are difficulties with finding the right respondents for an interview.<br>[c] Questionnaire items that *describe* ("indirect") the construct are interpreted differently than items that literally *display* ("direct") the meaning of the items.<br>[d] Many results contradict the literature or certain expected effects are totally absent.<br>[e] Regression models lack explanatory power.<br>[f] Completed questionnaires often favour the right side of the scale, which, in the majority of cases is the higher values of the five or seven point Likert scale.<br>[g] The findings are greatly shaped by the very typical African sample that is subject of the study.<br>[h] The respondents have a poor comprehension of the items: asking the researcher "what does [the item] means?"<br>[i] There is a recall bias among the respondents.<br>[j] The respondents typically provide socially desirable answers.<br>[k] The respondents perceive the researcher as a journalist and/or completing the questionnaire is perceived as a once-in-a-lifetime event for the entire neighbourhood or village.<br>[l] The respondents are anxious and suspicious of the researcher's intentions.<br>[m] The respondents only complete the questionnaire on the basis of incentives that are offered by the researcher. |

2 For an extensive literature review of the theoretical subjects in Table 2.1, see Eijdenberg (2016a,b), Eijdenberg and Masurel (2013) and Eijdenberg et al. (2015, 2017).

sector (for example, commercial banks); local academic researchers; and even, on one occasion, the Burundian Minister of Trade and Industry, Postal Services and Tourism. The number of experts was limited within the local communities in East African LDCs. Therefore, a snowball sampling technique was used in which one expert highlights the next (Saunders et al. 2012).

### *Experienced Challenges with Qualitative Data Collection in East African LDCs*

First, there are language difficulties while doing research in East African LDCs (Table 2.1, [a]). Arranging interviews, and communication with local people who are involved with the previously mentioned methodologies often takes place through interpreters. Thus, a "lost in translation" situation often arises, already at the organising phase, while the actual interview about the content was still to come. Misunderstandings about the time, date and location of the set-up with the interviewees frequently occurred. In addition to the language difficulties, there was a variety of difficulties with organising the interviews on location. Some notable examples are: no-shows of interviewees; not replying to e-mails, phone calls and text messages; demands for different sorts of incentives for the interview, ranging from pens and pencils to money and cell phones; interrupting and leaving the interview abruptly; and attending the interview with uninvited individuals, such as family and friends. Occasionally, the respondents insisted that these uninvited people participated in the interview.

Second, there are difficulties in finding the right people for an interview (Table 2.1, [b]). Although there was not always the evidence to prove so, I often had the feeling that I was directed to interviewees who were friends, family or acquaintances of the local research assistants or of the people at the office that I first approached for contact. In certain cases, the use of the people's local social networks delivered outstanding interviewees, such as the Burundian Minister of Trade and Industry, Postal Services and Tourism and city mayors; but in other cases it led to clearly the wrong people for an interview, such as unexperienced policy officers with limited knowledge of my topic of interest. Furthermore, while it was expected that certain interviewees at mid-senior or senior level of experience would have mastered the English language, the reality was that many were unable to speak and understand English. This difficulty led in some cases, again, to a "lost in translation" situation with regard to communication between the researcher, the interpreter and the interviewee. For example, at one interview in Iringa, a city in Southern Tanzania, the interviewee (the city mayor) responded extensively, over several minutes, to the researcher's question "What motivates people in this city to start a small business?" However, the interpreter translated the interviewee's explanation from Kiswahili to English in only a couple of words, commenting that the mayor's answer amounted to just a few words in English.

### *Quantitative Data Collection in East African LDCs*

The main studies in the East African LDCs entailed quantitative data collection of samples with between 100 and 160 respondents. In each of the East African LDCs, I conducted the questionnaires with small business owners who often operate in so-called small- and medium-sized enterprises (SMEs) and the previously discussed MSEs. The respondents were small business owners in both the formal and informal economy. In the formal economy, the respondents were predominantly owners of mini-markets and handicraft shops. The small business owners were producing and selling groceries, utensils, beverages, prepared food, airtime credits for mobile phones, small furniture and handcrafted products for tourists, such as wooden masks and necklaces. For the informal economy, I administered the questionnaires on the previously discussed typical Tanzanian small business: the "*mama lishe*".

The choice for each sample of small business owners was based on: (a) the suggestions from the experts in the pre-studies, and (b) achieving a sufficient number of these suggested small business owners in the region to ensure statistical power for the analysis: using the rule of thumb of "$N$ must be at least $50 + 8m$", where $m$ represents the number of independent variables in the study (Tabachnick and Fidell 2007). The most effective type of sampling was the snowball sampling methodology, which involves going from one respondent to the other (Saunders et al. 2012). The help of local assistants was crucial: they helped with conducting the quantitative survey, in terms of language translation and introducing me to the respondents. Without the help of the local assistants, most likely the rounds of data collection would not have been so successful. As I had face-to-face contact with the respondents and let the respondents complete the questionnaire on the spot, I achieved very high response rates (approximately 95%–99%). The few small business owners who caused the non-response rate refused cooperation because of lack of time and worries about confidentiality.

### *Observed Limitations with Quantitative Data Collection in East African LDCs*

First (1), there is a difference in interpretation by the respondents between *direct* and *indirect* phrased items in the questionnaire (Table 2.1, [c]). *Direct* items concern items including the word that covers the theoretical concept. For example, when the respondent is asked in the questionnaire about their necessity motivation, a *direct* item would be "Have you started your business out of necessity?" In contrast to *direct* items, *indirect* items, or descriptive items, describe the content of the theoretical concept without using the word that covers the theoretical concept. For example, when the respondent is asked in the questionnaire about their necessity motivation, an *indirect* item would be "Have you started your business because you needed to sustain your family?" Frequently, the respondents filled out the *direct* and *indirect* questions in a contradictory manner: for example, while the *direct* item was answered with "Agree" or "Strongly agree", the *indirect* item was answered with "Disagree" or "Strongly disagree" on the same five-point Likert scale of ascending order responses (i.e. the value "1" represents "Strongly disagree"; the value "2" represents "Disagree"; the value "3" represents "Not sure"; the value "4" represents "Agree"; and the value "5" represents "Strongly agree").

Second (2), while there was reason to believe on the basis of the literature that there were generally positive effects on small business growth from entrepreneurial motivation, effectuation and causation orientations, and entrepreneurial orientation, a number of effects were significantly negative and in some cases, the effects were totally absent (Table 2.1, [d]). For example, in one of the studies in the East African LDCs, there are only a few significant (and negative) effects from the effectuation and causation orientations on small business growth.

Third (3), concerning small business growth, many of the small business growth items were included in the questionnaire on the basis of a pre-study with experts and a pilot study among small business owners. However, while the owners mainly indicated that their small business *has* grown over a certain period of time, often the small business growth measures turned out to be irrelevant in the regression models, because there was no model significance reached (Table 2.1, [e]) (see, for example, Eijdenberg 2016b).

Fourth (4), in general, many items in the questionnaires are responded to at the positive end of the five- or seven-points Likert scale (Table 2.1, [f]). For example, concerning entrepreneurial motivation in the study of Eijdenberg and Masurel (2013), the items were measured on a five-point Likert scale where 1 represents "Strongly disagree" and 5 represents "Strongly agree". The majority of the items were reported by the respondents as higher than a mean of 3.5. Another example, concerning entrepreneurial orientation is that the items were measured on a seven-point Likert scale, where 1 represents "Strongly disagree" and 7 represents "Strongly agree". Again, the majority of the items were reported by the respondents at the higher, positive end of the seven-point Likert scale (Eijdenberg 2016b).

Finally (5), most of the findings are shaped by their sample in terms of the size, the sampling method, the characteristics of the sector, the applied analysis methodology, the location of the data collection and the time of the data collection (Table 2.1, [g]). Therefore, the findings should be interpreted with some reservations. As discussed in the previous section on empirical studies, decisions concerning the data collection on location were predominantly theoretically driven, but inevitably pragmatic choices were also made, because many challenges needed to be dealt with. For example, I needed to consider my own time limits, personal safety, climate, local cultural habits such as national holidays and working hours, the dispersion of the respondents across the region or the city, the availability of the respondents, the attainability of the respondents by the – sometimes scarce – availability of transportation modes and the input of local support such as language interpreters, and the assistance of the local authorities, such as the municipality and the Chamber of Commerce.

#### *Possible Explanations for the Limitations*

There are a number of reasons that can cause one or more of the previously mentioned research limitations. Two reasonable explanations stem from the economic and cultural context in which the data collection has taken place. This can lead to several response biases, in particular concerning the interpretation of items, the ability to recall certain events, the social desirability of responding, and the perceptions and expectations from both the respondents and the researcher.

#### *Economically Determined*

The economic context of the East African LDCs is one possible reason why the used literature on entrepreneurial motivation, effectuation and causation orientations, and entrepreneurial orientation, from Western studies largely do not apply to East African LDCs. The data collection took place in four of the world's poorest countries. These countries have very low scores of gross national income per capita; a very low score on the human asset index on the basis of the percentage of the population malnourished, the mortality rate among children up to five years, the secondary school enrolment ratio, and adult literacy; and a high economic vulnerability, which comprises the structural vulnerability to exogenous economic and environmental shocks, such as the instability of the exports of goods and services and the risk of becoming victims of national disasters (United Nations 2015). These countries, as far back as comparisons can be made with more advanced economies in Western society, have almost always been economically underdeveloped and, while making progress, the prospects are not very prosperous for the not too distant future. Unlike Western society, people in East African LDCs are generally less educated, in terms of the degree to which they have obtained or the quality of their education, and have been exposed to less, or at least different, opportunities from environmental change and technological innovations. As a consequence of these pressing circumstances, people have little influence on the growth of their small businesses. Therefore, it can be assumed that these people generally do not fit with the Austrian economists' conception of the acting individual who operates as an independent economic entity, and that the society's conditions are largely influenced by the individual's own actions (Kirzner 1997; Schumpeter 1934). On the contrary, in East African LDCs the society's conditions, such as the poor economy, largely influence the individual's actions and how eventually their businesses grow (Liedholm 2002). Hence, the respondents might give different answers from the reality or from what was expected from the literature, and the interviews in the pre-studies.

#### *Culturally Determined*

Another possible reason relates to the cultural aspects of the context of East African LDCs. The respondent's ability to interpret the item (Table 2.1, [h]); the ability to recall (Table 2.1, [i]); and the pressure to give a socially desirable answer (Table 2.1, [j]) might disturb the results. Apparently in the studies in the East African LDCs, *direct* items may be "too direct" for the respondents; while the *indirect* items describe an event that covers the theoretical concept where the respondents feel more related to. *Direct* items can be answered negatively, because the respondents feel too proud to admit, while *indirect* items can describe an event on which the respondent knows how to answer such items socially desirable. Furthermore, also responding at the higher, positive ends of the five- or seven-point Likert scales can be due to social desirability (the tension to answer positively) and this can also be sector-dependent (e.g. sectors that are visibly on the rise, such as the mobile telecom industry between 2000 and 2010). The interpretation of the questionnaires by the respondents can differ per sample: it is likely that samples with higher-educated respondents, for example in the financial service sector, have different abilities in item interpretation than respondents from samples used in the studies in the East African LDCs, such as the *mama lishe*. In addition, many items in the questionnaires were assessed to measure the phenomenon *at the start of the business*. Therefore, there can be a recall bias/memory effect with the respondent, in particular concerning the small business growth measures such as the value of the housing or the value of the sales over a certain period of time. Most of these measures were often forgotten by the respondents. However, the change in the number of employees was often easy for the respondents to recall. Moreover, there is a possibility of misinterpretation due to the loss of content that may occur after translation from English to the other languages. The majority of the respondents in the studies in the East African LDCs were lower-educated. It is likely that the respondents were not familiar with research methods, such as filling out the questionnaires. Therefore, many respondents did not know precisely what to do at the start of completing a questionnaire. Instructing the respondents on the questionnaires took a substantial effort from me, as the researcher, and the assisting team. Eventually, although the respondents assured us that they understood the items in the questionnaire, often questions on practicalities (e.g. the expected time to finish the questionnaire) were still raised by the respondents. This can decrease the validity.

Another possible explanation might stem from the respondent's perception of the data collection and the respondent's expectations of the researcher. It is possible that the different perceptions have their roots in sub-Saharan Africa's *Ubuntu*, in particular sharing and collectivism (Saule 1998) and other typical African values and beliefs (see Munene et al. 2000: 342), such as seeing advancement or success as being dependent on loyalty to powerful others. These values and beliefs might also be the reason why small business growth is not explained by the theoretical subjects: the fruits of growth are shared first among relatives, i.e. the extended family (Khavul et al. 2009) before they influence the growth of the small business. Thus, owners do not feel the urge to grow their small business from the start. The dependency on the loyalty to powerful others might explain why many small business owners are impervious to entrepreneurial motivation, effectuation and causation orientations, and entrepreneurial orientation: none of this matters as long as their success is dependent on others in their network. These "others" can be people or organisations in the small business owner's network (as illustrated by, for example, Khavul et al. 2009; Khayesi et al. 2014; Kiggundu 2002; Luke et al. 2004; McDade and Spring 2005; Ramachandran and Shah 1999; Rutashobya and Jaensson 2004). Hence, the respondents might give answers in the questionnaires that differ from the reality or from what is expected on the basis of the pre-studies and the literature review.

Finally, an explanation can be found in African cultural attitudes, such as to "fully trust relatives but not strangers" (Munene et al. 2000: 342). My experience at the time of the data collection was that I was perceived by the respondents more as a journalist than as a researcher (Table 2.1, [k]). During the different rounds of data collection in the East African LDCs, I found that the rounds of data collection often attracted much attention from others in the immediate surroundings, which may have caused social pressure on the respondent while filling out the questionnaire. In regard to the respondent's misperception of me, the researcher, being a journalist, the respondents often experienced the data collection on the spot either as a positive event, to which many people from the local community were invited, or as a negative event, in which the respondents refused to cooperate because of suspicions about my integrity, even though I was accompanied by local assistants (Table 2.1, [l]). In addition, as I was the researcher and not a local person, the respondents often perceived the event of the data collection as an opportunity to take advantage and to demand incentives, i.e. money, for filling out the questionnaires (Table 2.1, [m]). Moreover, there was a difference in the expectations of the researcher, on the basis of the literature and the perception of the reality by experts in the pre-studies, and the small business owners in the main studies about certain events. For example, with regard to the effectuation and causation orientations: small business owners were expected to be predominantly effectuation-oriented (as indicated by the local experts in the pre-study and as expected by me, the researcher, on the basis of the literature), but the small business owners reported themselves to be mainly causation-oriented (Eijdenberg et al. 2017).

## Recommendations for Future Research

With regard to the previously mentioned methodological concerns, a number of recommendations for future research can be made. The first recommendation concerns the context of the East African LDCs. Scholars are encouraged to study the theoretical subjects from Table 2.1 beyond the context of East African LDCs in order to increase generalisability and make cross-country comparisons, for example with non-African LDCs, such as Cambodia or the Lao People's Democratic Republic in South East Asia (United Nations 2015).

Second, the main causes of the previously mentioned methodological concerns are that they are embedded in the construct validity and scale reliability, and the respondent's perception of the data collection and the respondent's expectations of the researcher. I recommend that other researchers consider and use alternative items and scales when conducting questionnaires. For example, avoid *direct* items in questionnaires and make use of a limited response possibility, such as a three-point Likert scale, as opposed to a seven-point Likert scale, to reduce complexity. Further, I invite other researchers to undertake more item construction together with the respondents. Although relying on the literature is considered to be the route for assessing convergent and discriminant validity, engaging the respondents to jointly create items that are applicable for their context might lead to more reliable results. Another recommendation is to use signs, symbols or emoticons, such as ☹ and ☺, in scales to express feelings. In addition, using more reversed items can test the respondent's answer consistency. This reduces the chances of content being lost in translation and interpretation biases. Therefore, construct validity can be increased, which decreases the likelihood of non-findings, such as the absence of the effects from entrepreneurial motivation, effectuation and causation orientations, and entrepreneurial orientation on small business growth; and the low explanatory power of coefficients in regression models.

Third, if certain theoretical subjects or indicators fail to show any significance, or causal effects remain absent, I would invite researchers to use theoretical subjects and indicators from other scientific disciplines that *do* work. This is referred to by Naudé (2010) as the "scholarly disconnection": for long, scientific disciplines have developed rapidly over the past five decades, but have failed to integrate. A valuable example of the integration of scientific disciplines could be the use performance indicators from development ... economics (for example consumer durables like owning a television and a refrigerator) (see, for example, Booysen et al. 2008; Filmer and Pritchett 2001; Pouw and Elbers 2012) in entrepreneurship literature. These indicators might be more relevant in the context of East African LDCs than indicators from entrepreneurship literature, such as the value of the sales.

Fourth, it is recommended that future research should go beyond the sample limitations of the studies in the East African LDCs. During the rounds of data collection, certain pragmatic choices were made, because I needed to deal with many previously-mentioned challenges for example, concerns about my personal safety; the climate; local cultural habits, such as national holidays and working hours; the dispersion of the respondents in a region or a city; the availability of the respondents; the availability of transportation modes; and the input from local support such as language interpreters and the assistance of local authorities such as the municipality and the Chamber of Commerce. Research on more and different samples, for example, the furniture sector in Tanzania (Isaga 2015; Isaga et al. 2015), would enrich the findings in terms of variety and generalisability.

Fifth, future researchers are encouraged to study beyond the time constraints of the data collections in the studies in East African LDCs. The collection of data at a different time might produce different findings; for example, because another type of business, which is dependent on social and economic developments, is present at that time. Furthermore, the availability of more time would give the researcher the opportunity to study the phenomena of interest at a different pace, or, for example, on a longitudinal basis. Data sets from longitudinal studies might be richer in content than the data sets from the cross-sectional studies in the East African LDCs.

Finally, while common research methodologies are applied in the studies of East African LDCs and the use of a certain methodology is largely dependent on the status of the literature that is being reviewed (Edmonson and McManus 2007), future researchers are encouraged to make use of different methodologies. Examples of different methodologies are experimental designs and observations. These methodologies could complement the use of questionnaires, interviews, and focus groups. There are examples of qualitative studies (e.g. Khavul et al. 2009; Langevang et al. 2012) that reveal rich insights into the theoretical subjects from Table 2.1. That is, the setting of the data collection should be a key element in the choice of a research methodology, despite what the status of prior theory and research prescribes researchers to use (Edmonson and McManus 2007).

## References

Ahiazu, A. (1995). "The Type A Method for Management Research in Africa. Enunciating a Culture-Specific Paradigm". *Paper presented at a regional seminar on Culture Dimensions to Appropriate Management in Africa.* Kampala, Uganda: Makerere University.

Akong'a, J. (1995). "The Growth-Positive and Growth-Negative Cultural Characteristics in African Societies". *Paper presented at a regional seminar on Culture Dimensions to Appropriate Management in Africa*, Kampala, Uganda: Makerere University.

Audretsch, D.B., Keilbach, M.C. & E.E. Lehmann (2006). *Entrepreneurship and Economic Growth.* New York: Oxford University Press.

Baker, T., Gedajlovic, E. & M. Lubatkin (2005). "A Framework for Comparing Entrepreneurship across Nations". *Journal of International Business Studies*, 36(5), 492–504.

Basu, R.R., Banerjee, P.M. & E.G. Sweeny (2013). "Frugal Innovation: Core Competencies to Address Global Sustainability". Journal of Management for Global Sustainability, 1(2), 63–82.

Baumol, W.J., Litan, R.E. & C.J. Schramm (2007). *Good Capitalism, Bad Capitalism and the Economics of Growth and Prosperity.* New Haven, CT: Yale University Press.

Blunt, P. & M.L. Jones (1992). *Managing Organizations in Africa.* Berlin: Walter de Gruyter.

Booysen, F., Van der Berg, S., Burger, R., Von Maltitz, M. & G. Du Rand (2008). "Using an Asset Index to Assess Poverty Trends in Seven sub-Saharan African Countries". *World Development*, 36(6), 1113–1130.

Brettel, M., Mauer, R., Engelen, A. & D. Küpper (2012). "Corporate Effectuation: Entrepreneurial Action and its Impact on R&D Project Performance". *Journal of Business Venturing*, 27(2), 167–184.

Central Intelligence Agency (2015a). *The World Factbook: Burundi*. Retrieved 30 March 2015, from Central Intelligence Agency: https://www.cia.gov/library/publications/the-world-factbook/geos/by.html.

Central Intelligence Agency (2015b). *The World Factbook: Rwanda*. Retrieved 30 March 2015, from Central Intelligence Agency: https://www.cia.gov/library/publications/the-world-factbook/geos/rw.html.

Central Intelligence Agency (2015c). *The World Factbook: Tanzania*. Retrieved 30 March 2015, from Central Intelligence Agency: https://www.cia.gov/library/publications/the-world-factbook/geos/tz.html.

Central Intelligence Agency. (2015d). *The World Factbook: Uganda*. Retrieved 30 March 2015, from Central Intelligence Agency: https://www.cia.gov/library/publications/the-world-factbook/geos/ug.html.

Collier, P. (2007). *The Bottom Billion: Why the Poorest Countries are Failing and What Can Be Done About It*. Oxford: Oxford University Press.

Dau, R.K. (2003). "Trends in Social Security in East Africa: Tanzania, Kenya and Uganda". *International Social Security Review*, 56(3–4), 25–37.

East African Community. (2014). One People One Community. Retrieved 10 October 2014, from East African Community: http://www.eac.int/.

Edmonds, M., Mills, G. & T. McNamee (2009). "Disarmament, Demobilization, and Reintegration and Local Ownership in the Great Lakes: The Experience of Rwanda, Burundi, and the Democratic Republic of Congo". *African Security*, 2(1), 29–58.

Edmondson, A.C. & S.E. McManus (2007). "Methodological Fit in Management Field Research". *The Academy of Management Review*, 32(4), 1246–1264.

Eijdenberg, E.L. (2016a). *Small Business Growth in East African Least Developed Countries – Unravelling the Role of the Small Business Owners*. PhD dissertation, Vrije Universiteit Amsterdam, Alblasserdam: HAVEKA.

Eijdenberg, E.L. (2016b). "Does One Size Fit All? A Look at Entrepreneurial Motivation and Entrepreneurial Orientation in the Informal Economy of Tanzania". *International Journal of Entrepreneurial Behavior & Research*, 22(6), 804–834.

Eijdenberg, E.L. & E. Masurel (2013). "Entrepreneurial Motivation in a Least Developed Country: Push Factors and Pull Factors among MSEs in Uganda". *Journal of Enterprising Culture*, 21(1), 1–25.

Eijdenberg, E.L., Paas, L.J. & E. Masurel (2015). "Entrepreneurial Motivation and Small Business Growth in Rwanda". *Journal of Entrepreneurship in Emerging Economies*, 7(3), 212–240.

Eijdenberg, E.L., Paas, L.J., & E. Masurel (2017). "Decision-Making and Small Business Growth in Burundi". *Journal of Entrepreneurship in Emerging Economies*, 9(1), 35–64.

Eisenhardt, K.M. (1989). "Building Theories from Case Study Research". *The Academy of Management Journal*, 14(4), 532–550.

Filmer, D. & L. Pritchett. (2001). "Estimating Wealth Effects Without Expenditure Data or Tears: An Application to Educational Enrolments in States of India". *Demography*, 38(1), 115–132.

Frese, M., Brantjes, A. & R. Hoorn (2002). "Psychological Success Factors of Small-Scale Businesses in Namibia: The Roles of Strategy Process, Entrepreneurial Orientation and the Environment". *Journal of Developmental Entrepreneurship*, 7(3), 259–282.

Frese, M., Krauss, S.I., Keith, N., Escher, S., Grabarkiewicz, R. & S. Tonje Luneng (2007). "'Business Owners' Action Planning and Its Relationship to Business Success in Three African Countries". *Journal of Applied Psychology*, 92(6), 1481–1498.

Gartner, W.B. & S. Birley (2002). "Introduction to the Special Issue on Qualitative Research Methods in Entrepreneurship Research". *Journal of Business Venturing*, 17(5), 387–395.

Glaser, B. & A. Strauss (1967). *The Discovery of Grounded Theory: Strategies of Qualitative Research*. London: Wiedenfeld and Nicholson.

Hagos, G. (2000). Gender Divide Stifles Women Entrepreneurs. Retrieved 5 December 2014, from *Pan African News Agency*.

Hanson, S. (2009). "Changing Places Through Women's Entrepreneurship". *Economic Geography*, 85(3), 245–267.

Hjorth, D., Jones, C. & W.B. Gartner (2008). "Introduction for 'Recreating/Recontextualising Entrepreneurship'". *Scandinavian Journal of Management*, 24(2), 81–84.

Hughes, M. & R.E. Morgan (2007). "Deconstructing the Relationship between Entrepreneurial Orientation and Business Performance at the Embryonic Stage of Firm Growth". *Industrial Marketing Management*, 36(5), 651–661.

Isaga, N. (2015). "Owner-Managers' Demographic Characteristics and the Growth of Tanzanian Small and Medium Enterprises". *International Journal of Business and Management*, 10(5), 168–181.

Isaga, N., Masurel, E. & K. van Montfort (2015). "Owner-Manager Motives and the Growth of SMEs in Developing Countries: Evidence from the Furniture Industry in Tanzania". *Journal of Entrepreneurship in Emerging Economies*, 7(3), 190–211.

Jackson, T. (2004). *Management and Change in Africa: A Cross-Cultural Perspective*. London: Routledge.

Joergensen, J.J. (1990). "Organizational Life-cycle and Effectiveness Criteria in State-owned Enterprises: The Case of East Africa". In: A.M. Jaeger & R.N. Kanungo, *Management in Developing Countries*. London: Routledge, 62–82.

Johns, G. (2006). "The Essential Impact of Context on Organizational Behaviour". *The Academy of Management Review*, 32(2), 386–408.

Khavul, S. & G.D. Bruton (2013). "Harnessing Innovation for Change: Sustainability and Poverty in Developing Countries". *Journal of Management Studies*, 50(2), 285–306.

Khavul, S., Bruton, G D. & E. Wood (2009). "Informal Family Business in Africa". *Entrepreneurship: Theory & Practice*, 33(6), 1219–1238.

Khayesi, J.N., George, G. & J. Antonakis (2014). "Kinship in Entrepreneur Networks: Performance Effects of Resource Assembly in Africa". *Entrepreneurship: Theory & Practice*, 38(6), 1323–1342.

Kiggundu, M.N. (1989). *Managing Organizations in Developing Countries*. Sterling, VA: Kumarian Press.

Kiggundu, M.N. (2002). "Entrepreneurs and Entrepreneurship in Africa: What is Known and What Needs to be Done". *Journal of Developmental Entrepreneurship*, 17(3), 239–258.

Kirkwood, J. (2009). "Motivational Factors in a Push-Pull Theory of Entrepreneurship". *Gender in Management: An International Journal*, 24(5), 346–364.

Kirzner, I.M. (1997). "Entrepreneurial Discovery and the Competitive Market Process: An Austrian Approach". *Journal of Economic Literature*, 35(1), 60–85.

Kolk, A. & R. van Tulder (2010). "International Business, Corporate Social Responsibility and Sustainable Development". *International Business Review*, 19(2), 119–125.

Krauss, S.I., Frese, M., Fiedrich, M. & J.M. Unger (2005). "Entrepreneurial Orientation: A Psychological Model of Success among Southern African Small Business Owners". *European Journal of Work & Organizational Psychology*, 14(3), 315–344.

Kriauciunas, A., Parmigiani, A. & M. Rivera-Santos (2011). "Leaving our Comfort Zone: Integrating Established Practices with Unique Adaptations to Conduct Survey-based Strategy Research in Non-traditional Contexts". *Strategic Management Journal*, 32(9), 994–1010.

Kristiansen, S. (2002). "Individual Perception of Business-Context: The Case of Small-scale Entrepreneurs in Tanzania". *Journal of Developmental Entrepreneurship*, 7(3), 283–304.

Kuzilwa, J.A. (2005). "The Role of Credit for Small Business Success: A Study of the National Entrepreneurship Development Fund in Tanzania". *Journal of Entrepreneurship*, 14(2), 131–161.

Langevang, T., Namatovu, R. & S. Dawa (2012). "Beyond Necessity and Opportunity Entrepreneurship: Motivations and Aspirations of Young Entrepreneurs in Uganda". *International Development Planning Review*, 34(4), 439–459.

Langevang, T. & K.V. Gough (2012). "Diverging Pathways: Young Female Employment and Entrepreneurship in Sub-Saharan Africa". *The Geographical Journal*, 178(3), 242–252.

Liedholm, T. C. (2002). "Small firm dynamics: evidence from Africa and Latin America". Small Business Economics, 18(1), 225–240.

Luke, N., Munshi, K. & M. Rosenzweig (2004). "Marriage, Networks and Jobs in Third World Cities". *Journal of the European Economic Association*, 2(2–3), 437–446.

Lyons, M., Brown, A. & C. Msoka (2014). "Do Micro Enterprises Benefit from the 'Doing Business' Reforms? The Case of Street-vending in Tanzania". *Urban Studies*, 51(8), 1593–1612.

Mbiti, L. & J. Maree (1996). *Ubuntu: The Spirit of African Transformation Management.* Randburg: Sigma Press.

McDade, B.E. & A. Spring (2005). "The 'New Generation of African Entrepreneurs': Networking to Change the Climate for Business and Private Sector-led Development". *Entrepreneurship & Regional Development*, 17(1), 17–42.

Minniti, M. & W.A. Naudé (2010). "What Do We Know About the Patterns and Determinants of Female Entrepreneurship across Countries?" *European Journal of Development Research*, 22(3), 277–293.

Molina-Azorín, J.F., López-Gamero, M.D., Pereira-Moliner, J. & E.M. Pertusa-Ortega (2012). "Mixed Methods Studies in Entrepreneurship Research: Applications and Contributions". *Entrepreneurship & Regional Development*, 24(5–6), 425–456.

Mufune, P. (2003). "African Culture and Managerial Behaviour: Clarifying the Connections". *South African Journal of Business Management*, 34(3), 17–28.

Munene, J.C., Schwartz, S.H. & P.B. Smith (2000). "Development in Sub-Saharan Africa: Cultural Influences and Managers' Decision Behaviour". *Public Administration & Development*, 20(4), 339.

Naudé, W.A. (2010). "Entrepreneurship, Developing Countries, and Development Economics: New Approaches and Insights". *Small Business Economics*, 34(1), 1–12.

Naudé, W.A. (2011). "Entrepreneurship is Not a Binding Constraint on Growth and Development in the Poorest Countries". *World Development*, 39(1), 33–44.

New Vision. (2007). The Rise and Rise of Lugabire. Retrieved 3 July 2016, from New Vision: http://www.newvision.co.ug/new_vision/news/1169407/rise-rise-lugabire.

Noorderhaven, N.G. & B. Tidjani (2001). "Culture, Governance, and Economic Performance: An Exploratory Study with a Special Focus on Africa". *International Journal of Cross Cultural Management*, 1(1), 31–52.

Nzelibe, C. 1986. "The Evolution of African Management Thought". *International Studies of Management and Organization*, 16(2), 6–16.

Onwuejeogwu M.A. (1995). "Development in Africa: Common Cultural Values Central for Effective Managerial and Administrative Training Programmes". Paper presented at a regional seminar on cultural dimensions and appropriate and effective management in Africa, Kampala, Uganda: Makerere University.

Otite, O. (1978). "The Introduction: The Study of Social Thought in Africa". In: O. Otite, *Themes in African Social and Political Thought*. Enegu: Fourth Dimension Publishers, 1–34.

Overå, R. (2007). "When Men Do Women's Work: Structural Adjustment, Unemployment and Changing Gender Relations in the Informal Economy of Accra, Ghana". *Journal of Modern African Studies*, 45(4), 539–563.

Pouw, N. & C. Elbers (2012). "Modelling Priority Patterns in Asset Acquisition: The Case of Smallholder Farmers in Three Rural Districts in Uganda". *Journal of Development Studies*, 48(9), 1360–1374.

Powell, B. (2008). *Making Poor Nations Rich: Entrepreneurship and the Process of Economic Development*. Oakland, CA: The Independent Institute.

Ramachandran, V. & M.K. Shah (1999). "Minority Entrepreneurs and Firm Performance in Sub-Saharan Africa". *The Journal of Development Studies*, 36(2), 71–87.

Rao, B.C. "How Disruptive is Frugal?". Technology in Society, 35(1), 65–73.

Rooks, G., Sserwanga, A. & M. Frese (2014). "Unpacking the Personal Initiative – Performance Relationship: A Multi-group Analysis of Innovation by Ugandan Rural and Urban Entrepreneurs". *Applied Psychology: An International Review*, 65(1), 1–33.

Rousseau, D.M. & Y. Fried (2001). "Location, Location, Location: Contextualizing Organizational Research". *Journal of Organizational Behavior*, 22(1), 1–13.

Rutashobya, L. & J.-E. Jaensson (2004). "Small Firms' Internationalization for Development in Tanzania". *International Journal of Social Economics*, 31(1/2), 159–172.

Sarasvathy, S.D. (1998). *How Do Firms Come to Be? Towards a Theory of the Prefirm*. PhD dissertation. Pittsburgh, PA: Carnegie Mellon University.

Sarasvathy, S.D. (2001). "Causation and Effectuation: Toward a Theoretical Shift from Economic Inevitability to Entrepreneurial Contingency". *The Academy of Management Review*, 26(2), 243–263.

Saule, N. (1998). "Images of Ubuntu in Essays of SEK Mqhayi in Umteteli Wzabantu". *South African Journal of African Languages*, 18(1), 10–19.

Saunders, M., Lewis, P. & A. Thornhill. (2012). *Research Methods for Business Students* (5th ed.). Essex: Pearson Education Limited.

Schneider, F. (2005). "Shadow Economies Around the World: What Do I Really Know?" *European Journal of Political Economy*, 21(3), 598–642.

Schumpeter, J.A. (1934). *The Theory of Economic Development*. Cambridge, MA: Harvard University Press.

Snyder, M. (2000). *Women in Africa Economies: From Burning Sun to Boardroom*. Kampala: Fountain Publishers.

Steyaert, C. (1997). "A Qualitative Methodology for Process Studies of Entrepreneurship: Creating Local Knowledge Through Stories". *International Studies of Management and Organization*, 27(3), 13–33.

Strier, R. (2010). "Women, Poverty, and the Microenterprise: Context and Discourse". *Gender, Work and Organization*, 17(2), 195–218.

Tabachnick, B.G. & L.S. Fidell. (2007). *Using Multivariate Statistics* (5th ed.), Boston: Pearson Education.

United Nations (2015). *UN Recognition of Least Developed Countries (LDCs)*. Retrieved 30 November 2015, from United Nations: http://www.un.org/en/development/desa/policy/cdp/ldc/ldc_list.pdf.

Van Gelderen, M. & E. Masurel (2012). *Entrepreneurship in Context*. New York: Routledge.

Vaunne, M. & T.J. Schoeneman (1997). "Individualism Versus Collectivism: A Comparison of Kenyan and American self-concepts". *Basic and Applied Social Psychology*, 19(2), 261–273.

Webb, J.W., Ireland, R.D. & D.J. Ketchen Jr. (2014). "Toward a Greater Understanding of Entrepreneurship and Strategy in the Informal Economy". *Strategic Management Journal*, 8(1), 1–15.

Welter, F. (2011). "Contextualzing Entrepreneurship: Conceptual Challenges and Ways Forward". *Entrepreneurship: Theory and Practice*, 35(1), 165–184.

Welter, F. & M. Xheneti (2013). "Reenacting Contextual Boundaries: Entrepreneurial Resourcefulness in Challenging Environments". In: A.C. Corbett & J. Katz, *Entrpereneurial Resourcefulness: Competing with Constraints (Advances in Entrepreneurship, Firm Emergence and Growth, volume 15)*. Emerald Group Publishing Limited, 149–183.

Whetten, D.A. (1989). "What Constitutes a Theoretical Contribution?" *The Academy of Management Review*, 14(4), 490–495.

World Bank. (2004). *World Development Report 2005: A Better Investment Climate for Everyone*. Washington, D.C.: World Bank and Oxford University Press.

Zahra, S.A. & M. Wright (2011). "Entrepreneurship's Next Act". *The Academy of Management Perspectives*, 25(4), 67–83.

Zahra, S.A., Wright, M. & S.G. Abdelgawad (2014). "Contextualization and the Advancement of Entrepreneurship Research". *International Small Business Journal*, 32(5), 479–500.

CHAPTER 3

# *Africapitalism*: A Management Idea for Business in Africa?

*Kenneth Amaeshi and Uwafiokun Idemudia*

*Africapitalism*, a term coined by the Nigerian banker and economist, Tony O. Elumelu C.O.N., is an economic philosophy that embodies the private sector's commitment to the economic transformation of Africa through investments that generate both economic prosperity and social wealth. Elumelu argues that "Africa's renaissance lies in the confluence of the right business and political action."[1] The concept is fast becoming a buzzword in Africa and expected to gain recognition even beyond the continent. It has continued to attract significant attention in both business and policy circles. For instance, on an invitation to a panel chaired by UN Secretary General Ban Ki-moon (9 April 2014), Elumelu shared his views on Africapitalism with the UN General Assembly and Economic and Social Council (ECOSOC).[2] *The World in 2015*, a key publication by *The Economist*, featured a piece on "The Rise of Africapitalism".[3] The Tony Elumelu Foundation has also established the Africapitalism Institute,[4] a research-based think tank to mainstream the understanding and practice of Africapitalism.

One of the projects funded by the Africapitalism Institute is the Edinburgh Project.[5] The Edinburgh Project, amongst others, aims to rethink capitalism in Africa by focusing on the role of business leaders, investors, and entrepreneurs in Africa's development. It is a four-country study – Cote d'Ivoire, Kenya, Nigeria, and South Africa – with an international partnership involving nine universities: Pan Atlantic University – Lagos Business School (Nigeria); Strathmore Business School (Kenya); University of Loughborough; University of

1 http://tonyelumelufoundation.org/africapitalisminstitute/driving-africas-renaissance-africapitalism/.

2 http://www.heirsholdings.com/tonyelumelu/tony-elumelu-addresses-the-un-general-assembly.

3 http://www.economist.com/news/21631956-entrepreneurs-will-transform-africa-says-tony-elumelu-chairman-heirs-holdings-and.

4 http://www.tonyelumelufoundation.org/africapitalisminstitute/.

5 http://www.business-school.ed.ac.uk/blogs/research-news/2014/09/22/africapitalism-african-business-leaders-and-africas-development/.

 | DOI 10.1163/9789004351615_004

Nottingham; University of Durham (UK); York University (Canada); University of Cape Town (South Africa); and University of Grand-Bassam (Cote d'Ivoire); with the University of Edinburgh (UK) overseeing the entire project.

In this chapter,[6] we seek to provide insight about this concept that, as explained above, has seen the birth of a dedicated institute and the commencement of a continent-wide research project. We link Africapitalism to the broader literature on business and society, and critically interrogate and explore it as a possible management idea for business in Africa in response to the onslaught of global capitalism. Coincidentally, the literature on the role of business in society often takes context for granted. When it takes context into consideration, it often adopts an (historical) institutional perspective, which tends to focus more on *why* firms behave the way they do, rather than on *how* firms *ought* to behave, especially in weak institutional contexts. This neutrality, arguably, reflects a dominant paradigm within the social sciences, which have had enormous influence on the field of business in society scholarship. Stepping out of this neutrality, we argue that Africapitalism, i.e. the need for the private sector in Africa to commit to the socio-economic development of Africa, is both an imaginative *management idea* and a creative moral-linguistic artefact that embodies a new space for appropriating and re-moralising capitalism in Africa. We situate Africapitalism in the broader conversation on global capitalism and highlight some of the salient principles that make it simultaneously an aspect of global capitalism but uniquely different in its situated contextualisation. In so doing, we try to reinstate the sense of place and belonging in the economic globalisation discourse as a form of economic patriotism, and we argue that this is the quintessential distinctiveness of Africapitalism in the global, economic world order. We also highlight emerging issues for further research, and seek to ignite a continued discussion on this theme.

## Introduction

Africa has a long and chequered history of colonialism, bad governance, and poverty. In addition, the continent suffers from weak institutions and distressed civil societies. Resuscitating Africa from near economic and social collapse has continued to remain a thriving business for multinational institutions, foreign governments, aid agencies, international NGOs, and international donors.

6 This chapter is a slightly amended version of a publication in the Africa Journal of Management, Vol. 1 (2015), issue 2. The Open Access published Journal version of this paper can be freely download from: http://www.tandfonline.com/doi/pdf/10.1080/23322373.2015.1026229.

Regrettably, some of these actors have also proven to be Africa's Achilles' heel. The latest to arrive among this foray of helpers are multinational corporations, which often (are forced to) take on public responsibilities in the form of Corporate Social Responsibility (CSR). Predictably, none of these have become the panacea to the myriad of challenges confronting the continent (see Idemudia 2014); rather, most of them continue to flounder at the margins. The crisis of "development" in Africa and the failure of either the state or the market to deliver has, in recent years, led to a call for better collaboration and partnership between the state, business, and civil society, if developmental challenges in the region are to be addressed (see Garforth et al. 2007; Idemudia 2014; Richey and Ponte 2014).

While the 1980s and 1990s were generally seen as the "lost decades" for development in most parts of the region, Africa is now supposedly on the rise (see *The Economist* 2011, 2013; Carmody 2008). This rise is largely driven by natural resources extraction, export of primary commodities, and the recent rediscovery of Africa as the last frontier of capitalism by the global market. This re-discovery and recognition has been intensified in the wake of the global financial crisis. Implicated in this rise are entrepreneurs who push the boundaries and explore new and innovative opportunities in the continent. The emergence of successful African entrepreneurs has also contributed to the new narrative of Africa rising. Recognising the power of the market for development and the key role of entrepreneurs as economic development change agents in unfettered markets, the nouveau economic elites in Africa have sought to engage with the sustainable development of the continent in a number of ways. One such attempt is the emergence of Africapitalism as a possible economic and management idea in Africa and beyond.

Elumelu's Africapitalism is an idea that emphasises the obligations of the private sector towards the socio-economic development of Africa and assumes the feasibility of such an undertaking. As an economic idea, it will require efficient economic coordination by diverse actors, such as the state, civil society, and markets. In order to do so, it will need to tap into the moral psychology of the actors (moral agents) and hypothesise human behaviours and needs. This may be contrary to the starting point of neoclassical economic thinking of the *homo economicus*, who is primarily driven by self-interest. Indeed, an Africapitalism perspective that is rooted in the values of Ubuntu[7] sees the purpose of management as neither to benefit one *collection of individuals*, as the

7 Ubuntu is simultaneously the foundation and edifice of African philosophy and its direct relevance to management theory and practice is covered extensively in the literature (see Lutz 2009; Prinsloo 2000; Mbigi and Maree 1995; and Karsten and Illa 2005).

shareholder theory would suggest, nor to benefit many collections of individuals, as the stakeholder theory proposes. Instead, its purpose is to benefit the community as well as the larger communities of which it is a part (Lutz 2009). As such, the *common good* becomes the principal target of managers (Ibid.). This is an entirely different perspective and will have implications for how the business-society relationship is understood in Africa.

The significance of Africapitalism stems from both the enormity of the developmental and governance challenges confronting Africa (see Mbaku 2004), and the fact that the continent requires a customised economic philosophy and business model that better allows it to meet her needs. This is particularly the case given what Ekeh (1990) has referred to as the "tyranny of borrowed paradigm," in which African realities are either ignored in theoretical debates or made to fit into Western constructs. Consequently, while Lutz (2009) notes that theories that were created within and for individualistic culture are often not at home within communal cultures, Blunt and Jones (1997) assert that Western approaches to management and leadership are often incompatible with the cultural context of Africa. Similarly, Zoogah (2008) has argued that there is a need for a contextualised approach to management theory that incorporates the African context, and the lived experience of its people in its theorising and modelling (see also Edoho 2001). In addition, Lutz (2009) suggested that such a theory is needed not only in the interest of moral integrity and social stability, but also in the interest of economic productivity.

After considering a variety of alternatives, Zoogah and Nkomo (2013) see research that is strong in differentiating Africa yet still highly similar to the West, i.e. that advocates for balanced identity as the most optimal space via which African management research can maintain its unique African identity while still contributing to global management theories. They assert that this is consistent with strategic balance theory, which suggests that a balance between differentiation and conformity leads to better outcomes. This is where Africapitalism comes in as a hybrid notion (i.e. a management idea – a "fairly stable bod[y] of knowledge about what managers ought to do" (Kramer, 1975: 47)) that is potentially an alternative to the status quo. Africapitalism seeks to avoid cultural romanticism that seems to see African culture as the panacea to solve African problems and Western universalist discourse that ignores subtle contextual particularities by reasserting the sense of place, culture, and emotion in capitalism. However, if Africapitalism is to be a meaningful idea and not to be conflated with other similar ideas (i.e. a CSR-esque phenomenon) and its true transformational potential is to be realised both in terms of management theory and practice in Africa, then there needs to be a clarification of its philosophical foundation and the underpinning associative ideas.

It is against this background that this chapter seeks to propose a series of associated ideas that might underpin the notion of Africapitalism as a basis for the socio-economic governance role of business and a management idea. It considers its implications for business and society relationships in Africa. The chapter starts by exploring the nature of global capitalism before dovetailing to the quintessential characteristics of Africapitalism as both a moral and a linguistic project.

## Global Capitalism: Prospects, Problems, and Paradoxes

Capitalism is one of the most creative ingenuities of mankind. Arguably, capitalism as a mode of economic coordination is fundamentally anchored on the principles of freedom (liberty), individuality (self-interest), diligence (thrift and self-discipline), rights (private property), and equity (fairness). Where each of these fundamentals or a combination of them is out of kilter, capitalism limps, wobbles, and could become dangerously wild if unchecked. The recent global financial crisis, which has been described as a crisis of capitalism, is a case in point. The different societal pathologies created by entrepreneurs and enterprises – for example, global warming, labour exploitation, inequality, pollution, and human rights infringements, etc. – are manifestations of unguarded capitalism. Nonetheless, capitalism in its completeness ought to be a benign force for good, driving human innovation for a progressive world.

In other words, capitalism is primarily a moral project, both as a process and as an outcome (Dunning 2003, 2005; Lundan 2011; Judge et al. 2014), underpinned by a "moral or ethical ecology" (Dunning 2005: 138) or what Donaldson and Dunfee (1999) characterise as a set of "hypernorms". At the heart of capitalism is the moral question of "what is produced, in what ways it is produced, and who benefits from the goods (and bads) created" (Dunning 2005: 136). Reinforcing the moral foundation of capitalism, Novak (1982: 56) argues that "each age of capitalism requires its own specific moral culture which nurtures the virtues and values on which its existence depends." Unfortunately, "[f]or too long capitalism, its institutions and morality have been kept separate from each other" (Dunning, 2005: 149) and the resultant successes and failures of capitalism have been treated as matters of mere technicalities (Hayek 1979).

That said, capitalism has strong cultural influences and undertones (Hall and Soskice 2001). The Continental-European form of capitalism is different from the Anglo-Saxon variant. While the former is socially oriented, the latter is highly economistic in outlook and orientation. These varieties are informed by distinct socio-cultural philosophies. The emergence of capitalism in China, for instance, is unique given the role of the state in furthering economic advancement. What is seen today as mere expressions of markets, are historical products of well-articulated socio-political philosophies. In most advanced capitalist societies, the state is instrumental to the shaping of the different forms of capitalism existing in these societies. For instance, French capitalism is different from both UK and German forms of capitalism (Kang and Moon 2012). Capitalism in these countries is a function of historical and cultural antecedents leading to what has been characterised as a "methodological national" (Smith 1979) approach to the study of capitalism. As Offe states:

> If there is anything distinctive about the "European" model of capitalism, it is the insight, congealed in a myriad of economic institutions and regulatory arrangements, that the interest of "all of us" will be served well if the pursuit of the interest of "each of us" is to some extent constrained by categorical status rights.
>
> OFFE 2003: 444

Nonetheless, the study of capitalism assumes strong institutional contexts and actors – for example, strong governments, civil society, effective or efficient regulations and governance. However, nation states and governments in Africa are weak. This weakness makes it difficult for the states and governments to play effectively the roles of protecting lives and properties, as well as ensuring social well-being, infrastructure development, and the development of enabling institutions for the production and consumption of goods and services within Africa. In addition, and unfortunately, the benefits of capitalism are unevenly, some may say, unjustly distributed, partly due to structural and power imbalances in the global polity and partly as a result of weak local (national) governance systems. Capitalism requires effective government, market, and civil society, to yield good societal outcomes. Where one or more of these are missing, the tendency of capitalism leading to societal pathologies is magnified. Thus, reflecting on the benevolence and malevolence of capitalism, Dunning writes:

> I would assert that capitalism, although possibly the best economic system currently known to man to create wealth, is sub-optimal. In its current state, it is perceived to result in, or continue to allow, an unacceptable level of poverty and social injustice, insufficient participation and a lack of democracy. It is also frequently associated with corporate malfeasance, misuse of economic and political power by governments, and a cavalier attitude by supranational entities towards environmental, security and cultural related issues.
>
> DUNNING 2005: 138

Consequently, Newell (2008) has stated that we are now at a critical crossroads, where we must choose between a laissez-faire approach to capitalism and regulated capitalism that would serve broader social and environmental goals, such as social justice and sustainability. In response, those that accept the realities of economic globalisation and liberalisation on ideological grounds, as well as on the market efficiency arguments, have called for capitalism with a human face as a strategy to deal with the contradictions of capitalism (Leisinger 2007). For instance, while Bill Gates has called for creative capitalism,[8] drawing on his notion of embedded liberalism, John Ruggie has also suggested principled pragmatism (United Nations 2006). In contrast, proponents of regulated capitalism, argue that economic globalisation and liberalisation have altered the balance of rights and obligations that structure corporate behaviour (Chang 2001). Indeed, while firms now enjoy enormous amount of freedom and protection of their rights, essentially secured by what Stephen Gill has labelled the "new constitutionalism" (Gill 2003), there seems to be a commensurate decline in their responsibility and obligations to society at large. These scholars thus argue that self-regulation, as espoused in the laissez-faire approach to capitalism, is unlikely to deliver in terms of addressing the contradictions of capitalisms without stronger regulations (See Utting 2005, 2008; Newell 2001, 2008; O'Laughlin 2008). However, McBarnet (2007) has also pointed out that the corporate accountability movement may be asking more of the law than the law can deliver, as corporations are very adept at circumventing regulatory control and creatively complying with legal requirements.

This laissez-faire approach to capitalism versus the regulated capitalism debate has been particularly insightful, especially as it highlights the strength and limitations of both sides to the debate. However, Crouch (2010) points out that the unintended consequence of this debate has been the tendency to neglect business as a fundamental institution in socio-economic governance. He argues that it is "essential that analysis of policy and politics of development takes full account of giant corporations as a form of governance in its own right." This is because, in the present context, the corporate hierarchies of big business are a major source of governance that rival both the state and the market. Thus, there is a need for attention to turn to the role of the firm as political actors, rather than simply being an entity to be regulated by public policy (Crouch 2010). It is therefore not surprising that, in the context of Africa, the discourse of Africapitalism has recently emerged as one way of engaging with the potential socio-economic governance role that business can play in Africa's

8 Through which business, especially the big ones, can improve the lot of the poor by better aligning their self-interest with the good of society (O'Laughlin 2008).

development. This is particularly important given that the discussions about the changing role of business in development in Africa are only just emerging (see Idemudia 2014). However, while recent works (see Geelhoed et al. 2014; Carney and Freeland 2014; Anyansi-Archibong and Anyansi 2014) on Africapitalism have been insightful, they have either tended to conflate it with other similar ideas like philanthro-capitalism – and thus undermine the innovative fresh perspective that the notion can bring to the analysis of business and society relationship in Africa (e.g. Anyansi-Archibong and Anyansi 2014) – or use it in an unspecified manner that belies its transformative possibilities.

## Africapitalism as an Imaginative Moral-linguistic Project

Africapitalism is an attempt to re-imagine entrepreneurship and reunite capitalism with its moral roots in Africa. This chapter takes the commitment of Africapitalism seriously and considers the necessary principles or values foundational to such a commitment. It identifies four possible principles: sense of progress; sense of parity; sense of peace; and sense of place and belonging, which are arguably rooted in the Ubuntu worldview. In this regard, Africapitalism implies the restoration of African-ness in capitalism, reflecting the economic and social practices implicit in African culture and tradition. To realise its goals, Africapitalism must bring its moral intuitions and principled commitments into alignment with modern economic practices. Here, the notion of Ubuntu or African traditional humanism comes to mind. In economic terms, it is a kind of humanism that does not proscribe self-enrichment, but requires the affluent to improve their community (Lutz 2009; Littrell et al. 2013). In this kind of voluntary wealth distributivism, one's economic and social power is measured by his or her economic empowerment of others.

Thus, if self-identity in the traditional Africa is a relational and transactional category, then a person is a creative articulation of his or her individuality within the matrix of the social community. In a fundamental sense, the community shapes identity. As such, an Africapitalism perspective sees the firm not as a mere collection of individuals, but as a community (Karsten and Illa 2005; McFarlin et al. 1999). "In a community the individual does not pursue the common good *instead* of his or her own good; rather pursues his or her own good *through pursuing* the common good" (Lutz 2009). This is because the values of Ubuntu are able to hold the paradox of individual and community in dynamic and interdependent tension by proposing the abrogation of the twin dangers of the subjugation of the individual to the collective, and the detached superordinacy of the individual (Littrell et al. 2013). Hence, drawing on the Ubuntu emphasis on group solidarity and relationship building, Africapitalism offers an alternative corporate culture that allows firms to strive for profit-making – but not the sort of profit-making at any cost that allows for the exploitation of human beings – because the ultimate goal of self-enrichment is to use it for the improvement of the community (Lutz 2009; Prinsloo 2000). At its core, the values of Ubuntu that might underpin the notion of Africapitalism include respect for the dignity of others, group solidarity, participation, sharing, the spirit of harmony and interdependency (see Mbigi 2002; Makhudu 1993). As mentioned above, we see the following four points as its cardinal values of Africapitalism: (1) sense of progress and prosperity; (2) sense of parity; (3) sense of peace and harmony; and (4) sense of place and belonging.

### *Sense of Progress and Prosperity*

Africapitalism is predicated on the creation of social wealth in addition to the pursuit of financial profitability. Wrapped around both social wealth and financial profitability is a sense of progress and prosperity that goes beyond just material accumulation to also include psycho-social human well-being. In this regard, progress and prosperity are not just the absence of poverty, but the presence of conditions that make life more fulfilling (e.g. access to quality education, health, social capital, democratic institutions, etc.) (Brundtland 1994). Accordingly, Brundtland stated that:

> Prosperity is more than the absence of poverty, pressing though that is. It means addressing sustainable development and careful husbandry of the world's resources, while recognising the rights of developing countries to break out from poverty. It means addressing population growth which leads to famine, destabilisation and war. It means quality of life achieved through education, employment, social justice and social security …. true world prosperity will remain a distant goal unless we pursue policies based on the concept of global solidarity.
>
> BRUNTLAND 1994: 57

This sense of progress and prosperity is nowhere more needed than in Africa, a continent riddled with extreme negative human conditions.

### *Sense of Parity*

The benefits of progress and prosperity need to be equitably shared. It is very easy for the accumulation of wealth to be lopsided. Most liberal economies have also led to high inequality (Piketty 2014). Inequality has become the new scourge and burden of success and the new poverty. Inequality in Africa is not necessarily created by liberalism, but the absence of it and the entrenchment of crony capitalism and corruption. Africapitalism is driven by a countercurrent of progressivism, which recognises that growth needs to be inclusive. In other words, it promotes a form of entrepreneurship that strives to create financial and social wealth for all stakeholders and not just for shareholders.

### *Sense of Peace and Harmony*

Capitalism can be very innovative, and at the heart of contemporary capitalism is the Schumpeterian quest for creative destruction. Framed as such, capitalism presents an arena of continuous struggle and contestations between the incumbents and the emergent; between old and new regimes; and between places and spaces. This quest for creative destrucion is often underpinned by the logic of self-interest (Adam Smith), which creates enormous rewards for firms and entrepreneurs, and has been proven to be one of the best drivers of entrepreneurial activities. Yet, it is riddled with imperfections – e.g. excessive inequality and market failure (Crouch 2011).

The quest for "[…] investments that generate both economic prosperity and social wealth," which is at the heart of Africapitalism, is a quest for balance, harmony, and peace. It is a recognition of the tendency of liberal market capitalism to lead to some form of socio-environmental imbalance, which is often dangerous to humanity. This sense of balance, which is expressed as the balance between economic prosperity and social wealth, could be further stretched to include the need to create a balance between the impacts of consumption and production on the ecological, environment, society, and economy. In this regard, Africapitalism shares similar values of balance and harmony with the sustainability movement (Schwartz and Carroll 2008), which can be summed up as the quest for peace and security: "[…] a process of achieving human development […] in an *inclusive, connected, equitable, prudent,* and *secure* manner" (Gladwin et al. 1995: 878, emphasis in original). Africapitalism is also underpinned by a stakeholder orientation insofar as it not only sees the creation of private wealth in the form of profits for shareholders, but strives to create social wealth for all stakeholders. It is a re-enactment of the modern management philosophy of harmony and balance (Kramer 1975).

### *Sense of Place and Belonging*

The sense of place and belonging is at the heart of the Africapitalism agenda. It is a direct response to globalised capitalism, which often takes place for granted and prioritises cost instead. Consequently, it is easy to outsource and for capital to follow the least cost-tolerant path. Arguably, therefore, globalisation trivialises place and promotes "placelessness". It reduces place to a mere resource, to the extent that the economic value of a place determines its situation in the scheme of things. Place is consumed and place is fluid. Globalisation reduces place to space, which, according to Gieryn (2000: 465), "[…] is what place becomes when the unique gathering of things, meanings, and values are sucked out." Lamenting the impact of globalisation on place, Escobar wrote:

> Place has dropped out of sight in the "globalization craze" of recent years, and this erasure of place has profound consequences for our understanding of culture, knowledge, nature, and economy. It is perhaps time to reverse some of this asymmetry by focusing anew – and from the perspective afforded by the critiques of place themselves – on the continued vitality of place and place-making for culture, nature, and economy.
>
> ESCOBAR 2001: 141

The focus on cost and not place renders the global economic order placeless, and this placelessness has implications for managerial framing of costs and opportunities. As such, Africapitalism is underpinned by the value of sense of place and rootedness (Tuan 1977). It strives to restore in managerial decision making the link between place and economics on the one hand, and between place and self-identity on the other hand. Economic transactions are emplaced in place, and place is intrinsically bound with self, for "there is no place without self and no self without place" (Casey 2001: 684). In other words, Africapitalism becomes an expression of *topophilia* (Tuan 1974) – "the effective bond between people and place" (Duncan and Duncan 2001: 41).

The sense of place and belonging can also manifest itself as an expression of patriotism, which "[…] attributes an intrinsic moral value to the defence of the homeland, even if it does not specify its boundaries" (Clift and Woll 2012: 314) and "[…] entails a significant degree of loyalty to one's country and an associated disposition to take pride in it, to be subject to emotions closely connected with one's perception of its well-being, and to give some degree of preference to its needs and interests over the needs and interests of other countries" (Audi 2009: 367–368). Within the context of Africapitalism, this expression of patriotism could be classified as a form of economic patriotism, which suggests "[…] that economic choices should be linked with concerns for one's homeland" (Clift and Woll 2012: 308). In this case, the focus of Africapitalism on Africa is not arbitrary since, "[…] economic patriotism, like economic nationalism, needs to be defined by its territorial references and its underlying conception of political economic space, not by its supposed policy content" (Ibid.). And at the firm level, it could lead to corporate patriotism:

"[…] those forms of corporate behaviour which contribute to the national welfare of citizens and elicit the supportive behaviour of consumers and other stakeholders" (Puncheva-Michelotti et al. 2014: 1–2). As such, Africapitalism is, arguably, an exercise in, and an acceptance of, economic and political pragmatism given that: "[…] economic patriotism is a universal phenomenon endemic within interdependent markets and economic jurisdictions" (Clift and Woll 2012: 309).

As a linguistic project, Africapitalism jolts conventional wisdom and repositions the development of Africa in the world firmly as an indigenous project in which Africans will play significant, active roles. We see this glimmer of audacious hope across the continent, whether engaging with business leaders in Lagos, Nairobi, Accra, or Johannesburg. The message and the sentiments it evokes are unique. The emotive power of Africapitalism is not necessarily a new phenomenon in economic history. Economic patriotism and nationalism played significant roles in the rebuilding of Western Europe after World War II, for instance. The same could be seen in the contemporary rise of China as an economic world power. This highlights the view that economic development is both a rational and an emotional project. As such, the resurgence of the behavioural perspective of economics and finance at the wake of the recent global financial crisis is not surprising. The behavioural turn emphasises the role of emotions, sentiments, and sometimes crass irrationality on the rational person of neoclassical economics – including entrepreneurs. And herein lies the distinctiveness of Africapitalism as a powerful emotional economic tool for Africa's sustainable development. Since "To live is to live locally, and to know is first of all to know the places one is in" (Casey 1996: 18; see also Escobar 2001), the emotive force of Africapitalism, which is embedded in the sense of place and belonging, lends it the ability to connect with the African identity in a way that is not easily reflected in the broad view of capitalism.

## Emerging Issues and Future Research

It is important to emphasise that this chapter seeks merely to highlight the foundational ideas that might underpin the notion of Africapitalism. It is not an attempt to establish an Africapitalism theory of management. Hence, there are three main emerging issues. First, clarifying these foundational issues stems from the fact that Africapitalism shares the ethos of *doing good to do well* with other, similar ideas like Corporate Social Responsibility, corporate citizenship (CC), bottom of the pyramid and triple bottom line. Yet, Africapitalism is sufficiently different from these concepts, in the sense that while these concepts attempt to address the problems of owner-wealth maximisation theories of the firm without addressing the root of the problem (i.e. individualism) (Lutz 2009), Africapitalism takes on this challenge by suggesting that the firm can be seen as a community (i.e. sense of belonging) rooted in a sense of place. Consequently, Africapitalism creates a space to challenge what Blowfield (2005) has labelled "the non-negotiable value of capitalism," which concepts such as CSR or CC take for granted. The implication thus is that although Africapitalism might share the ameliorative potential of concepts like CSR or philanthropy, potentially it offers a much more transformative agenda.

Second, by reasserting the role of *place* and *emotion* in capitalism, Africapitalism offers an alternative basis for the socio-economic governance role of business that goes beyond the often limited business case argument that underpins many other concepts in the field of business and society. Crucial here is the fact that Africapitalism is not just an African-only project; rather, it is a mentality that is inclusive of different agents and actors that share the emotional attachment to the place. Thirdly, the discrepancy between traditional African cultures and theories taught to African managers and future managers remains a serious problem (Lutz 2009). Similarly, Zoogah (2008) has also pointed out that it has been suggested that Africans lack the confidence to generate meaningful, significant, and unique management knowledge. Africapitalism offers a potential space to begin to address these challenges.

There is a need, then, to further clarify what Africapitalism might mean as a *management idea* (Birkinshaw et al. (2008); Kramer 1975) in practice and the need to formulate hypotheses that can be tested using empirical data. This chapter is an attempt to spark a debate in this area. There is a need for other scholars with an interest in Africa to join the debate and subject the concept to more rigorous analyses that might spur further innovation.

## Conclusion

Africapitalism is capitalism by Africa-oriented entrepreneurs for Africa. It allows for a space to re-appropriate the discourse of capitalism in a manner that puts Africa, its culture, and people front and centre of any possibility of capitalist development in the region. Articulated as such, it comes across as a force for good. It is a creative and novel way of domesticating and unleashing the power of capitalism in Africa. It is a concept that can easily unleash the emotive imagination of Africans and refocus their minds on what it means to be African in Africa. In this regard, Africapitalism becomes an expression of economic patriotism.

Africapitalism is a creative push back on the disadvantages of globalisation. It is an entrepreneurial quest and mindset that challenges the conventional win-lose mentality of entrepreneurs and businesses in Africa to create shared value (i.e. win-win outcomes) in and for Africa instead. The idea of capturing national governments for personal gains, which seems rather prevalent in the continent, is anachronistic, unfair to African society, and ultimately unsustainable. Economic patriotism, which is at the core of Africapitalism, is unashamedly good for Africa, and should be promoted within and for the continent.

Africapitalism without a strong philosophy behind it runs the risk of being hollow and ungrounded. Entrepreneurs and firms are at the very heart of capitalism. Any change in the way capitalism runs today should involve these actors. For Africapitalism to succeed, it needs to permeate the entrepreneurial mindset and the boardroom. Given its normative base, it also needs supporting governance mechanisms. Africapitalism requires Africa-consciousness and a form of re-imagined Afrocentricism that places the interests of Africa and Africans at the epicentre of business decisions, and that will guide Africa's renaissance. Afri-consciousness is a socio-mental awareness of Africa, putting Africans before the market. The sudden characterisation of the continent as the last frontier of capitalism bears the hallmarks of the exploitative form of capitalism, which will not be good for the continent. Afri-consciousness helps to neutralise the onslaught of globalisation and redirects the positive energy of capitalism in Africa to meeting the genuine development needs of African people.

However, Africapitalism can only thrive in a politically stable and environmentally sustainable Africa. It should be open to the natural and unnatural contingencies of the modern market and robust enough to carve a separate and distinct niche for itself in the face of globalisation and globalised Western capitalist market structures. Furthermore, Africapitalism can be both secular and non-secular in orientation. It can be informed by the ethos of both indigenous and non-indigenous religions in Africa. That said, African entrepreneurs must work creatively with the different governments to achieve this goal. This is where responsible business-government relations become a critical strategic option for businesses in Africa. Yet, Africapitalism can potentially serve as the common discourse for collective action and a space to redress the imbalance in management research and theory on Africa. This is particularly important given that Zoogah and Nkomo (2013) have indicated how the predominance of Western epistemology in the production of management knowledge about Africa has led to the exclusion of African voices.

## References


Agnew, J.A. (1987). *Place and Politics: The Geographical Mediation of State and Society*. London: Allen and Unwin.

Anyansi-Archibong, C. & P.M. Anyansi (2014). "African Entrepreneurs and their Philanthropies: Motivations, Challenges and Impacts". In: M. Taylor, R.J. Strom & D.O. Renz (eds) *Handbook of Research on Entrepreneurs Engagement in Philanthropy Perspectives*. Cheltenham and Northampton: Edward Elgar, 267–297.

Audi, R. (2009). "Nationalism, Patriotism, and Cosmopolitanism in an Age of Globalization". *The Journal of Ethics*, 13: 365–381.

Birkinshaw, J., Hamel, G. & M. Mol (2008). "Management Innovation". *Academy of Management Review*, 33: 825–845.

Blowfield, M. (2005). "Corporate Social Responsibility: Reinventing the Meaning of Development?" *Journal of international Affairs*, 81(3): 515–524.

Blunt, P. & M.L. Jones (1997). "Exploring the Limits of Western Leadership Theory in East Asia and Africa". *Personnel Review*, 26(1/2): 6–23.

Brundtland, G.H. (1994). "What is World Prosperity?" *Business Strategy Review*, 5: 57–69.

Carmody, P. (2008). "Exploring Africa's Economic Recovery". *Geography Compass*, 2(1): 79–107.

Carney, D. & C. Freeland (eds) (2014). "Making Capitalism more Inclusive: Selected Speeches and Essays from Participants at the Conference on Inclusive Capitalism", 27 May, London.

Casey, E. (1993). *Getting Back into Place: Toward a Renewed Understanding of the Place-World*. Bloomington, IN: Indiana University Press, (cited in Escobar 2001).

Casey, E. (1996). "How to Get from Space to Place in a Fairly Short Stretch of Time. Phenomenological Prolegomena". In: S. Feld & K. Baso, *Senses of Place* 27: 14–51. Santa Fe: School of American Research.

Casey, E.S. (2001). "Between Geography and Philosophy: What Does it Mean to Be in the Place World?" *Annals of the Association of American Geographers*, 91(4): 683–693.

Chang, H.J. (2001). Breaking the Mould: An Institutionalist Political Economy to Neoliberal Theory of the Market and the Sate, program paper (SPD) No 6. Geneva: UNRISD.

Clift, B. & C. Woll. (2012). "Economic Patriotism: Reinventing Control over Open Markets". *Journal of European Public Policy*, 19 (3): 307–323.

Crouch, C. (2010). "CSR and Changing Modes of Governance: Towards Corporate Noblesse Oblige". In: P. Utting & J.C. Marques (eds) *Corporate Social Responsibility and Regulatory Governance: Towards Inclusive Development*, London: Palgrave Macmillan: 26–49.

Crouch, C. (2011). *The Strange Non-Death of Neoliberalism*. Cambridge: Polity Press.

Donaldson, T. & T.W. Dunfee (1999). *Ties that Bind: A Social Contracts Approach to Business Ethics*. Boston, MA: Harvard Business School Press.

Duncan, J. & N. Duncan (2001). "Sense of Place as a Positional Good: Locating Bedford in Place and Time". In: P.C. Adams, S. Hoelscher & K. Till (eds) *Textures of Place: Exploring Humanist Geographies*. Minneapolis, MN: University of Minnesota Press: 41–54.

Dunning, J.H. (ed.) (2003). *Making Globalization Good*. Oxford: Oxford University Press.

Dunning, J.H. (2005). "Is Global Capitalism Morally Defensible". *Contributions to Political Economy*, 24 (1): 135–151.

Dunning, J.H. (2008). "Corporate Social Responsibility: An Institutional Perspective". In: R. Strange & G. Jackson (eds), *Corporate Governance and International Business: Strategy, Performance and Institutional Change*. Basingstoke and New York: Palgrave-Macmillan, 168–195.

Edoho, F.M. (2001). "Management in Africa: The Quest for a Philosophical framework". In: F.M. Edoho (ed.) *Management Challenges for Africa in the Twenty-First Century: Theoretical and Applied Perspectives*, Westport, CT: Praeger, 73–90.

Ekeh, P. (1990). "Social Anthropology and Two Contrasting Uses of Tribalism in Africa". *Comparative Studies in Society and History*, 34(4): 660–700.

Escobar, A. (2001). "Culture Sits in Places: Reflections on Globalism and Subaltern Strategies of Localization". *Political Geography*, 20: 139–174.

Garforth, C., Philips, C. & S. Bhatia-Panthaki (2007). "The Private Sector, Poverty Reduction and International Development". *Journal of International Development*, 19: 723–734.

Geelhoed, J., Samhoud, S. & I. Smolders. (2014). *Creating Lasting Value: How to Lead, Manage and Market your Stakeholder Value*. London/Philadelphia/New Delhi: Kogan Page.

Gieryn, T. (2000). "A Space for Place in Sociology". *Annual Review of Sociology*, 26: 463–496.

Gill, S. (2003). *Power and Resistance in the New World Order*. Basingstoke: Palgrave Macmillan.

Gladwin, T., Kennelly, J. & T. Krause (1995). "Shifting Paradigms for Sustainable Development: Implications for Management Theory and Research". *Academy of Management Review*, 20(4): 874–907.

Hall, P.A. & D. Soskice (eds) (2001). *Varieties of Capitalism – The Institutional Foundations of Comparative Advantage*. Oxford: Oxford University Press.

Hayek, F. (1979). *Law Legislation and Liberty*, Vol. 3, London: Routledge and Kegan Paul.

Idemudia, U. (2014). "Corporate Social Responsibility and Development in Africa: Issues and Possibilities". *Geography Compass*, 8/7: 421–435.

Judge, W.Q., Fainshmidt, S. & J.L. Brown III (2014). "Which Model of Capitalism Best Delivers both Wealth and Equality?" *Journal of International Business Studies*, 45: 363–386.

Kang, N. & J. Moon (2012). "Institutional Complementarity between Corporate Governance and Corporate Social Responsibility: A Comparative Institutional Analysis of Three Capitalisms", *Socio-Economic Review*, 10: 85–108.

Karsten, L. & H. Illa (2005). "Ubuntu as Key African Management Concept: Contextual Background and Practical Insights for Knowledge Applications". *Journal of Managerial Psychology*, 20(7): 607–620.

Kramer, H. (1975). "The Philosophical Foundations of Management Rediscovered". *Management International Review*, 15(2–3): 47–55.

Leisinger, K.M. (2007). "Capitalism with a Human Face: The UN Global Compact". *Journal of Corporate Citizenship*, 28: 113–132.

Littrell, R.F., Wu, N.H., Nkomo, S., Wanasika, I., Howell, J. & P. Dorfman (2013). "Pan-Sub-Saharan African Managerial Leadership and Values of Ubuntu". In: T.R. Lituchy, B.J. Punnett & B.B. Puplampu (eds), *Management in Africa: Macro and Micro Perspectives*, New York: Routledge: 232–248.

Lundan, S.M. (2011). "An Institutional Perspective on the Social Responsibility of TNCs". *Transnational Corporations*, 20(3): 61–77.

Lutz, D.W. (2009). "African Ubuntu Philosophy and Global Management". *Journal of Business Ethics*,84: 313–328.

Makhudu, N. (1993). "Cultivating a Climate of Co-operation through Ubuntu". *Enterprise* 68 (August).

Mbaku, J.M. (2004). *Institutions and Development in Africa.* Trenton and Amara: Africa World Press.

Mbigi, L. (2002). "The Spirit of African Leadership: A Comparative African Perspective". *Journal of Convergance*, 3(4): 18–23.

Mbigi, L. & J. Maree. (1995). *Ubuntu, the Spirit of African Transformation Management.* Randburg: Knowledge Resources.

McBarnet, D. (2007). "Corporate Social Responsibility beyond the Law, through Law, for Law: The New Corporate Accountability". In: D. McBarnet, A. Voiculescu & T. Campbell (eds), *The New Corporate Accountability: Corporate Social Responsibility and the Law.* Cambridge: Cambridge University Press.

McFarlin, D.B., Coster, E.A. & C. Mogale-Pretorius (1999). "South African Management Development in the Twenty-First Century", *Journal of Management Development*, 18(1):63–78.

Murton, B. (2012). "Being in the Place World: Toward a Maori 'Geographical Self'". *Journal of Cultural Geography*, 29(1): 87–104.

Newell, P. (2001). "Managing Multinationals: The Governance of Investment for the Environment". *Journal of International Development*, 13(7): 907–919.

Newell, P. (2008). "CSR and the Limit of Capital". *Development and Change*, 39(6): 1063–1078.

Novak, M. (1982). *The Spirit of Democratic Capitalism*. Lanham, MA/New York: Madison Books.

Offe, C. (2003). "The European Model of 'Social' Capitalism: Can It Survive European Integration?" *The Journal of Political Philosophy:* Vol. 11, No. 4, 2003, 437–469.

O' Laughlin, B. (2008). "Governing Capital? Corporate Social Responsibility and the Limits of Regulation". *Development and Change*, 39(6): 945–957.

Piketty, Th. (2014). *Capital in the Twenty-First Century*. Cambridge MA/London: Harvard University Press.

Prinsloo, E.D. (2000). "The African View of Participatory Business Management". *Journal of Business Ethics*, 25: 275–286.

Puncheva-Michelotti, P., McColl, R., Vocino, A. & M. Michelotti. (2014). "Corporate Patriotism as a Source of Corporate Reputation: A Comparative Multi-Stakeholder Approach". *Journal of Strategic Marketing*, 22 (6): 471–493.

Richey, L.A. & S. Ponte. (2014). "New Actors and Alliances in Development". *Third World Quarterly*, 35(1): 1–21.

Schwartz, M. & A.B. Carroll. (2008). "Integrating and Unifying Competing and Complimentary Frameworks: The Search for a Common Core in the Business and Society Field". *Business and Society*, 47: 148–186.

Smith, Anthony D. (1979). *Nationalism in the Twentieth Century*. Oxford: Martin Robertson.

*The Economist*. (2011). "The Hopeful Continent: Africa Rising", http://*www.economist.com*/node/21541015/print, last accessed 1 December 2014.

*The Economist* (2013) "The Hopeful Continent: Africa Rising", http://*www.economist.com*/node/21572377/print, last accessed 1 December 2014.

Tuan, Y.F. (1974). *Topophilia: A Study of Environmental Perception, Attitudes, and Values*. Englewood Cliffs, NJ: Prentice Hall.

Tuan, Y.F. (1977). *Space and Place: The Perspective of Experience*. Minneapolis, MN: University of Minnesota Press.

United Nations. (2006) *Promotion and Protection of Human Rights: Interim Report of the Special Representative of the Secretary-General on Issues of Human Rights and Transnational Corporation and Other Business Enterprise* (UN Document No. E/CN.4/2006/97) Commission on Human Rights, 22 February New York: United Nations Economic and Social Council.

Utting, P. (2005). "Corporate Responsibility and the Movement of Business". *Development in Practice*, 15(3/4): 375–388.

Utting, P. (2008). "The Struggle for Corporate Accountability". *Development and Change*, 39(6): 959–975.

Zoogah, D.B. (2008). "African Business Research: A Review of Studies Published in the Journal of African Business and a Framework for Enhancing Future Studies". *Journal of African Business*, 9(1): 219–255.

Zoogah, D.B. & S. Nkomo. (2013). "Management Research in Africa: Past, Present and Future". In: T.R. Lituchy, B.J. Punnett & B.B. Puplampu (eds) *Management in Africa: Macro and Micro Perspectives*, New York: Routledge: 9–31.

CHAPTER 4

# Inclusive Business in Africa: Priorities, Strategies and Challenges

*Addisu A. Lashitew and Rob van Tulder*

*Inclusive business* is a newly emerging concept that refers to purpose-driven businesses that aspire to achieve societal impact or to create "shared value" (Porter and Kramer 2011). Only recently has the concept been introduced in development and business literature [cf. Van Tulder and Da Rosa (2011) for a literature review and Halme et al. (2012) and Hahn (2012) for early adoptions of the concept]. "Inclusiveness" can be understood narrowly as referring to societal impact and inclusion, or more broadly as comprising both societal and environmental considerations. Inclusive businesses are thus businesses that not only generate financial returns to their shareholders, but also explicitly include societal and environmental considerations in their core operations.

The importance of inclusive businesses for achieving sustainable and inclusive development is receiving attention at national, regional, and international policy fora (UNDP 2013; Mignano and Ishikawa 2014). Among policymakers, business-based approaches to poverty alleviation are appealing for their capacity to sustainably finance themselves and achieve scale. Among businesses, inclusive approaches represent an opportunity to give a "humane face" to their operations by allowing them to generate financial returns while simultaneously addressing societal issues that adversely affect the community in which they operate. Inclusive business strategies have the potential to seize new opportunities in yet unchartered markets (Prahalad 2004). The convergence of financial, strategic and societal considerations are thus presented as a win-win scenario for companies and societies – although the increasing attention it is receiving perhaps stems from a number of concurrent societal issues, including widespread and rising income inequalities and the recent financial crisis that adversely affected the legitimacy of business. The emergence of the "inclusive business" concept also reflects the increasing demand for sustainable business practices that address concerns of environmental sustainability and resource efficiency.

Academic discourse on the multi-faceted relationship between business and society is extensive and with a long history (Clarkson 1995). Several conceptual and theoretical approaches have been introduced to understand the

 | DOI 10.1163/9789004351615_005

motivations, mechanisms, and performance of business engagement with society. Stakeholder theory offers a paradigm that situates the firm within the context of a diverse set of stakeholders with and towards whom it has different types of relationships, interests, and responsibilities (Freeman 2010). The instrumental perspective of this approach concurs that successfully managing these diverse relationships and interests is critical for reducing opportunism and maximising competitive advantage (Jones 1995). The alterative paradigm of "corporate social performance" looks into the organisation's principles of social responsibility, the processes of its social responsiveness, and the outcomes they produce (Wood 1991). Just as financial performance indicates outcomes towards shareholder interests, properly quantified measures of corporate social performance would also indicate the organisation's success towards meeting its societal accountability. A large body of empirical research assesses whether higher levels of corporate social performance lead to greater financial performance (Waddock and Graves 1997), with meta-analytical reviews documenting a positive relationship (Orlitzky et al. 2003; Van Tulder et al. 2013).

Two specialised streams of literature can claim the legacy of studying the conceptual predecessors of what we call here "purpose-driven" or "inclusive" businesses. The social entrepreneurship literature is a relatively distinct domain that analyses entrepreneurship that gives primacy to social over business ambitions (Mair and Marti 2009; Mair et al. 2012). The common thread in this literature is the aim to understand how entrepreneurs create societal value by providing solutions to social problems, focusing on themes such as motives, processes, and challenges (Dacin et al. 2010). Understanding the likes of the Grameen Bank of Bangladesh, whose model spawned a microfinance revolution around the world, has been the main concern of the social entrepreneurship literature.

More recently, the fields of international business and strategy have started to take interest in societal issues such as poverty and sustainability. More classical approaches in this domain focused on the role of foreign direct investment on sustainable development in general, for instance through technology transfer and spillover effects (cf. Dunning and Fortanier 2007). Only a few studies have devoted systematic empirical attention to the level of the firm (Fortanier and Kolk 2007 Fortanier 2008). Corporate interest on the subject was initiated through case-based arguments, in particular following the publication of books such as *Fortune at the Bottom of the Pyramid* (Prahalad 2004) and *Capitalism at the Crossroads* (Hart 2005). These books have received a fair deal of criticism for "commercialising" and "romanticising" poverty (Karnani 2009; Munir et al. 2010). But they are also recognised for reshaping the discourse on poverty by challenging multinationals to consider developing economies as potential market opportunities (Kolk et al. 2014; Van Tulder et al. 2014). Recent advances in the literature (Caneque and Hart 2015) call for greater engagement with the poor as co-creators, and also enhanced partnerships with civil society and other indigenous actors. The focus of this literature is primarily on multinationals that, often in partnership with local civil society organisations, are expected to create "mutual value" that straddles societal and financial bottom-lines.

As such, "inclusive business" can be seen as the convergence of the Bottom of the Pyramid (BoP) and social entrepreneurship values and practices within mainstream business. This convergence, and the increasing attention given to inclusive business in national and international policy fora, also highlights the rising "developmental" imperative attributed to the private sector. The aim is not only to positively impact the communities in which the business operates, but also to create a virtuous cycle that boosts business productivity and performance through these interventions.

## Inclusive Businesses in Africa

The image of Africa as the continent bypassed by globalisation is already changing rapidly, giving way to the "Africa rising" narrative that highlights promising trends of economic transformations. In the decade since 2000, economic growth in the African region was second only to East Asia, averaging 5.1% per annum (Mckinsey and Company 2012). Africa has become an important destination of foreign investment, creating tens of millions of jobs, allowing millions of African consumers to join the middle-class consumer group (EY 2015). In spite of this progress, manifold structural challenges constrain African economies from reaching their full potential, including poor economic governance, inadequate infrastructure, underdeveloped financial services, low levels of literacy and, in many cases, fragile political institutions (GIZ 2013). As much as two thirds of Africans of working age are estimated to lack stable employment opportunities, showing that by far the majority of Africans still live in abject poverty (McKinsey and Company 2012). Companies that invest in the continent often come to realise that they need to address issues of inclusiveness, either as threat or as opportunity. A systematic research on the strategies that Dutch companies employ in Africa to gain a sustainable competitive advantage found that more than two thirds of these companies search for ways to achieve greater inclusiveness (Lem et al. 2013).

Insofar as inclusive businesses thrive by translating social needs into (marketable) business ventures (Mair and Marti 2009), Africa's extensive socio-economic issues and the institutional voids (Khanna et al. 2005) provide a great deal of business opportunities. The challenge, however, remains in exploiting the continent's resources to achieve inclusive growth that reaches Africa's young, rising population that is in search of new opportunities in a technologically connected world (UNDP 2013). Africa hence offers great scope for entrepreneurship that leverages technological advances to address pressing social needs.

There is indeed evidence that inclusive and socially-oriented businesses are playing a crucial role in Africa's development, as highlighted by a number of emerging examples from the continent. Ignitia, a young business in Lagos, uses advanced weather forecast models to provide affordable, SMS-based daily weather forecasts for tens of thousands subsistent farmers. Safaricom, Kenya's largest telecom operator, is best-known for its M-Pesa service, which is an SMS-based platform for transferring, saving and borrowing money using basic mobile phone devices. In less than a decade, M-Pesa has managed to reach more than 20 million Kenyans, extending financial services to millions of otherwise financially excluded individuals. Sole Rebels is a business from Ethiopia that specialises in eco-friendly, hand-crafted shoes made from locally-available materials using traditional artisanship and empowered women. It aspires to be "the new Nike of Africa", and already sells its products in over 30 countries through online channels, while also distributing through more than ten retail shops in cities as diverse as Athens, Barcelona, and Taipei.

These examples illustrate the power of "inclusive" business models for transforming lives and connecting Africa to global markets. They also indicate how the challenges of doing business in Africa can be surmounted by leveraging new and innovative, technology-driven business models.

But what are the kinds of approaches or strategies that are used by inclusive businesses in Africa? And what societal issues are given greater attention? What kinds of challenges do these businesses face? Little is currently known regarding the strategies, priorities, and challenges challenges of African entrepreneurs in the domain of inclusive business. The purpose of this study is to provide exploratory evidence on inclusive business practices in the continent. Using a survey tool designed for this purpose, we collected responses from 75 organisations operating in six East-African countries, namely: Ethiopia, Mozambique, Rwanda, Kenya, Tanzania, and Uganda. The survey covered, in particular, organisations from The Netherlands that were active in addressing social issues in these African countries as part of their core business strategies. This chapter presents the main findings from this survey.

The rest of the chapter is organised as follows: the second section describes the methods of data collection and analysis. Subsequently, we present the results of our analysis on the approaches and strategies that organisations adopt to become inclusive. A fourth section compares the level of policy attention given to inclusiveness among organisations by type of organisation and industry. We then examine the types of disadvantaged groups and social exclusion issues that are targeted by the organisations in our survey. This is followed by a look at the challenges inclusive businesses face before we present our conclusions.

## Data and Method

In the second half of 2015, an open-ended questionnaire was distributed among a large number of organisations operating in Africa.[1] The purpose of the data collection was to gain insight on how organisations understand and approach the multi-faceted issue of "inclusiveness". The questionnaire was exploratory in nature, and was developed using insights from literature reviews in the fields of international business in Bottom of the Pyramid (BoP) markets and social entrepreneurship.

Efforts were made to include "frontrunner" organisations that explicitly mention societal impact as their strategic orientation. The survey also covered organisations that did not define themselves as "inclusive", but nevertheless indicated "contributing to society" as one of their objectives. By covering a diverse set of organisations, we hoped to get a relatively diverse and representative response, thus supporting the exploratory aims of this study.

Data collection was conducted between June and October 2015 in organisations that were active in six East-African countries: Ethiopia, Mozambique, Rwanda, Kenya, Tanzania, and Uganda. We also covered 13 organisations from the Netherlands that were active in these and other African countries. All responses from the Netherlands were received by email. Research assistants personally filled in the survey in each of the African countries. The data collection elicited responses from 75 organisations. The respondents come from a wide range of industries and from the non-profit sector (Table 4.1). The majority

1 The survey was a part of a larger research projected funded by NWO-WOTRO on the subject of inclusive business models in Africa. The research project further looks into the various definitions and operationalisations of inclusive business and the process of transitioning strategies towards greater inclusiveness.

TABLE 4.1 *Number of respondents by country and industry*

| Industry | Ethiopia | Mozambique | Rwanda | Kenya | Tanzania | Uganda | The Netherlands | Total |
|---|---|---|---|---|---|---|---|---|
| Construction | | 3 | 2 | | 1 | 2 | 2 | 10 |
| Energy | | 1 | 1 | 1 | | 1 | | 4 |
| Finance | 1 | | | 4 | 1 | 1 | 2 | 9 |
| Agribusiness | 5 | | 1 | 1 | | 3 | | 10 |
| Health | | | | 2 | 1 | | 2 | 5 |
| ICT | 1 | | 1 | 1 | 1 | | | 4 |
| Transport & logistics | | | 1 | | 1 | 1 | 1 | 4 |
| Other Businesses | 1 | 1 | 2 | | 1 | 2 | 2 | 9 |
| NGOs | 1 | 2 | | | 4 | 5 | 3 | 15 |
| Govt agencies & Associations | | 1 | 1 | 1 | | 1 | 1 | 5 |
| Total | 9 | 8 | 9 | 10 | 10 | 16 | 13 | 75 |

(55) of the organisations were businesses, whereas NGOs – including aspiring "social enterprises" – constituted 15 of these respondents, the remaining five being government agencies and inter-organisational associations.

The front page of the survey included an example definition for "inclusive business". Such a definition was deemed necessary to provide a comparable framing of the subject. Although this also has a risk of biasing the respondents, it was considered useful given the newness of the concept to many participants and the diverse ways in which it could be understood. The following definition was provided:

> According to UNDP, inclusive businesses are businesses that include poor people on the demand side as clients and customers, and on the supply side as employees, producers and business owners at various points in the value chain. Inclusive businesses also work actively to benefit other socially and economically disadvantaged groups such as women, ethnic and religious minorities and handicapped people.

While useful as a benchmark, this definition is, in some ways, more specific than other alternative definitions since, for example, it includes SME development among inclusiveness strategies. The survey, therefore, also included other general questions that recognise the diverse approaches organisations could adopt for becoming inclusive.

## Inclusiveness Strategies and Approaches

The strategies that could be used by businesses to engage their communities are diverse and multifaceted. Since not all approaches are equal in their capacity to achieve impact, studies have sought to understand major approaches for inclusiveness. Munir et al. (2010) identifies four typologies with increasing levels of knowledge transfer potential: market-driven, distribution-driven, production-driven, and knowledge-driven. Compared to market driven approaches in which the producer targets the BoP simply as target buyers, production and knowledge driven approaches directly engage the BoP as co-producers and thus have greater potential to achieve impact.

Jenkins et al. (2010) outline five thematic areas in which inclusive businesses can achieve impact: extending reach through distribution networks, facilitating financial access for suppliers and consumers, increasing demand by changing mindsets, designing relevant products and services, and developing the right pricing and payments policies. While these typologies are more specific as to the strategy of inclusion, they are not informative regarding the level of inclusiveness of each approach.

Nelson et al. (2013) pinpoint the following four general approaches in which businesses can contribute to inclusive development:

- *Inclusive core business* whereby businesses directly impact upon society through their core operations; for example, through the goods and services they produce, the employees they hire, or by developing their value chain members such as suppliers and distributors.
- *Hybrid models* that combine social and commercial capital and/or public and private resources.
- *Corporate social investment and strategic philanthropy* including strengthening of public services, civil society organisations and communities, and investments on key social services such as health and nutrition, education and skills, infrastructure, including by indirect means through sharing know-how and technology.
- *Public policy engagement and advocacy* including strengthening institutional capacity through investments on the development of governance, ethical, social, and environmental standards.

The first two of these four typologies appear to be more sustainable the rest considering their potential capacity to create societal and shareholder value simultaneously. This classification also recognises that not all societal issues can be integrated with core business operations, necessitating diverse approaches that include strategic philanthropy, social investment and public policy engagement.

Van Tulder and Da Rosa (2011) defined four general requirements for inclusive business strategies that need to be addressed in order to establish a link with inclusive growth: (1) *Mission*: an active and identifiable approach (or narrative) towards poverty and income inequality; (2) *Impact*: accountability beyond the direct effects of the business model (including indirect effects and unintended consequences); (3) *Inclusive business cases*: a clear link to the core activities and competencies of the corporation (both in production and sales); (4) *Stakeholder involvement:* pro-active partnerships with NGOs and government in a firm's portfolio of primary and secondary stakeholders.

Given the diverse ways in which the concept of inclusive business is defined, understood, and operationalised, one of the goals of our research was to understand how organisations approached the concept. The survey, therefore, included the following two related questions: "What does inclusive business mean to your organisation?" and "What are the approaches or strategies your organisation uses to becoming inclusive?" As indicated earlier, we asked these questions after providing a specific definition for inclusive business in order to frame the issue more tightly.

The responses to these questions showed that organisations nevertheless define and frame inclusiveness in many different ways. The following summaries highlight some of the most commonly cited ways in which organisations frame the subject of inclusive business:

- Inclusive business means maximising triple bottom-line goals of serving people and the planet while remaining profitable.
- Inclusive business means providing affordable and tailored products for disadvantaged people (e.g. loans without collateral for women, accessible financial services for low-income people, and providing advance payment for suppliers).
- Inclusive business means economically empowering poor people at the bottom of the pyramid by giving them trainings, by hiring them directly, or by selling to them affordable products.
- Inclusive business means giving back to society (e.g. scholarships for girls, distributing solar lights, and supporting rural workers).

The extent to which an organisation's core business model directly tackles critical social issues is an important characteristic of a successful inclusive business model (Nelson et al. 2013; Van Tulder and Da Rosa 2011). Our data, however, shows that inclusive business is, in many cases, still seen as a corporate social responsibility (CSR) initiative that is not directly linked to core operations. We find that particularly among African respondents inclusive business is characterised as the responsibility of the CSR department, whereas inclusiveness strategies appear relatively well integrated within the organisation among Dutch respondents. However, many African organisations also indicate that they tailor their products to meet the needs of disadvantaged people. This seems a typical sign of organisations that are in a relatively early (and often reactive) stage of transition to a more inclusive business model – despite of their frontrunner status (cf. Van Tulder et al. 2013). The transition literature argues that these companies face a number of additional barriers to change in their internal organisation as well as in their relations with external stakeholders.

A few organisations appear to be ahead of the curve in terms of promoting inclusiveness. One tourism organisation, for example, defined its vision of promoting "the five Ps", which, in addition to the triple P's of Planet, People and Profit, includes Passion and Pleasure. Likewise, a number of organisations pointed out that they actively reach out to partner with other stakeholders to maximise social impact. In contrast, a few other organisations indicated difficulty in becoming inclusive, either because they do not directly operate in developing countries or because they are Business-to-Business companies (B2B) only dealing with other businesses and not with consumers (for example logistics services or import and export business). Several organisations also pointed out that they do not (yet) have clearly articulated strategies for becoming inclusive. In these cases, socially-oriented practices appear to be confined to occasional CSR initiatives.

Taking the transition stage that companies are in – between strategic intent and realisation – thus provides an important context through which to assess their inclusive business strategies. The critical CSR literature argues that companies that have not successfully linked their CSR (inclusiveness) ambitions to actual realisation are engaged in "window dressing" (cf. Frynas 2010). This argument, however, fails to appreciate the importance of the transitioning process that companies have to go through and which requires ambitions first and implementation later – often under challenging circumstances (cf. Mintzberg et al. 2009).[2]

The respondents also identified a number of strategies used for promoting inclusion, such as improving access to education, inclusive finance, value chain development, inclusive/frugal innovation, and making available affordable products. Among these, providing affordable products appears to be the most widely used strategy, especially in Africa, which perhaps reflects the pressing challenge of satisfying customers with low purchasing power. Developing different aspects of the value/supply chains is also among the most frequently cited approaches for inclusiveness. The importance of value chain development could be reflective of the fact that agriculture and agribusiness are important sources of livelihood for millions of subsistence farmers in Africa (GIZ 2013).

## Levels of Inclusiveness

Do organisations differ in the emphasis or priority they give to inclusiveness? To answer this question, the survey included a question that asks: "On a scale of one to ten, how would you evaluate the extent to which becoming 'inclusive' is a policy priority in your organisation?"

2 The research in this chapter is a part of a larger research project that aims to reveal the conditions under which inclusiveness intentions can materialise in specific sectors and in African countries. Analytically, we thus have to make a distinction between "real" intentions and "window dressing" intentions. In other studies, we have made the distinction between (1) intrinsically and (2) extrinsically motivated strategies and between (a) reactive and (b) active strategies. This will be further elaborated in the present research project (Van Tulder et al. 2013).

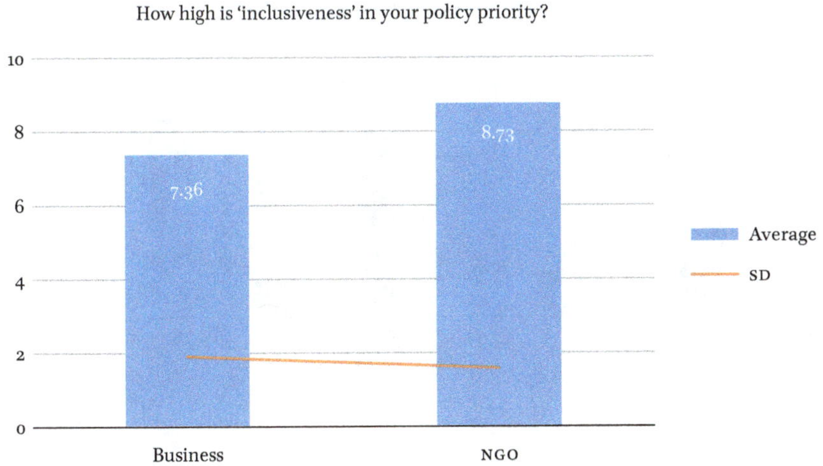


FIGURE 4.1 *Policy priority of inclusiveness: Businesses vs NGOs*

The average response for this question across all respondents is 7.7. This relatively high value of the response reiterates that our sample contains organisations with above average awareness in societal issues and an intention to become inclusive. The centrality of social causes among many of the organisations is apparent from their responses, which characterise being inclusive as their "*raison d'être*" or "part of their DNA", or the "only way to operate".

Comparison of businesses and NGOs shows that NGOs give notably higher priority to inclusiveness (Figure 4.1). The relatively low level of standard deviation among NGOs also indicates that the adoption of inclusiveness policies is unanimous among civil society organisations compared to businesses. This result confirms the pioneering role NGOs can play in promoting socially-oriented policies.

The level of priority given to inclusiveness also differs among industries in terms of adopting inclusiveness (Figure 4.2). The energy industry (N = 4) gives the highest level of priority for inclusiveness, followed by food (N = 10) and finance (N = 9) industries. In contrast, the transport and logistics industry (N = 4) gives by far the lowest level of priority for inclusiveness.

A potential reason for these variations is the nature of the industries, especially their proximity to and embeddedness with local communities. For example, businesses in the food industry by definition have to engage directly with farming communities from whom they source their raw materials. In contrast, industries such as transportation and logistics that often serve business customers are less likely to have strong ties with local communities. In addition, the adoption of inclusiveness themes in management discourse is likely

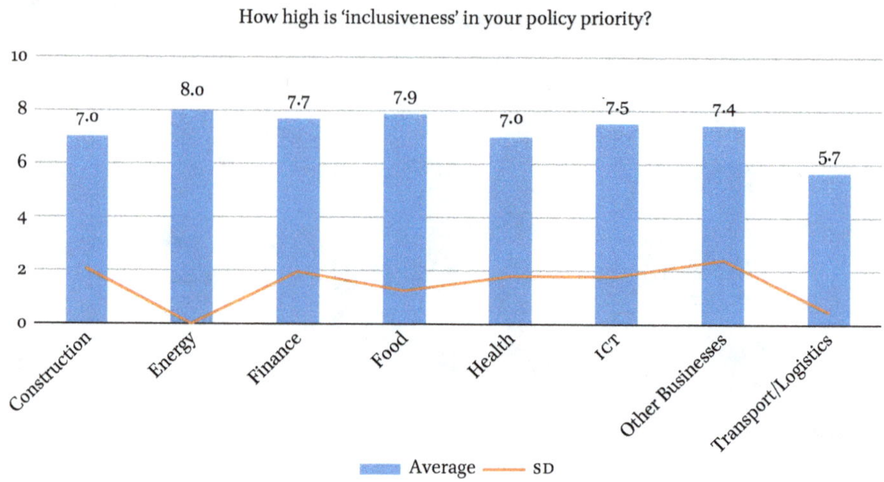


FIGURE 4.2 *Average levels of policy priory for inclusiveness by industry*

to differ across industries, depending on their exposure and the level of their engagement with broader debates on social policy.

## Priority Disadvantaged Groups and Exclusion Issues

### *Priority Disadvantaged Groups*

One way of characterising inclusive or social businesses is identifying the disadvantaged groups or societal issues their business models aim to address (Mair et al. 2012). We, therefore, include the following question in our survey: "Which potentially disadvantaged groups are most relevant for your organisation?" Respondents were given the option of indicating more than one answer when deemed necessary.

The responses to this question across the whole sample are summarised in Figure 4.3. The figure shows that empowering women to foster gender equality is considered to be the most important goal of inclusiveness. As indicated in the note under the figure, 36 organisations, or about half of the total sample, consider women priority social groups. Owners of small enterprises and poor people (employees) are the next most important disadvantaged groups. The focus on these disadvantaged groups is perhaps not surprising considering the prevalence of significant informal economic activity, poverty, and gender inequities in East-Africa.

Next to the above-mentioned "top-priority" disadvantaged groups, a number of other groups were given moderate level of priorities. These include rural inhabitants, illiterate people, (owners of) medium-sized enterprises, and

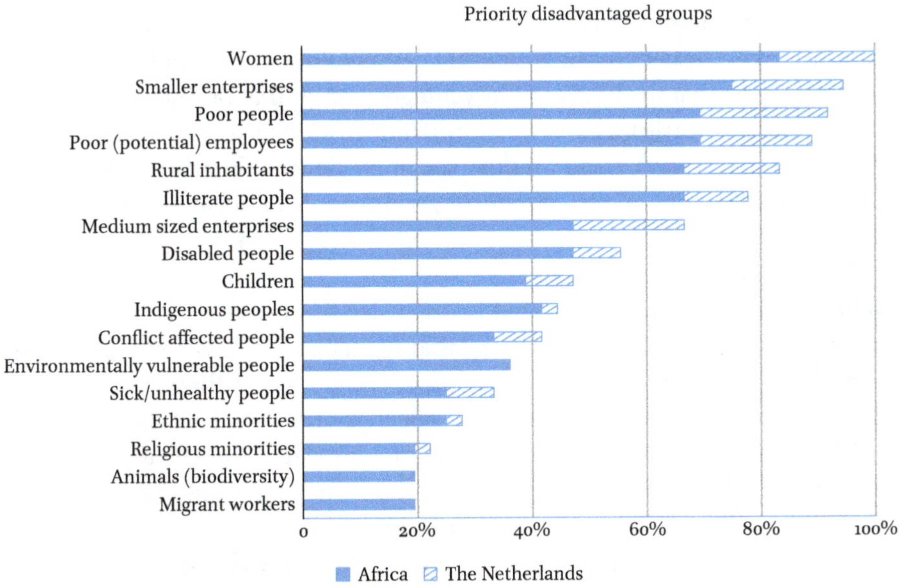


FIGURE 4.3 *Priorities given to different disadvantaged groups*
Note: The maximum response (1) is 36 (of the total sample of 75 organisations)

disabled people. The remaining excluded groups receive less than 50% of the maximum response, suggesting they are the least prioritised groups. The low-level of priority given to children, indigenous peoples, sick people, conflict-affected people, ethnic and religious minorities suggests that issues of health, conflict, and social justice are not considered focal areas for inclusive businesses.

Figure 4.3 also allows comparison of responses among African and Dutch organisations. The solid-filled bars indicate responses among African organisations, whereas the pattern-filled ones indicate the responses of Dutch organisations. The two groups of respondents seem to agree with the top-level priorities (women, small enterprises, and poor people/employees). However, empowering illiterate people seems to receive more attention among African organisations than their Dutch peers, whereas the reverse is true for medium-sized enterprises.

Further investigation of the responses suggests some important variations across countries. For example, organisations from Tanzania and Uganda consider illiterate people as top priorities, whereas those from Mozambique and Rwanda consider them among the least prioritised groups. Likewise, respondents from Kenya and Tanzania consider, respectively, disabled people and indigenous people as top priorities, although these groups fall much lower in the ranking in other African countries. There is also little consensus across countries with respect to the importance of medium-sized enterprises. These results suggest that the kind of disadvantaged groups that businesses prioritise differ across countries. This is not surprising given that African countries are diverse in many ways, including the social challenges they face, the level of public engagement in policy discourses, and the role of businesses therein.

### *Priority Societal Issues*

Which societal issues are targeted by inclusive businesses? This question already hints at the value propositions that inclusive business could offer with regard to social inclusion and development. Our survey, therefore, included a question whereby respondents could select priority social exclusion issues.

The responses to this question are reported in Figure 4.4. The top three priority societal issues are employment generation, access to finance, and capacity building. Closely following them are the issues of access to information, access to education, and income and productivity growth. These results tally with the results reported in the previous section, suggesting that organisations use employment generation and income/productivity improvement to target

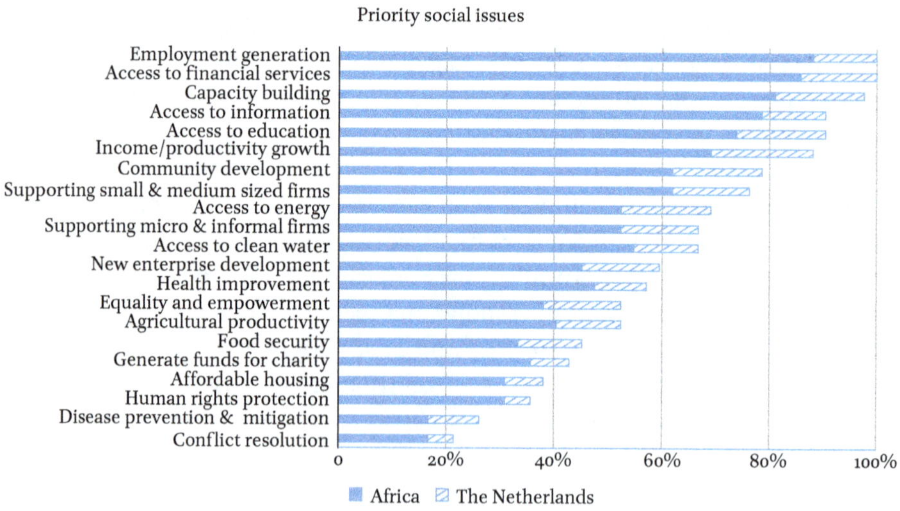


FIGURE 4.4 *Priorities given to different societal issues*
Note: The maximum response (1) is 42 (of the total sample of 75 organisations)

poor people and financial service provision and capacity development for supporting women and small enterprises.

A large number of societal exclusion issues receive medium-level priority. These include community development, medium and small firms and microenterprises, access to energy, access to clean water, new enterprise development, and health services. Finally, a number of issues related to social justice and security receive the least level of response. Overall, these results indicate that "inclusiveness" is more strongly associated with economic empowerment rather than other (social and political) aspects of development.

Comparison between African and Dutch organisations does not indicate any large priority differences. Two minor exceptions are income and productivity growth, which received greater response from Dutch organisations compared to Africans. By contrast, African organisations give greater priority for access to information than their Dutch counterparts.

Comparison of the results across countries indicates notable differences in the importance attributed to "access to information". The issue receives significantly higher level of priority in Ethiopia, Mozambique, Uganda, and Tanzania, whereas it is among the least priorities in Rwanda and Kenya. Likewise, there is limited cross-country unanimity on the importance of employment generation, which is a top priority in Ethiopia, Kenya, and Rwanda, but much lower in the list in Mozambique, Tanzania, and the Netherlands. Dutch organisations also focus on a broader range of exclusion issues compared to other African organisations. Again, these findings suggest heterogeneity across countries and thus point to the importance of addressing country- and sector-specific factors to understand the types of social issues taken up by inclusive businesses.

## Challenges Faced by Inclusive Businesses

To find out the most important challenges that organisations face in their efforts to implement inclusive business practices, the survey posed the following question: "What are the most important managerial, organisational, technical or external obstacles that hinder your organisation from becoming more inclusive and contributing to society?"

The question was open ended so that respondents could provide their own responses for each category of challenges. The respondents identified dozens of challenges with varying degrees of importance. Word frequency analysis revealed that factors such as policy, capacity, resources, and government are most frequently mentioned. However, many words describe the same

TABLE 4.2 *Categories of challenges that inclusive businesses face*

| Category | Type of obstacle |
|---|---|
| A. Technical obstacles | – Shortage of skills, knowledge and know-how |
| B. Organisational obstacles | – Limited organisational capacity<br>– Insufficient organisational resources<br>– Lack of financial resources |
| C. Managerial obstacles | – Bureaucracy within organisation |
| D. External obstacles | – Poor government policy<br>– Access to energy, electricity, and road<br>– Corruption<br>– Poor infrastructure<br>– Constraining laws and regulations |

idea – for example, the words knowledge, skills, education, and training all describe more or less the same concept.

Table 4.2 summarises the identified challenges more systematically by grouping them into four major categories. Among technical obstacles, shortage of trained and skilled manpower is the most important obstacle that organisations face. A larger number of organisational obstacles were identified, including lack of financial resources and limited organisational capacity. Bureaucracy within the organisation was also found to be an important hindrance. Finally, an even greater number of external obstacles were pointed out, including inhibitive government policy, insufficient access to electricity and road networks and, more generally, to public infrastructure, high levels of corruption and unfavourable laws and regulations.

We use a word frequency graph to assess the importance of these challenges. Figure 4.5 presents the results of the word frequency, also subdividing the total frequency between African and Dutch respondents. Shortage of skilled and knowledgeable manpower was identified as the most important performance obstacle, followed closely by limited financial resources. African and Dutch organisations unanimously identify these two issues as by far the most important challenges to becoming inclusive.

These responses are not different from findings in other surveys. For example, a UNDP report finds that the five primary constraints in the market environment of developing countries are lack of market information, ineffective regulatory environments, inadequate physical infrastructure, limited

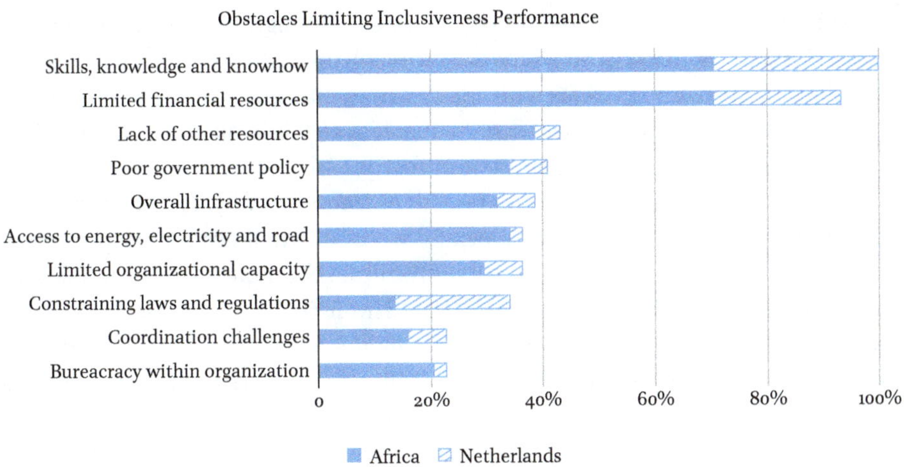


FIGURE 4.5 *Major challenges faced by inclusive businesses*
Note: The maximum response (1) is 44 (of the total sample of 75 organisations)

knowledge and skills, and limited access to financial services (Gradl and Jenkins 2011). Similarly, a survey by Mckinsey and Company (2012) that covered 1,373 business leaders in Egypt, Kenya, Nigeria, Senegal, and South Africa, identified the following three challenges as the most important barriers for firm growth: poor macroeconomic conditions (55%); potential political instability (40%); and access to finance (32%). Our results, therefore, seem to apply to the broader region of Africa as well.

A second-tier list of challenges in terms of importance includes shortage of resources, poor government policy, insufficient infrastructure, lack of access to energy, limited organisational capacity, and constraining government laws and regulations. The level of emphasis given to these constraints is generally comparable between African and Dutch respondents. One exception is constraining laws and regulations, which are perceived to be more important by Dutch organisations. In contrast, access to electricity and roads is considered to be of greater importance by African respondents.

## Discussion and Conclusion

This chapter provided exploratory results on different aspects of inclusive business practices in Africa. The chapter highlighted major approaches and strategies towards inclusiveness, priority disadvantaged groups and exclusion issues, and the kinds of challenges faced by frontrunner inclusive businesses.

The organisations in our sample give relatively high priority to inclusiveness. However, some organisations are more advanced than others in integrating their inclusiveness efforts with their core operations. NGOs give relatively greater emphasis than businesses to inclusiveness, while businesses also differ from one another depending on their industry.

Inclusiveness is generally understood as economically empowering disadvantaged groups of people, especially women, small-scale entrepreneurs, and poor people, but also, to some extent, rural inhabitants, illiterate people, and owners of medium-sized enterprises. The focus is mostly on improving income and productivity for these people by means of employment creation, improving access to finance, capacity building, and access to information and education.

The survey identified a large list of internal and external obstacles that limit the ability of organisations to implement their inclusiveness policies. Shortage of skilled manpower and limited financial resources are found to be the two most important constraints In addition, a number of organisational factors, such as lack of capacity and bureaucracy as well as external factors, such as poor infrastructure, low levels of access to energy and roads, and prohibitive laws and regulations were identified as critical obstacles.

What kind of policy lessons can be extracted from this analysis? While our results indicate a number of ways in which the private sector is contributing to inclusive growth, they also suggest significant technical and organisational challenges that limit its ability to achieve social impact. In this last section, we consider potential policy interventions that could alleviate the most important challenges for inclusive businesses, namely inadequate technical and managerial know-how and shortage of financial resources.

### *Building Inclusive Ecosystem*

The topic of ecosystems is related to a number of strands of literature, particularly to studies on business partnerships, (global) value chains, business networks and clusters, ecosystems and systems theory (Gradl and Jenkins 2011; Porter and Kramer 2011). The literature on ecosystems was pioneered by Moore (1996, 2006), where ecosystems were defined as

> An economic community supported by a foundation of interacting organizations and individuals – the organisms of the business world. [...] The member organisms include [consumers,] suppliers, lead producers, competitors, and other stakeholders. Over time, they coevolve their capabilities and roles, and tend to align themselves with the directions set by one or more central companies.

In order to succeed, inclusive businesses need to be embedded in a larger innovation ecosystem, which would give them easy access to potential technology providers, funders, capacity builders, on-the-ground partners, and supply chain players (Gradl and Jenkins 2011). Developing supportive inclusive ecosystems is hence one of the key factors for successful shared value creation at the BoP. Caneque and Hart (2015) argue that the move from stand-alone ecosystem-based strategies is crucial for the success of BoP initiatives.[3]

Supporting institutions are largely absent in many African countries, which could adversely affect performance in many ways. For example, poorly developed "framework conditions", such as public education, could expose businesses to productivity losses and remedial-training costs (Porter and Kramer 2011). Since most firms do not have the resources and the capacity to build inclusive business ecosystems single-handedly, they need to rely on collaborative efforts that are able to mobilise sufficient resources and technical know-how (GIZ 2013; Gradl and Jenkins 2011). From the lead company's perspective, the best approach would be identifying gaps and deficiencies that represent the greatest constraints to productivity and growth (Porter and Kramer 2011). The company can then distinguish those areas where it is best equipped to lead cost effective collaborative efforts. Gradl and Jenkins (2011) identified three strategies in which multinationals could strengthen their inclusive business ecosystems: (i) Unilateral initiative, e.g. educational, or infrastructural interventions; (ii) Project-based alliances between a company and one or more organisations and; (iii) Platforms that allow many different players to coordinate with each other. There is also great potential for partnership strategies (Lem et al. 2013), which requires proper partnership management practices, but also requires national legal conditions under which cross-sector partnerships can materialise. The link between the inclusiveness strategy of companies and the macro-outcome on the national level in terms of inclusive growth is achieved through the creation of new institutions of which partnerships seem to be an important form. Further research is thus needed to identify how African countries can provide better legal, cultural, and institutional conditions than others for "inclusive partnerships".

3 There are several examples of inclusive ecosystems in the BoP including mobile money ecosystems (Jenkins 2008), financial services (Ehrbeck et al. 2012), and agricultural value chains (GIZ 2013; Chung et al. 2004). Examples of successful ecosystems include IT in Silicon Valley, North Carolina's Research Triangle, cut flowers in Kenya, and diamond cutting in Surat, India. The "Silicon Savannah" technology ecosystem in Nairobi, as well as the Konza Techno City that is under construction, are other recent examples of emerging business ecosystems.

### *Inclusive Financing*

The financial sector in Africa is uncompetitive and often state-dominated, which limits access to external financing that is critical for the development of a vibrant private sector. External financing is especially likely to be scarce for inclusive businesses that also take up social issues, and thus appear to be relatively more risky (Gradl and Jenkins 2011). Inclusive businesses may take longer to become profitable, and therefore have long-term investment horizons, which would discourage private investors pursuing only financial return (Jenkins et al. 2010; GIZ 2013). It is, therefore, imperative to avail targeted financing schemes that are especially designed to meet the needs of socially-oriented businesses. Firstly, governments and other policymakers could encourage and invest in venture capital schemes that fund start-ups. Providing initial seed money for innovative solutions with significant social impact can be fruitful, as has been shown by the UK Department for International Development's (DFID) experience of investing in M-PESA, the now famous mobile-based banking system in Kenya. Local governments need to provide regulatory support for impact investors, while also encouraging local entrepreneurs to capitalise on emerging financing schemes such as crowdsourcing. Secondly, policymakers could support the development of local financing sources for aspiring inclusive businesses. Many African countries have state owned development banks. These banks are shielded from competition and are often slow to adopt new lending modalities that foster the development of inclusive businesses. Institutions with greater expertise on inclusive business financing, such as the World Bank, could collaborate with local development banks to enhance their ability to fund inclusive businesses. Finally, providing further support to microfinance institutions could improve financial access for small and micro-businesses, especially those owned by women and those in rural areas. Apart from direct financial provision, governments could provide policy and regulatory support and capacity development for smaller microfinance institutions to help them deliver financial services with greater potential for social impact.

### *Knowledge Generating and Sharing*

There is great scope for generating and sharing practical knowledge to enhance the capacity of the private sector to achieve greater social impact. One potentially fruitful approach is establishing and strengthening *resource centres* that specialise in generating and sharing applied knowledge. Well-run, sector-specific centres of excellence could serve as knowledge portals that generate, consolidate, and disseminate market and technological know-how for practitioners. Such knowledge and information portals can expand their reach by taking advantage of expanding mobile access in Africa. The type of information that can be dispensed through such portals includes market price data, weather forecasts, international commodity prices, and professional advice including medical, legal, and technical support (Jenkins 2008).

Business incubation centres have the same advantage of serving as portals for creating and disseminating practical knowledge on business development. Business incubation hubs can provide a safe space where aspiring entrepreneurs can experiment with new business concepts, share experiences, and learn from one another. They can be important nods for connecting entrepreneurs, especially in countries where support services are scarce and knowledge and expertise is geographically scattered. Experiences in developing countries (iHub in Nairobi and Impact Hub around the world) illustrate the usefulness of open spaces for business incubation and innovation.

## References

Caneque, F.C. & S.L. Hart. (2015). *Base of the Pyramid 3.0: Sustainable Development through Innovation and Entrepreneurship*, Greenleaf Publishing Limited, Sheffield, UK.

Chung, W.W., Yam, A.Y. & M.F. Chan (2004). "Networked Enterprise: A New Business Model for Global Sourcing". *International Journal of Production Economics*, *87*(3), 267–280.

Clarkson, M.E. (1995). "A Stakeholder Framework for Analysing and Evaluating Corporate Social Performance". *Academy of Management Review*, *20*(1), 92–117.

Dacin, P.A., Dacin, M.T. & M. Matear (2010). "Social Entrepreneurship: Why We Don't Need a New Theory and How We Move Forward from Here". *The Academy of Management Perspectives*, *24*(3), 37–57.

Dunning, J.H. & F. Fortanier. (2007). "Multinational Enterprises and the New Development Paradigm: Consequences for Host Country Development", *Multinational Business Review*, vol.15 (1), 25–46.

Ehrbeck, T., Pickens, M. & M. Tarazi (2012). Financially Inclusive Ecosystems: The Roles of Government Today. Available online at: http://www.cgap.org. (last accessed 1 June 2016).

EY (2015). EY's Attractiveness Survey Africa 2015: Making Choices. Available online at: www.ey.com (last accessed 1 June 2016).

Fortanier, F. (2008). *Multinational Enterprises, Institutions and Sustainable Development*, PhD Dissertation, University of Amsterdam.

Fortanier, F. & A. Kolk. (2007). "On the Economic Dimensions of CSR: Exploring Fortune Global 250 Reports", *Business and Society*, *46*, (4), 457–478.

Freeman, R. (2010). *Strategic Management. A Stakeholder Approach,* Cambridge: Cambridge University Press.

Frynas, G. (2010). *Beyond Corporate Social Responsibility Oil Multinationals and Social Challenge,* Cambridge: Cambridge University Press.

GIZ (2013). Value Chain Development by the Private Sector in Africa: Lessons Learnt and Guidance Notes. Available online at: https://www.giz.de. (last accessed 10 May 2015).

Gradl, C. & B. Jenkins. (2011). *Tackling Barriers to Scale: From Inclusive Business Models to Inclusive Business Ecosystems.* CSR Initiative, Harvard Kennedy School, Cambridge.

Hahn, R. (2012). "Inclusive Business, Human Rights and the Dignity of the Poor: A Glance beyond Economic Impacts of Adapted Business Models", *Business Ethics: A European Review,* Vol. 21 (I1), 47–63.

Halme, M., Lindeman, S. & P. Linna. (2012). "Innovation for Inclusive Business: Intrapreneurial Bricolage in Multinational Corporations", *Journal of Management Studies,* Vol. 49 (4), 743–784.

Hart, S.L. (2005). *Capitalism at the Crossroads: The Unlimited Business Opportunities in Solving the World's Most Difficult Problems.* Upper Saddle River, NJ: Pearson Education.

Jenkins, B. (2008). *Developing Mobile Money Ecosystems.* Washington, DC: IFC and the CSR Initiative at the Harvard Kennedy School.

Jenkins, B., Ishikawa, E., Geaneotes, A. & J. Paul (2010). *Scaling Up Inclusive Business: Advancing the Knowledge and Action Agenda.* Washington, D.C.: IFC and the CSR Initiative at the Harvard Kennedy School.

Jones, T.M. (1995). "Instrumental Stakeholder Theory: A Synthesis of Ethics and Economics". *Academy of Management Review*, *20*(2), 404–437.

Karnani, A. (2009). "The Bottom of the Pyramid Strategy for Reducing Poverty: A Failed Promise", *DESA Working Paper* No. 80.

Khanna, T., Palepu, K.G. & J. Sinha (2005). "Strategies that Fit Emerging Markets". *Harvard Business Review*, 83(6), 4–19.

Kolk, J., M. Rivera-Santos & C. Rufín (2014). "Reviewing a Decade of Research on the 'Base/Bottom of the Pyramid' (BoP) Concept". *Business & Society*, *53*(3), 338–377.

Lem, M., Van Tulder, R. & K. Geleynse (2013). *Doing Business in Africa. A Strategic Guide for Entrepreneurs,* The Hague: Berenschot, PrC and NABC.

Mair, J. & I. Marti (2009). "Entrepreneurship in and around Institutional Voids: A Case Study from Bangladesh". *Journal of Business Venturing*, 24(5), 419–435.

Mair, J., Battilana, J. & J. Cardenas (2012). "Organizing for Society: A Typology of Social Entrepreneuring Models". *Journal of Business Ethics, 111*(3), 353–373.

McKinsey & Company. (2012). Africa at Work: Job Creation and Inclusive Growth. Available online at: www.mckinsey.com. (last accessed on 20 May 2015).

Mignano, K.G. & E. Ishikawa. (2014). "Shared Prosperity through Inclusive Business: How Successful Companies Reach the Base of the Pyramid". *International Finance Corporation* 2014. Washington DC.

Mintzberg, H. Lampel, J. & B. Ahlstrand (2009). *Strategy Safari: A Guided Tour through the Wilds of Strategic Management,* Minnesota, MN: The Free Press.

Moore, J. (1996). *The Death of Competition: Leadership and Strategy in the Age of Business Ecosystems.* New York: Harper Business School.

Moore, J.F. (2006). "Business Ecosystems and the View from the Firm". *Antitrust Bulletin, 51,* 31.

Munir, K., Ansari, S. & T. Gregg (2010). "Beyond The Hype: Taking Business Strategy to the 'Bottom of the Pyramid'". In: A.C. Baum Joel & Joseph Lampel (eds) *The Globalization of Strategy Research* (Advances in Strategic Management, Volume 27). Bingley: Emerald Group Publishing Limited, 247–276.

Nelson, J., Torres-Rahman, Z. & D. Stibbe (2013). A New Global Partnership with Business: Building a Post-2015 Development Framework to Achieve Sustainable Prosperity in Africa. Available online at: https://www.hks.harvard.edu. (last accessed on 15 May 2016).

Orlitzky, M., Schmidt, F.L. & S.L. Rynes (2003). "Corporate Social and Financial Performance: A Meta-Analysis". *Organization Studies, 24*(3), 403–441.

Porter, M.E. & M.R. Kramer (2011). "Creating Shared Value". *Harvard Business Review,* 89 (1/2), 62–77.

Prahalad, C.K. (2004). *The Fortune at the Bottom of the Pyramid.* Philadelphia: Wharton School Publishing.

UNDP (2013). *Realizing Africa's Wealth: Building Inclusive Businesses for Shared Prosperity.* A UNDP African Facility for Inclusive Markets Report United Nations Development Programme. New York.

Van Tulder, R. & A. Da Rosa (2011). "Inclusive Business through Partnerships", Contribution to the High-Level meeting, Busan: Partnerships Resource Centre.

Van Tulder, R., Van Tilburg, R., Francken, M. & A. Da Rosa (2013). *Managing the Transition to a Sustainable Enterprise. Evidence of Dutch Frontrunner companies,* London: Earthscan.

Van Tulder, R., Verbeke, A. & R. Strange. (2014). *International Business and Sustainable Development,* Vo. 8 Progress in international Business Research, Bingley: Emerald Publishing Group.

Waddock, S.A. & S.B. Graves (1997). "The Corporate Social Performance-Financial Performance Link". *Strategic Management Journal, 18*(4), 303–319.

Wood, D.J. (1991). "Corporate Social Performance Revisited". *Academy of Management Review, 16*(4), 691–718.

CHAPTER 5

# Innovation as a Key to Success? Case Studies of Innovative Start-ups in Kenya and Nigeria

*Miguel Heilbron, André Leliveld and Peter Knorringa*[1]

## Introduction

Innovations are a dominant force in economically transforming societies. Schumpeter (1934) coined the idea of creative destruction, where the introduction of new (innovative) products and production processes wipes out the markets for existing products or production processes, leading to innovation rents for innovative entrepreneurs. According to Schumpeter, creative destruction is a continuous and main driver of economic growth and transformation in capitalist societies. In his early work, Schumpeter expected creative destruction to come mainly from newly established entrepreneurs operating in competitive markets. Innovation processes are, however, erratic and risky. The uncertainty of innovation processes induces innovating entrepreneurs or firms to control their external environment by growing in size. Larger firms are better able to control their external environment. Moreover, they have more financial means and they are able to spread Research and Development (R&D) costs over a higher turnover, thereby reducing fixed costs per unit product. The idea of large firms being in a better position to produce innovations is referred to as Schumpeter II (Schumpeter 1942), which juxtaposes the "older" Schumpeter I, which expected newly established entrepreneurs to take the lead.

Schumpeter's ideas refer to capitalist economies in Western Europe and Northern America. Are they relevant for African economies when we try to understand successful entrepreneurship in today's Africa? For a long time, the

1 Correspondence to: André Leliveld, a.h.m.leliveld@asc.leidenuniv.nl. We thank the following individuals for providing insight through questionnaires or during interviews: two entrepreneurs in Kenya and one entrepreneur in Nigeria, who participated on the basis of anonymity, and Mr. Ben White (CEO & Founder VC4Africa), Mr. Bankole Oluwafemi (CEO & Founder Big Cabal Media / TechCabal), and Ms. Saskia Reus-Makkink (CEO & Founder Africa Funded). We thank VC4Africa (Venture Capital for Africa) for allowing us to use data from their database for this chapter. The authors are responsible for any error of interpretation that may have occurred.

 | DOI 10.1163/9789004351615_006

role of innovation in Africa's economies and enterprises has been neglected in academic and policy discourses. This was related to a rather pessimistic view that African economies were lagging behind when it comes to innovation. This impression has been fostered by indices such as the Global Innovation Index in which the majority of African countries can be found at the lower end of the ranking. We argue this view needs revision. Critical scholars point out that African economies have always been sources of creativity and innovation, but these innovation manifestations – in particular from the informal sector – have remained largely "below the radar" in official statistics and reports (Kaplinsky 2011; Badhuri 2016). Secondly, like elsewhere across the globe, the innovation landscape is changing dramatically in many African countries. New developments in ICT have been picked up rapidly by innovative entrepreneurs in many African economies. For example, in 2014, the ICT sector contributed more than 10 per cent to gross domestic product (GDP) in countries like Kenya, Nigeria, South Africa, Tunisia, Senegal, and Morocco (World Development Indicators). M-Pesa has become an exemplary and well-documented case of a successful innovation in Africa, which fully exploits the opportunities offered by the ICT revolution. Events like DEMO Africa show a variety of innovations built by African innovators across the continent.[2] iHub in Kenya has become an internationally recognised innovation space. In fact, across the African continent, technology hubs, hacker spaces, co-working spaces, ICT business incubators, Fab-Labs, and other innovation centres are mushrooming, spurring, and supporting new manifestations of innovation and entrepreneurship. Currently, over a hundred such spaces exist across Africa, and more than half of Africa's economies have at least one (World Bank 2016). In Kenya, the government has started the construction of Konza Techno City, with the ambition to become a "Silicon Savannah" for the East African region, in response to San Francisco's "Silicon Valley" in the US. In Nigeria, the Lagos State Government initiated plans to enhance Lagos' Yaba area as a high-tech economic hub of Africa. Other African countries and cities have initiated similar plans.

In sum, the innovation landscape in many African countries is changing dramatically. However, to date, little empirical knowledge exists on how

2 The annual DEMO Africa event provides the most innovative companies from African countries a platform to launch their products and announce to Africa and the world what they have developed. Innovations presented at the DEMO Africa Conferences in recent include innovative touchscreen stickers, game studios, solar power products, smartphones, e-commerce platforms, finance products and services, media companies and products, apps focused on various issues, among other innovations. (DEMO Africa 2016).

domestic firms in Africa operate in this changing environment.[3] Moreover, given the changing innovation landscape, a view is needed that has much more of an eye for the diversity of innovation trajectories of Africa-based companies; a view not solely confined to small- and medium enterprises in the informal sector, which has been the focal point in studies on African entrepreneurship up to now, or to large companies traded on stock markets, but also including the "missing middle" (Staley and Morse 1965) in both the informal and formal sector. This explorative chapter aims to contribute to a more nuanced picture on innovation and (successful) entrepreneurship in Africa by presenting some cases of innovative entrepreneurs that are exemplary for a new generation of companies started and managed by African entrepreneurs. We will consider the determinants of their success, in which innovation and the recent changes in the innovation landscape have played a major role. The structure of this chapter is as follows. First, we will set the context by describing the changing innovation landscape in twenty-first-century Africa and by briefly presenting the main body of literature to which this chapter relates. Then, we briefly discuss the data and methodology used for this chapter. This is followed by a presentation of cases of 14 successful innovative companies, of which three cases will be analysed more in depth. Finally, we summarize our conclusions and discuss the determinants behind the success of the presented firms in which innovation has played a major role.

## Setting the Context: Changing Innovation Landscape in African Economies

The innovation landscape in many African countries has undergone dramatic changes since the beginning of the twenty-first century. Among others, four major developments or drivers stand out: the fast spread of new information and communication technology (ICT); the transfer of R&D activities of multinational enterprises (MNES) to Africa, the rise of Global Value Chains (GVCS), and changes on the demand side due to population dynamics. These developments are briefly explained below.

3 A notable exception is an ongoing research project on innovation for productivity growth in low income countries (among which six African countries), commissioned by the UKS Department for International Development (DFiD) and conducted by Tilburg University, the Netherlands. Research outcomes and publications can be found at https://www.tilburguniversity.edu/research/economics-and-management/dfid-innovation-and-growths.

One of the biggest changes has been the fast spread of new ICT across the African continent. In Africa, internet access, the use of computers, and mobile networks have grown dramatically during the last two decades. The new ICT has opened new opportunities for African domestic firms to gain relatively easy access to technologies that could help them to embark on innovation-driven growth trajectories. The notions of the Third Industrial Revolution and the Internet of Things have been introduced, which would enable a democratisation of technology across regions and societies (Howard 2015; Rifkin 2011). Across African countries, many examples can be found of individual entrepreneurs who have managed to set up innovative companies with the use of open access ICT applications (see also in this chapter). This could make innovative domestic firms potentially less dependent on technology transfer, for instance through Foreign Direct Investment by MNEs. At the same time, the new opportunities offered by ICT developments should be looked upon with care. The 2016 World Development Report warns for a digital divide, in which a happy few reap all the benefits while a majority of people lag behind (World Bank 2016).

A second global trend in recent years has been the internationalisation of R&D activities by MNEs (UNCTAD 2006). This leads to "polycentric innovation", which designates the global integration of specialised research and development capabilities across multiple regions to create novel solutions that no single region or company could have completely developed on its own (Singh 2011; Radjou 2009). Greater product and technology complexity has increased costs and risks for innovators such that these can barely be dealt with by relying on one firm's own limited resources and capabilities alone. In addition, the globalisation wave of the last two decades has opened more possibilities for cross-national alliances that contribute to creating competitive advantage in foreign markets (Lavie and Miller 2008). This trend of polycentric innovation can also be observed in some African countries. Notably, countries like Nigeria, South Africa, Kenya, Rwanda, and Senegal have become "hubs" for MNEs, such as IBM and Google, but also non-ICT companies like Philips, Siemens, and Unilever, to establish innovation centres, in addition to innovation centres that emerged locally. However, little is known about the effects on and entrepreneurial opportunities this offers for domestic firms. On the one hand, there is an optimistic view that polycentric innovation can indeed lead to more chances for domestic firms; on the other hand, there is a critical view that points out possible crowding out or exploitation of (informal) domestic firms (see Knorringa et al. 2016 for this discussion). Both views lack empirical evidence though when it comes to the African continent.

The rise of Global Value Chains (GVC) is a third significant global development that also involves African farms and firms (Kaplinsky 2011). Generally, it is thought that for those domestic firms that succeed to integrate into a GVC, this could have a significant effect on innovation capabilities and grasping associated entrepreneurial opportunities (Fu et al. 2011). For domestic firms in Africa, GVCs not only represent a new market for their produce, but they also play a growing and crucial role in acquiring knowledge and enhancing learning and innovation. However, also in this case, we know very little about how this works out for domestic firms in Africa. For example, Fu et al. (2011: 1209) observe that "the literature has not yet clearly settled how innovation systems and GVCs interact, and how this interaction is likely to affect enterprise learning."

The fourth big change is related to the population dynamics of Africa and the emerging class of middle-income consumers, which have led to the rapid growth of consumption in Africa, creating new markets for both international and domestic firms. High population growth in many African countries, in combination with persistent high income inequalities, have led to a dramatic growth of the number of consumers at the so-called Bottom/Base of the Pyramid (BoP). The idea that a "fortune" can be found at the BoP (Prahalad and Hart 2002) has been firmly rooted during the last decade in corporate business studies and practices. The World Resource Institute estimates the current BoP market in Africa at $US 429 billion. In addition, there is a growing and emerging middle class that is receptive and willing to spend money on quality products, provided these are suitable, well made and reasonably priced. Since the 1980s, the middle class has tripled in Africa and currently constitutes 30 per cent of the population.[4] In 2008, annual consumer demand in Africa was estimated at $US 680 billion. Forecasts predict that this figure will be $US 2.2 trillion in 2030. This will lead to a rising demand for good quality but relatively low cost products, services, and systems. In the innovation literature, the concept of frugal innovation has been introduced to identify these innovations.[5] Successful frugal innovations ask for a good understanding of living conditions, preferences, and aspirations of the BoP and the emerging middle class. Domestic firms that operate in local environments have a comparative advantage to

4 Ravallion (2009: 11) estimated the "middle class" in Sub-Sahara Africa as 27.6 per cent, in a range of 2–13USD/capita/day.

5 *The Economist* coined the term "frugal innovation" in the article "First break all the rules: The charms of frugal innovation" (*The Economist* 2010). The term has since been picked up in academic literature on innovation.

MNEs regarding this local knowledge. Frugal innovations are therefore thought to offer better opportunities for domestic firms to become involved in the design, production, and distribution chain of frugal products and services.

## The "missing middle" and Success Factors for Firm Performance

The above developments, which underlie the changing innovation landscape in many African countries, have renewed attention for the role of innovation and technology in private sector development, and the private sector is also increasingly recognised by both African governments and donors as an important engine of growth. The above developments are thought to offer opportunities and threats for different groups of entrepreneurs in Africa. Our argument is that the opportunities offered by the changing innovation landscape are increasingly grasped by an emerging class of entrepreneurs, of which a number of cases are presented in this chapter, and whose group is usually referred to as "the missing middle" in the private sector development literature. This is a group of entrepreneurs that neither has the full characteristics of micro- and small enterprises, nor the full features of corporate business.

Staley and Morse (1965), in their classic book *Modern Small Industry for Developing Countries*, introduced the idea of modern small- and medium enterprises as a key element in a dynamic industrial structure and as an intermediate category between the modern large corporate sector and a large group of more traditional artisans and other informal sector businesses (Fafchamps 1994). This was and still is an important observation as most African economies, at least in some of their key sectors, continue to be characterised by a so-called dual industrial structure, with a small segment of large, often (partly) foreign-owned corporations on the one hand, and a large segment of informal businesses on the other.

In between these two segments, what is missing is an intermediate segment of dynamic and modern small- and medium-scale businesses, domestically owned and significantly contributing to innovation in the domestic economy.[6] This is not only or even most importantly simply a matter of the desire to have more formally registered small- and medium-scale businesses in a country, more registered production, employment and export earnings. The often

6 One should be aware that "domestic" is a politically sensitive term in many African countries, because a significant portion of the existing small- and medium scale businesses are owned by people descending from Indian, Arab or Lebanese immigrants, and recently many Chinese small-scale entrepreneurs have also come to Africa.

implicit connection to Schumpeter I innovation thinking is that this middle segment would, as it has in developed economies, also be the catalyst for a more creative, innovative, and thus dynamic industrial structure. Also in the context of this chapter, the key point is that this middle segment would consist of a class of strong-minded and independent entrepreneurs and innovators that bring a qualitatively distinctive and additional element to a countries' knowledge base.

This classification is clearly not clear-cut in practice, and empirical research shows in between categories and processes of graduation from one category to another. For example, Staley and Morse (1965) already recognise that some informal sector "artisans could manage to modernize and grow into dynamic small industries" (Fafchamps 1994: 2). Moreover, research has emphasised that within the informal sector one might distinguish between growth-oriented entrepreneurs and survivalists (Berner et al. 2012; Tellegen 1997), while others see again an intermediate category within the informal sector, so-called constrained gazelles (Grimm et al. 2012). These studies also show that individual graduation from one segment to another is possible, but is an exception, not the rule (Berner et al. 2012). More likely are somewhat longer-term intergenerational graduation processes, in which better-educated children of informal sector entrepreneurs are able to become co-owners or managers of formal dynamic small- and medium enterprises.

The above insights will be used to assess whether the case studies presented in this chapter provide indications that these new successful businesses can actually be seen as the frontrunners in the emergence of a dynamic intermediate segment of formal small- and medium enterprises that are "filling" the middle. One way to do this is to look at success factors for firm performance. These are often divided into internal and external factors. Internal factors include issues like leadership and entrepreneurial ability, attitude to risk, availability of working and investment capital, marketing and management knowledge and know-how, the availability of appropriate technology, and the skill set of the workforce (Nichter and Goldmark 2009; Philips and Bhatia-Panthaki 2007).

The list of external factors is even longer and ranges from rather direct to more indirect contextual factors. Rather direct are the forward and backward linkages, the ability to link up in larger and (inter)national value chains, tax regimes, industrial policy, and government attitude and policy towards SMEs. More indirect but still potentially very important in influencing firm performance are issues like macro-economic conditions, public sector capacity and willingness to cooperate with business, the legal framework and implementation, targeting by donors and government, and level and appropriateness of services offered by the financial sector (Philips and Bhatia-Panthaki 2007).

We will return to these internal and external success factors in the discussion section of this chapter, after the presentation of the case studies.

## Data

### *VC4A Database*

This chapter largely builds on findings and cases that have been selected from a dataset collected by VC4A (Venture Capital for Africa). VC4A is a global peer-to-peer network of African and Africa-focused entrepreneurs, investors and others. Since 2013, VC4A has reached out annually to its community of entrepreneurs and investors with a survey, to find out more about their progress. The end of 2015 VC4A survey was completed by 462 entrepreneurs from the VC4A community, in 41 African countries. The majority of the cases presented in this chapter was selected from this dataset.

At the time of the survey, the VC4A community had over 20,000 members spread across 159 countries, and over 2,000 African start-ups presented their companies on the VC4A website. The founders of these start-ups were included in the survey. VC4A indicates that most of the ventures in its network are purposed for growth, "either by leveraging technology or through the application of a disruptive business model." VC4A also indicates that "most of the companies are early stage and require investments between USD 10K and 1 million" (VC4A 2016a).

In the survey, VC4A asked entrepreneurs to report on their revenue, profit, team size, capital requirements, progress in fundraising, and other indicators. Below, we present some descriptive figures to give an idea of the composition of the 462 entrepreneurs listed in the VC4A database and to show that the VC4A companies in general, and the specific cases further discussed in this chapter, are in a different "league" than companies that, for instance, emerge from surveys among micro- and small enterprises in the informal sector. An overwhelming majority of companies is registered and part of the formal sector, and they represent a variety of examples of missing middle companies.

A striking feature of this missing – or, should one say, emerging – middle is the high level of education of the entrepreneurs. 91.7 per cent of the respondents have a university degree level of education, 7.7 per cent has secondary school and less than 1 per cent only has primary education as the highest completed level of education. 25.3 per cent has an MBA on top of their university degree. The high level of education suggests founders of African innovative growth ventures also have access to resources and networks. Also striking is the number of female founders. More than 25 per cent of the ventures have a female founder or co-founder. VC4A indicates this is higher than the average in New York City (21 per cent) or San Francisco (16 per cent) for similar ventures. VC4A does not ask respondents about the nationality and ethnic heritage of entrepreneurs. VC4A lists both local African founders, founders from global African diaspora, and other founders from outside Africa who are setting up a venture in Africa. The majority of founders, 53.5 per cent, is below 35 years old. 21 per cent is between 35 and 44 years; 7.5 per cent is between 45 and 55; and 4.1 per cent is above 55 years. 13.8 per cent is under 25.

Sector-wise (founders could indicate more than one sector) 40 per cent of the ventures are in ICT; 21 per cent in agriculture; 15 per cent in e-commerce; 13 per cent in mobile services; 11 per cent in education; 10 per cent in diversified services; 9 per cent in clean technology; 9 per cent in financial services; 7 per cent in media; 7 per cent in manufacturing; 7 per cent in renewable energy. 69 per cent of the ventures indicate they are in a start-up phase, while 30.7 per cent say they are in a growth stage. VC4A defines the start-up stage as "focused on solution validation, product market fit, survival," and the growth stage as "focused on expanding product line, growing revenue, growing team." The average team size for a venture is 8.9 FTE (Full Time Equivalent).

45 per cent of the ventures indicated generating revenue in 2015. 26 per cent generated less than USD 50,000; 10 per cent generated USD 50,000–100,000; 3 per cent generated USD 100,000–500,000; and 5 per cent generated more than USD 500,000. 48 per cent of ventures have secured outside investment. 92.7 per cent of all investments are less than USD 500,000. 65.8 per cent of investments is between USD 10,000 and USD 50,000. 26.9 per cent of investments fall in the range of USD 50,000 and USD 500,000; and only 3.6 per cent of the investments are over $US 1 million. The difference in investment sizes varies between the different types of investors. Angel investors are typically investing between $US 25,000 and $US 100,000, whereas venture capitalists and social impact funds are typically investing over $US 100,000.[7] The ICT sector is the most attractive for investors, securing 61 per cent of all investments. 57 per cent of invested capital comes from founders themselves. Grants and competitions account for 13 per cent, family and friends for 11 per cent, and

---

7 An angel investor is an affluent individual who provides capital for a business start-up, usually in exchange for convertible debt or ownership equity. A venture capitalist is also an individual or a group of individuals, or a company, that invests in a business venture, providing capital for start-up or expansion. Unlike venture capitalists, angel investors often operate in a group and play a direct role as advisers in the operations of the investee firm. They often demand a substantial part of the ownership to exercise control over the investee firm to offset their high risk.

angel investors per cent, whereas venture capitalists and social impact funds only account for 3 per cent. Bank loans and SME lenders represent 5 per cent (VC4A 2016b).

## Case Selection

We chose to select and present nine cases from the VC4A database in more detail as illustrative cases for the discussion presented in this chapter. The companies include: a cooking fuel company; a mobile sports betting website; an education products company; two mobile payments companies; two solar power product companies; a media company; and an exotic fruits and vegetables company. In addition, we selected five cases that are not part of the VC4A database. These companies include: a mobile payment company; an online hotel booking company; an ICT services company; an online shopping company; and an online entertainment company. These companies are generally in a later growth stage, and are exemplary of where "missing middle" startup companies could end up. In line with the objectives of this volume, we have selected successful cases. For this, we used growth in revenues, external investments, FTEs and exposure in the last few years as key indicators. After selecting around 40 cases that fitted the criteria, it became clear that the successful cases predominantly could be found in South Africa, Nigeria and Kenya. We selected 12 of the 14 firms in Nigeria and Kenya, which we sent a brief questionnaire with open questions to retrieve additional information to what we already knew through the VC4Africa database and public sources, going into more depth on the educational background of the founders, innovation, finance, performance, and growth trajectories of the companies. Three firms responded and filled in the questionnaire. In addition, we also spoke to three experts who know the practice of the "missing middle" very well on determinants of success for African innovative start-up entrepreneurs, the role of innovation, differences between Kenya and Nigeria, and needed policies.[8]

In the remainder of this chapter, we will first present general data of the 14 selected companies; subsequently, we will present the three cases in more detail, followed by a discussion on what the empirical cases can tell us about determinants of success for innovative start-ups.

8 Mr. Ben White (CEO & Founder VC4Africa), Mr. Bankole Oluwafemi (CEO & Founder Big Cabal Media / TechCabal), and Ms. Saskia Reus-Makkink (CEO & Founder Africa Funded).

## Cases of Innovative Start-ups in Kenya and Nigeria

### *Fourteen Cases*

Table 5.1 presents descriptive figures of the 14 cases that have been selected for this chapter. In this section, we point out some of the major findings from Table 5.1 and present more background where relevant. If we look at the year of registration, some of the companies (3, 8, 9 and 11) are over ten years old, which questions whether these companies can still be called start-ups. However, two of them reached break-even point only in 2016, which suggests that these companies have been struggling to enter the market and reach a growth stage. When the start-up stage is defined as "focused on solution validation, product market fit, survival," and the growth stage as "focused on expanding product line, growing revenue, growing team," most entrepreneurs in this sample did not call their companies start-ups, but referred to their companies as being in a growth stage.

All companies have been started by a limited number of people: they all have between one and three founders. Four of the teams include one or more female co-founders. Most of the founders are between 25 and 35 years of age. All of the founders have university degrees, and five of the teams include one or more co-founders with an additional MBA. Only two of the companies were established with support from an incubator, innovation hub, or other enterprise promoting entity. The nine companies from the VC4A data indicated some form of independent collaboration with an MNE, either by selling to, sourcing from, or connecting with an MNE. Only company 2, engaged in mobile sports betting, is partly financed by an international company.

In terms of finance, most companies in the sample got their money from their own savings in combination with securing external capital. The latter ranges from $US 10–20,000 to $US 125,000. For most companies the founder has been the main source of funding. The other main capital sources include friends and family, angel investors, grants, and competitions. While the funding types include both equity and debt, microfinance institutions did not play a role in securing capital and a bank loan only played a role for company 8. All companies except one are looking for external funding, but some of the owners indicate that this is difficult. Having moved from being a start-up to a growing company, they need more finance to sustain their development.

The companies have been quite successful in their respective operations. As the figures in Table 5.1 show, most companies reached their break-even point within five years, and became profitable soon thereafter, or are expected by the owner to become profitable in the near future. The company growth allowed for most companies to employ more people, as the figures on FTEs show. In

TABLE 5.1 *Key figures on 14 innovative start-up companies in Kenya and Nigeria*

| Figure | 1 | 2 | 3 | 4 | 5 | 6 |
|---|---|---|---|---|---|---|
| **Country** | Nigeria | Nigeria | Nigeria | Nigeria | Kenya | Kenya |
| **HQ** | Lagos | Lagos | Abuja | Lagos | Nairobi | Nairobi |
| **Industry** | Energy | E-commerce | Education | E-commerce | Fin Serv | Clean Technol |
| **Founders** | 3 | 1 | 2 | 3 | 3 | 3 |
| **Female Founders** | 1 | 0 | 0 | 1 | 1 | 2 |
| **Education of Founders** | One MBA, others unknown | MBA or higher | All university or college | Two MBA, one univ or coll. | All university or college | All MBA or higher |
| **Stage** | Growth | Growth | Growth | Growth | Growth | Start-up |
| **B2B/C/G*** | B/C/G | C | B/C/G | B/C | B/C | B |
| **Market** | West Africa | Nigeria | Nigeria | Nigeria | Kenya | Kenya |
| **Urb / rur** | Both | Urban | Both | Both | Urban | Urban |
| **Year reg.** | 2011 | 2013 | <2006 | 2012 | 2014 | 2008 |
| **Total inv.**** | 1.580K | 400K | 296K | 63K | 20K | 125K |
| **Revenue 2015** | >500K | >500K | n.a. | <50K | <50K | >500K |
| **Breakeven** | 2012 | 2016 | 2016 | 2017 | 2016 | <2010 |
| **Profitable** | 2013 | 2016 | 2016 | >2017 | <2010 | 2014 |
| **FTE 2015** | 55 | 10 | 0 | 4 | 4 | 4 |

* B2B/C/G = Business to Business/Consumer/Government

** Sum of investments (in $US)

SOURCE: DATABASE VC4AFRICA (COMPANIES 1–9) AND PUBLIC SOURCES, ONLINE BLOGS, PERSONAL COMMUNICATION (COMPANIES 10–14).

| 7 | 8 | 9 | 10 | 11 | 12 | 13 | 14 |
|---|---|---|---|---|---|---|---|
| Kenya | Kenya | Kenya | Kenya | Kenya | Nigeria | Nigeria | Nigeria |
| Nairobi | Nairobi | Nairobi | Nairobi | Nairobi | Lagos | Lagos | Lagos |
| Media | Clean Technol | Agribusiness | E-commerce | ICT | Creative industry | E-commerce | E-commerce |
| 2 | 2 | 1 | 2 | 1 | 2 | 2 | 1 |
| 0 | 0 | 0 | 1 | 0 | 0 | 0 | 0 |
| All university or college | One MBA, one univ or coll. | University or college | n.a. | n.a. | n.a. | n.a. | n.a. |
| Growth | Growth | Growth | Growth | Growth | Growth | Growth | Growth |
| B/C | B/C | B/C | B/C/G | B/G | B/C | B/C | B/C |
| Central / West Africa | Kenya | Kenya | Internat | Internat | Internat | Africa | Internat |
| Urban | Rural | Urban | Both | Both | Both | Both | Both |
| 2011 | 2006 | 2007 | n.a. | 1999 | 2010 | 2012 | 2013 |
| 0 | 500K | 10K | n.a. | n.a. | n.a. | n.a. | n.a. |
| >500K | 50–100K | 100–500K | n.a. | >50 mln | n.a. | >28 mln | >500K |
| 2013 | <2010 | 2016 | n.a. | n.a. | n.a. | n.a. | n.a. |
| 2014 | <2010 | 2016 | n.a. | n.a. | n.a. | n.a. | n.a. |
| 18 | 9 | 70 | n.a. | 100+ | 100+ | 1800 | 49 |

particular, company 1 (involved in solar cooking stoves) has shown spectacular growth in terms of FTE, given the relatively few years that it has been in business.

It is interesting to observe, when we look at the businesses and the sectors they are involved in, that some of the trends sketched above can be seen among these start-ups. One has to do with the opportunities created by the ICT revolution. Company 13 very quickly became one of the biggest online shopping companies in Nigeria, and company 14 has become a successful online hotel booking company. Company 11 became one of Kenya's biggest IT companies, and also Company 2, involved in mobile sports betting, is successful because of the ICT revolution in Nigeria. And companies 4 and 10 are involved in forms of e-commerce (having developed an application for mobile credit payments and to enable mobile orders for delivery and pickups of products respectively), which very much relies on the latest ICT innovations.

That said, a company needs customers. The ICT revolution can only lead to successful outcomes if there are customers who want to make use of products or services that result from new ICT applications. Most of the companies in this study target urban consumers, only one focuses on rural consumers, and some do both (see Table 5.1). The nature of goods and services sold by the companies are such that a rising middle-class consumer might be interested in and can afford the products and services. This also partly explains the urban orientation of most companies. The customers may well be outside Africa as well, as is the case with company 9, which sells exotic fruits and vegetables to the European market. Also, company 3, which develops and sells e-books to, among others, Nigerians in the diaspora who want to learn local languages, and company 12, which has become the largest distributor of African movies around the globe, target customers outside Africa. Other companies thrive on the wave of interest regarding the social and environmental impact of corporate business. For example, company 1 is involved in converting waste-based biomass into cellulosic ethanol (cooking fuel). The company serves urban and rural based clients. In terms of social impact, the company has sold over 200,000 clean-cook stoves in West Africa to date and its product has now logged over two million stove-use days. It has been introduced by the national Nigerian programme for clean-cook stoves and adopted by many state and local governments as the preferred stove in over ten states in Nigeria. This also shows that (local) governments in African countries can be customers as well, despite the perception sometimes that these governments are poor and dysfunctional.

Another successful example in the social and environmental impact range is company 6, which produces and sells 2-in-1 roofing tile technologies that integrate solar cells in roof tiles. The company is based in Nairobi, Kenya, was registered in 2008, reached break-even point in 2009, and became profitable in 2010. However, it is also indicated there was no revenue until 2014. It is indicated in 2015 that its revenue was over $US 500,000 and this is also expected for the subsequent years. Before 2015, the company had no paid staff; from 2015, the company employed 4 FTES. In 2016 and 2017, this is expected by the founders to be 15 FTES and 40 FTES, respectively. In 2015, the company secured $USD 125,000 in external capital. The company is currently looking to raise $US 3.5 million in investments.

A diverse picture also emerges geographically. While some of the companies stay in their home markets, others have chosen to extend their business beyond the national borders. This may be within Africa itself (1 and 7), and/or beyond Africa (10, 11, 12 and 14). There is not necessarily a link between being more internationally oriented and ICT. Although e-commerce facilitates reaching out to international markets (for instance companies 11, 12 and 14), company 1 successfully sells a non-ICT related technology (converting waste-based biomass into cellulosic ethanol) to an ever-growing market in West Africa. ICT may have helped to identify foreign markets, but this has not been explored in the case studies.

The presented cases may already provide hints about what determinants of successful innovative start-ups might be, but before we discuss this, we have elaborated on three company cases studies in more detail below, based on additional interviews with the owners of these companies.

## Three In-depth Cases

### *Company 9, Kenya*

Company 9 is an exotic fruits and vegetables producer, packer, supplier, and exporter based in Nairobi, Kenya, registered in 2007. The company produces for international export markets outside Africa (Europe, USA, Asia, Middle East). The single founder of the company (current age 33) can be classified as a local entrepreneur. His origins are in the rural Kiegoi area in the Meru region of Central Kenya, near to Mount Kenya, 320 km from Nairobi. The respondent finished his education to college level. After secondary school in Kiegoi, he started a college education track in 2001, which he completed in 2012 while simultaneously holding down employment. From 2003 to 2006 he worked at multiple local companies, for example as a field manager for a company involved in farming and export and as a sales and marketing officer at a transport company, where he was able to achieve good results.

Company 9 was started from "doing some informal business" and remained informal for the first five years following its registration in 2007. The initial idea for the company was to market the products coming from the respondent's rural area, thus empowering local low-income families economically. With this in mind, the respondent went to Nairobi in search of a market for the products. However, in Nairobi it soon became clear the market was already flooded. Consequently, and having gained a few years of experience in the horticulture sector, the respondent also looked at market opportunities in Europe.

He registered the company and applied for export licences plus other certifications to comply with international food standards. Then he started looking for markets in Europe, a process that he says was not easy. In the end, he says, his work paid off: he secured a number of contracts from client companies and started producing and exporting the products. "At first it was hard," he said, but as he progressed, "things became easier."

The respondent said that, to begin with, he funded the venture from his own savings and that he has been able to grow by reinvesting profits to expand the company. To date, the company has not received any substantial outside investments, although he does want to raise external funds.

The company has developed a structure with appropriate quality checks at both the farm and packing house level. The produce for export includes beans, peas, chilies, aubergines and other vegetables, baby vegetables such as baby carrots, baby leeks, baby courgettes, bimi (tender stem broccoli), passionfruit, avocados and a large selection of fair trade certified flowers.

The company started by shipping small volumes of one to three tons a week and now is shipping three to twenty tons a week. The company has been looking for a stronger partner in the market to work with, to ship volumes for distribution to foreign countries, but so far without success.

Working with smallholder farmers and fair trade and sustainability certifications, the company achieved a large social/environmental impact. At the time of the interview, the company employed 90 people. Before 2014, the company had no paid employees. In 2014, it employed 50 FTEs and in 2015 70 FTEs. The founder expects this will rise to 200 FTEs in 2016 and 300 FTEs in 2017. The company secured $US 10,000 in external investments in 2015. In 2014, the company generated between $US 50,000–100,000 in annual revenue, in 2015 between $US 100,000–500,000, and in 2016 and 2017 revenues are expected to be above $US 500,000. They expect to reach break-even point and become profitable in 2016.

The company did not use an accelerator or incubator. Innovative elements the company introduced are adding value to existing horticulture products (innovating new value adding techniques to the products), developing new projects at the farm level, and using technology to improve operations at the farm level. The respondent said turnover increased by 40 per cent in the last year due to new or strongly improved products.

Of the packers, farmers, and other workers involved, 80 per cent are women and 20 per cent are men. According to company documents, the aim is to revolutionise the industry in terms of farmers' and employees' welfare, with fair trade compliance benefiting the community. Small-scale farmers owning one to three acres mainly grow the produce. They are provided with seeds, fertilisers, chemicals, and technical assistance to meet the required quality standards that the market demands. Once the produce is at the packing house, it is processed and packed according to the client's order, specifications, procedures, and standards and then exported to Europe, USA, the Middle East and Asia. The produce is exported to the wholesalers/distributors importers who then supply the produce to big supermarkets like Tesco, Morrison's, J&S and other retailers.

The respondent said he is the only small business in Kenya offering sea shipping for vegetables to Europe. He said he has developed brands that are now widely accepted in the market. The company developed new and better products on their own, in consultation with customers and clients, in order to get an idea about how the market would receive the products and to get with taking the brands to market. On competition in the sector he said: "The competition is high amongst the players both big and small locally plus competition from other countries. The competition is healthy. What keeps us as unique is that Kenya has good weather that supports full year production compared to competing countries who grow in seasons because of not conducive weather."

The respondent mentioned "economic and social impact to the community, the workers and the consumers" as the most important indicator to determine achieved success of African start-ups/companies. In response to the question of whether he considers his own company successful, he replied: "Not yet successful, because I have not achieved the full potential to where I would want to be." He said "we haven't reached where we want to be, neither have we achieved our goals." According to the respondent, the most important reasons the company became successful include securing and sustaining markets and its workforce. He sees "securing markets and the ability to produce what the market requires" as the most important indicators showing the company is successful.

The respondent suggested that government/policymakers should support small companies financially, as this is the greatest obstacle for many. He suggested that other entrepreneurs should "first of all identify the need they want to address, know their markets well, do due diligence and be ambitious and most of all be visionary."

### *Company 12, Nigeria*

Company 12 is a creative industry company based in Lagos, Nigeria, founded and registered in 2010, targeting low-to-middle-income consumers in Africa and in the diaspora with creative content. Two co-founders started the company. The founder interviewed here (current age 35), who is the initiator of the company and its current CEO, can be classified as a diaspora entrepreneur, born in the UK and of Nigerian descent. After school and studies in Nigeria and the UK, (he holds a Master's degree), he says he had jobs but never stayed in them for very long as he was "always looking to set up my own venture."

The idea for the venture emerged when the respondent noticed how much his mother was watching Nigerian movies at home, but when realised that there was a lack of online services to buy or stream new movies. His first step was to do some research, in order to get a better understanding of the content, the industry and the wider market – first online from the UK, later also on the ground in Lagos, Nigeria. It became clear the distribution infrastructure was very limited. "When I saw that there was an opportunity to develop it," the respondent said, "I started purchasing the online licenses for some movies, direct from the producers, so that I could legally stream them on our YouTube channel."

The company was started in 2010 with investments from a UK-based friend who became co-founder of the company. The respondent says they started a Limited Company in order to be taken seriously by other local and international organisations, for example YouTube. "We needed a professional structure in order to function." The respondent indicated the initial partnership with YouTube was brokered via personal networks.

After a US-based technology news website published an article on the company in 2011 they were approached by a big international investment fund and, following conversations, due diligence and negotiations, they successfully closed a deal worth $US 3 million. Subsequently, they have secured one other investment with this investment fund, two with other international investment companies and one with another company. Amounts were not disclosed in the interview.

Without making use of an accelerator or incubator, the company developed a product/service that was new and was the first in the market. The product evolved from a YouTube channel to an online platform, to an Android App produced by the company. The new product/service was developed together with other parties, i.e. an external supplier was used to build the online platform. The company continues to improve their products and the respondent said the turnover increased in the last year as a result.

Before they introduced the product, there were other ways of streaming Nigerian movies on YouTube or online, but illegally. In contrast, the new company paid for online rights to the content – making a fair deal for content producers, who previously were losing out to online revenue models. The respondent added: "We totally reshaped and redefined the entire distribution model for Nollywood, Africa's most popular form of entertainment. We brought Nollywood online, opening up a huge content catalogue to millions more people, both in Africa and in the Diaspora. I consider that to be innovative." He described the most innovative aspect of his company as "creating a beautiful platform for African content – making it more accessible than ever before."

In five years, the company became one of the world's largest distributors of African-made creative content, employing over a hundred people. The respondent did not disclose details, but other sources indicate that the company is valued at tens of millions of US dollars, with multi-million-dollar revenues. Outside sources also indicate that the company has attracted tens of millions in investments.

Regarding competition in the sector he said: "A lot of competitors who initially came into the video on demand space have fallen by the wayside, as they've realized how complicated and capital-heavy the market is. In terms of other content distributors, more well established entities, we are seeing more competition as more and more come into the digital sphere."

The respondent mentioned "continuing to build year-on-year" and "adding value to the market" as the most important indicators for achieving success for African start-ups/companies. In response to the question of whether he considers his own company successful, he replied: "We are still working hard to be 'successful' – a lot of people know about us, a lot of consumers use our products and consume the content we distribute and we've successfully raised venture capital – however, there's a long way for us to go, in terms of growth and profitability, before we would declare ourselves as successful." He considers Innovation, determination, and hard work the most important reasons for his company's success, and indicated growth and profitability the most important indicators of a company's achievements.

The respondent suggests government/policymakers could make it easier to do business and cut down administration time for entrepreneurs. To other entrepreneurs he suggests: "Lower your expectations of what being an entrepreneur is – it is the hardest, hardest thing you'll ever do. Unless you're willing to give up everything to make your business into the beast it needs to be to weather the market, you will not achieve the sort of success you want to."

### *Company 7, Kenya*

Company 7 is a media company based in Nairobi, Kenya, registered in 2011. Its main customers are broadcasters and it serves regional markets. The company was started by two founders. The founder interviewed here (current age 50), who initiated the company and is its current CEO, can be classified as an entrepreneur from outside of Kenya. The respondent was born in South Africa where he also completed his education, (he has an Arts degree). This provided him the basis for his media skills, but did not prepare him for starting a company. The respondent says management experience was as useful in this regard as his media experience. After graduation, the respondent worked for a large multinational media company for almost twenty years. This involved working in many parts of the world and he was relocated within Africa around ten years ago.

After being posted to Africa, after more than a decade away from the continent, the respondent said he realised "change was coming fast to the continent" and he wanted to "bring change to media on the continent." His work for the multinational media company showed him the potential and the opportunities of the rapidly changing media environment. He mentions the "push" of potential relocation and the prospect of his contract coming to an end as the motivation to put some of his innovative ideas into practice.

After he left his regular job, it took about eight months to start the new company. Registration in 2012 coincided with initial discussions with a potential client to produce African news content. This first deal was agreed verbally and it took almost a year before a contract emerged. In early 2013, the company launched a daily video news service providing African news content on a subscription basis; this required hiring four people as news staff. A few months later, the company started producing another show and hired a creative director and a graphics designer. This grew potential to create graphics and, later, animated graphics and full animation. Currently, the company produces three TV shows, partners to create a Sports News show and produces a daily news "feed", in addition to some animation. The idea of engaging African media producers across the continent, using cutting edge technology and an African "media hub" to create ready-to-air content and selling that content to broadcasters, has been proven. The company now needs considerable financing to scale up and is looking for outside investments.

The respondent said local (Kenyan) financing, even from so-called business-friendly institutions, is prohibitively expensive, with interest rates between 17–19 per cent per annum and with prohibitive guarantees. To date, the entire business has been bootstrapped, with the respondent having provided all financing in personal loans to the company from the beginning.

The company currently has revenues of over $US 500,000, employs 18 people and is active in multiple countries across Africa. The company has not yet secured any outside investment, but is still looking. In 2012, the company employed six FTEs, which rose to 12 in 2013, 15 in 2014, and 18 in 2015. The company's workforce is expected to rise to 20 FTEs in 2016 and 24 FTEs in 2017. The company reached break-even point in 2013 and became profitable in 2014. In 2012 and 2013, it made between $US 100,000–500,000 in annual revenue. In 2015, this rose above $US 500,000 and revenues have remained above this level ever since.

The respondent mentioned a media space in Nairobi, where offices can be rented, as crucial to the company's development. As a media company creating African content for broadcast, online and corporate clients, the company's promise is to deliver cutting edge African news, creative, and animated content. The respondent considers the company innovative in the sense that their content is "truly Africa-wide and groundbreaking, the use of technology constantly evolving and we do so from a highly creative media hub." He indicates that the most innovative element is the "merger of digital technologies and African media creation to develop great African broadcast content, quickly and competitively." He indicates developing an innovative and creative media space from a "frontier market hub" as groundbreaking: creating African content that speaks to pan-African audiences and taps into local capacity and increasingly available digital technology.

The company developed the new products on their own, using feedback from early clients. Turnover increased 10 per cent in the last year due to new or strongly improved products. This was slower than previously, due to the loss of a major client. He also mentioned competition in the sector is growing fast.

The respondent sees access to capital as the most important indicator for determining the success of African start-ups/companies. In response to the question of whether he considers his own company successful, he replied: "We are told we have been extremely successful. We are a long way from where we want to be." He considers the focus on producing great African content the most important reason his company is successful, and new contracts for multi-episode TV shows (three new contracts in the past year) to be the most important indicator of the company's achievements.

He suggests that government/policymakers should provide funding to institutions and/or financiers so that they can provide competitive financing (at less than 10 per cent interest per annum), and provide more sectoral support (as, for example, South Africa's Industrial Development Corporation and regional business development councils do). To other entrepreneurs he suggests: "Try to line up financing before starting out."

## Discussion

In this section, we use insights from the case studies and the interviews with experts[9] to discuss the determinants behind the success of the firms that have been examined. We make a distinction between the internal and external factors, as explained in previously.

A first important internal success factor that emerges from the case studies, but also from the wider VC4A database, is the level of education of the founder entrepreneurs. Most of them have a university degree, in some cases combined with an MBA degree. While the contents of the studies may not have contributed a great deal in terms of how to set up and run a company, for many of them education has probably helped in building "entrepreneurial competences" such as ITC literacy, presentation and communication skills, networking skills, and negotiation skills. In addition, the high education level is also a reflection of social class, though it does not necessarily imply that the entrepreneurs originate from higher social strata in society. That said, the fact that they have completed university enables them to participate in social and economic networks, both nationally and internationally, that go beyond the level of kin and friendship relations. In terms of sustainable livelihoods studies, one could argue that the high level of education has helped these entrepreneurs to build and extend their social capital.

A second internal determinant for success is the registration and formalisation of the company. Being a formal enterprise – i.e. being registered at the Chamber of Commerce, paying taxes, abiding with all other requirements set by statutory law – not only opens up access to sources of finance that go beyond microfinance, but also enables the entrepreneurs to engage in or catch the attention of larger (international) investment funds and ventures. This can help growth-oriented firms to overcome one of the big constraints they generally face: access to finance and working capital. There is a downside to

9 Mr. Ben White (CEO & Founder VC4Africa), Mr. Bankole Oluwafemi (CEO & Founder Big Cabal Media / TechCabal), and Ms. Saskia Reus-Makkink (CEO & Founder Africa Funded).

formalisation, though, which might work against registered companies. Those competitors in the sector who remain informal can often operate with lower transaction costs, and thus might have more room to manoeuvre when it comes to financial accountability, taxes, and exploring the grey areas between legality and illegality. Formal companies are more clearly "on the radar" of other agents, such as local authorities, national government agencies, banks, accountants, etc. The transaction costs that come with this may actually reduce their competitiveness compared to informal firms operating in the same business. This also qualifies, to some extent, the appraisals in existing literature that suggest that the informal sector is a source of creativity and growth in African economies. While this may be true on one level, the informal sector can also result in a process of creative destruction among emerging firms in the "missing middle" segment of the formal sector. In terms of contributions to economic growth and transformation, the latter are generally ascribed as having larger potential than the millions of micro- and small entrepreneurs in the informal sector.

A third internal factor that is relevant to the cases presented in this chapter is the access to capital. Many of the respondents used their own savings to invest in the start-up of their business, and rarely used external finance. In the growth stage, the entrepreneurs have, however, been able to attract capital in various ways, as the case studies show. Consequently, an important constraint to further firm growth is overcome. The formalisation of the company in combination with other entrepreneurial competences, skills, and networks have helped to attract this finance. That said, the entrepreneurs in our case studies also mention that attracting finance is hard and some of them are still seeking larger investment funds to finance their growth ambitions. Moreover, a "missing middle" exists in financial services. While in many African countries it is much easier to either access micro-finance loans for informal entrepreneurs or formal bank loans for large corporations with political contacts, access to finance is extremely difficult to the intermediate-sized loans needed by the segment of enterprises that have been presented here. The emergence of platforms such as Venture Capital for Africa, and the rise of Angel investments, etc., has broadened the scope for finance for these types of enterprises. Nevertheless, venture capitalists still look at Africa with some caution. Although business climate and investment risk indicators in many African countries show a steady trend upwards, investing in African companies is still considered a risky and uncertain business, different from Asia or Latin America. A perceived lack of adequate (financial) market regulations and governance in Africa, and a high-risk assessment of insecurities related to the political and economic conditions in African countries means investors remain reluctant to invest in innovative and, by definition, high-risk business. This may slow down the emergence and further growth of a middle segment of enterprises in African economies.

The cases also reveal a fourth and undeniable success factor: an entrepreneurial spirit and attitude among the founders of the firms. Many of the companies appear to be pioneers in their respective markets and sectors, having identified and grasped market opportunities, and having developed innovative products and services. The innovations they develop are not always disruptive, in a sense that they are breakthroughs for society as a whole, but, in most cases, they are new to the market and, in all cases, new to the company. This reflects the reality of innovation. Breakthrough and disruptive innovations are scarce. Frequently, innovation comes from the cumulative effect of implementing small-scale ideas over prolonged periods of time. It is a process that encompasses the acts of numerous individuals, not only the original inventors, but also the producers, consumers, and middlemen that transmit and operationalise the innovations, making them acceptable to society. What the presented cases show is that this cumulative innovation is widely manifest in African societies as well through the recombination or innovative use of ideas, knowledge, and technology (see also Gewald et al. 2012). The entrepreneurial spirit, which is manifest in, among other things, the innovative products and services, gives companies a "first mover" advantage in their respective markets, through which they can accrue innovation rents. Some of the entrepreneurs indicate that competition is increasing, others copy what they are doing, but certainly entrepreneurs set in motion a process of creative destruction, as indicated by Schumpeter.

As already touched upon in the case descriptions, the adequate and innovative use of available new technology is a clear factor behind the success of many of the firms presented in this chapter. While the availability of new technologies is largely an external factor, it ultimately depends on an internal factor, namely being capable of making use these new technologies, which is a key to success. In this sense, the availability of new technologies in Africa is only a mediating factor, offering new chances and opportunities, which still have to be captured by innovative entrepreneurs. From the case studies, it becomes clear that new ICT has enabled many entrepreneurs to explore more easily and get better insights into (new) market developments and identify new business opportunities. It has also helped them to increase the scale of their business, be that national, regional, or international. Finally, it has led to innovative products and services, which have made many of the entrepreneurs presented in this chapter forerunners in the respective markets and (sub-)sectors.

That said, the presentation of success stories in this chapter may overlook the fact that, to date, only a small section of entrepreneurs have been able to profit from the ICT revolution in Africa in such a way that it has helped them to realise an innovative, growth-oriented enterprise. This is despite media rhetoric that claims otherwise. The World Development Report 2016 refers to the digital divide, which occurs across countries and continents (World Bank 2016). In addition, arguments from the technological capability school, a prominent line of thinking in the 1980s on technology and innovation in developing economies, might be relevant today as well. Their argument is that (firms in) developing economies need to undertake well-articulated searches in terms of the adaptation and assimilation of the transferred technologies, outside of formal R&D labs (Badhuri 2016: 3). The main point is that, without proactive indigenous innovation efforts, imported technology remains static technology, which will never turn into real indigenous technological capability (Fu et al. 2011: 1210). Fu et al. (2011) conclude that the technology gap in many developing economies remains large. The consequence for local innovative firms might be a "locked in" or path dependent trajectory that prevents them from embarking on trajectories for further innovation and growth.

More research is needed to further explore determinants behind the success of the innovative start-up and growth companies we have focused on in this paper. Moreover, we are aware that in this exploratory paper we were only able to present a select number of cases and could not cover the full variety of companies. For example, while the VC4A data and other sources indicate female founders start many successful innovative companies in the sphere, all three cases explored in-depth were owned by male entrepreneurs. Another example of an issue debated in the context of African start-ups is the presumed advantage American and European entrepreneurs, or entrepreneurs with American or European education and networks, have over local African entrepreneurs in terms of access to funding, relevant networks, language, and skills for pitching to investors and other factors. While we were able to show cases of successful innovative companies by local African entrepreneurs, this could be explored in greater depth too.

As we mainly concentrated in this chapter on the start-up and growth trajectory of the companies itself, we have paid less attention to the external environment that may have influenced a firm's performance. A few things stand out though. Firstly, at least three of the developments identified in the landscape of innovation created opportunities for the companies discussed in this paper. Many made use of the new technologies that have become available, one succeeded in becoming part of a GVC (fruits and vegetables), and an emerging middle class of consumers has created sufficient and effective demand for the products and services that the firms under study supply. The internationalisation of R&D activities by MNEs has had little influence on the success of the firms. The companies that have been studied have relations with MNEs in some cases, but these are client relations, and not in the area of R&D collaboration and co-creation of products and services. Some of the companies did make use of local incubators, accelerators, or other enterprise promoting entities.

Secondly, clearly Kenya and Nigeria are different in many respects, be it tax regimes, industrial policy, or government attitude and policy towards SMEs. But also macro-economic conditions, societal conditions, public sector capacity, and willingness to cooperate with business, the legal framework and implementation, the level and appropriateness of services offered by the financial sector differ. This almost certainly has an effect on the performance of the firms discussed in this chapter, but we however have not explored this in detail. On the other hand, both countries are known for being innovation hubs in Africa, and historically they have been among the few African countries that, following independence, have succeeded in building and sustaining a segment of strong small- and medium-sized local firms in the formal sector. In addition, Nigeria and Kenya have become major entry points for investors and companies aiming to serve regional markets in West and East Africa, respectively. This also suggests that the economic and political environment is currently conducive to business, probably also for local start-ups and growth-oriented local firms.

To conclude, this chapter has shown that there is an emerging and growing generation of enterprises in Kenya and Nigeria that come near to what has been formerly defined as "the missing middle", and that innovation and the recent changes in the innovation landscape play a major role in their success. Both internal factors and external factors have had a role in this. Important to note here is that the interaction between the internal and external factors also matter. Mead (1994) showed the crucial importance of bust-boom cycles in some African economies on informal-sector firm performance. While internal factors offer micro-level insights into which firms are able to perform more successfully in a given setting, the external factors provide macro- or meso-level insights into factors that hinder or enable firm growth more generally. In order to promote the missing middle, one would need to look at both internal and external factors. Certain external conditions would need to be in place for a forerunners to be able to exploit opportunities to fill the middle and benefit from it, and to start providing role models for other less catalytic entrepreneurs to follow in their footsteps.

## References

Badhuri, S. (2016). "Frugal Innovation by the 'Small and the Marginal': An Alternative Discourse on Innovation and Development", Inaugural lecture Prince Claus Chair in Development and Equity, 23 May 2016, Erasmus University Rotterdam.

Berner, G.E., Gomez, G.M. & P. Knorringa. (2012). "Helping a Large Number of People Become a Little Less Poor? The Logic of Survival Entrepreneurs", *European Journal of Development Research*, vol. 24 (3), 382–396.

DEMO Africa (2016), www.demo-africa.com, accessed 21 June 2016.

Fafchamps, M. (1994). "Industrial Structure and Microenterprises in Africa", *The Journal of Developing Areas*, 29/1, 1–30.

Fu, X., Pietrobelli, C. & L. Soete (2011). "The Role of Foreign Technology and Indigenous Innovation in the Emerging Economies: Technological Change and Catching-up", *World Development*, vol. 39 (7), 1204–1212.

Gewald, J.B., Leliveld, A. & I. Peša (eds) (2012). *Transforming Innovations in Africa: Explorative Studies on Appropriation in African Societies*, Leiden/Boston: Brill.

Grimm, M., Knorringa, P. & J. Lay (2012). "Constrained Gazelles: High Potential in West Africa's Informal Economy", *World Development*, vol. 40 (7), 1352–1368.

Howard, Philip N. (2015). *Pax Technica: How the Internet of Things May Set Us Free or Lock Us Up*. New Haven, CT: Yale Press.

Kaplinksy, R. (2011). "Schumacher meets Schumpeter: Appropriate Technology Below the Radar", *Research Policy*, vol. 40, 193–203.

Knorringa, P., Peša, I, Leliveld, A. & C. van Beers (2016). "Frugal Innovation and Development: Aides or Adversaries?" *European Journal of Development Research*, vol. 28 (2), 143–153.

Lavie, D. & S.R. Miller (2008). "Alliance Portfolio Internationalization and Firm Performance", *Organizational Science* 19(4): 623–646.

Mead, D. (1994). "The Contribution of Small Enterprises to Employment Growth in Southern and Eastern Africa", *World Development*, vol. 22 (12), 1881–1894.

Nichter, S. & L. Goldmark (2009). "Small Firm Growth in Developing Countries", *World Development*, vol. 37 (9), 1453–1464.

Phillips, C. & S. Bhatia-Panthaki (2007). "Enterprise Development in Zambia: Reflections on the Missing Middle", *Journal of International Development*, vol. 19, 793–804.

Prahalad, C.K. & S.L. Hart (2002). "The Fortune at the Bottom of the Pyramid", *Strategy and Business*, First Quarter 2002, Issue 26.

Radjou, N. (2009). "Managing the New Trajectory of Global Innovation", Centre for India and Global Business, Cambridge Judge Business School, Cambridge, UK. http://www.cfr.org/content/meetings/New_Global_Trajectory.pdf, accessed June 2016.

Ravallion, M. (2009). "The Developing World's Bulging (But Vulnerable) Middle Class". *World Development*, 38(4), 445–454.

Rifkin, J. (2011). *The Third Industrial Revolution: How Lateral Power is Transforming Energy, the Economy, and the World',* New York: Palgrave Macmillan Ltd.

Schumpeter, J.A. (1934). *The Theory of Economic Development: An Inquiry into Profits, Capital, Credit, Interest and the Business Cycle*, Cambridge: Harvard University Press. Translated from *Theorie der wirtschaftlichen Entwicklung* (1911).

Schumpeter, J.A. (1942). *Capitalism, Socialism and Democracy*, HarperCollins 3rd edition (1951).

Singh, M.G. (2011). "Innovation in India: Affordable Innovations". In: S. Dutta, *The Global Innovation Index 2011, Accelerating Growth and Development*, Geneva: INSEAD, 77–86.

Staley, E. & R. Morse. (1965). *Modern Small Industry for Developing Countries*, New York: McGraw Hill.

Tellegen, N. (1997). *Rural Enterprises in Malawi: Necessity or Opportunity?*, Aldershot: Ashgate Publishing Ltd.

*The Economist* (2010), "First Break all the Rules: The Charms of Frugal Innovation", 15 April 2010. www.economist.com/node/15879359, accessed 20 April 2016.

UNCTAD (2006), *World Investment Report*, Geneva: United Nations.

VC4A 2016a, www.vc4a.com, accessed 21 July 2016.

VC4A 2016b, *Venture Finance in Africa 2016 Research*, https://vc4a.com/venture-finance-in-africa/2016-research/, accessed 21 July 2016.

World Bank (2016) *Digital Dividends*, World Development Report 2016, Washington, DC: The World Bank.

World Development Indicators, http://data.worldbank.org/data-catalog/world-development-indicators.

CHAPTER 6

# Innovation in Manufacturing SMEs in Kenya, Ghana and Tanzania: A Grounded View on the Research and Policy Issues

*Jaap Voeten*

## Introduction

The promotion of entrepreneurship and innovation in the private sector in Africa has entered the agenda of the economic and development research community and policymakers. All agree that innovative and dynamic businesses are crucial for catching up with global economic growth and development (Chaminade *et al.* 2010). A focus on promoting innovation and productivity in small and medium-sized enterprises (SMEs) in manufacturing would have a particularly positive development impact (Szirmai *et al.* 2011). This is because formally established SMEs in general provide employment and create a middle class in society, stabilising the overall economy. Moreover, economic development brings a shift from economic activity in agriculture to manufacturing, thus providing additional value in terms of a "structural change bonus".[1] The present economic contribution of the manufacturing sector to the overall economy in many African countries, compared to the agriculture and services sectors, is typically low. For instance, in Kenya and Ghana, the share of manufacturing to total GDP in terms of value added was 11.3 per cent and 5 per cent respectively in 2015.[2] The actual situation of SMEs in Africa, however, is one of low productivity and low economic significance, termed the "missing middle".[3] Innovation is considered the best way to promote the stagnating manufacturing SME sector, because value creation results in a better-balanced economic structure, and increased competitiveness is the route towards import

1 Any shift of labour and other resources from agriculture to manufacturing results in an immediate increase in overall productivity and income per capita. This is referred to as the "structural change bonus".

2 http://data.worldbank.org/indicator/.

3 This phrase has been used relatively loosely in economic development discussions, meaning a lack of SMEs, particularly in the developing world. See: http://www.africa.com/blog/investing_in_africa_defining_themissing_middle_/.

 | DOI 10.1163/9789004351615_007

substitution and export promotion. This is a somewhat classical view on development that still holds in the globalising world today.

Current research and theory development in innovation have mainly built on advanced economies in Western countries. Only recently have research projects started to address innovation, its processes and conditions in countries elsewhere. One such example is a research project funded by the UK's Department for International Development (DFID) "Enabling Innovation and Productivity Growth in Low Income Countries" (EIP-LIC). The research explores innovation in manufacturing SMEs in ten African and Asian countries and assesses relationships with internal capabilities and external institutional factors.[4]

During the research design of the project, several basic conceptual and theoretical issues emerged, such as the unclear definition and complicated measurement of innovation in developing countries. In research in advanced economies, innovation is typically measured by research and development (R&D) expenditures and the numbers of patents of new products or production technologies, as proposed in the Oslo Manual, for instance (OECD 2005). Çapoğlu (2009) already observed that, despite increasing interest in the literature, the exact definition of innovation in developing and emerging economies remains an unresolved issue. This is because innovation in African manufacturing SMEs often manifests itself differently, not necessarily via high profile technological and radical "new to the world" breakthroughs involving explicit R&D investments and patents. Innovation often concerns incremental adoption and adaptation or new combinations of existing technologies (Szirmai *et al.* 2011). Many of these innovations involve "an aggregation of small insights and advances through learning by doing rather than on major technological inventions" (Carayannis *et al.* 2003). These forms of innovation, new to the company, are perhaps equally important for raising productivity and competitiveness of SMEs. In their initial efforts to formalise innovation in developing countries in a theoretical framework, Fagerberg *et al.* (2010) confirm that there is "another way to look at innovation that goes significantly beyond this high-tech picture. In this, broader perspective, innovation – the attempt to try out new or improved products, processes or ways to do things – is an aspect of most if not all economic activities. In this sense, innovation may be as relevant in the developing part of the world as elsewhere."

Further EIP-LIC analysis into innovation processes within SMEs in developing countries also revealed some divergence between theory and reality.

4 The research and the development of the argument in this chapter was funded in the framework of DFID (EIP-LIC/PO5639): https://www.tilburguniversity.edu/dfid-innovation-and-growth/.

While the process is often seen in the literature "as carried out by highly educated labor in R&D intensive companies with strong ties to leading centers of excellence in the scientific world" (Fagerberg *et al.* 2010), the African reality of SMEs is not based on explicit links with science and technology institutions. The process is more commonly an experience-based learning process within the boundaries of the firm. SME entrepreneurs initiate, interact and learn by doing, much depending on their internal capabilities (Lundvall *et al.* 2009). A notable implication of managing and owning the innovation process within the firm is the likelihood of owning the innovation benefits as well.

The EIP-LIC research design with regard to the external conditions and the institutional context in which innovations evolve faced conceptual issues. In their analyses in advanced economies, Lundvall (1992) and Freeman (1987) suggest that innovation takes place within a relatively stable institutional context, "controlled" and supported by established formal actors and innovation policies, which they termed an "innovation system". The innovation process is linked to a co-evolutionary network of supporting institutions: financial and legal institutions, technology development and research agencies, universities, education and training systems, governance structures and innovation policies (Edquist 1997).

In the Sub-Saharan African context, however, many of such formal institutions and links are typically not well developed. Instead, many enterprises are supported in their innovation activities by less visible or less commonly known informal institutional links. Informal institutions are broadly understood as links and ties with networks of friends and family and social capital, but are also considered as the informal "rules of the game" including traditions, culture, habits and mental models (Scott 2001). Informal institutions may include personal and family contacts, community and social networks, informal credit for incremental innovation and adoption. This reality of how innovation evolves within informal institutional contexts in Africa has just started to be acknowledged in recent innovation systems literature (Lundvall 2009; World Bank 2010).

With a view to addressing the conceptual issues mentioned above, amongst others, the EIP-LIC research included a qualitative research component, a series of case studies. This concerned an inductive exploration of how innovation in manufacturing SMEs materialises on the ground. The aim of the case studies series was to complement the quantitative EIP-LIC research design, in particular in identifying, validating and complementing existing theories and hypotheses with contemporary realities, as perceived by manufacturing SME owners and managers. In this chapter, a selection of three cases from the EIP-LIC cases series are presented and analysed, addressing three overall research questions: what and how do innovations materialise within manufacturing SMEs? What are the firms' strong and weak internal capabilities? How does the external business and institutional context play a supporting or hampering role in the innovation process? This chapter identifies patterns and trends in the cases and concludes with some reflections on policy implications.

## Approach and Method

In the ten countries of study within EIP-LIC,[5] we identified and interviewed 15 to 20 innovative manufacturing SMEs to develop the series of cases. To assure homogeneity, enabling comparison between companies and countries, we selected the SMEs by applying the following criteria: (i) formally registered SMEs in manufacturing; (ii) between ten and 150 employees (turnover, assets and capital formation are not considered), and: (iii) owned by African and Asian entrepreneurs.[6]

We obtained the data for developing cases via holistic "semi-structured" interviews with SME owners and managers.[7] We visited the enterprise premises and asked open questions about how they survive and expand, solving daily issues with new solutions, production techniques, processes or investments in new products and ways of marketing. More specifically, we followed the innovation typology of Kaplinsky and Morris (2001): (i) process innovation aiming at improving the efficiency of transforming inputs into outputs; (ii) product innovation leading to better quality, lower price and/or more differentiated products; (iii) business practice innovation, implying new ways to organise the business and attract new clients; (iv) functional innovations – assuming responsibility for new activities in the value chain, such as design, marketing and logistics; and (v) inter-chain innovations, moving to new and profitable chains.

5 Ethiopia, Ghana, Kenya, South Africa, Tanzania, Uganda, Bangladesh, India, Indonesia and Vietnam.

6 In Africa, one should be careful about talking about "African entrepreneurs". Many businesses in African countries have Indian (or other Asian) owners. The owners and their families have been in these countries for generations and gained local nationality. They are well integrated in the local economic life and society.

7 EIP-LIC has a case study database developed in the framework of qualitative research activities in the African and Asian countries of study.

After clarifying the types and processes of innovation, we then asked how the entrepreneurs perceive the company's capabilities, or the lack thereof, in enabling the entrepreneur to innovate. We subsequently addressed the issue of how innovating entrepreneurs perceive and cope with the (ever-changing) external business and institutional context. We wrote the case studies based on transcribed interview recordings and on visual observations complemented with grey materials. The qualitative data were systematically stored in the EIP-LIC qualitative dataset. The analysis of the data, inductively and systematically identifying patterns and trends, was an iterative process with the data collection. Lastly, we reviewed the findings against literature for comparison and validation or to signal theoretical differences.

Regarding the validity of the research, qualitative research in general does not claim to collect and analyse data from a representative sample. Instead, on a case-by-case basis, qualitative analysis provides exploratory (inductive) insights into issues, processes and systems in a bottom-up way that helps to suggest theoretical concepts for the local context (Denzin and Lincoln 1998). Against this background, the selection of cases involved "information-oriented" sampling, as opposed to random sampling. Next, we present three selected cases from Kenya, Ghana and Tanzania manufacturing SMEs. In the analysis, we also refer to other cases in the series of DFID qualitative studies.

## Cases

### *Food Processing – Palm Oil, Mixes, and Palm Cream* (*Ghana – 110 Employees*)

The company started in 1994 with the production of various palm oils and related products. It is located on the northern side of Accra. The production processes, carried out in three large production halls, entail palm seed cleaning, cooking and milling, followed by extracting oils, drying the powders and cooking the creams as final products. A separate packaging and canning section is also a recent part of the company. To secure supply of the palm seeds used in production, the company has acquired 350 acres of land in different locations near Accra and in the Eastern Region. It cultivates oil palm, cassava, maize and other crops. The company has 110 employees.

Initially, the company focused on the domestic market. However, the owner soon realised the export potential of his products through his network of contacts. Moreover, distribution in the domestic market took a lot of effort – "Maintaining contacts and managing the logistics in the three regions outside Accra were very time consuming compared to the returns." The owner had previous overseas experience in the retail food sector during a five-year stay in the UK. This helped him a lot in using his network of good contacts among companies, importers and distributors, and to understand export requirements.

The company started exporting their products in the year 2000. Today, the company only deals with four principal importers overseas: in Europe (Netherlands, Germany and Norway), the USA, Canada and Australia.

### Innovation and Internal Capabilities

The owner sees a constant need to develop new palm oil and other related products. The demand is changing continuously and technological developments make new products possible. In recent years, many new products – beyond palm oil – have been introduced as a result. The current range includes banku mix, gari, cereal mix, kokonte and hausa koko powder, canned palm cream concentrate and canned eggplants. In the future, the owner foresees new products "because day in day out our customers and importers ask if there is anything new."

In this dynamic business context, the owner tries to keep well informed of trends, which "helps me to be one step ahead of the competition." Most of the competing companies are Ghanaian companies. The owner has the advantage of exchanging new products within his international network of contacts and "by so doing we are always ahead, and that has really worked for us."

Product innovation goes hand in hand with new technologies in processing, labelling and packaging. The establishment of the canning section in 2003 was one key technological innovation. Considering whether to make this investment, the owner realised that there were only a few canning companies in Ghana, while the demand was high. The new machines enabled the company to launch new products with a longer shelf life. The owner believes that part of the success of the canned products was "the existing and well-established reputation of the company brand in the market."

The growth strategy of the company focuses on expanding the production volume and range of products. This involves innovation and technology, enabling the firm to process raw materials into high quality food products.

The expansion of the range of products will create more employment in the near future – "These innovations are not about saving on labour costs, but about the ability to produce new products that the customers want. Therefore, we envisage growth in terms of both machines and personnel."

The owner recognises the positive effect of employment creation, in particular for women – "We have about 30 women employed directly, and the impact on their children is very positive. They are able to give good meals to the children and pay school fees, so the children get educated and learn about good hygiene: it is a multiple effect."

The owner considers himself a real entrepreneur. When he sees opportunities and other products overseas, he says, "If others can do it, like producing some special type of product, I believe I can do it." Once an opportunity arises, the owner reviews the financial implications and consequences. At the same time, he is aware that one can never be certain about a business plan, financial calculations and forecasts – "I am an entrepreneur, so I am able to smell an opportunity; that good feeling helps in taking some of these decisions."

When a new product is first proposed, by a customer for instance, the owner and the principal product developer first brainstorm about the overall idea and sort out the technical details of the process and the ingredients. Sometimes company staff from the factory come forward with additional ideas. There has been input from employees in one way or another in all the new products so far. The owner also travels two to three times a year abroad (The Netherlands, Germany and Belgium) and studies new products in the various shops. He often goes just "to see products in the shops and to see how our products match with other products on the market in terms of presentation and pricing, and also to get customer feedback." If the owner sees an interesting product, he brings it back. He feels that every suggestion from a customer could be useful – "We put it on the shelf since we cannot implement it immediately, even though it's a good idea."

The required minimum education level for staff is basic junior high school and the ability to read and write – "We also have some university educated staff in product development and quality monitoring." The company undertakes quarterly training for their employees within the framework of a UNDP and UNIDO programme "Sustaining Competitive Enterprise". Trainers from local institutions discuss production techniques and practices for the highest possible quality and current product trends in the industry. They show videos and give participating staff the opportunity to present their own innovation ideas.

Indeed, quality has been one of the important areas of attention to assure continued access to the export market. Internally, the company has an agreed practice and culture of everyone being responsible for quality assurance – "You are on the machine working but you should open your eyes and observe." Quality means, among other things, that the product looks traditional and natural.

This is what the average consumer wants to see in the product – "The palm oil they remember from their grandmother's time."

The company does not yet have any formalised bonus or reward system. However, some years back a staff member came up with the idea for a new and successful product and "we gave him a bonus."

### External Business and Institutional Environment

Regarding the external business environment, the owner is facing several challenges. One major challenge perceived by many manufacturing companies in Ghana, according to the owner, is the unreliable electricity supply and frequent power cuts, which become more of a problem by the day. Without the generators purchased half a year ago, the company would not be able to survive. The generators can power the whole plant, but this brings with it a much higher cost "which could have been invested into the product or raw materials. In a day, the generators use almost 1000 Ghana cedi (300 USD) to keep the machines working and maintain production at the required level."

The owner feels that the location of the company's plant is not very good. Previously, the company was located in the outskirts of Accra, which is a more residential area. He tried to expand, but land acquisition was difficult and not well regulated – "You acquire a plot of land and before you know it, someone else is claiming ownership." The current location provides space, but it is some distance from the central district, and road conditions are poor. The owner is trying to lobby for investments in infrastructure by local government, "but no matter how much you talk, you don't get anywhere."

In an effort to protect the brand name, the company has registered its name as a trademark, "despite the fact that enforcement is weakly implemented by the government." The owner feels that government officials and politicians are usually looking at short-term policies and programmes that will bring them power and benefits rather than really helping the companies.

The owner is not very positive about the banking sector in Ghana. The interest rate for credit is about 35 per cent per year, "which is simply too high for any kind of business." The company got credit because otherwise it was impossible to grow – "Certainly for at least a number of years you cannot do without credit. You definitely need credit to be able to meet all the industry standards." The credit issue prevents the owner from doing things that he would like to do. Repayment is an ever-present challenge.

The company monitors the international firms in Ghana: their new and existing products, marketing, types of packaging, machines used, etc. The company sees Nestlé and Unilever as its main role models. The company recently collaborated with the Food Research Institute in a yam preservation project.

However, the cooperation was established through an informal contact, which ended when the person left the institute. The owner has just signed a Memorandum of Understanding (MoU) with the Food and Nutrition Department of a Polytechnic College. The students are working on developing food products and "it's one of the things we are trying to do. They are studying food products and they have quite a number each year, so we can get many more ideas for product development."

### *Wood Processing – Furniture (Tanzania – 40 Employees)*

The company produces furniture and is situated on a busy road on the south side of Dar es Salaam. It also sells different kinds of wood for construction projects. The company has an open workshop including a number of heavy sawing machines. The company also saws wood and parts for other furniture producers, as a paid service.

The owner started in 1995 as a trader, buying wood from villages in the country and selling to wholesalers in Dar es Salaam. However, organising and implementing the transportation became increasingly complicated over the years. Despite the fact that he always had the required paperwork, the police and government officers from the Ministry of Natural Resources made the transport difficult – "they did not trust the documents, so there were extra costs to make sure the timber reached town." In 2003, he decided to change his trading activity – "because in everything I was doing I faced challenges. I asked myself, why don't I become a manufacturer of furniture myself?" Shortly thereafter, he started making furniture and immediately secured orders.

To buy his first sawing machine, the owner took out a loan from a private commercial bank, which was possible because he had an established and registered office of trading business, a plot of land and some furniture as collateral. Initially, the bank paperwork was too difficult to complete. The bank then simplified it because "they lowered the amount of money I wanted." Eventually, he secured the loan with an interest rate of 23 per cent for six months. The owner was very much aware that the loan was not very attractive – "but it was a must to get money to start manufacturing." He had confidence in the market for furniture.

#### Innovation and Internal Capabilities

Since 2003, despite ups and downs, the business has been growing steadily. With the profits and savings, the owner managed to buy six large and 12 small hand machines. He had confidence to invest in the machines because his network of clients had provided him with sufficient orders thus far. The production techniques improved and became more refined. The business practice also changed in the sense that, previously, the owner just produced furniture without having orders. However, the hardwood became very expensive, so he switched to only producing after having received an order, which is much easier – "if you produce without an order, you need a bigger place or a showroom where you can keep furniture well-arranged and clean." He considers himself well known in the area. He has a good reputation and people trust him.

The sawing machines enable the owner to produce pieces faster and of higher quality than local competitors. He bought the large machines second-hand from the UK. Before he did so, he visited several small companies in Dar es Salaam that use similar models. Then, a contact in the UK helped him to find second-hand machines for sale and checked their condition and operational efficiency. The owner is very satisfied with these machines. The small hand machines were bought new from the local agent of a Japanese importer.

The company employs an average of 40 workers, although currently only has 12 workers (when we visited the company for this research project). The workers do not have fixed employment contracts. Instead, the owner recruits workers once he receives orders. He negotiates payment depending on the number of pieces to be produced and concludes a short-term contract. The 12 current workers work most of the time in the company. They know beforehand how much they will earn – "they know once there is a large order, then they will earn a lot." The owner does not train his workers. It is not difficult get good skilled workers and the required skills for furniture making are not very difficult to obtain. Most of the workers can produce what the clients want. The owner mentions that there is no education or school to increase their knowledge and skills.

To design the furniture, the owner has a large collection of printed pictures of products (tables, chairs, cupboards, drawers, etc.) – "but that was before the coming of smartphones. Now, I have lots of pictures on my mobile phone." When a new client comes to the workshop, the owner first listens to what design he or she wants. Sometimes the owner shows pictures to get ideas. Before making a more detailed design drawing of the furniture, the owner visits the customer's home and takes measurements. The owner drafts several drawings with the sizes. Then once the customer agrees, the owner discusses with the workers how to best produce it. They sit down and the workers also provide ideas.

### External Business and Institutional Environment

The clients of the company are mostly private households. Occasionally, the owner receives orders from schools for classroom furniture from other areas in

Dar es Salaam. There is some competition for these orders in the neighbourhood from other furniture producers. The owner's strategy is to prioritise client satisfaction – "because if the client is satisfied then he will become my ambassador and bring other customers." He is hardworking, even at night sometimes, to make sure that he delivers on time.

Lately, there is more competition from larger shops on the outskirts of Dar es Salaam that import furniture from China. In large showrooms, this imported furniture is on display – "and because of the imported furniture it is more difficult to get orders from the government offices. Most government agencies prefer imported furniture." The owner wonders why the government is buying imported instead of local products – "people from the government usually say that they will buy furniture from Tanzania, but I have never seen them actually buying local furniture." The owner considers that Chinese products are not very good and lack durability. He wonders why Tanzanian clients buy this lower quality Chinese furniture at a much higher price.

Regarding the business environment, the owner does not receive support from the government – "most of the time when government officers come here, they are coming for their official issues. They want me to pay tax." The owner finds the government more of a hindrance than a support. Many government officials visit: an official from the municipality regarding business registration, a representative from the Ministry of Natural Resources inspecting the wood – "I never see them coming here to talk or ask how the business is going or what problems I am facing."

He has some advice for the government. One important issue is that the government should establish a single set of consistent rules and regulations for business operation. Many government officials come to collect payment of different taxes – "and it is changing all the time." The same applies to the owner's experience of the Tanzanian Revenue Authority (TRA) – "you might go there and pay tax but they will come here again for something else." The owner would like to see a government consensus on regulations for starting and running a business.

The owner does not receive external advice or expertise. When he faces technical or design challenges, he solves the matter himself or calls friends for help. There are no contacts with formal institutions, vocational training or technology centres – "one example yesterday, I had a piece of marble work to do for a kitchen cabinet. I asked a friend who specialises in this. I wanted to see how he does it, so I called him and asked him to do the work while I was watching."

His friends or family do not support the business, which relies on the owner entirely. He hopes to modify his work in future, because it is his only employment. He manages to take care of his family – "and that is very important for me." He hopes to move to bigger manufacturing premises and also to purchase a showroom to display some of his furniture. He is currently saving but he does not know where he might buy, since he prefers premises close to the main road. It is very important for a workshop like his to be close to the main road, to make marketing easier – "we keep the furniture outside so it is easier for people to see it."

### *Textile and Clothing – Company Uniforms and Accessories Tailoring (Kenya – 30 Employees)*

The company is a Kenyan-owned textile and garment manufacturer located in a commercial area in South Nairobi. It has a small workshop with one production line and 30 employees. The company is involved in the stitching, tailoring and branding (printing logos) of company and school uniforms and work clothes. Occasionally, other promotional items such as T-shirts and polo shirts, caps and reflective jackets are produced. The enterprise usually deals with big private companies, hotels, NGOs and schools in Nairobi and the surrounding area, because this involves a certain level of mass production: only 20 pieces or more are cost-effective. The company does not export, but there are buyers from Tanzania and Southern Sudan, who themselves take the products back to their countries.

The textile inputs and fabrics come from suppliers in Nairobi. The company has an agreement with the suppliers allowing payment after a certain period of time. This is because most of the clients do not pay cash upfront or directly after delivery, but usually after 30 days or more.

This new enterprise is only 18 months old. Its young owner is motivated to develop his company and committed to developing business more widely in Kenya. As a child, he lived with his family in the USA for a time. However, the Western world was not what they expected, and so the family returned. The owner is happy that he gained exposure to the outside world, which helps him to do business today in Kenya.

Despite the fact that Kenya is a developing country, the owner sees great opportunities. Most of the successful businessmen he knows started small, and he is aware that starting a business is not only about money – "If you are only money oriented your business will never live on." In his opinion, an entrepreneur has to like what he or she is doing – "If you like what you are doing, you will come up with new inventions which people will really like. Then the money will follow."

#### Innovation and Internal Capabilities

He started the business in 2013. Previously, he tried to get a regular job, but without success. He started to explore other opportunities, such as starting a business by himself. The idea of a textile business came from a friend who owns a textile company. Visiting this company gave him the inspiration to start the uniforms business.

Initially, he started a "briefcase" company by acquiring orders from corporates and hotels for uniforms. Once he got an order, he subcontracted it to a friend who had a small tailoring workshop. He subsequently delivered the product to the client and earned a small commission. After a while, he realised that he could get a much higher profit margin by manufacturing the textiles himself. The sewing and printing machines are usually expensive to buy, but luckily, he was able to borrow a machine from a client asking to have 200 shirts stitched. Shortly after, more clients placed orders for clothes, enabling him to buy another machine and expand the company.

His growing client base has forced the owner to innovate and expand. He plans to increase production capacity and move to a larger production hall in the industrial area, where he will get double the amount of space for the same rent. By installing two more production lines, he will be able to handle a big order of, for instance, 1000 or more overalls or dustcoats. At the same time, he will be able to handle other orders. The owner sees the necessity to innovate. He is aware that if an entrepreneur wants to survive in Kenya, he or she has to be innovative and think outside the box – "Because if you don't, somebody else will and they will kick you out." He knows that if he does not come up with new machinery, the company will have to close down. The owner also mentions that Chinese traders, with modern machines, may take over the market soon. It is better that Kenyan firms capture the market right now.

He is making arrangements and investigating possibilities. He has found an Asian supplier of the new machinery, which is technologically advanced and much more efficient. He is also exploring the possibility of producing leather products, such as handbags and women's shoes, the latter currently imported from China. He is considering importing the raw materials and manufacturing shoes locally.

The business currently has 30 employees. Most came without previous knowledge or experience, and were trained on the job. Some are qualified, and train others in how to tailor new products. There is no formal training within the company. The supplier of the sewing machines provides instruction on how to use the machines.

Generally, clients ask for specific pre-designed products. However, the owner would like to do more of his own design work in the future – "It's not the client who drives me, it's me who drives the client." He develops his own ideas and researches internet retail sites to see what is available on the market in other countries.

He has a designer meeting twice a week. Some new designs are successful, while others are not. The experienced staff also come up with ideas that are worth trying. On a few occasions, the designer improved a design proposed by the client, much to the satisfaction of this client. However, there is little time to think about innovation and testing new ideas on the work floor, where the staff are under pressure to meet tight production deadlines every day.

#### External Business and Institutional Environment

The owner finds the business environment in Kenya hard – "It is every man for himself." He feels that the government is letting small companies down because of the many taxes and laws. Government officials visit often and deliberately look for administrative mistakes. The government creates an uncertain and hostile business environment. A company never knows when the government officials will visit, and "when they show up, you go down." The owner's critical opinion grew from witnessing more challenges as his company was growing – "If the government officials were doing what they were supposed to do we would be doing well." What really upsets the owner is that there are so many young people in Kenya with great ideas and energy, but stuck in a political system that prevents them from taking initiative and growing new businesses.

The owner is concerned about the increasing imports of cheap, low quality products. He thinks that the advantage of being located in Kenya is the quick delivery time of tailor-made products, last-minute production and close proximity to the client.

Without the financial and emotional support of his family and friends, he could not have set up his business. They were very supportive in overcoming initial insecurities. He attributes much of the success of his business to his wife and parents. They help him in developing ideas and running a business – "we go through these problems together."

### *Analysis of Trends and Patterns*

#### Innovation

While some reports about the African economic situation sketch a pessimistic picture of the manufacturing SME sector, the enterprises analysed in the EIP-LIC qualitative series of cases innovated, expanded and started exporting. In further analysing the firms' innovation in terms of incremental adoption and adaptation or new combinations of existing technologies (Szirmai *et al.* 2011), it is evident that the interviewed SMEs' owners introduced a number of product, process and business practice innovations.

The palm oil company in Ghana initially manufactured products for the local market, then successfully accessed the export market, along with the introduction of several new products and new production processes. The furniture company in Tanzania changed from trading wood into manufacturing, which would qualify as functional innovation. This enabled the company to introduce new products and gradually new technology. The Kenyan textile company started as a briefcase company, then established a production line with new machines and new design.

Applying the innovation typology of Kaplinsky and Morris (2001), however, is not so straightforward. The reality shows a combination of several types of innovations within the SMEs, where one type of innovation often interacted with or triggered another. This pattern was observed in all SMEs subject to the qualitative research in EIP-LIC.

Although the innovations in the cases are not radical or "new to the world", they were new for the companies. They mostly concern product innovations involving new technology; value is created by expanding the range of products with higher quality while using locally available raw materials. Against this background, all cases comply with the characteristics of innovation in factor-driven economies (Porter *et al.* 2002). In these economies, low-cost labour and unprocessed natural resources are the dominant basis of competitive advantage and exports. The next stage would be an efficiency-driven economy, where products and services become more advanced and production highly efficient. This is not yet happening in the cases in Ghana, Kenya and Tanzania.

### Internal Capabilities

With regard to the internal capabilities, all companies are informally organised. None of them has an innovation or R&D specialised department. Typically, the companies possess old and outdated machinery, often purchased second-hand from Europe (or in other cases from China). Owners are aware of the necessity to innovate and pursue efforts to do so. They have numerous innovation ideas and initiated tests and trials. The resilience of the owners is notable in this respect. They all have determination and persistence in setting up their business as well as a "drive" to continually improve their operations. Several owners among the SMEs interviewed in EIP-LIC explicitly mentioned that they did not establish the company for profit reasons only. The sense of fulfilment and achievement gained from setting up the business is valued, regardless of how difficult it is to make ends meet.

The internally managed innovation processes observed in the cases do not follow a linear and "projectified" approach involving a strategic plan, a cost-benefit analysis and a timeframe for the implementation, as often described in technology-push innovation approaches (Godin 2006). Instead, the owners of the interviewed companies work step-by-step and see what works and what does not. This innovation process is earlier described by Kline and Rosenberg

(1986) in their chain link model, acknowledging the disorganised feedback loops between iterative stages of the innovation process, including idea generation, testing and implementation.

Regarding the workforce of the SMEs, companies in the three cases presented in this chapter do not face difficulties in recruiting staff. However, in many other companies interviewed within EIP-LIC, owners report the problematic recruitment of skilled craftsmen and operators to work with modern machines in particular. Younger generations lack relevant experience and are not very motivated to do manufacturing work. Regarding innovative ideas, the owners indicate that most of their employees have little knowledge or exposure to new technologies, products and other outside information. Although ideas from the workers and production managers are generally appreciated, they only suggest occasional improvements on the production level. Teece *et al.* (1997) suggest that the focus needs to be defined in terms of distinctive competences or capability of the workforce. Products, for that matter, are the manifestation of competence. Innovation in a dynamic context depends in large measure on internal technological, organisational, and managerial processes inside the firm. Organising the SME effectively and efficiently is generally more fundamental to innovation than is strategising in, for instance, engaging in business conduct that keeps competitors off balance, raises rivals' costs, and excludes new entrants (*Ibid*).

The owners mention that the skills and knowledge gained through formal education do not match the company's requirements. Practical skills and an entrepreneurial and creative attitude is a particular area for improvement, according to the owners. Despite the shortcomings, no interviewed company provides additional external formal training for the workers, opting instead for on the job training. Some owners are reluctant to provide any training at all because of past experience of workers moving to other jobs.

Most owners in the cases demonstrate social awareness and a sense of responsibility towards the community and environment in which they operate. Owners take environmental and social considerations into account, and go "beyond compliance" in terms of employment creation for the community stakeholders, and women in particular, and contribute to poverty alleviation. The concept of Social Corporate Responsibility (CSR) is definitely not exclusively for large companies in Western countries (Quazi *et al.* 2007).

### External Business Environment and Formal and Informal Institutions

All the SME owners indicate that the business environment in their respective country is challenging. They all see promising market opportunities on the one hand but a harsh institutional context on the other, which makes business operations, innovation and development problematic. The companies face competition from local firms, which is not mentioned as a key problem; the SME owners understand that competition forces companies to stay sharp and to look for innovative ways to do better than their competitors. However, the companies face serious and unfair competition from imports. China and India in particular ship in cheap counterfeit products of inferior quality, according to the owners. Rossouw *et al.* (2015) confirms that the perceptions of Africans towards Chinese business are rather negative, in particular with respect to the quality of Chinese products and services. Employment practices of Chinese companies as well as their environmental and economic responsibility are considered problematic.

### Business Context

Regarding ideas for innovation, and available technology in particular, suggestions come from the suppliers' side, amongst others. Most owners and managers are well informed about the technology possibilities and alternatives for their manufacturing through suppliers of machinery and equipment. They research suppliers' websites abroad and travel to fairs, identifying existing technology that could be adapted or adopted in their local context. In addition, interviewed owners are client-oriented and get innovation ideas via the demand side. The customers often come with requirements and suggestions, to which most owners are attentive. In fact, the buyers and clients are a strong force for the so-called market-pull types of innovation in the cases, corresponding to the theory distinguishing buyer-driven from producer-driven value chains (Gereffi *et al.* 2005).

There are no links observed with Western multinationals in the form of subcontracting or supplier arrangements; the interviewed companies operate independently. There is no spill-over of technology as a result of cooperation within value chains.

### Formal Institutional Context

All SME owners have a more or less negative perception about the formal institutional context. Dealing with government agencies involves various political and bureaucratic challenges. In general, the SME owners keep the government at a distance.

On the one hand, the owners do not see a consistent regulatory or policy framework for manufacturing SMEs (nor an explicit long-term overall economic development plan). Many ministries and governmental agencies have different regulations, which makes the institutional context conflicting and unpredictable. The situation is reported to be difficult because of bribery and corruption. As a result, most companies are careful to avoid external exposure, which would attract government officials. Entrepreneurs mention that the government is after a "quick buck" by earning on imports rather than investing, and later yielding tax, in local manufacturing.

On the other hand, owners also see that staff within ministries and agencies are motivated and engaged in efforts to develop and promote innovation policy. Increasingly, policy frameworks and associated documents are being developed. Despite considerable effort in developing strategies and plans, actual implementation is only just beginning in Ghana, Tanzania and Kenya, due to the limited availability of public budgets and knowledgeable staff.

Interaction with existing technology institutions, as formal innovation system actors, is virtually non-existent. Many SMEs indicate that they would like to cooperate with universities to undertake research at their premises, sharing the research insights obtained. The technological focus of universities is often different and very much focused on theory development rather than practical application within SMEs. The interviewed companies did not enjoy the support of these formal innovation system institutions in their efforts to innovate. They do not feel supported at all by the government, and feel that they have to survive on their own.

The banking system was often discussed as the last element of the interviews. The owners do not consider formal banks as an attractive source of finance for SMEs. The most problematic issues here concern high interest rates, collateral requirements and complex paperwork. The owners mention interest rates ranging from 16 to 35 per cent per year, which is difficult to cover, given the low profit margins of their operations.

### Informal Institutions

The company owners mentioned that friends and family were critical in the set-up and innovation efforts of the business. Previous working experience overseas or in export further strengthened their informal networks, as well as informal contacts via social media and elsewhere. These networks provide a safety net as well as encouragement and stimulation, also described in the theoretical framework of social capital (Knight, 2003).

The interviewed companies source credit mostly from informal financial institutions. Most of the companies were given informal loans and gifts by family and friends. Informal money lenders, or "Shylocks", demand even higher interest rates, but provide flexibility. Beyond family and friends, in some cases informal channels and contacts within the business sector and some government agencies are essential sources of technical advice, orders and tenders, amongst other benefits.

## Concluding Remarks with Regard to Policy Issues

The official figures, in the World Bank databases amongst others, indicate that the manufacturing sector in many African countries including Ghana, Tanzania and Kenya is diminishing, whereas this sector could bring significant benefit for overall development, as explained in the introduction to this chapter. Manufacturing SMEs choose, or are forced, to close down their business in the harsh business environment. This results in African countries exporting raw materials while importing processed and manufactured products, thus missing the added value of a manufacturing sector, and the structural change bonus it brings. This remains an issue to be further examined by policymakers within government, civil society and development organisations as well as the manufacturing sector itself (Aubert 2005).

One of the critical reasons for the diminishing manufacturing sector, as explained by various SME owners, is that they lose out to cheap imports. Innovation would be one way to make more efficient use of resources and processes and compete with imports on the local market. Thus, innovation within local manufacturing SMEs could be precisely the response needed: introduce local higher quality products at lower costs. Several owners do see the low quality of imported products as a motivation to innovate, focusing on affordable durable consumer goods. The reality, however, is that many local manufacturing SMEs have limited capacity to innovate and stagnate or give up as a result. Limited firm level capabilities are one problem, but the difficult institutional context and lack of innovation support and policies appear to be more critical.

Innovation policies in Western countries are typically based on innovation systems theory, which states that innovation is not considered as a firm-level effort only. The support of a network of formal institutions (Freeman 1987; Lundvall 1992) is critical. The underlying idea of the associated Science-Technology-Innovation (STI) policies is to link innovation within firms to science and technology via research and development organisations and technical universities, innovation and research funds, the financial and banking sector, education institutes, patent registration bureaus and certification offices (OECD 2005).

In fact, many African countries have started to develop and adopt STI policies (Ozor 2011). STI policy aims to understand the innovation system structure, identify failures and develop "corrections" (Bergek *et al.* 2008). The conceptual idea of STI policy and the innovation system is thus to orchestrate the set-up of the required institutions. However, while this approach may be conceptualised and implemented in high-tech advanced economies, the reality on the ground in countries like Tanzania, Ghana and Kenya is different. On the one hand, the types of innovation relevant to development impact in the short run, typically do not involve the development of advanced "new to the world" technology, but rather the incremental adoption of existing technologies, since most of the technology is already available elsewhere in the world and accessible via the internet.

Once acquired, the companies themselves refine and adapt the existing technology. The innovations observed in the cases are the product of experiential learning and a process of doing, using and interacting (DUI) in an informal way, earlier described by Lundvall *et al.* (2009). Learning by doing and interaction with suppliers, clients and informal networks, and experiential and social learning (Kolb 1984; Beers *et al.* 2010) is more useful for building a broader understanding of innovation systems in developing countries. DUI focuses on innovations, on interactive and on the job learning through informal structures and relationships, which Lundvall considers highly relevant for developing countries. Instead, using the STI approach as a blueprint, policymakers within government agencies could opt for a broader view of innovation systems based on the DUI concept.

The informal context is also critical in the DUI concept. Informal institutions in DUI practices described by Lundvall (2009) take on the role of the insecure formal institutional context and provide stability and predictability. The role of informal institutions in supporting innovation is increasingly acknowledged in innovation in Africa (World Bank 2010). Policy could also allow and strengthen the informal institutional context instead of overruling informality.

Apart from government innovation policies, the World Bank (2010) recently reported an alternative market ideology, taking the view that innovation occurs naturally in a good business climate and most of all through interactions in the business system. Innovation thus is fundamentally the task of the private sector and of entrepreneurs, and occurs through horizontal and vertical linkages of businesses, spillover and actors' networks, involving subcontracting, interactive learning within supplier and buyer value chains and foreign direct investment.

Finally, yet importantly, is the impact of a hostile and unfriendly government, as it is often engaged in bribery and corruption. Despite their good intentions in formulating innovation policies written by government agencies, the entrepreneurs prefer to keep the government at a distance. While entrepreneurs need a formal institutional context that assures stability and predictability, the reality in Ghana, Kenya and Tanzania seems to be the reverse, bringing extra uncertainty and risk. Many firms stay micro and informal and use simple technology that does not require extensive use of the formal institutional context. The institutional context, providing trust, predictability, stability and access to finance is more of a problem in preventing investment in technology and innovation. Before considering explicit innovation policies, addressing this hostile institutional environment as a first step could already bring significant benefit. Spontaneous innovation can be expected only if the government can be trusted to provide a basic reliable institutional context without the uncertainties of corruption.

## References

Aubert, J.-E. (2005). *Promoting Innovation in Developing Countries*. Policy Research Working Paper 3554. Washington, D.C.: World Bank.

Beers, P., Sol, J., & A. Wals. (2010, July 4–7). *Social Learning in a Multi-actor Innovation Context*. Paper presented at the Ninth European IFSA Symposium "Building sustainable rural futures – the added value of systems approaches in times of change and uncertainty", Vienna, Austria.

Bergek, A., Jacobsson, S., Carlsson, B., Lindmark, S. & A. Rickne, (2008). "Analyzing the Functional Dynamics of Technological Innovation Systems: A Scheme of Analysis". *Research Policy 37*, 407–429.

Çapoğlu, C. (2009). "The Meaning of Innovation and Entrepreneurship in Developing Countries". *International Studies in Entrepreneurship 21*, 85–91.

Carayannis, E., Gonzalez, E. & J. Wetter. (2003). "The Nature and Dynamics of Discontinuous and Disruptive Innovations From a Learning and Knowledge Management Perspective". In: L. Shavinia (ed.), *The International Handbook on Innovation*. London: Elsevier Science Ltd, 115–138.

Chaminade, C., Lundvall, B.-Å., Vang, J. & K.J. Joseph. (2010). "Designing Innovation Policies for Development: Towards a Systemic Experimentation Based Approach". In: B.-Å. Lundvall, K.J. Joseph, C. Chaminade & J. Vang (eds), *Handbook of Innovation Systems and Developing Countries*. Cheltenham: Edward Elgar, 360–379.

Denzin, N.K. & Y.S. Lincoln. (1998). *The Landscape of Qualitative Research: Theories and Issues*. Thousand Oaks, CA: Sage Publications.

Edquist, C. (1997). *Systems of Innovation: Technologies, Institutions and Organisations*. London: Pinter Publishers.

Fagerberg, J., Srholec, M. & B. Verspagen. (2010). "The Role of Innovation in Development". *Review of Economics and Institutions*, 1 (2), Article 2. Retrieved from http://www.rei.unipg.it/rei/article/view/15.

Freeman, C. (1987). *Technology Policy and Economic Performance: Lessons from Japan.* London and New York: Pinter Publishers.

Gereffi, G., Humphrey, J. & T. Sturgeon. (2005). "The Governance of Global Value Chains". *Review of International Political Economy 12*(1), 78–104.

Godin, B. (2006). "The Linear Model of Innovation: The Historical Construction of an Analytical Framework". *Science, Technology* and *Human Values 31*, 639–667.

Kaplinsky, R. & M. Morris. (2001). *A Handbook for Value Chain Research.* Brighton: Institute of Development Studies (IDS), University of Sussex.

Kline, S.J. & N. Rosenberg. (1986). "An Overview of Innovation". In: R. Landau & N. Rosenberg (eds), *The Positive Sum Strategy: Harnessing Technology for Economic Growth.* Washington, D.C.: National Academy Press, 275–305.

Knight, J. (2003). "Trust, Institutions, and Institutional Change: Industrial Districts and the Social Capital Hypothesis". *Politics and Society 31*(4), 537–566.

Kolb, D. (1984). *Experiential Learning.* Englewood Cliffs, NJ: Prentice Hall.

Lundvall, B.-Å. (1992). *National Systems of Innovation: Towards a Theory of Innovation and Interactive Learning.* London: Pinter Publishers.

Lundvall, B.-Å., Vang, J., Joseph, K.J. & C. Chaminade. (2009, October 6–8). Bridging Innovation System Research and Development Studies: Challenges and research opportunities. Paper submitted for the 7th Globelics Conference, Senegal.

OECD. (2005). *The Measurement of Scientific and Technological Activities, proposed guidelines for collecting and interpreting technological innovation data – Oslo Manual.* Paris: Organization for Economic Co-operation and Development (OECD), Eurostat.

Ozor, N. (2011, February 16–18). "Linking Science and Technology Research to Policy and Practice: Issues and the Role of African Governments". In: N. Ozor, K. Urama, M. Bolo, L. Sibanda, E. Brown & G. Reid (eds), *Proceedings of the Stakeholders Workshop on Strengthening Linkages between Policy Research and Policymaking for African Development.* A Publication of the African Technology Policy Studies Network (ATPS). Retrieved from: http://www.atpsnet.org/Files/Linking_Research_to_policy_Proceedings_of_Stakeholders_Workshop_Kenya.pdf.

Porter, M., Sachs, J. & J. McArthur. (2002). "Executive Summary: Competitiveness and Stages of Economic Development". In: M. Porter, J. Sachs, P. Cornelius, J. McArthur & K. Schwab (eds), *The Global Competitiveness Report 2001.* New York: Oxford University Press, 16–26.

Quazi A., Rahman, Z. & B. Keating. (2007, December 3–5). "A Developing Country Perspective of Corporate Social Responsibility: A Test Case of Bangladesh". In: M. Thyne, K. Deans & J. Gnoth (eds), *3Rs – Reputation, Responsibility* and *Relevance.* Conference proceedings. Dunedin, New Zealand: Australia and New Zealand Marketing Academy.

Rossouw, G., Geerts, S. & N. Xinwa. (2015). *Africans' Perceptions of Chinese Business in Africa: A survey*. Ethics Institute of South Africa, retrieved from http://www.ethicsa.org/phocadownloadpap/Research_Reports/AfricanPerceptionSurveyChinese BusinessWEBSITEVERSION.pdf (accessed 24 August 2015).

Scott, R.W. (2001). *Institutions and Organizations* (2nd ed). Thousand Oaks, CA: Sage Publications.

Szirmai, A., Naudé, W. & M. Goedhuys. (2011). "Entrepreneurship, Innovation, and Economic Development: An Overview". In: A. Szirmai, W. Naudé, & M. Goedhuys (eds), *Entrepreneurship, Innovation, and Economic Development*. Oxford: Oxford University Press, 3–32.

Teece, D.J., Pisano, G. & A. Shuen. (1997). "Dynamic Capabilities and Strategic Management". *Strategic Management Journal 18*, 509–533.

World Bank. (2010). *Innovation Policy: A Guide for Developing Countries*. Washington, D.C.: The World Bank. Retrieved from https://openknowledge.worldbank.org/handle/10986/2460.

# PART 2

## *Entrepreneurship Development, Country Studies*

CHAPTER 7

# An Institutional Analysis of Entrepreneurship Development in Nigeria

*Abel Ezeoha and Afam Ituma*

## Introduction

Entrepreneurship as a field of study has grown immeasurably in importance and has attracted significant research and policy attentions in the past two decades. This has largely been due to its impact on innovation, economic growth, poverty alleviation and public goods delivery, particularly in developing countries. The adoption of institutional theory in entrepreneurship studies has equally helped to highlight the interactive roles of institutions and individuals in entrepreneurship development.

Although there is an unusual absence of the term "institution" in conventional definitions of entrepreneurship, such definitions are always embedded in the context of the presumed interaction between individuals and socio-economic institutional structures on which the society operates. Earlier definitions as cited in Iversen et al. (2008) and Zimmerman (2008), for instance, focused on the role and contributions of entrepreneurs in the larger economy. Popular among the definitions are that of Cantillon (1959), an Irish merchant based in France, who presented an entrepreneur as one who was "responsible for all exchange and circulation in the economy"; and Baptiste Say (1767–1832)[1] who saw an entrepreneur as "the main agent of production in the economy" (cited in Iversen et al. 2008).

The quest for a more authoritative and inclusive definition of the concept in the globalised business environment has thus provided a fertile ground for the current growth in entrepreneurship literature. A working definition of entrepreneurship that is consistent with the modern business environment, according to Stevenson of the Harvard Business School, *presents the concept as "the pursuit of opportunity beyond resources" (cited in* Eisenmann, 2013). Drawing on Hitt et al.'s (2011) conceptualisation, entrepreneurship refers to a "context specific social process through which individuals and teams create wealth by

1 Say, J.B. (1855). *A Treatise on Political Economy*, trans. Clement Biddle. Philadelphia: Lippincott, Grambo & Co.

 | DOI 10.1163/9789004351615_008

bringing together unique packages of resources to exploit marketplace opportunities" (Ibid.: 59). It equally includes new-venture creation that is growth oriented and generates employment, as well as small businesses and microenterprises that may provide self-employment (Bhide 2000).

Historically, an entrepreneur has always been regarded as an innovative productive agent with a difference. In this sense, a neoclassical economist, Alfred Marshal (1842–1926) was the first to refer to an entrepreneur as an innovator, stressing that such a businessperson is always in constant search for opportunities to minimise cost[2] (Van Praag 1999). Subsequent scholarly efforts, according to Swedberg (1991) and Zimmerman (2008), were built on this innovative role of an entrepreneur, with Joseph Schumpeter, the then student of Bohn-Bawerk, who later became one of the most influential entrepreneurship scholars, illustrating that a businessman who undertook either of the following tasks qualified as an entrepreneur and innovator: creation of a new good or a new quality; creation of a new method of production; opening of a new market; the capture of a new source of supply; or creation of a new organisation or industry. The entrepreneurship networks thus contribute towards building the required institutional platforms for the smooth and efficient functioning of the national economy (Acs, Szerb, and Autio 2015).

Despite the valid acknowledgement that entrepreneurship is shaped and constrained by the socio-cultural and economic factors embedded in different national contexts (Ibid.), the entrepreneurship literature has largely neglected to account for entrepreneurship development in diverse institutional characteristics. Most extant studies in this area have focused largely on entrepreneurship in Anglo-Saxon Western countries (e.g. United Kingdom and United States) and other Western countries that share comparable cultural values and business environment. Studies on this subject in Africa have been rare and we know comparatively little about the dynamics of entrepreneurship development in Nigeria in particular. The Nigerian context represents an important but relatively neglected context that can enrich and contribute to the global entrepreneurship discourse due to its unique geographical, political, economic and cultural characteristics. In response to an earlier call by entrepreneurship scholars (e.g. Herbig 1994; Shane 1992), this paper draws on Institutional Theory to discuss some key factors that shape and constrain entrepreneurship development in Nigeria. The paper highlights the context-specific nature of entrepreneurship and attempts to reveal the influence of various factors and

2 Marshall, Alfred (1890), Principles of Economics: An Introductory Volume, 1st Ed., London: Macmillan.

variables on entrepreneurship development. This is expected to contribute to the development of contextually relevant policies, practices and theories of entrepreneurship development. The rest of the paper is organised as follows. The next section provides brief insights on the entrepreneurship context in Nigeria. A third section outlines the theoretical framework of the paper. This is followed by a look at the strategies for building effective institutional structures for entrepreneurship development. Finally, we present the summary and conclusion.

## Nigeria's Entrepreneurship Context

The Nigerian business environment is largely described as difficult and unfriendly. The country lags behind in key measures of quality of business environment. The 2014 Doing Business Report in Nigeria revealed that the country fell from its 138th position in 2013 to the 147th position in 2014. Nigeria's context is a confirmation that the economic hardship and social discrimination that create opportunities for the birth of entrepreneurship businesses, ironically threatens entrepreneurship incubation and business survival. For instance, the country does relatively well in terms of rate of new business registration (with the level rising from 65,074 in 2010 to 81,144 in 2012); the cost of business startup procedures (% of GNI per capita) (declining from 75.9 per cent as at 2010 to a low level of 31.6 per cent in 2014); and the ease of doing business (scoring 175 as against the Sub Sahara African average of 142 in 2013) (World Bank Doing Business Report, 2015). In contrast, the country lags far behind in the indices for business survival and sustainability – performing poorly in terms of ability to resolve insolvency in business (with a score of 107 out of 189 countries covered in the 2014 Doing Business Report).

The Africa Heritage Institute, an independent economic think-thank in Nigeria, developed an environmental matrix termed BECAN Model, as a tool for benchmarking the quality of Nigeria's business environment, reflecting some negativities in the business environments both at the national and subnational levels. The matrix is represented in the box below:

## Business Environment Matrix in Nigeria

In essence, profiting from a high risk, volatile and unprofitable business environment is rather the main window of opportunities for true entrepreneurs. Entrepreneurial success is, for instance, tied to the quality of an entrepreneur's

| Infrastructure and utilities: | Legal and regulatory services |
|---|---|
| · Energy<br>· Water<br>· Access to information<br>· Transportation<br>· Social infrastructure | · Business registration<br>· Tax administration<br>· Contract enforcement<br>· Land registration and property rights |
| **Business support and investment promotion:** | **Security:** |
| · Entrepreneurship promotion<br>· Access to finance<br>· Investment promotion<br>· Industrial clusters<br>· Public-private partnership adoption | · Major crimes<br>· Minor crimes<br>· Police coverage<br>· Perception of security |

SOURCE: CONSTRUCTED FROM THE BECAN REPORT 2007

decision-making under extreme uncertainty and ambiguity (McVea 2009). An entrepreneur focuses on affordable loss and not on the conventional rate of business returns.[3] In the foreseeable future, the goal of the entrepreneur is that return on capital would over-run the affordable risk.

While it is not contestable that Nigeria ranks amongst the worst in most strategic measures of the quality of the business environment, available evidence reveals the thick presence of the country in the global entrepreneurship environment. In effect, the country is still ranked among the top investment destinations in the Sub Sahara African region (UNCTAD, World Investment Report 2015). This is confirmed in a report by AllWorld Network Inc., where in 2012, 50 top Nigerian private companies broke many AllWorld records in a contest involving companies from 15 other countries in the Middle East, North Africa, India, Pakistan, South Africa and Turkey. Nigeria was adjudged to have the highest number of well-established women entrepreneurs at the level of 16 per cent. The top 50 Nigerian entrepreneurs were also found to break many of the records in terms of the growth rate, the size of companies and diversity of industries.[4] Some of the factors responsible for this scenario are based on the claim that the country is a high risk high return destination

3 The 10 Myths of Entrepreneurship, http://www.youtube.com/watch?v=G8gRkJ9cnzo.

4 http://www.allworldlive.com/nigeria-fast-growth-50-winners.

(Ventureafrica.com);[5] and optimistic entrepreneurs with an eye on high returns find the country as a viable destination for investments.

## Institutional Theory and the Entrepreneurship Premise

Modern theoretical postulations on the meaning and role of entrepreneurs are different from the early days practice. The central attempt in the modern practice is to conceptualise entrepreneurial activities in the changing global economic system. Core emphases of the modern theorists, starting from the late 1990s, for instance, are identified to include: an interception between available profitable opportunities and enterprising individuals; and expertise in decision-making uncertainty (Shane and Venkataraman 2000). The theoretical views about modern entrepreneurship practices are thus weaved into an emerging neo-institutionalism school, which sees both the entrepreneur and the institution as practically inseparable.

The theoretical context of neo-institutionalism (championed by John Meyer and Brian Rowan in 1977, Lynne Zucker also in 1977, and later reshaped by Richard Scott in 1983)[6] revolves around how the institutional structures in the society shape the behaviour of micro-agents, and how the agents (particularly the individuals) strive to manage prevailing threats, while at the same time exploiting opportunities in the larger business environment. The application of neo-institutionalism therefore seeks to explain the socio-political dynamics prevailing in the operational spaces of individual agents in the society. Applying this neo-institutional theoretical framework, the formal organisational structure of an enterprise is adjudged to be shaped by "the technical demands and resource dependencies," and "by institutional forces, including rational myths, knowledge legitimated through the educational system and by the professions, public opinion, and the law" (Powell 2007: 1).

Attempts at incorporating institutional theory in modern entrepreneurship studies therefore centre on the position of an individual either as a dormant business person, whose orientations and actions are defined by institutional forces outside his control, or as an active agent, who exploits institutions and redirects institutional policies and courses of actions to his/her credit. In doing this, the entrepreneurial agent sees himself in a constant struggle to strike an optimal balance between the judgements of the structuralists and those of the

5 http://venturesafrica.com/five-african-countries-that-offer-the-greatest-investment-opportunities-in-real-estate/.

6 For a source of this emphasis, see Powell (2007: 1).

agency theorists. From the perspective of structuralism, entrepreneurship development is shaped by prevailing framework and rules; while from the agency perspective, human agents are viewed "as ontological primitive and view institutions as structures that created by goal-maximizing individuals" (Clark 1998: 245). It is this dichotomy between the structuralists and the agency theorists that gave birth to the problem of the *paradox of embedded agency* – with an attempt to address the problem leading to the postulation of the new institutional theory. The *paradox of embedded agency* essentially arises because entrepreneurs who are constrained by institutional challenges and pressures face little chance of transforming the institutions in their favour. By implication, the freedom of entrepreneurs operating in a socio-economically difficult and unstable environment is likely to be constrained by the same environment (for more insight on this see Lawrence, Suddaby, and Leca 2009).

Resolving the arising conflicts between the structuralists and the agency theorists within the framework of neo-institutionalism requires a clear understanding of the meaning, context and tenets of modern institutions. This is more so considering that the term "institution" is not just imprecise, but also complex. Institutions may be defined as "the rules of the game in a society or the humanly devised constraints that shape human interaction" (North 1990: 3). They are generally conceptualised as deep aspects of social structure, which act as authoritative guidelines and constraints on behaviour (Scott 2008). Institutions can be either formal, such as rules, laws and constitutions, or informal, such as norms of behaviour and conventions (Boettke and Coyne 2009; North 1994). Formal institutions refer to the objective constraints and incentives arising from government regulation of individual and organisational actions (Bruton et al. 2009). Informal institutions are "the norms, customs and mores that enable us to cooperate with strangers in the marketplace," through "the norms and values of trust and reciprocity" (Boettke and Coyne 2009: 6). In reality, both the formal and informal institutional environments play a crucial role in socio-economic development. As Boettke and Coyne put it, "informal rules are often codified in practice to become formal law"; and that "the enforcement of the formal and informal institutions determines how binding the rules are in any given society" (Ibid.). However, the degree of influence each of the two has on the economic landscape depends on the levels of economic development in a country, and specifically on the strength of the socio-political structures in place.

The premise of the traditional institutional theory posits that whereas the formal institutions dwell on existing economic, political and legal structures in place, the informal institutions focus on the socio-cultural contexts in the society. The former addresses issues relating to the role of national institutions such as national labour laws; trade unions; politics; educational and vocational training systems; labour market; professional bodies; international institutions; employers' federation; consulting organisations; placement organisations; trade bodies; government institutions; local authorities; and voluntary bodies (Budhwar and Debrah 2001). In contrast, the latter explains how individual and firm behaviours are shaped and regulated by social and economic institutions. This theory suggests that individual and firm's behaviours reflect and mimic societal conventions, values, beliefs and norms.

## Institutional Pillars and Entrepreneurial Development: The Nigerian Context

Over the years, institutional theory has gained prominence as a popular and influential explanation for organisational and individual behaviour (Dacin et al. 2002). The institutional approach has been adopted by different disciplines and the extant literature on institutional theory is too extensive to be adequately summarised here (for a more comprehensive review see Hodgson 1994). Although institutionalists vary in terms of their emphasis, inherent to all their work is a claim that organisations operating in similar environments are likely to seek legitimacy and recognition by adopting practices, processes and structures that are prevalent in their environment (Fogarty 1996). This general proposition has been the foundation on which a number of institutional mechanisms have been conceptualised. A particularly useful conceptual framework for understanding how entrepreneurship development is shaped and constrained by institutional setting is Scott's (2004) "pillars" of institutional processes. Scott posits that there are three "pillars" of institutional processes: the regulative pillar, the normative pillar and the cognitive pillar. These pillars shape and circumscribe the actions of individuals and organisations within a given institutional environment. We draw on the three pillars to illustrate the context dependent nature of entrepreneurship; and how institutions can shape and constrain entrepreneurship development in a developing society such as Nigeria.

### Regulative Institutional Pillar

The regulative institutional pillar refers to the "existing laws and rules in a particular national environment, which promote certain types of behaviours and restrict others" (Kostova 1997: 180). It involves "rule-setting," "monitoring," and "sanctioning" activities (Scott 2008: 2). It equally focuses on government policies and programmes aimed at stimulating and developing the productive capacities of entrepreneurs in a country. Legal structures transcend beyond rules and regulations, extending to "government attitudes toward markets and freedoms and the efficiency of its operations are also very important" (World Economic Forum 2015: 4).[7]

There are key legally-linked factors that can affect entrepreneurship development. Some of these include government activism, legal frameworks for lending and borrowing, environmental rules, protectionist policies that favour (or are biased against) certain classes of businesses or ethnic groups, access to education as well as property ownership rights. Government activism, for instance, reflects the extent to which a nation's formal institutions redistribute economic wealth through progressive tax structures and spending to provide for the common welfare of its citizens (Aidis et al. 2012). It thus reflects a government's ability to address social issues and provide public goods. In Nigeria, government activism remains somewhat low. This is considering the existence of limited government support for social programmes and national welfare provisions. In essence, government inactivity is likely to motivate many entrepreneurs to set up social enterprises to fill this gap. This view is consistent with broader literature (e.g. Mair, Battilana, and Cárdenas's 2012), which recognises that social enterprises frequently appear where governments fail to provide for social needs, such as adequate healthcare, children's social services or environmental protection.

In a multi-class, multi-ethnic society like Nigeria, entrepreneurship spirits and practices have emerged as a way of coping with the inherent discrimination tendencies by dominant groups. The same is the case in countries with racial bias, where minority races are naturally considered more enterprising than the majority racial groups. Under this scenario, marginalised groups that are discriminated against and are socially deprived strive to overcome such stigmatisation by breaking new business grounds and building protective entrepreneurial empires (Cuervo 2005). This is essentially the case in Nigeria, where the Igbo ethnic group is considered to have drawn its entrepreneurship strength from an attempt to break away from the difficulties imposed by the 1966–69 Civil War between Biafra (largely dominated by the Igbos) and the Nigerian government. The Igbo ethnic group is ranked as one of the two most educated ethnic groups in Nigeria and one of the most industrious and business-oriented, together with the Yoruba in the Western Region (see, for instance, a detailed account of this claim in Mwakikagile 2007: 274).

7 http://reports.weforum.org/global-competitiveness-report-2014-2015/methodology/.

Along similar lines, the argument is that a larger, wealth-redistributing welfare state crowds out private pro-social initiatives (Warr 1982) and thus fewer individuals are likely to be motivated to engage in social entrepreneurship. The rentier nature of the Nigerian state, in this sense, can be linked to its characteristic under-productivity and underdevelopment (Falola, 2004); it can also be responsible for the high level of informality in the country's entrepreneurial space. As established by Herb (2005), the fact that rentier states need not tax their citizens creates a disconnection between the people and the government. At the sub-national level, apart from Lagos (in the South) and Kano State (in the North), there is generally an inverse link between the flow of oil revenue and economic productive tax capacity (Ezeoha et al. 2016).

That the legal environment in Nigeria has not provided a favourable ground for entrepreneurship development does not, however, imply absence of government's supporting institutional structures for entrepreneurship growth. Some programmes have indeed been initiated and implemented by the government as outlined in table 7.1 below. While it is outside the scope of this paper to give a full evaluation of the success or failure of the various government interventions in the previous years, it is evident that the level of unemployment and poverty has remained relatively high, in spite of the expectations of Nigerians regarding the benefits of the various intervention programmes.

Figure 7.1 below shows the rate of unemployment by state in the country.

The regulatory institutional pillar is also anchored on measurable indices like ease of doing business; level of economic freedom; rule of law; prevailing copyright and patent laws; efficiency of the financial system infrastructure; fiscal policy direction of the government; and the nature of the labour market regulation. Nigeria's ranking on these indicators reveals a comparatively poor stance in the Sub-Sahara African region. A number of researchers confirm the significant influence of these factors on entrepreneurship development. Stel et al. (2007), for instance, find some of the key constraints to include minimum capital requirements and labour market regulations. Nystron (2008) finds the efficiency of the regulatory frameworks on property rights, access to credits and labour as being the lubricants for entrepreneurship growth; and Powell and Rodet (2012), in a multi-country case study, find that "freedom from big government" is an important driver of entrepreneurship growth and development.

In Nigeria, other critical regulatory issues against entrepreneurship development border on legal and governance challenges, which reflect particularly on the prevalence of bureaucratic bottlenecks, corruption and fraud,[8] policy

8 For historical insights into the world of corruption and frauds in Nigeria, see for instance Ellis (2016).

TABLE 7.1 *Macro policy programmes of the Nigerian government to encourage entrepreneurship*

| | Programme | Objective |
|---|---|---|
| 1 | Agricultural Development Project (ADP) | The main purpose of the ADP is to stimulate increased food production and enhance the income of the rural population. |
| 2 | National Directorates of Employment (NDE) | Responsible for vocational skills development and small-scale enterprises programmes designed to combat unemployment. |
| 3 | National Economic Reconstruction Fund (NERFUND) | Provides long-term loans at concessionary interest rates to promote small- and medium-scale industrial projects. |
| 4 | Family Economic Advancement Programme (FEAP) | Established to provide micro-facilities for entrepreneurs. |
| 5 | People's Bank and Community Bank Programmes | Designed to make banking services more accessible and extend credit to the poor. |
| 6 | Better Life Programmes/ Family Support Programme (BLP/FSP) | Aimed at providing micro-credit facilities for women entrepreneurs. |
| 7 | National Poverty Eradication Programme (NAPEP) | Aimed at providing vocational skills development and small-scale enterprises programmes designed to combat unemployment. |
| 8 | National Empowerment and Economic Development Strategy (NEEDS) | To eradicate poverty and unemployment. |
| 9 | Small and Medium Enterprises Development Agency of Nigeria (SMEDAN) | To promote the development of Nigeria's SMEs. |
| 10 | Youth Enterprise with Innovation in Nigeria (You WiN!) Programme | The main objective of the programme is to generate jobs by encouraging and supporting aspiring entrepreneurial youth in Nigeria to develop and execute business ideas that will lead to job creation. The programme provides business training for up to 6,000 aspiring youth entrepreneurs spread across all geo-political zones in Nigeria. |

SOURCE: ABIMBOLA ET AL. (2011)

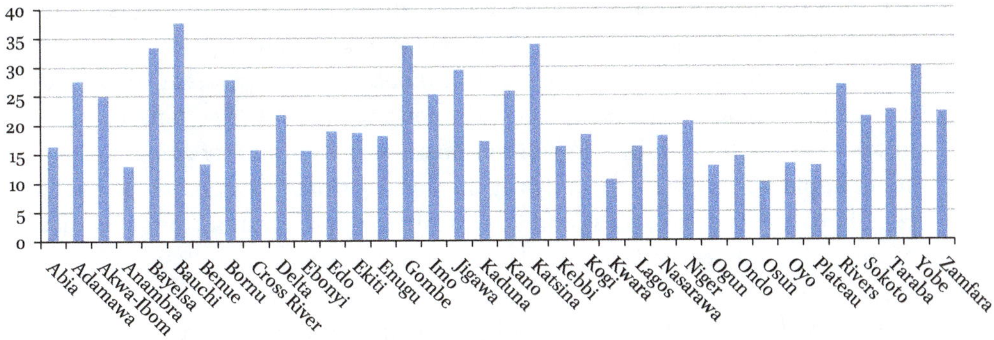


FIGURE 7.1 *Unemployment rates across Nigerian states*
SOURCE: NATIONAL BUREAU OF STATISTICS, SOCIAL STATISTICS IN NIGERIA, 2015

inconsistency, ethnic segregation, archaic land governance practices, judicial delays as well as the absence of formal legal tool for the promotion, protection and governance of entrepreneurial businesses. For instance, the higher rate of piracy faced by Nigerian artists[9] succinctly demonstrates the inability of the legal system to promote entrepreneurship growth and development in the country.

Also in the international business environment, Nigerian entrepreneurs are challenged by the poor economic competitiveness of the country as a whole. The country is largely dependent on crude oil exportation for its foreign exchange earnings, with the proportion of oil revenue to total export revenue standing at about 75 per cent. Aided by the country's porous land borders and seaports, this import-dependency syndrome is such that virtually everything is loosely imported into the country (Omoh 2011). The implication is that the products of local entrepreneurs are left to compete with those of other entrepreneurs in countries where the business environment is friendly and where the cost of production is much cheaper. Evidence shows that in other jurisdictions (such as the USA), "larger firms feed the fish instead of eating it" (Acs and Armington 2006: 166), as opposed to the Nigeria case where larger firms (sometimes with wider access to foreign resources and markets) feed on the fish by crowding out small firms.

Nigerian entrepreneurs do not enjoy good reception in neighbouring African countries either. Key examples are the Ghanaian-Nigerian business squabble, where the Ghanaian government enacted and tried to enforce a policy compelling Nigerian businessmen and traders to pay a minimum capital of

9 For more insight on the intensity and the threatening impact of piracy in the country, see Oguntola (2016).

$300,000 or have their businesses shut down (*Business Day*, 10 August 2012; Akinyoade 2015). This is similar to the recent Zimbabwean declaration against foreign African businesses, where the Zimbabwean government, under its black empowerment law, gave foreign shopowners (mostly Nigerians and Chinese) an ultimatum to shut down their businesses by 1 January 2014. The 2015 xenophobia attacks in South Africa against other African nationals (especially Nigerians and Zimbabweans) and their businesses are again further evidence of the unfriendly reception of Nigerian entrepreneurs within the Sub-Sahara African region.

The unstable and fragile nature of the Nigerian financial system poses another setback to entrepreneurial growth and sustainability in Nigeria. This is especially considering the existence of financial barriers such as high lending rates, excessive demand for mortgage-backed collaterals, high incidence of financial exclusion, credit rationing, and lack of protection for minority businesses that tend to crowd out small savers and borrowers in the financial system (Ezeoha and Amaeshi 2010).

### Normative (Social) Context

The normative pillar refers to "a prescriptive, evaluative, and obligatory dimension into social life" (Scott 2008: 54), based on social interactions, social obligations and shared understanding of what is appropriate (Wicks 2001). Normative elements are the values and social norms that define the "rules of the game" – that is, "what is right to do around here" (Marquis et al. 2007: 934). The normative frameworks set the standards for, and encourage conformity to that which is deemed to be acceptable corporate behaviour (Campbell 2006).

Nigeria is a country with a rich cultural heritage. One of the main features of Nigeria's distinctive culture is the importance attached to the extended family system. Nigerians are connected by a network of social relationships based on lineages and genealogical lines (Ituma and Simpson 2007). Within the kin system there is an emphasis on interdependence, sharing and reciprocal obligations. Here, close and not so close family members (e.g. distant cousins and their spouses and children) form a social network of relationships that serves as a form of social insurance. This network has multifaceted dimensions (e.g. gift giving, financial support, care for children), and is built around ethnic lines (Ituma and Simpson 2009). The extended family system reinforces values such as sharing and mutuality, adherence to social obligations and the need to maintain strong social and personal relations. These values and practices exert normative pressures toward behaviours oriented towards obligations and commitments, which, to some extent, take the place of the established social security and welfare systems of more developed countries.

The aforementioned normative features of the Nigerian society are found to exact significant influence on entrepreneurship growth and development; and that is essentially because of their influence in decision-making processes and in risk behaviours of indigenous entrepreneurs. Studies (for example Babatunde 1992; Obayan 1995) suggest that the extended family phenomenon could, in essence, be a barrier to entrepreneurship development. The empirical premise of such studies is that the expectations of the extended family system from its members are incongruent with entrepreneurial ideals based on the purely economic principle of rationality and profit maximalisation. The Nigerian extended family system seems to encourage dependence of other family members on the successful member, thereby impacting negatively on the invested fund. This is in contrast with the case of Asian entrepreneurship, which thrives on familial ties (Reddings 1980), where every member of the family engages in productive activities, towards the actualisation of the set business goals.

Further views on the impact of the normative institutional pillar in the case of Nigeria are captured in the undoubtedly near lack of a culture of business succession in the country (Onuoha 2013; Ogundele 2012), usually resulting in an unsustainable family business system. There is, for instance, a known history of closure of large family business empires due to the death of the family heads. A good example here is the case of Alhaji Moshud Abiola, whose Concord Group (his business name) controlled the landscapes of the news media, airlines and communication businesses in the country up until the start of the 1990s; the Odutola Business Empire (then controlled by two blood brothers; Alhaji Jimoh Odutola and Timothy Adeola Odutola), which laid the "foundation for modern commerce and industry in Nigeria," but could not survive beyond the founders because "none of their children was interested in reviving their businesses";[10] the Ekene Dili Chukwu Group (owned by Chief Ilodibe), whose successful transport and haulage, and automobile distribution businesses suddenly vanished "following the death of the super-rich patriarch."[11]

A growing level of insecurity – arising from political crisis, ethnic and religious unrest, civil conflicts, a high crime rate, kidnapping, and armed insurgence equally constitute another major threat to entrepreneurship growth in

10 Lanre Alfred (2016), "Dwindling Fortunes of Homes of Super-Rich in Nigeria", *ThisDay Newspapers*, 6 March.

11 *The Nations Newspaper*, "Receding Fortunes of Business Empires, Special Report", 30 August 2015.

the country. Civil conflicts and political instability have the tendency to threaten the survival of the majority of entrepreneurs. This arises when conflict induces business displacements (Benassy-Quere et al. 2007), dispossesses people of their means of livelihood (Faria and Mauro 2009), dampens entrepreneurial spirit and escalates poverty by distorting the government's fiscal incentives, undermining human development efforts at all levels, and causing the destruction of socioeconomic infrastructure (Wharton and Oyelere 2011; Serneels and Verpoorten 2015; Ezeoha and Ugwu 2015). In conflict situations, minority populations and women are more adversely affected, leading particularly to the destruction of the female entrepreneurial class.

The Boko Haram insurgence in the country since 2009 specifically demonstrates how conflicts can induce business migration and cause some displacements in the development patterns of entrepreneurship. A popular Nigerian media outlet in 2012 described the impact on the host cities as "a systemic distortion of existing economic patterns and structure in the Northern region" (*Business Day*, 18 April 2012). More worrisome is the destabilising impact on local business and entrepreneurial groups that have provided a significant platform for poverty mitigation and employment in the country.

### Cognitive (Cultural) Pillar

The cognitive pillar refers to "shared conceptions that constitute the nature of social reality and the frames through which meaning is made" (Scott 2008: 57). A particular cognitive pillar that has influenced the pattern of entrepreneurship development in Nigeria is the gender role stereotype, which perceives women as the "weaker" sex. Nigeria is a masculine society and there are traditional gender-based differences in role allocation (Udegbe 2003). Women are primarily defined through childcare and domestic responsibility, while men are viewed as breadwinners and, as such, their career development is generally given more priority (Chovwen 2006; Ituma and Simpson 2009). The masculine stereotypes may discourage some women from attempting to set up new business in Nigeria, because entrepreneurs are often viewed as bold, aggressive, calculative, risk-taking men (Abimbola et al. 2011). Gender bias is more prevalent in Muslim-dominated Northern states, where women are, traditionally, least expected to be engaged in overt socio-economic activities. For example, in a good number of the Northern states, women are nearly absent in the ownership of farms. In the predominantly Christian Southern states (excluding Lagos and a few other States in the South-West that have a relatively even distribution by the two major religions), the proportion of female farmers ranges from 24 per cent in Imo State to 82.8 per cent in Anambra State; but in the predominantly Islamic States in Northern Nigeria, the proportion of female farmers is relatively lower at 0.3 per cent in Bauchi or Jigawa State to slightly over 50 per cent in Katsina. See figure 7.2 below, where States in the first half of the graph (Adamawa to Zamfara) represents the Northern states and the other half (from Abia to Rivers) represents Southern states.

Even in educational institutions, courses of studies are gender determined – with some courses assumed to be exclusive reserves for the women and some for men. Gender-related challenges are of concern, especially in light of the fact that competition in the business environment has no special consideration for the weakness or fragility of newcomers. It is an environment where those who enter are expected to have the ability to survive, and whoever is not able to do so should just be allowed to die off. Survival is considered only for the fittest, the smartest and the die-hards; where the big fish are eager and ready to feed on the small fish as a strategy for growth. Such features, in an environment without adequate institutional protections, are a deterrent against the emergence and sustainability of female entrepreneurs.

Other key factors that have shaped entrepreneurship development and sustainability in Nigeria include governance challenges, such as: bureaucratic corruption, ethnicity, land governance policy and policy inconsistency. A good example of the effect of policy inconsistency is the removal of the fuel subsidy in Nigeria, which is believed to have adversely affected businesses through the increase in the costs/prices of production inputs. The case of persistent subsidy reforms shows how unfavourable government policies can retard entrepreneurship growth and survival in an oil-dependent society. Structural defects in the country are also reflected in prevalent multiple taxation practices – due to the federal structure of the country, weak tax laws and institutions, corruption; and poor access to business finance – due to the unwillingness of lending

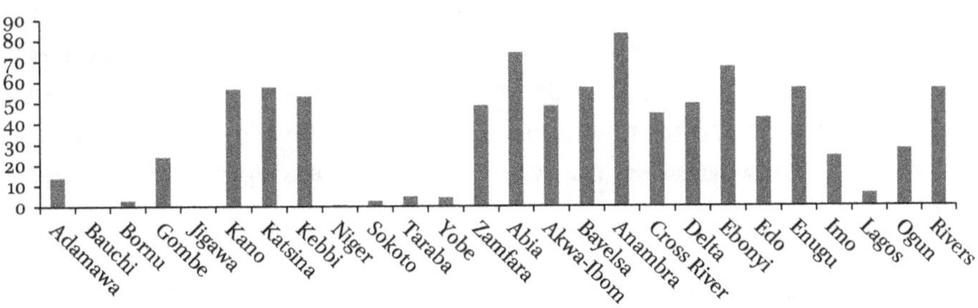


FIGURE 7.2 *Percentage distribution of female farmers in some selected states in Nigeria*
SOURCE: NATIONAL BUREAU OF STATISTICS, SOCIAL STATISTICS IN NIGERIA 2012

institutions to extend credits to SMEs and new ventures, high interest rates, and overly demand for collateral; infrastructural deficiency – bearing on bad road condition, erratic electricity supply, inefficient and costly transport system, telecommunication network problems, and similar.

## Institutionalised Strategies for Entrepreneurship Development

A number of studies find a strong positive correlation between the soundness of the business environment and entrepreneurial success (Agboli and Ukaegbu 2006). In the case of Southeast Nigeria, the study by Agboli and Ukaegbu finds that, when premised on the quality of infrastructure, access to credit, bureaucratic practices and regulatory policies, the business environment in southeast Nigeria is stressful, and so constrains the scope of entrepreneurial development in the area.

The unwavering nature of the enterprise performance and business environment nexus has equally been anchored on the fact that whatever happens in that environment determines the degree of competitiveness and success of all enterprises (BECAN Report 2007). The importance of ensuring a stable and friendly environment is highlighted in the 2007 BECAN report. The report amplifies that the background challenges created by lingering widespread poverty and unemployment in Nigeria should serve as a wake-up call for government to build a viable competitive private sector-led business environment capable of creating jobs, generating wealth, and fostering sustainable growth and poverty reduction (Ibid.).

Another strategic effort at institutionalising entrepreneurship development in Nigeria and other developing nations is education. The relevance of entrepreneurial education is premised on the notion that entrepreneurs are made and not born. Bechard and Toulouse (1998) defines entrepreneurship education as a collection of formalised teachings that informs, trains and educates anyone interested in business creation or small business development. Its central aim is "to provide students with the knowledge, skills and motivation to encourage entrepreneurial success in a variety of settings."[12] In the words of Unachukwu (2009), the whole essence of entrepreneurship education is to

> prepare people especially youths to be responsible and enterprising individuals; to develop deep thoughts on entrepreneurship and consequently

12 http://en.wikipedia.org/wiki/Entrepreneurship_education.

contribute to economic and sustainable development of their communities; and to encourage creative thinking and promotes a strong sense of self-worth and accountability.

There has been a paradigm shift in the practice of entrepreneurship education in Nigeria. The shift has occurred in the following order:

- From a focus on the informal traditional apprenticeship model, which was the case up to the late 1970s, to a much more formalised educational model.
- Emphasis on technical education, which was initiated in the late 1970s, following the enactment of The Federal Polytechnic laws (Decree No. 33 of 1979 as amended by Decree No. 5 of 1993). The Decree was aimed at producing the middle-level manpower needed for industrial and technological development of the country.
- Introduction of entrepreneurial education in university and higher education in 2006 "to continuously foster entrepreneurship culture amongst students and faculty, with a view of not only educating them but to also support graduates of the system towards establishing and also maintaining sustainable business ventures, including but not limited to those arising from research."[13]

Undoubtedly, entrepreneurial education has a number of advantages and has proven to be highly impactful in developing countries such as India, China, Brazil and other emerging economies in the world. Not only have these countries produced domestic entrepreneurial capital, they have also recently come top among entrepreneurship exporting countries. This explains the presence of Indian and Chinese entrepreneurs in all parts of Africa and the Middle East. The major benefits of entrepreneurship education, especially in the area of resolving conventional entrepreneurial challenges, are tied to the belief that such a system has the capacity to induce entrepreneurial culture and understanding in a wide range of individuals, enhance positive entrepreneurial behaviour and personalities, instigate entrepreneurial and innovative thinking amongst the youth, and lay a strong foundation for the realisation of the goals of Nigerian education policy.

---

13 This position was declared by Hajiya Uwani Yahy, the Director for Students Support Services Department of National Universities Commission (NUC), at a consultative meeting with Vice Chancellors of the nation's universities in Abuja in February 2011.

## Summary and Recommendation

In most developed and emerging economies, the strength of the entrepreneurship class is the strongest propelling force for socio-economic development. The level of economic development is also determined by the volume of entrepreneurial activities going on therein. Thus, countries that have excelled in employment creation and poverty reduction are those that have strategically invested in entrepreneurship development. In Nigeria, macro-economic entrepreneurial benefits are yet to be optimised due to the hostile and chronically problematic nature of the internal and external business environment in the country.[14] Business performance is still greatly constrained by institutional weaknesses such as: poor infrastructure; insecurity; weak legal structure; near absence of structured government supports; and poor access to external finance. At the micro-scale, many Nigerians lack the requisite skills and entrepreneurial spirit to excel. Ironically, entrepreneurial activities in the country have been given a significant boost by persistent economic challenges, such as poverty, unemployment and institutional weaknesses. While economic challenges might have presented significant opportunities for resolute individuals to succeed, it is necessary to note that it is only by providing the right institutional environment for business that the country can expand its entrepreneurial scope, tap into its huge human and natural resources, and meaningfully and effectively fight the scourge of poverty, youth unemployment and civil conflicts.

This paper has provided an institutional explanation of entrepreneurship development in the Nigerian context. An important implication of the analysis is that individuals and firms do not always take rational decisions; rather, decisions and behaviour are framed by certain presupposed expectations. These expectations, in turn, legitimise individual actions and determine behaviour. Thus, we should not think of entrepreneurship development as primarily driven by individual free choice, but should take into consideration the wider contextual factors that create opportunities and barriers for individual career development. Researchers should give greater attention to the interactions among the institutional pillars and the simultaneous influence of these pillars on aggregate entrepreneurship.

---

14 For a commentary on the challenges against entrepreneurship development in Nigeria, see the *Vanguard* [Newspaper] article on "Entrepreneurship, Nigeria and its Operating Environment", 1 August 2015 as well as *The Guardian* article on "Entrepreneurship Development in Nigeria", 1 September 2015.

## References

Abimbola, O.H., Adekeye, O.A., Ajayi, M.P. & A.S. Idowu. (2011). "Some Socio-cultural Issues in Entrepreneurship Development Among Some Groups in Nigeria". *Gender and Behaviour*. 19, 2, 268–282.

Acs, Z.J. & C. Armington. (2006). *Entrepreneurship, Geography, and American Economic Growth*, Cambridge: Cambridge University Press.

Acs, Z.J., Szerb, L. & E. Autio. (2015). *Global Entrepreneurship and Development Index 2014*, Springer Briefs in Economics, Springer.

Agboli, M. & C. Ukaegbu. (2006). "Business Environment and Entrepreneurial Activity in Nigeria: Implications for Industrial development", *Journal of Modern African Studies*, 44(1), 1–30.

Aidis, R., Estrin, S. & T.M. Mickiewicz. (2012). "Size Matters: Entrepreneurial Entry and Government". *Small Business Economics*, 39(1), 119–139.

Akinyoade, A. (2015). "Nigerians in Transit: The Trader and the Religious in Jerusalem House, Ghana." In: Akinyinka Akinyoade & Jan-Bart Gewald (eds), 2015, *African Roads to Prosperity*, Leiden/Boston: Brill, 211–231.

Babatunde, E.D. (1992). *Culture, Religion, and the Self: A Critical Study of Bini and Yoruba Value Systems in Change*. Lewiston, NY: Edwin Mellen Press.

BECAN Report (2007). *Business Environment and Competitiveness Across Nigerian States: National Synthesis Report*, Enugu: African Institute for Applied Economics.

Bechard, J.P. & J.M. Toulouse. (1998). "Validation of a Didactic Model for the Analysis of Training Objectives in Entrepreneurship", *Journal of Business Venturing, 13* (4), 317–332.

Benassy-Quere, A., Coupet, M. & T. Mayer. (2007). "Institutional Determinants of Foreign Direct Investment", *The World Economy*, 764–781.

Bhide, A. (2000). *The Origin and Evolution of New Business*. New York: Oxford University Press.

Boettke, P.J. & C.J. Coyne. (2009). *Context Matters: Institutions and Entrepreneurship*, Boston, MA: Now Publishers Inc.

Bruton, G.D., Ahlstrom, D. & T. Puky. (2009). "Institutional Differences and the Development of Entrepreneurial Ventures: A Comparison of the Venture Capital Industries in Latin America and Asia". *Journal of International Business Studies*, 40(5), 762–778.

Budhwar, P. & Y. Debrah. (2001). "Rethinking Comparative and Cross National Human Resource Management Research", *The International Journal of Human Resource Management*, 12(3), 497–515.

Campbell, J.L. (2006). "Institutional Analysis and the Paradox of Corporate Social Responsibility", *American Behavioral Scientist* 49(7), 925–938.

Cantillon, R. (1959). *Essay on the Nature of Trade in General*, London: Frank Cass and Company.

Chovwen, C. (2006). "Barriers to Acceptance, Satisfaction and Career Growth, Implications for Career Development and Retention of Women in Selected Male Occupations in Nigeria". *Women in Management Review*, 22(1), 68–78.

Clark, W.R. (1998). "Agents and Structures: Two Views of Preferences, Two Views of Institutions", *International Studies Quarterly*, 42(2), 245–270.

Cuervo, A. (2005). "Individual and Environmental Determinants of Entrepreneurship", *International Entrepreneurship and Management Journal*, 1, 293–311.

Dacin, M.T., Goodsstein, J. & W.R. Scott. (2002). "Institutional Theory and Institutional Change: Introduction to the Special Research Forum", *Academy of Management Journal*, 45, 45–57.

Eisenmann, T.R. (2013). "Entrepreneurship: A Working Definition", *Harvard Business Review*, 10 January.

Ellis, S. (2016), *Present Darkness: A History of Nigerian Organised Crime*, Oxford: Oxford Press.

Ezeoha, A.E. & K. Amaeshi. (2010). "Banking Development, Small Businesses and Minority Lending in Nigeria", *International Journal of Financial Services Management*, 4(4), 281–297.

Ezeoha, A.E. & O.J. Ugwu. (2015). "Interactive Impact of Armed Conflicts and Foreign Direct Investments in Africa", *African Development Review*, 27(4), 2015, 456–468.

Ezeoha, A., Igwe, A., Onyeke, C. & C. Uche. (2016). "Relevance Lost? The Petroleum Equalization Fund in Nigeria", *Energy for Sustainable Development*, 31, 152–162.

Falola, T. (2004). *Economic Reforms and Modernization in Nigeria, 1945–1965*, Kent, OH: Kent State University Press.

Faria, A. & P. Mauro. (2009). "Institutions and the External Capital Structure of Countries", *Journal of International Money and Finance*, 28, 367–391.

Fogarty, T.J. (1996). "The Imagery and Reality of Peer Review in the US: Insights from Institutional Theory", *Accounting, Organizations and Society*, 21(2/3), 243–268.

Herb, M. (2005). "No Representation without Taxation? Rents, Development, and Democracy", *Comparative Politics*, 37(3), 297–316.

Herbig, P. (1994). *The Innovation Matrix: Culture and Structure Prerequisites to Innovation*. Westport, CT: Quorum.

Hitt, M.A., Ireland, R.D., Sirmon, D.G. & C.A. Trahms. (2011). "Strategic Entrepreneurship: Creating Value for Individuals, Organizations, and Society". *Academy of Management Perspectives*, 25(2), 57–75.

Hodgson, G.M. (1994). "The Return of Institutional Economies". In: N.J. Smelser & R. Swedberg (eds), *Handbook of Economics Sociology*, Princeton, NJ: Princeton University Press & Russell Sage Foundation, 58–76.

Ituma, A.N. & R. Simpson. (2009). "The 'Boundaryless' Career and Career Boundaries: Applying an Institutionalist Perspective to ICT Workers in the Context of Nigeria", *Human Relations*, 62(5), 727–761.

Ituma, A.N. & R. Simpson. (2007). "Moving Beyond Schein's Typology, Career Anchors of Information Technology workers in Nigeria", *Personnel Review*, 36(6), 978–995.

Iversen, J., Jørgensen, R. & N. Malchow-Møller. (2008). *Defining and Measuring Entrepreneurship*, Boston, MA: Now Publishers Inc.

Kostova, T. (1997). "Country Institutional Profiles: Concept and Measurement". *Academy of Management Best Paper Proceedings*, 180–189.

Lawrence, T.B., Suddaby, R. & B. Leca. (2009). *Institutional Work: Actors and Agency in Institutional Studies of Organizations*, Cambridge: Cambridge University Press.

Mair, Johanna, Battilana, Julia & Julian Cardenas (2012). "'Organizing for Society: A Typology of Social Entrepreneuring Models'. Special Issue on Social Entrepreneurship Theory and Practice", *Journal of Business Ethics* 111(3), 353–373.

Marquis, C., Glynn, M.A. & G.F. Davis (2007). "Community Isomorphism and Corporate Social Action", *Academy of Management Review* 32(3), 925–940.

Marshall, A. (1890), *Principles of Economics: An Introductory Volume*, 1st Ed., London: Macmillan.

McVea, J.F. (2009). "A Field Study of Entrepreneurial Decision-making and Moral Imagination", *Journal of Business Venturing*, 24(5), 491–504.

Meyer, J.W. & B. Rowan. (1977). "Institutionalized Organizations: Formal Structure as Myth and Ceremony", *American Journal of Sociology*, 83, 340–363.

Mwakikagile, G. (2007). *Nyerere and Africa: End of an Era*, Pretoria: New Africa Press.

National Bureau of Statistics (2012). Social Statistics in Nigeria.

North, D.C. (1990). *Institutions, Institutional Change and Economic Performance*. Cambridge: Cambridge University Press.

North, D.C. (1994). "Economic Performance Through Time", *American Economic Review*, 84, 359–369.

Nystrom, K. (2008). "The Institutions of Economic Freedom and Entrepreneurship: Evidence from Panel Data", *Public Choice*, 136, 269–282.

Obayan, A.O.I. (1995). "Changing Perspectives in the Extended Family System in Nigeria: Implications for Family Dynamics and Counselling", *Counselling Psychology Quarterly*, 8(3), 253–257.

Ogundele O.J.K. (2012). "Entrepreneurial Succession Problems in Nigeria's Family Businesses: A Threat to Sustainability", *European Scientific Journal*, 8(7), 208–227.

Oguntola, T. (2016). "How Piracy is Wrecking Nigerian Entertainment Industry", *Leadership Newspapers*, 19 May.

Omoh, G. (2011). "For How Long Will Nigeria Continue with this Import (Syndrome), Madness", *Vanguard Newspapers*, 20 February.

Onuoha, B.C. (2013). "Challenges and Problems of Professionalizing Family Businesses in South-East Nigeria", *American International Journal of Contemporary Research*, 3(4), 130–139.

Powell, W.W. (2007). "The New Institutionalism". In: S. Clegg & J.A. Baily (eds), *The International Encyclopedia of Organization Studies*, London: Sage Publishers.

Powell, B. & C.S. Rodet. (2012), "Praise and Profits: Cultural and Institutional Determinants of Entrepreneurship", *Journal of Private Enterprise*, 27(2), 19–42.

Redding, S.G. (1980). "Cognition as an Aspect of Culture and its Relation to Management Processes: An Exploratory View of the Chinese Case", *Journal of Management Studies* 17(2), 127–147.

Say, J.B. (1855). *A Treatise on Political Economy*, trans. Clement Biddle. Philadelphia, PA: Lippincott, Grambo & Co.

Scott, R.W. (1983). "Introduction: From Technology to Environment". In: J.W. Meyer & W.R. Scott (eds), *Organizational Environments: Ritual and Rationality*, 13–17, Beverly Hills, CA: Sage.

Scott, W.R. (2008). "Approaching Adulthood: The Maturing of Institutional Theory", *Theory and Society*, 37(5), 427–442.

Scott, W.R. (2004). "Institutional Theory, Contributing to a Theoretical Research Program". In: G. Ken & A. Michael (eds), *Great Minds in Management: The Process of Theory Development*, Oxford: Oxford University Press, 460–484.

Serneels, P. & M. Verpoorten. (2015). "The Impact of Armed Conflicts on Economic Performance: Evidence from Rwanda", *Journal of Conflict Resolution*, 59(4), 555–592.

Shane, S. (1992). "Why Do Some Societies Invent More Than Others?" *Journal of Business Venturing*, 7, 29–46.

Shane, S. & S. Venkataraman. (2000). "The Promise of Entrepreneurship as a Field of Study", *Academy of Management Review*, 25(1), 217–226.

Stel, A.V., Storey, D. & R. Thurik. (2007). "The Effect of Business Regulations on Nascent and Young Business Entrepreneurship", *Small Business Economics*, 28, 171–186.

Swedberg, R. (1991). *Joseph A. Schumpeter: His Life and Work*, Cambridge: Policy Press.

Udegbe, I.B. (2003). "The Realities of Nigerian Organisational Health Policies and Practices for Female Employees". In: I.B. Udegbe (ed.), *Transforming Health Policies for Gender Equity in Nigerian Organisations*. Lagos: Macmillan.

Unachukwu, G.D. (2009). "Issues and Challenges in the Development of Entrepreneurship Education in Nigeria", *African Research Review*, 3(5), 213–226.

UNCTAD (2015). World Investment Report – Reforming International Investment Governance, Geneva: United Nations.

Van Praag, M. (1999). "Some Classical Views on Entrepreneurship", *De Economist*, 147(3), 311–335.

Warr, P. (1982). "Pareto Optimal Redistribution and Private Charity", *Journal of Public Economics*, 19(1), 131–138.

Wharton, K. & R.U. Oyelere. (2011). "Conflict and Its Impact on Educational Accumulation and Enrolment in Colombia: What We Can Learn from Recent IDPs", *IZA DP* No. 5939, August.

Wicks, D. (2001). "Institutionalized Mindsets of Invulnerability: Differentiated Institutional Fields and the Antecedents of Organizational Crisis", *Organization Studies*, 22(4), 659–692.

World Bank (2015), Doing Business 2015 – Going Beyond Efficiency Washington DC: The World Bank Group.

World Economic Forum (2015), The Global Competitiveness Report 2015–2016, Geneva: World Economic Forum.

Zimmerman, J. (2008). *Refining the Definition of Entrepreneurship*, Michigan: ProQuest.

Zucker, L.G. (1977). "The Role of Institutionalization in Cultural Persistence", *American Journal of Sociology*, 42, 726–743.

CHAPTER 8

# Entrepreneurship Development in Africa: Insights from Nigeria's and Zimbabwe's Telecoms

*Nnamdi O. Madichie, Knowledge Mpofu and Jerry Kolo*

## Introduction

This chapter explores the challenges and opportunities for entrepreneurship development in Nigeria and Zimbabwe. The cross-national comparative analysis provides insights on the diverse and unique configuration of institutional logics that promote or constrain entrepreneurship development in these two sub-Saharan African (SSA) economies (Ajai 2015: 153). The contextual opportunities and barriers in the two countries are explored by drawing from institutional theory (Pache and Santos 2010; Smith and Lewis 2011), and using the telecommunications sector to highlight the issues that shape the current and future trends in entrepreneurship development championed by a "new generation of African entrepreneurs" (McDade and Spring 2005). Comparatively, Nigeria has been covered considerably more than Zimbabwe in existing literature on entrepreneurship development in Africa. Nigeria's Globacom, founded by Mike Adenuga, and Econet Wireless, founded by Zimbabwean Strive Masiyiwa, are two case studies from the telecommunications sector led by a new generation of African entrepreneurs and used in this chapter to illustrate enterprise development (Carter and Wilton 2006a, 2006b). Both case studies provide critical analysis of emerging issues through compelling success stories of entrepreneurship initiatives despite infrastructure challenges and unstable economic and political landscapes experienced in the two SSA countries in recent years.

The choice of countries is based on trends in the telecommunications sector,[1] and trends in entrepreneurship beyond the small business sector. Furthermore, the skewed nature of entrepreneurship research in both contexts is evident. On the one hand, Nigeria is well reported in the entrepreneurship literature; Zimbabwe, on the other hand, is largely unreported. Following on from the country level analyses in the second section, the chapter focuses on

1 Telkom SA is discussed under "Profile of the companies" with a history of success in the South African market and several African countries (see Ajai 2015: 155).

 | DOI 10.1163/9789004351615_009

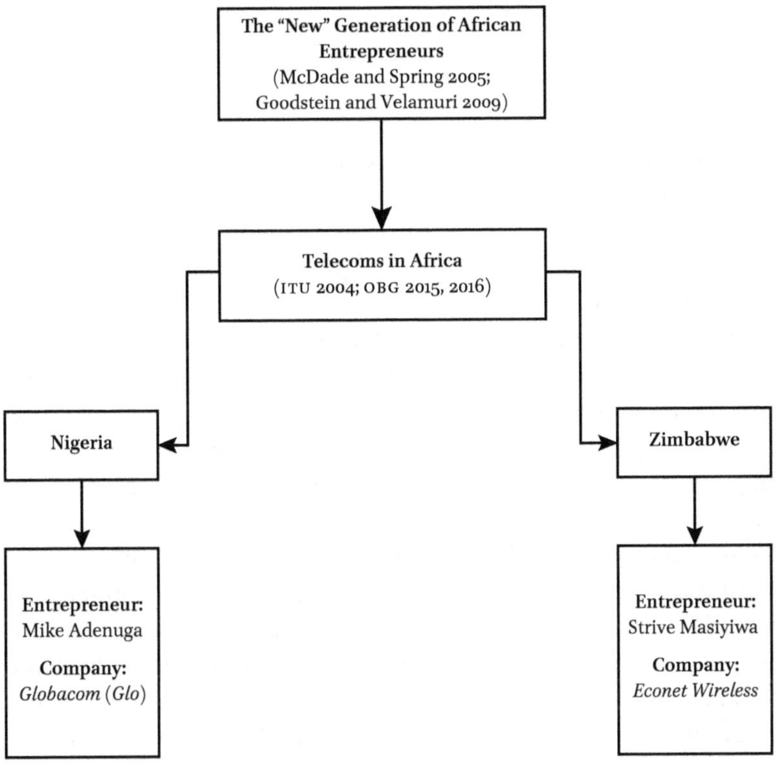


FIGURE 8.1 *Chapter framework*

key entrepreneurial developments in the important mobile telecoms sector. The chapter interrogates the entrepreneurship literature alongside trends in the telecoms sector in both countries. This sets the context for the case studies,[2] providing illustrations of enterprise development, starting with a profile of the entrepreneurs themselves (see Figure 8.1) – Mike Adenuga (featured in *Forbes* as the second richest man in Nigeria, behind billionaire portfolio entrepreneur, Aliko Dangote) and Strive Masiyiwa (Zimbabwean Telecom tycoon

2 Despite the limitations of the research approach in the development of the chapter, it is consistent with what already exists in the public domain (see Gillwald and Mureithi 2011; Sutherland 2011; Curwen and Whalley 2011; Curwen and Whalley, 2008; Karabag and Berggre 2011; Majumdar 2011). For example, in developing a detailed case study on mobile operator roaming charges in East Africa, Gillwald and Mureithi (2011: 32) relied on "empirical evidence acquired through in-depth interviews and market analysis." According to them "[...] despite Zain being unable ultimately to dominate its competitors, it had a sustained disruptive effect on the entire market."

also featured in *Forbes Magazine*) – before exploring the companies these entrepreneurs founded, Globacom or Glo, and *Econet Wireless*.

## Entrepreneurship Development in Africa: Issues, Challenges and Opportunities

The seminal article by Tom Forrest (1994) entitled "*The advance of African capital: The growth of Nigerian private enterprise*", sets a good tone for Entrepreneurship Development in sub-Saharan Africa (SSA). The article is arguably the most extensive account of medium- and large-scale African business published on the topic in the 1990s. It examines the strategies and patterns employed by enterprises from the colonial period to the post-independence decade, and provides specific profiles of Nigeria's key entrepreneurs. The study is not only a valuable digest of business activities, but also challenges existing views about SSA enterprise development (see Madichie 2016). It also raises a series of questions about the challenges of SSA Enterprise development – a topic worthy of re-examination in the current economic dispensation confronting the region. Two decades on, in 2016, the region is facing the same questions; notably, what role have the political conditions played in shaping the general conditions for accumulation (i.e. private/indigenous)? How important have state policies been in the formation and rate of private accumulation (of private capital)? Do social and economic spaces exist within which private enterprises are sufficiently independent of political and state control to allow the pursuit of private, large-scale accumulation of capital and economic growth and development?

In a bid to address these questions, McDade and Spring (2005) identified characteristics of a supposedly "new generation" of entrepreneurs from the region. These authors evaluated the goals and achievements of the enterprise networks of these new breed of players, and conclude that, despite the limitations (especially from the political class and institutions), these entrepreneurs have gone on to create intra- and cross-national networks that strengthen private-sector-led economic growth in SSA (see McDade and Spring 2005: 17). As these authors point out in the interdisciplinary volume *African Entrepreneurship: Theory and Reality*, there is a spectrum of entrepreneurs ranging from illiterate owners of micro-enterprises to wealthy founders of large manufacturing firms and their MBA-educated managers (see McDade and Spring 2005:18).

The entrepreneurial landscape in SSA accommodates a multitude of micro-enterprises that provide marginal employment for a single individual as well as a small number of large corporations employing hundreds of people.

The configuration includes informal and formal sector businesses, traditional and modern, indigenous and foreign-owned enterprises geographically dispersed in rural and urban areas. The characterisation of SSA businesses also spans a small large-scale sector and a large small-scale sector. In between is the medium-scale sector, which has been called the "missing middle" in the context of SSA (McDade and Spring 2005: 20). However, a study of modern SSA entrepreneurs in six countries (Botswana, Cote d'Ivoire, Ghana, Kenya, Malawi, and Tanzania) profiled medium-scale firms and concluded that "the middle is not missing" (Marsden 1990: 5). For example, it identified 5000 formally registered road transport companies in Tanzania, and reported that over 2000 Ghanaian businesses applied for loans from financial institutions where the average investment project funded was US$1.5 million. As McDade and Spring surmised, "these are not micro- or small-scale enterprises." (McDade and Spring 2005: 20). Indigenous medium-to-large-scale formal sector enterprises are an important part of the entrepreneurial landscape in spite of their small percentage. Also, there has been the argument that this precedent was set by colonialism, which stifled the growth of an indigenous formal private sector; most SSA governments have, post-independence, continued to limit the expansion of indigenous entrepreneurship. Government leaders were suspicious that a strong private sector comprised of their own citizens might threaten their own powers and privileges. Hence, during the 1960s to 1980s, many SSA states stepped into the role of business owner. State-owned enterprises (SOEs) assumed the responsibility of building the infrastructure of newly independent countries to meet the demand for goods and services. Most SOEs were unproductive and failed; so, by the late 1980s, many SSA governments reverted to donor-driven policies that promoted private sector-led economic development.[3]

3 According to McDade and Spring (2005: 21), the SOEs were sold to civil servants or businessmen, many of whom came to be known as "business bureaucrats", who depended on the patronage of governments to remain viable (Janssens-Bevernage 2002: 12). During the 1980s, donor mandated structural adjustment programmes (SAPs) called for economic liberalisation to open both private and state-owned domestic firms to external competition. Most large firms in Africa manufacture beverages, clothing, furniture, rubber, leather products, plastics, soap/toiletries, pharmaceuticals, or are in construction and transportation. Many of these large-scale firms in Africa are owned by ethnic minorities such as Asians, Syrians/Lebanese and Europeans. There are also multinational companies. Indigenous Africans own one-third or less of large industrial firms. The amount varies among countries. In Kenya, black Africans own only 3.6 per cent of large firms, whereas in Zimbabwe it is more than 30 per cent (Ramachandran and Shah 1999). In Zimbabwe, a number of party-linked businessmen emerged through these organisations, such as Roger Boka, Enock Kamushinda, Philip Chiyangwa, Supa Mandiwanzira, Strive Masiyiwa, Peter Pamire, and Chemist Siziba. They

However, the "new generation of African entrepreneurs" had some common traits – they used cell phones, laptop computers, international credit cards, and e-mail accounts. In the case of Nigeria, the industrial sector has, in the last decade, come to be dominated by small-scale enterprises that constitute 66 per cent of industrial establishments (Singh *et al.* 2011: 205). The dominance of these small businesses is also reflected in a push for curriculum development tailored to the sector.[4] Furthermore, research seems to have conflated entrepreneurship with small business. For example, Inegbenebor (2006: 2) posited that entrepreneurs of small- and medium enterprises help to "raise the level of productivity in the economy by harnessing and utilizing resources more effectively." As champions of change and initiators of development activities, entrepreneurs are arguably a rare breed of people with rare abilities to identify and exploit opportunities, as well as the capacity to improve society, while maximising benefits from their *venturesomeness* (*see* Inegbenebor 2006: 2). As Inyang & Enuoh (2009: 66) points out,

> the entrepreneurs usually start as a downtown corner shop, or business outfit of a family size, to grow to become a big business concern like the Dangotes[5] [...] these are well-known and successful Nigerian entrepreneurs with large conglomerates or business empires under their control. What helps them going over the years despite obstacles, are the development of special skills, attitudes and behaviour, which enable them to preserve and perform their roles in society [...] The Nigeria entrepreneurs must acquire the requisite entrepreneurial competencies through

used their access to the state to develop significant business interests. It was at that time that Masiyiwa faced major obstacles when he tried to establish his own mobile phone company.

4 For example, one study highlighted "The National Universities Commission's 1989 Approved Minimum Academic Standards for teaching of courses in business schools at the undergraduate level has a compulsory course on Entrepreneurial Development" (see Inyang and Enuoh 2009: 65) in a bid to create opportunities for graduating students of business management and related disciplines to learn entrepreneurial skills to help them venture into setting up businesses. The programme is also intended to assist the government in reducing unemployment through self-employment. The government is, therefore, heavily concerned about developing small-scale business operators or indigenous entrepreneurs that can assist in economic/national development – being self-employed and reducing unemployment, creating more employment opportunities and given the citizens a sense of self-worth and confidence.

5 Referring to Alhaji Aliko Dangote, Nigerian entrepreneur and Africa's richest man according to *Forbes Magazine*.

regular training and development programmes to avoid entrepreneurial failures in their business ventures.

However, most entrepreneurship-related studies, and especially in the context of Africa, have focused mainly on the small business sector or the informal economy (see notable studies in Table 8.1).

In the case of Zimbabwe, like any other country in the developing world, the country faces numerous constraints to enterprise development, which still linger after almost four decades of independence. Despite the successes, particularly in the first decade after independence in 1980, the political and economic failures experienced in Zimbabwe from the mid-1990s have been widely and largely attributed to poor governance, corrupt and ineffective leadership, lack of capacity, and/or unwillingness to embrace democratic institutions. This has been exacerbated by the challenges of political pluralism in a growing democracy and the emerging diverse institutional logic and complexity of competing demands of both internal and external stakeholder groups. In the following decades, the State strengthened its machinery in response to growing dissent. This was evident in different ways that included avoidance, Machiavellian manipulation through coercive power, creating and breaking the 'rules of the game', ignoring explicit norms and values, disguising non-conformity, assaulting sources of institutional pressure from political opposition and dominating institutional power, space and processes. However, as was noted in the context of Nigeria, most scholarly research on entrepreneurship in Zimbabwe has revolved around small business and/or the informal economy as illustrated in the studies in Table 8.2.

Nonetheless, the unpredictability of the complexities in Zimbabwe has resulted in multi-levels of distinct logics characterised by *conflict over the ends*, which have continuously been replaced by *conflict over the means*. Political conflict, corruption, poverty, and resentment are cutting deep, consequentially precipitating serious constraints to entrepreneurship development potential in Zimbabwe (and indeed across SSA). The economic narrative of the ruling elite has failed to offer solutions to millions of unemployed Zimbabweans for nearly thirty years, resulting in mass migration. Over three million have been displaced into the diaspora looking for economic space and opportunities in other countries such as South Africa, the UK and the US. Entrepreneurship development increasingly depends on remittances from Zimbabweans in the diaspora and economic space is gained through political connections (see Jones 2010).

The *Doing Business 2016 Report* (see Table 1.1 on p. 5 of the report) ranks Mauritius at 32, which is the highest ranking for an SSA country. Rwanda is ranked

TABLE 8.1 *Summary of entrepreneurship research in Nigeria*

| Author/Year | Title | Focus/Emphasis |
|---|---|---|
| Akinyoade and Uche (2016). | "Dangote Cement: An African Success Story?" | Corporate entrepreneurship |
| Adelowo, Ilori, Siyanbola and Oluwale (2015). | "Technological Learning Mechanisms in Nigeria's Technology Incubation Centre", *African Journal of Economic and Management Studies*, 6(1), 72–89. | Business support/ SMES |
| Madichie, N. (2011b). | "Setting an Agenda for Women Entrepreneurship in Nigeria: A Commentary on Faseke's Journey through Time for 'The Nigerian Woman'", *Gender in Management: An International Journal*, 26(3), 212–219. | Women entrepreneurship |
| Singh, Simpson, Mordi, and Okafor (2011). | "Motivation to Become an Entrepreneur: A Study of Nigerian Women's Decisions", *African Journal of Economic and Management Studies*, 2(2), 202–219. | Women entrepreneurship |
| Inyang and Enuoh (2009). | "Entrepreneurial Competencies: The Missing Links to Successful Entrepreneurship in Nigeria", *International Business Research*, 2(2), 62–71. | SMES |
| Madichie and Nkamnebe (2008). | Entrepreneurial emergence in a typical sub-Sahara African context, Nnewi | Indigenous small firms |
| Aruwa (2006). | Entrepreneurial development, small and medium enterprises. Kaduna: Entrepreneurship Academy Publishing. | SMES |
| Ogundele (2006, May–July). | "Entrepreneurship studies and development in Nigeria: The missing link", *Lagos Organisation Review*, 2 (4): 69–74. | Unstated. |
| Nwachukwu (2005). | The practice of entrepreneurship in Nigeria. Onitsha: Africana-First Publishers Limited. | SME Development |

| | | |
|---|---|---|
| Ojong (2005). | "Starting a new business". In: S.N. Udo (ed.). *Entrepreneurial Development: Principles and Practice,* 43–45, Calabar: Wusen Press. | Financial Management |
| Nigeria Investment Promotion Commission (2004). | Overview of small and medium scale enterprises in Nigeria. An Information Booklet, Abuja. | Unstated (government support for SMES) |
| Anyanwu, Adebusuyi and Okafor (2003). | The slow pace of disbursement of small and medium industries equity investment scheme (SMIEIS) fund and the need for remedial measures. Central Bank of Nigeria, Research Department, Occasional Paper No. 30. | SMEIEIS (Small businesses). |
| Ilesanmi (2000). | Entrepreneurial development. (1st Ed). Ilorin, Nigeria: Kola Success Publications. | Leadership |
| Owualah (1999). | Entrepreneurship in small business firms. (1st Ed). Lagos: G-MAG Investment Ltd (Educational Publishers). | Small Business Firms |
| Ogundele and Oni (1995). | "The controversial dimension of organisational effectiveness: With specific reference to a sample of SME in Nigeria". In: A.T. Ojo (ed.) *Management of small and medium enterprises in Nigeria,* 22–29. Ikeja: Pumark Nigeria Ltd. | SME in Nigeria |
| Onuoha (1994). | Entrepreneurial development in Nigeria. Okigwe: Avan Global Publications. | SMES |
| Fadahusi (1992). | "Entrepreneurship and small industry development in the Commonwealth: An overview", *Nigerian Management Review,* 7(1&2):443–454. | SMES |

TABLE 8.2 *Summary of entrepreneurship research in Zimbabwe*

| Author/ Year | Title | Focus/Emphasis |
|---|---|---|
| Charles Makanyeza and Gilbert Dzvuke (2015) | The influence of innovation on the performance of small and medium enterprises in Zimbabwe. *Journal of African Business,* 16(1–2), 198–214. | SMES; Innovation and enterprise performance |
| Wilton (2015) | Want to support enterprise development in developing countries? Think about the other salient factors. An investigation of Zimbabwe and Pacific Island countries. *International Journal of Entrepreneurship & Small Business*, 25(3), 282. | SMES and Entrepreneurship development in Zimbabwe and Pacific Island countries |
| Nyamwanza, Mavhiki, Mapetere and Nyamwanza (2014) | An Analysis of SMES' Attitudes and Practices Toward Tax Compliance in Zimbabwe. *Sage Open Publication.* | SMES, Entrepreneurship, Tax compliance |
| Chivasa (2014) | Entrepreneurship culture among SMES in Zimbabwe: A case of Bulawayo SMES. *International Journal of Economics, Commerce and Management Vol* 2(9). | Entrepreneurship, SMES in Zimbabwe |
| Dawson and Kelsall (2012) | Anti-developmental patrimonialism in Zimbabwe, *Journal of Contemporary African Studies*, 30:1, 49–66. | Entrepreneurship; Economic rent management system in Zimbabwe |
| Magure (2012) | Foreign investment, black economic empowerment and militarised patronage politics in Zimbabwe. *Journal of Contemporary African Studies*, 30 (1), 67–82. | Black economic empowerment and patronage system in Zimbabwe |
| Ncube and Gómez (2011) | Local economic development and migrant remittances in rural Zimbabwe: building on sand or solid ground? *Working Paper No. 523. Institute of Social Studies. University Institute of the Erasmus University Rotterdam* (EUR). | Enterprise development in Zimbabwe. Zimbabwean Diaspora remittances |

| | | |
|---|---|---|
| Chikweche and Fletcher (2011) | Franchising at the Bottom of the Pyramid (BOP): An alternative distribution approach. *The International Review of Retail, Distribution and Consumer Research,* 21 (4), 343–360. | Entrepreneurship, SMEs, Franchising and Bottom of the Pyramid (BoP) in Zimbabwe |
| Goodstein and Velamuri (2009) | States, Power, Legitimacy, and Maintaining Institutional Control: The Battle for Private Sector Telecommunication Services in Zimbabwe. *Organization Studies*, 30(5), 489–508. | SMEs and Telecommunications sector development |
| Carter and Wilton (2006a) | Enterprise culture: Necessary in promoting enterprise. Lessons from enterprise development in Zimbabwe. *Journal of Enterprising Culture*, 14(3), 177–198. | SMEs and Enterprise development in Zimbabwe |
| Carter and Wilton (2006b) | Don't blame the entrepreneur, blame government: The centrality of government in enterprise development. Lessons from enterprise failure in Zimbabwe. *Journal of Enterprising Culture*, 14(1), 65–84. | SMEs and Enterprise development in Zimbabwe |
| Daniels (2003) | Factors that influence the expansion of the micro-enterprise sector: Results from three national surveys in Zimbabwe. *Journal of International Development*, Vol 15, 675–692. | SMEs and Enterprise development |
| Pedersen (1992) | Entrepreneurs and managers in Zimbabwe's District Service Centres. *Entrepreneurship & Regional Development*, 4(1), 57–72. | Entrepreneurship, SMEs, Corporate strategies |

62, making it the second country in SSA. Then there is Botswana at 72 and South Africa at 73 in the rankings. In broader Africa terms (i.e. North Africa), Tunisia and Morocco are ranked 74th and 75th respectively. Seychelles comes in at 95 and is followed by Zambia at 97th. Namibia is ranked 101, Swaziland 105, Kenya 108, and Ghana and Lesotho are jointly ranked at 114 (ahead of Brazil at 116). Uganda is ranked at 122 and Cape Verde at 126. Egypt comes up next at 131 and Mozambique at 133 (recall the study by Braathen (2004) on telecom development in Mozambique and Zimbabwe). Zimbabwe was ranked at 155 and Nigeria is disappointingly ranked at 169 out 189 countries profiled. These are below the rankings of Ethiopia and Sierra Leone at 146 and 147, respectively. However, the *Doing Business* methodology must be interpreted with caution as it clearly measures trends in the SME sector:

> Since 2003 Doing Business has been publishing annual quantitative data on the main regulatory constraints affecting domestic small and medium-size enterprises throughout their life cycle.
>
> *Doing Business*, 2016: 9

Furthermore, by measuring the "ease of starting a business" rather than "sustaining a business," the rankings would still require some cautionary interpretation:

> This year's report presents data for 189 economies and aggregates information from 10 areas of business regulation – starting a business, dealing with construction permits, getting electricity, registering property, getting credit, protecting minority investors, paying taxes, trading across borders, enforcing contracts and resolving insolvency – to develop an overall ease of doing business ranking. (*Ibid.*)

As further justification for this chapter's focus on telecoms, we are not only referring to voice calls, but also data and especially in relation to the internet and internet penetration. This is evidenced in the most recent *Doing Business* Report published by the World Bank, where it is clearly stated that:

> The proliferation of information and communication technologies has transformed how businesses operate and how they are regulated in every region of the world. The internet provides a new platform for delivering government information and services – and new opportunities for enhancing the efficiency and transparency of public administration. Indeed, the internet is a tool that governments can use to support businesses at

> every stage in their life cycle, whether applying for a business permit, registering property, paying taxes or trading internationally. (*Ibid.*)

The role of the information communications technology (ICT) in economic development is also captured in the report, with some emphasis on the role of the internet in actualising such processes:

> Beyond starting a business, the internet offers many opportunities for efficiency gains in other areas of business regulation measured by Doing Business. Among the 189 economies covered [...] more than 80% (152 in total) use web-based applications to process export and import documents. [...] Yet while the internet has the potential to promote inclusiveness, reduce corruption and improve regulatory efficiency, its impact on the quality of domestic governance is subject to political, infrastructural, social and economic factors [...].[6] (*Ibid.*: 11)

As a departure, therefore, this chapter focuses on the telecoms sector, broadly defined as including voice and data.

## Contextual Opportunities and Barriers: Insights from the Telecoms Sector

Mobile telecoms is a global industry that has transformed how we communicate. Since the industry started in the early 1980s, successive technological generations have improved the quality of mobile communications and the range of products and services that can be provided through mobile devices. As markets were liberalised, foreign direct investment (FDI) emerged as a key factor shaping the industry's development. Through foreign investment, telecoms-focused multi-national corporations (MNCs) emerged. These companies, such as Vodafone or Deutsche Telekom, invested in and developed mobile telecommunication markets around the globe. Various aspects of the growth of telecoms-focused MNCs have been explored in the literature. The strategies of companies from early liberalising countries (e.g. the United States) or small countries (e.g. Norway and Sweden) into Asia-Pacific markets has been explored, as have those of Asian operators like Hutchison Whampoa

6 See also pp. 14–17 of the *Doing Business* Report for the praise showered on Rwanda as the champion for SSA.

or NTT DoCoMo. Largely overlooked, however, has been the liberalisation and internationalisation that has occurred within SSA. Although Africa liberalised relatively late compared to other regions, it has embraced liberalisation on the one hand and mobile technologies on the other. What has emerged is a complex, increasingly pan-continental market, where MNCs, often headquartered elsewhere, play a key role. Hoffman, in a 2006 study, highlighted the mobile telecom landscape in Africa, which pitched South Africa and Nigeria as key players. According to him (Hoffman 2006: 86):

> Africa has three dominant mobile phone operators who are active across the continent, South African companies [...] occupy the top two positions [...]. Nigeria has proven to be "The growth market" in Africa for mobile telecommunications.

Hoffman also points out that, "Vodacom's South African rival MTN has shown just how important first mover advantage can be when entering a market, while Vodacom's decision not to enter the market shows how costly business decisions are." The experiences of both South African mobile giants have shown how lucrative internationalisation can be, especially when focusing on markets disregarded by other international players (see Hoffman 2006). Over the past decade, Nigeria has become the largest telecoms market in Africa and the Middle East, with more than 140 million active telecoms subscribers in 2015, according to the Nigerian Communications Commission (NCC), the federal telecoms regulator.[7] As is the case elsewhere in frontier and emerging markets, mobile subscribers accounted for over 99 per cent of this total, with virtually all of that segment controlled by the country's four GSM operators: MTN Nigeria, Airtel Nigeria, Globacom, and Etisalat Nigeria (see also Madichie 2011a). Nigeria's overall telecoms capacity is relatively high – a number of high-capacity submarine cables come ashore in the country – but bringing this capacity into people's homes remains a major hurdle. Despite the challenges, most indicators point to continued expansion. Taking into account the nation's large population and solid economic fundamentals, most local players are counting on continued rapid telecoms uptake. In the past five years, Nigeria has grown into one of Africa's largest and most vibrant markets for ICT products and services, with an ecosystem that ranges from software start-ups to infrastructure firms. According to the Federal Ministry of Communication Technology, the federal oversight body, the nation accounts for 29 per cent of all internet usage on the continent, and this figure is expected to rise. Despite

7 Culled from Oxford Business Group (24 April 2015) *A handful of mobile operators dominate.*

the rapid pace of growth in recent years, the industry faces a host of challenges, including low penetration in terms of both usage and infrastructure access, high operating costs, and a lack of local content. Nevertheless, most Nigerian ICT players remain optimistic due, in part, to the significant scope for expansion in terms of potential bandwidth – thanks to a total capacity of nearly 10 Terabytes per second (Tbps), most of it unused, through the existing submarine cables.

According to the Oxford Business Group's (OBG) recent report on Nigeria's shifting telecoms landscape (see OBG, 22 April 2016), a new mobile operator, Ntel, commenced 4G LTE (i.e. Fourth Generation Long-term Evolution) services in Lagos and Abuja in April 2016, increasing competition in the 170 million population telecoms market.[8] Operating on the 900-MHz and 1800-MHz bands, Ntel is looking to challenge the four major telecoms operators in Nigeria – South Africa's MTN, India's Bharti Airtel, UAE's Etisalat, and local Globacom – with the promise of internet speeds of up to 230 Megabytes per second (Mbps).[9] Smile Communications, a broadband service provider, is also making a push into the Nigerian 4G LTE space, with particular emphasis on voice over LTE (VoLTE), which allows users to make calls through an application or VoLTE-enabled handsets. The company unveiled its network, which operates on the 800-MHz band, in March 2016. The entry of Ntel and Smile underscores the potential for growth in the Nigerian telecoms industry, particularly in the mobile broadband space. According to Frank Li, Managing Director

8 However, Ntel's entrance comes at a time when operators are grappling with slowing revenues, and looking to data coverage to improve income. Flattening average revenue per user (ARPU) rates are being seen throughout the African continent, as competition and regulation drive down tariffs for voice services. MTN Nigeria's ARPU fell by 11.5 per cent year-on-year, for example, dropping to N994 (U$5) in the third quarter of 2015. As a result, data is becoming increasingly important to maintaining margins. Operators across Africa have benefited from the rollout of new 3G and 4G LTE networks, and Nigeria is no exception, with subscribers on data networks providing significantly higher revenues. According to MTN Nigeria, ARPU for smartphones is roughly 3.5 higher than for non-smartphones, suggesting there could be significant return on investment if operators develop the necessary infrastructure to support growing data use.

9 Ntel first announced it would be entering the market in the autumn of 2015, beginning with coverage in Lagos, Abuja and Port Harcourt, and eventually spreading out to smaller cities and towns across Nigeria. The first phase of the firm's operations is set to begin with 800 tower sites and is intended to grow to 2000. The company has ambitious targets, with plans to attract more than $1bn worth of investment by 2020 to expand its mobile broadband network, Kamar Abbas, CEO of Ntel, told local media in April.

of Huawei in Nigeria, "with a market of more than 170 million, the potential for ICT is massive and, like many other major multinational companies, it is one of our most important markets […]." Although the figure includes users with multiple SIM cards – a common trend in emerging markets – the number of mobile subscribers is projected to increase from 148.6 million to 229 million by 2020, driven by growth in mobile internet. Mobile broadband users are expected to number close to 200 million by the end of the decade, compared to just 30–35 million at present. According to the World Bank, this trend could have significant economic benefits, with a doubling in the usage of mobile broadband data typically resulting in a 0.5 percentage point increase in annual GDP per capita growth.

According to the International Telecommunications Union (ITU) report "*African Telecommunication Indicators 2004*", mobile telephone subscriptions in Africa have increased by over 1000 per cent over a five-year period during 1998 to 2003. At the end of 2003, Africa had 51.8 million users compared to fixed line users which numbered 25.1 million. Market penetration is low at 6.2 per cent but still more than fixed line, which have a market penetration of three per cent. Mobile usage and popularity has been the result of sector reform, emergence of investors (mobile phone companies), demand, and the licensing of new operators (Hoffman 2006: 86). In the mid-2000s, Africa had three dominant mobile phone operators who were active across the continent, South African companies MTN and Vodacom occupied the top two positions followed by Celtel. Nigeria has also proven to be "the growth market" in SSA for mobile telecoms. Indeed, the experiences of both South African mobile giants have shown how lucrative internationalisation can be, especially when focusing on markets disregarded by other international players (*Ibid.*: 84). India's Bharti Airtel's Nigerian unit, Airtel Nigeria (a telco we will revert to in the specific case analysis later on in this chapter) won three industry awards at the eighth edition of the Nigerian Telecoms Awards – as the most innovative telecom company, telecom brand and customer friendly operator of the year. As a company statement put it:[10]

> Airtel emerged overall best in the three categories following its enviable strides in charting new paths in meeting the demands and needs of its esteemed stakeholders through superior brand experience, a rich portfolio of innovative products and services ranging from exciting voice solutions to inventive data packages.

10 See http://www.indiaafricaconnect.in/index.php?param=news/4900/the-big-story/114.

Given the so-called credit crunch, the recent absence of high-value takeover bids comes as no great surprise, but it is again of interest that the only takeover bids during 2008 involving a target with assets (as against debt) worth over US$10 billion comprised France Télécom's unsuccessful offer for TeliaSonera and Vivendi Universal's unsuccessful bid for Zain Africa.[11] According to the Initiative for Global Development (IGD), a Washington DC-based non-profit organisation that engages and harnesses the power of the private sector to create sustainable growth and alleviate poverty in Africa, "The top 30 [SSA multinationals] span industries varying from financial services and petroleum to telecommunications and transport."[12] That report also underlined the private sector's pivotal role in raising living standards in emerging markets. As Daniel Altman, Director of Thought Leadership at Dalberg Global Development Advisors, put it:[13]

> These homegrown multinational companies bring the best practices in management, operations and governance wherever they go in the Sub-Saharan region [...] They can professionalize markets in ways that boost income and employment for entire sectors.
>
> IGD 2011

The entrepreneurship potential of the aforementioned "Top 30 SSA multinationals" to providing the direction of economic development is also evidenced by their annual rate of profit of about 30 per cent between 2006 and 2009, which far outpaced that of their global competitors, including Standard and Poor's 500 biggest US firms. According to James Mwangi, CEO and Managing Director of Equity Bank, Kenya, and a member of IGD's *Frontier 100* network, "there is so much untapped potential in these markets-potential for revenue as well as opportunity to create jobs and reduce poverty [...]." He adds that:

> Partnerships are critical to achieving a company's full potential, as Equity Bank's success has shown. By using the strategies outlined in this report, and by thinking long-term, other companies can grow and help change policies that will encourage additional economic development.
>
> IGD 2011

11 Zain, once again under offer during 2009 (but this time in the form of a 46 per cent stake in the company itself), remains unsold, as does (for now) MTN despite its active pursuit by Bharti Airtel.

12 http://www.igdleaders.org/about/overview/.

13 http://www.igdleaders.org/wp-content/uploads/IGD-Dalberg-Pioneers-on-the-Frontier.pdf.

Some notable key success factors include taking time for due diligence, looking for the right policy environment, being conscious of cultural differences and seeking long-term anchor clients and partners. According to Patrick Devenish, Group Chief Executive, AICO Africa Ltd., "expanding beyond our base in Zimbabwe played an important part in AICO Africa's growth and success. At the same time, it has benefitted millions of Africans who depend on agriculture for their livelihoods." (IGD 2011). Companies are headquartered in countries with significant differences in population and economic output. At the two ends of the spectrum are Nigeria, a US$200 billion economy home to more than 150 million people and almost half of the top 30 MNCs, and Mauritius, which has a population of fewer than 1.3 million people but boasts one of the highest gross domestic products in Sub-Saharan Africa of more than US$7,000 per capita.[14] The top 30 MNCs span five different industries, in addition to those with diversified businesses whose portfolios range from construction to hotel chains, retail companies, and agribusinesses. Main players were in financial services, followed by petroleum, telecom, transport, and tourism,[15] with annual revenues ranging from US$240 million for Kenya Commercial Bank to US$2.4 billion for Oando, a Nigerian-based energy company. For the purpose of this chapter, however, our focus is on the telecommunications sector, which has been reported to be amongst the top three main players in SSA's economic development.

In the case of Zimbabwe, from the 1990s, the route to success for most indigenous entrepreneurs was through affiliations to organisations such as the Indigenous Business Development Centre (IBDC), which was established in 1991 with Strive Masiyiwa as Secretary General. The original indigenisation and empowerment vision espoused by the IBDC was not premised on the racially motivated asset stripping currently defining Zimbabwe's indigenisation culture. As Raftopoulos and Compagnon (2003: 22) point out, the IBDC sought to fight unemployment by increasing the size of the country's economy through the creation of new black businesses as opposed to "taking over existing

14 *2010 Africa Development Indicators*, World Bank Group.

15 Indeed, borrowing from McDade and Spring (2005), we describe these entrepreneurs in the Telecoms sector as the "new generation", and following in the footsteps of the decade old seminal book by Iliffe (1983), which cited pioneers of indigenous African business such as Chief Alhaji Yinka Folawiyo, founder of Nigerian Green Lines shipping company (1979); the Dantata family in Kano (Nigeria) renowned merchants and arguably the wealthiest in tropical Africa (see pp. 2–3); Njenga Karume, a Kenyan who in 1974 was Director of 36 firms as well as a shoe manufacturing company that challenged multinationals in his native, Kenya; and Senegalese billionaire Alhaji Momar Sourang. See Iliffe, J. (1983). *Emergence of African Capitalism*. London: The MacMillan Press.

companies owned by Whites". However, over time, the IBDC changed course as a result of factionalism engineered by ZANU PF-aligned politicians-cum businessmen,[16] who were more concerned with getting rich overnight. This is consistent with Sandbrook's (1985: 72) characterisation of the African political elite's aspiration to become a bourgeoisie as "an opportunistic exploitation of *insider privileges* [...] not the development of the classic risk-taking entrepreneurial behaviour."[17] In other words, many black businessmen were too risk averse to startup "hard-core" capitalist projects or ventures that would bring about sustainable development in SSA. Ironically, in 1992, Jonathan Moyo, now a key member of the government implementing the indigenisation regulations supporting this class, implored the emergent African *petit-bourgeoisie* to strive to become "hard-core capitalists" creating wealth for the benefit of future generations instead of being "phony capitalists" content with merely retailing goods produced by others (see Moyo 1992: 323). However, not all entrepreneurs are phony capitalists as some have succeeded despite of the political constraints. For example, in one study entitled "*Resisting Political Corruption: Econet Wireless Zimbabwe*", Velamuri (2007) highlighted the plight of one of the entrepreneurs profiled in this chapter, Strive Masiyiwa, as he sought to create Econet. This is also instructive in the light of the study by Jones (2010) entitled "*The Rise of the Kukiya-kiya Economy 2000–2008*", in which the author himself described it as "[...] a new logic of economic action in post-2000 Zimbabwe." Evidently, there is a story that develops over a 15-year period between 1993 and 2008, characterising the challenges of private sector (entrepreneurship) development in Zimbabwe Davies, 2004; Raftopoulous, 1996, 2000; Devarajan, Easterly, & Pack. 2001; Maphosa, 1998) and, by extension, SSA McCormick, D. (1999; Madichie, 2009, 2010). As Velamuri points out:

16 By 1994, IBDC had extracted some access rights from the state such as a quota for building contracts, but its internal dynamics gave rise to a more militant groups such as the Affirmative Action Group (AAG), which was chaired by Philip Chiyangwa. The state funded both organisations, although it later complained about accountability.

17 As picked up from a separate study, Zimbabweans are not opposed to indigenisation per se, but they want the process to be carried out in a rational and fair manner to avoid a situation where the initiative is hijacked to benefit a privileged few. ZANU PF's militarised patronage system under the guise of indigenisation provides a perfect opportunity to well-connected members of the Zimbabwean ruling party-state complex to become rich overnight. Indications so far are that the implementation of the empowerment policy is vindictive and lacks transparency. The fast-track indigenisation programme across all sectors of Zimbabwe's economy is likely to have a knock-on negative effect on economic growth and poverty alleviation. In the long runs it can be argued that patronage politics are both economically and financially unsustainable as they run against the very basic notions of wealth creation meant to alleviate poverty and redistribute wealth. Current indigenisation policies in Zimbabwe seem to continue that trend.

> This case study documents the story of Zimbabwean Entrepreneur Strive Masiyiwa in his quest to obtain a mobile telecommunications license. First the Post and Telecommunications Corporation of Zimbabwe (PTC) and then the Ministry of Information, Post and Telecommunications of the government of President Robert Mugabe place obstacle after obstacle in his path, but Masiyiwa challenges their decisions and actions in the High Court and the Supreme Court. Throughout this five-year process (1993–1998), he remains determined to obtain the license through ethical means. A number of individuals and organisations impressed by his values come to his help and this assistance, along with the independence of the Judiciary, is instrumental in his firm being given the license in July 1998. The case represents an in-depth study of a successful example of resistance to political corruption (2003).

The above quote leads us to our next area of focus in this chapter – a critical evaluation of opportunities and barriers of mobile telecoms as an economic development tool in SSA.

## Critical Analysis of Emerging Issues: Introduction to the Case Studies[18]

The opportunities and barriers of mobile telecoms in Africa are taken from *Forbes*. After several years of steady growth in Africa, some sectors of the economy recently started to stagnate. Lower prices for oil and other commodities led to a smaller number of African billionaires than a year ago in *Forbes*' new list of Africa's 50 Richest – 23 billionaires in 2015, down from 28 in 2014 As a group, the continent's wealthiest 50 are worth US$95.6 billion, a decline of US$15 billion from a year ago. Aliko Dangote of Nigeria retains his spot as number one richest African for the fifth year in a row, but his US$16.7 billion net worth is nearly US$5 billion lower than a year ago, a result of a drop in the stock

18 We exclude South Africa for a number of reasons. First, it is widely reported on. Second, it dominates the southern African sub-region. Third, it is no longer the #1 economy in SSA (Nigeria has taken over). Fourth, it is home to Africa's #1 Telco, MTN. *Forbes* points out in its "Africa's 50 Richest 2015: South African Tycoons Overtake Nigerians Amid Economic Weakness" that "South Africans made the best showing on the Africa's richest list this year, occupying 16 spots, up from 11 last years. Nigerians had a smaller representation, with 10 members of the list, down from 13. Eight members hail from Morocco, 7 from Egypt, 3 from Tanzania and 3 from Kenya. There was one each from Algeria, Angola and Uganda." [*Forbes*, 18 November 2015].

price of his Dangote Cement and a weaker Nigerian currency. The methodology of the report clearly indicates the profiling of leading entrepreneurs in the continent:[19]

> Our list tracks the wealth of African citizens who reside on the continent, thus excluding Sudanese-born billionaire Mo Ibrahim, who is a U.K. citizen, and billionaire London resident Mohamed Al-Fayed, an Egyptian citizen. We calculated networths using stock prices and currency exchange rates from the close of business on Friday, November 13 [2015]. To value privately-held businesses, we couple estimates of revenues or profits with prevailing price-to-sales or price-to-earnings ratios for similar public companies.

*Forbes* also reports in its most recent publication that "seven members of the 2014 list dropped off, including mining mogul Desmond Sacco of South Africa and telecom tycoon Strive Masiyiwa of Zimbabwe." (*Forbes*, 18 November 2015). The minimum net worth required to make the list this year was US$330 million, down from US$510 million in 2013.

## The Entrepreneurs Unravelled

### *Mike Adenuga*

Dr. Michael Adeniyi Ishola Adenuga Jr. (CON) was born in 1953, in the ancient city of Ibadan, to Chief Mike Adenuga Senior (his father) a school teacher and the mother, Chief Mrs. Onyindamola Adenuga, a successful businesswoman in Ibadan. It is argued that Mike was influenced by his late mother's business acumen (see Keluro 2011). He attended the famous Ibadan Grammar School, in Oyo State in Southwest Nigeria. He studied Business Administration at Northwestern State University in the United States and went on to earn a Master's degree at Pace University, New York, majoring in Business Administration with emphasis on Marketing. He is also reported to have worked as a taxi driver to support himself while undertaking his MBA in New York. He returned to Nigeria and made his first fortune trading lace and Coca-Cola. Along the way, he made friends with Nigerian military bigwigs who awarded him lucrative state

19 *Forbes* (18 November 2015) Africa's 50 Richest 2015: South African Tycoons Overtake Nigerians Amid Economic Weakness. Retrieved from: http://www.forbes.com/sites/kerryadolan/2015/11/18/africas-50-richest-2015-south-african-tycoons-overtake-nigerians-amid-economic-weakness/#51b20f2772d7.

contracts, which turned out to be the foundation of his fortune.[20] At 63 years of age, Mike Adenuga is the second richest man in Nigeria, with a fortune currently estimated by *Forbes* at US$4.2 billion.[21] He built his fortune in telecom and oil production. Reports show that Mike Adenuga oversees what is generally regarded as one of the continent's largest business empires comprising oil and gas, telecoms, aviation, banking, and real estate. In each of these sectors, Adenuga has moulded his companies into major, if not dominant, players. In the oil and gas sector, for instance, Conoil Plc is one of the largest and most profitable oil marketing companies in Nigeria. His exploration outfit, Conoil Producing, operates six oil blocks in the Niger Delta. Conoil Producing, the downstream arm of the conglomerate, made history by becoming the first Nigerian company to strike oil and produce it in commercial quantity in 1991. He also owns real estate firm Proline Investments, which has hundreds of properties across Nigeria. In the banking sector, Equatorial Trust Bank (ETB) was one of the few banks that effortlessly met the N25 billion capital requirement during the 2005 banking consolidation exercise without going to the stock market and by merging with Devcom Bank, which was also owned by Adenuga. In 2015, ETB merged with Sterling Bank.

In telecoms, his mobile phone network, Globacom (or Glo), is the second largest operator in Nigeria with 32 million subscribers. It also has operations in Ghana and the Republic of Benin. A higher estimate of Glo's revenues led *Forbes* to increase the value assigned to it. Glo is not only the most innovative network in Nigeria, it also, in its first year of operation, became the fastest growing in Africa and the Middle East, with operations in Nigeria, Ghana, Benin Republic, Senegal, Gambia, and Cote d'Ivoire. Adenuga also has a multi-billion-dollar investment in real estate. These companies provide direct employment to thousands of workers and millions of others indirectly. Glo also has operations in Ghana and the Republic of Benin. A higher estimate of Globacom's revenues led *Forbes* to increase the value assigned to it. His latest achievement has been the laying of an international submarine cable, *Glo-1*, which has gigantic capacity, directly from Africa to Europe and America. The fibre optic cable provides excess bandwidth to all the cities connected to the cable, and has led to a much faster and robust connectivity for voice, data, and video. The name Adenuga means different things to different people. A husband, father, team leader, role model, an *entrepreneur par excellence*! Though he has made giant strides in several business categories, Nigerians would probably remember him more for his timely intervention in the telecommunications arena, where he seems to

20 *Forbes* (no date) Profile: Mike Adenuga. Retrieved from: http://www.forbes.com/profile/mike-adenuga/.

21 Ibid.

hold the aces that determine the pace of play. Globacom's historic introduction of Per Second Billing was the first time any network had launched on the billing platform. His network also pioneered such revolutionary products as Blackberry, vehicle tracking, mobile internet, and mobile banking services in Nigeria.

Mike Adenuga is undoubtedly one of the most recognisable names on the African continent. He has been described as "a *quintessential businessman* who has made his mark so distinctly that world leaders speak glowingly about him."[22] In recognition of his accomplishments in business and outstanding contributions to the economic growth of Nigeria, he was awarded an honorary doctorate degree by the Ogun State University. He was also honoured by the Federal Republic of Nigeria with the National Awards of the Officer of the Order of the Niger (OON) and later with the award of Commander of the Order of the Niger (CON). During Nigeria's 50th anniversary celebrations, Adenuga was one of the 50 pre-eminent Nigerians who were conferred with the Special Golden Jubilee Independence Anniversary Awards by the Federal Government of Nigeria. Among his awards was the national honour of Grand Commander of Niger (GCON). As Chairman of the revered Mike Adenuga Group, an entity that has been described as "probably the biggest business empire in Africa," which can "fittingly be summed up as the story of African enterprise."[23] Adenuga has won numerous awards in recognition of his personal and business accomplishments, including the African Telecoms Entrepreneur of the year for his courageous and rapid investment in the telecoms sector. Finally, Adenuga is rarely out of the news on account of several patriotic initiatives. Glo is also the biggest supporter of football in Africa and has raised the profile of football in Nigeria and Ghana with the sponsorship of the English Premier League and national football teams. It has spent over N6 billion on Nigerian football and has also transformed the annual Confederation of African Football (CAF) Awards and made it the most glamorous sports event on the continent. In addition, Glo sponsors the CNN *Inside Africa* programme as well as Manchester United Football Club in England.

---

22 See *News of the People*. Retrieved from: http://www.newsofthepeople-ng.com/mike-adenuga-complete-story-of-the-new-grand-commander-of-business/.

23 Adenuga's nomination was as a result of his immense contributions to the growth of oil and gas, banking, and the telecoms industries in the country. Press briefings praised him for having re-invented the country's telecoms industry. He is also a highly respected entrepreneur and one of the biggest employers in the country. In the last two decades, he has established a pedigree as a well-focused and prudent manager of people and resources, with an uncanny ability to successfully transform ideas and dormant businesses to highly viable enterprises (*Ibid*).

BOX 8.1 AWARDS AND RECOGNITIONS

- 2007 – African Entrepreneur of The Year at the maiden African Telecoms Awards (ATA) on August 15, 2007.
- 2007 – Named *African Entrepreneur of The Year* at the maiden African Telecoms Awards (ATA) on 15 August 2007 (see Keluro, 2011).
- 2010 – Voted Nigeria's Most Outstanding Business Personality in the last 50 years.
- In an online poll conducted by *This Day*, he polled 4272 votes to edge out the Chairman, Dangote Group, Alhaji Aliko Dangote who scored 4156. Founder of Diamond Bank, Mr Pascal Dozie, polled 3316, Ologorun Michael Ibru got 3073 while the Chairman, First City Monument Bank, Otunba Subomi Balogun polled 2801.
- 2009 – Adenuga won the coveted Silverbird Man of the Year Award, polling over 75% of the votes cast to edge out other eminent personalities such as the Governor of Central Bank of Nigeria, Mallam Sanusi Lamido Sanusi, Foreign Affairs Minister, Odein Ajumogobia, and the Akwa Ibom State Governor, Godswill Akpabio, among others. The annual award is facilitated by Silverbird Communications, owners of Silverbird TV and Rhythm 93.7 FM. Similarly, several other media organisations have also honoured the Globacom Chairman with their Man of the Year Award within the last few years.
- CAF has awarded Adenuga, the Pillar of Football in Africa for his strong support for African Football at both national and continental levels. At the 2nd edition of the Glo-CAF Awards held in Ghana, former President John Kufour declared Adenuga Africa's No.1 Businessman for his promotion of the continent through his business empire.
- 2016 – Nigerian Vanguard African Business Man of the Year Award (Osuagwu, 2016).

***Strive Masiyiwa***

Born in 1961 in Southern Rhodesia (now Zimbabwe), Strive Masiyiwa represents a great success story of one of the most prominent Zimbabwean entrepreneurs. Described as a visionary leader, entrepreneur, and philanthropist Masiyiwa attended primary school in Zambia and completed his secondary in Scotland. He went on to obtain a degree in Electrical Engineering in Wales before returning to Zimbabwe in 1984. After working briefly as a telecoms engineer for the state-owned telephone company, he quit his job and set up his own company, Econet Wireless.[24] However, this was not without obstacles, with numerous court battles initially blocking the venture take-off (see Velamuri 2007). Masiyiwa spotted an opportunity in the global rise of cell phone usage, but the government, which had a monopoly in telecommunications, thwarted his plans and refused to grant him a business licence. Masiyiwa appealed to the Constitutional Court of Zimbabwe, on the basis that the refusal constituted a violation of "freedom of expression". After a five-year legal battle, which took him to the brink of bankruptcy, the Zimbabwean court ruled in his favour.

In spite of these issues, Masiyiwa has won numerous accolades (see Box 8.1 for a summary) and gained international recognition for his business expertise and philanthropy. Moreover, he is considered one of Africa's most generous humanitarians and is generally recognised as one of the most prolific philanthropists to ever come out of Africa.

### BOX 8.2 SUMMARY OF MASIYIWA'S HONOURS AND AWARDS (2016)

- 1990 – Zimbabwean Businessman of the Year Award (youngest ever recipient of the award)
- 1998 – Zimbabwean Manager and Entrepreneur of the Year Award.
- 1999 – Junior Chamber International (JCI) – Ten Most Outstanding Young Persons of the World
- 2002 – Times Global Business Influentials List.
- 2003 – CNN/*Time* magazine Poll – 15 Global Influentials of the Year.
- 2010 – Builder of the Modern Africa Award
- 2011 – Forbes Magazine – 20 Most Powerful Business People in African Business.
- 2011 – Times of London – 25 Leaders of Africa's Renaissance Award.
- 2012 – Invited by President Barack Obama to attend G-8 Summit at Camp David, USA.
- 2014 – Fortune Magazine – 50 most influential leaders in the world
- 2015 – Forbes Magazine – 10 Most Powerful Men in Africa list for 2015.
- 2015 – African Business Awards – Lifetime Achievement Award.
- 2015 – Brand Africa Awards – Lifetime Achievement Award.
- 2015 – Freedom Award – International Rescue Committee.

24 The company he created is known to have operations and investments in more than 20 countries, including the UK, US, Latin America, New Zealand, United Arab Emirates, and

He reportedly used his own family fortune to build one of the largest support programmes for educating orphans in SSA. Masiyiwa is also involved in supporting a diverse range of health issues including campaigns against HIV/AIDS, cervical cancer, malnutrition and, more recently, Ebola. He is an avid environmentalist and together with Sir Richard Branson founded the environmental group, the Carbon War Room. Masiyiwa recently took over the chairmanship of AGRA, an organisation that supports Africa's smallholder farmers, a position previously held by the former UN secretary general, Kofi Annan. Masiyiwa is also co-chair of Grow Africa, the investment forum for Africa's agriculture, which has helped mobilise over US$15 billion in investments for African agriculture. He has used his wealth to provide scholarships to over 100,000 young Africans over the past 20 years through his family foundation, as well as providing support for over 40,000 orphans with educational initiatives, in addition to sponsoring students at universities in the US, UK and China. Masiyiwa also funds initiatives in public health and agriculture across the African continent. He is a member of the Bill Gates and Warren Buffett, initiative known as the Giving Pledge. *Forbes Magazine* puts Masiyiwa's personal wealth at US$600 million. *Ventures Africa* recently estimated Masiyiwa to be worth over US$1.4 billion.

### The Companies

#### *Globacom (Glo) Nigeria*

Globacom is Nigeria's second largest mobile phone network after South Africa's MTN.[25] Globacom Limited (or Glo) is a Nigerian multinational telecommunications company headquartered in Lagos, Nigeria. Glo is a privately owned telecommunications carrier that started operations on 29 August 2003.

---

China. Masiyiwa also has interests in the US having partnered with one of America's leading telecoms entrepreneurs, John Stanton, in a venture called Trilogy International Partners, which built New Zealand's third mobile network operator, 2 Degrees. Masiyiwa's investment in Seattle-based Trilogy International has also helped him secure interests as an investor in businesses in Bolivia and the Dominican Republic. Masiyiwa also has a controlling interest in a company based in Vermont, USA, which manufacture nano-fibre carbon products, called Seldon Technologies. One of Masiyiwa's most successful ventures is the London-based privately held Liquid Telecom Group, Africa's largest satellite and fibre optic business spanning over 14 countries.

25 According to *Forbes'* estimates, Mike Adenuga, who is worth US$5.1 billion, made his fortune in mobile telecoms, banking, and oil. Globacom Limited is headquartered at Mike Adenuga Towers, 1, Mike Adenuga Close, Off Adeola Odeku Street, Victoria Island, Lagos. Nigeria. See Globacom's Official Website online at: http://www.gloworld.com/ng/about-us/.

In 2016, the company operates in four countries in West Africa, namely Nigeria, Republic of Benin, Ghana, and Côte d'Ivoire (Efem 2008). As of June 2009, the company has employed more than 2,500 people worldwide. Glo has an estimated 25 million subscribers (June 2009) and it is entirely Nigerian owned. *Glo Gateway* (a subsidiary of Glo arising out of an expansion programme in 2008) is the International Wholesale Voice and Data Exchange Trading Business Unit, which now covers 140 countries under its roaming services, and is currently connected to 235 networks.[26] Since 2008, the growth in Glo's data roaming for mobile phones, laptops, and BlackBerry handsets[27] has now spread to 72 networks in 29 countries (see Remmy 2008), thus making Glo the largest roaming coverage for voice and data in SSA.[28] Glo has two strategic business units, Glo Mobile and Glo Gateway as well as the Glo-1 submarine cable. In its first year of operation, Glo Mobile, a subsidiary of Glo and its Mobile Network Unit, had one million subscribers in over 87 towns in Nigeria, and over N120 billion in revenues (Anon 2009). Glo Mobile has now spread to other African countries, namely Benin (Efem 2008) and Ghana (Remmy 2008). In August 2003, Glo Mobile was launched in Nigeria. Although Glo Mobile was the fourth GSM operator to launch in Nigeria, within seven years of the company's operation, its subscriber base had grown to over 25 million.[29] Glo Mobile is credited with pioneering lower tariffs and the introduction of Per Second billing (which charges subscribers for the exact airtime used) alongside other value-added services such as MMS (Multimedia Messaging Service; see e.g. Madichie 2011a). Others include Glo Magic Plus news and information, vehicle tracking, musical ring-back tones, and mobile banking. In 2009, Glo Mobile launched Blackberry prepaid services giving subscribers options to pay daily, weekly, or monthly for the service including free Yahoo mail access and free Blackberry messenger services. The company also launched 3G High Speed Internet services through the sale of its 3G modem. Glo Mobile 3G network is available in Lagos, Abuja, Benin, and Port Harcourt. Glo Mobile internet service was also launched to provide subscribers with high speed access to all popular internet sites which have been customised for mobile phone browsing.

In 2005, Glo Mobile introduced the Glo Fleet Manager, a comprehensive vehicle tracking solution. Glo Fleet Manager helps transporters/fleet operators manage their fleet. Glo Gateway recently acquired a licence in Côte d'Ivoire.

---

26 See Nweke, Remmy. "eReadiness: Nigeria ranks 94". *Daily Champion*, 25 June 2008.

27 In his analysis of the distribution strategies of Blackberry handsets in Nigeria, Uzo (2015: 216), pointed out that GSM operators such as MTN, Airtel (formerly Econet), Etisalat, and Glo Mobile should be cautiously courted.

28 "Globacom leads Africa, Middle East mobile market with 5.8m subscribers". *IT News*, (http://www.itnewsafrica.com/?p=29).

29 All Africa. Retrieved from: http://allafrica.com/stories/200609140507.html.

As a part of Glo's service offering, Glo Broad Access was launched on 24 November 2009, offering landline telephones, broadband internet, and video, all on a single digital wire line. Glo built a US$800 million high-capacity fibre optic cable known as Glo-1, a submarine cable from the United Kingdom to Nigeria. In May 2008, Glo acquired an operating licence through its Glo Mobile division in Ghana and plans to capture 30 per cent of the current 11 million subscriber market within 18 months of launch. The telco also plans to achieve this goal by launching bundled voice and internet services for Ghana and by specifically targeting "un-serviced" areas outside Ghana's two major cities, Accra and Kumasi. Glo Mobile was set to launch in Ghana in the first quarter of 2010. This has, however, was postponed to the third quarter of 2011, and again to 2012. In June 2008, Glo Mobile was launched in Benin. Glo Mobile demonstrated an unprecedented growth through the sale of 600,000 SIM cards in the first ten days of operation. In October 2009, Glo acquired submarine cable landing rights and International Gateway Services in Côte d'Ivoire. On 8 April 2011, Glo launched the sub-marine optical fibre Glo-1, one part of its maiden operation in Ghana, to usher in another major player in the Ghana telecommunication industry.[30] Glo-1 is the first successful submarine cable from the United Kingdom to Nigeria, and Glo is reportedly the first individual African company to embark on such a project. Glo-1 has the potential to provide high speed internet services and faster, more reliable, and cheaper telecom services. Glo-1 will potentially facilitate foreign investment and employment opportunities especially to Africans. The 9,800-km-long cable originates from Bude[31] in the UK and is laid from this location to Alpha Beach in Lagos, where it will have its landing station. Glo-1 will also improve teleconferencing, distance learning, disaster recovery and telemedicine among several other benefits for Nigerians and the people of West Africa.

### *Econet Wireless*

Founded in 1993 in Zimbabwe by Strive Masiyiwa, Econet Wireless is a diversified telecoms group with operations and investments in Africa, Europe, South America, and the East Asia Pacific Rim. It provides products and services in the core areas of mobile and fixed telephony services, broadband, satellite, fibre optical networks, and mobile payments. Econet's other activities include enterprise networks, financial services, renewable energy, and solar-powered solutions (Solarway Industries). By 1998, Econet Wireless Zimbabwe had its first mobile phone subscribers and was listed on the local stock exchange. Within a few years it was the second largest company in the country. In 2000,

30 In January 2012, Glo Ghana launched the "Reserve your number" campaign, but still without opening the network.

31 A seaside town in Cornwall, UK.

Masiyiwa moved to South Africa and founded the Econet Wireless Group, an organisation entirely separate from the Zimbabwean company with partners in Botswana, Kenya, Lesotho, Nigeria, Rwanda, and Burundi. He has interests in mobile phone operations in more than 20 countries on several continents. Some of the key businesses that he established with partners include Econet Wireless International, Econet Wireless Global, Mascom Wireless Botswana, Econet Wireless Nigeria (now Airtel Nigeria), Econet Satellite Services, Lesotho Telecom, Econet Wireless Burundi, Rwanda Telecom, Econet Wireless South Africa, Solarway, and Transaction Processing Systems (TPS). Masiyiwa also has interests in mobile operations in New Zealand, Bolivia, and the Dominican Republic.

## Summary, Conclusions and Implications

The main focus of this chapter has been to highlight the current state and challenges of enterprise development in SSA from the standpoint of two entrepreneurial ventures in a sector that has a key role to play in the region's economic development, i.e. the telecoms sector. Two divergent markets – Nigeria and Zimbabwe – were used as case studies. In the first case, the literature on entrepreneurship or enterprise development in Nigeria is replete (Abereijo, 2015; Abubakar, 2015; Abimbola, & Agboola, 2011; Alarape, 2009; Aderemi et al., 2008). However, the same cannot be said of the under-researched Zimbabwean context. In both cases, the focus of entrepreneurship research has been primarily on the SME sector, as highlighted in Tables 8.1 and 8.2. By extending the entrepreneurship discourse to the large business sector, epitomised by the two telecom giants in this chapter,[32] it is possible to argue that the value of this chapter lies in its ability to explore the less known from the context of the well-known.

As demonstrated in this chapter, the entrepreneurial landscape is fraught with challenges, which are, more often than not, institutional in their configuration. Whether it is Nigeria or Zimbabwe, economic environment is largely dictated by the political ruling class – the latter dictating the pace and scope of enterprise development. In the case of Zimbabwe for instance, the ruling political party, ZANU-PF, reportedly abandoned its pre-independence revolutionary promises of fundamental structural change (while retaining the rhetoric) in favour of a pragmatic accommodation of the capitalist sector, at the same time implementing a welfare social policy and boosting the peasant economy with

32 Similar to the methodology adopted for this chapter, Ajai (2015) adopted a case study approach in his investigation of African firms from South Africa and Nigeria examining other SSA markets such as Nigeria, Kenya and Ghana.

subsidies and infrastructural development (Government of Zimbabwe, 2007a, 2007b, 2009, 2010, 2011a, 2011b). This paved the way for a complex network of patrons and clients mediating the allocation of scarce resources. This "neo-patrimonial" process meant that the reciprocal needs and expectations of individuals, corporate entities, and the state are asymmetrically negotiated, with businesses needing to be close to powerful politicians in order to create and protect their investments. This practice seems common across SSA. As Handley (2008: 5) pointed out, "in Zimbabwe and other African countries, it is generally easy for a clique of state-based elites to promulgate policies furthering their own interests." In the specific case of Zimbabwe, the regime attempted to establish a new business class by issuing foreign currency licences to aspiring black businesses (what can be described as aggressive indigenisation). However, anyone obtaining licences could charge a massive premium merely by "selling" them to established businesses – without the attendant costs or other business risks. This ultimately led to the development of a class of "briefcase businessmen" hustling for the "best bidder" and reaping enormous returns in the process – thus bringing about an elite of political businessmen whose positions and profits depended, not on productivity, but on connections to the ruling Party and other political connections (Otieno 2009).[33]

Going forward, there is urgent need to establish a dynamic balance of the diverse institutional logics with a view to redefining an effective turnaround strategy for sustainable entrepreneurship development in SSA. There remains an urgent need to support, and not vilify, the observed entrepreneurial initiatives of not just small firms, but also medium to large enterprises, and especially indigenous enterprises with the potential to bring about an economic transformation of the region. It is also evident that the telecoms sector has far-reaching implications for other sectors, such as the financial institutions (micro-finance houses, banks, and mobile-payment firms), media and entertainment, as well as the agricultural sectors that have been identified as SSA's new frontiers for economic development.

33 At the other end of the spectrum, a challenge to the regime coalesced around the Zimbabwe Congress of Trade Unions (ZCTU). Created in 1980 by the state, the ZCTU was essentially a department of ZANU headed by Mugabe's brother, but by 1989, it had achieved some independence with Morgan Tsvangirai as its General Secretary. The ZCTU became instrumental in the formation of the National Constitutional Assembly in 1997 and then the Movement for Democratic Change (MDC) in 1999. The MDC was able to aggregate a disparate range of forces opposed to ZANU-PF: workers, students, middle-class urbanites, white commercial farmers and, combining the financial resources of both urban black and rural white capital with the numerical strength of the working class, mounted a significant challenge to the monopoly on power that ZANU-PF had enjoyed for 20 years.

## References

Abereijo, I.O. (2015). "Transversing the 'Valley of Death': Understanding the Determinants to Commercialization of Research Outputs in Nigeria", *African Journal of Economic and Management Studies*, 6(1), 90–106. Doi: http://dx.doi.org/10.1108/AJEMS-10-2012-0066.

Abimbola, O.H. & G.M. Agboola. (2011). "Environmental Factors and Entrepreneurship Development in Nigeria", *Journal of Sustainable Development in Africa*, 13(4), 166–176.

Abubakar, H.A. (2015). "Entrepreneurship Development and Financial Literacy in Africa", *World Journal of Entrepreneurship, Management and Sustainable Development*, 11(4), 281–294.

Adelowo, C., Ilori, M., Siyanbola, W. & B. Oluwale. (2015). "Technological Learning Mechanisms in Nigeria's Technology Incubation Centre", *African Journal of Economic and Management Studies*, 6(1), 72–89. Doi: http://dx.doi.org/10.1108/AJEMS-10-2014-0071.

Aderemi, H.O., IIori, M.O., Siyanbola, W.O., Adegbite, S.A. & I.O. Abereijo. (2008). "An Assessment of the Choice and Performance of Women Entrepreneurs in Technological and Non-Technological Enterprises in South-Western Nigeria", *African Journal of Business Management*, 2(10), 165–176.

Ajai, O. (2015). "Failure of Africa-to-Africa Internationalization: Key Factors and Lessons". In: I. Adeleye, K. Ibeh, A. Kinoti & L. White (eds) *The Changing Dynamics of International Business in Africa*, London: Palgrave, 148–168.

Akinyoade, A. & C.U. Uche. (2016). "Dangote Cement: An African Success Story?" ASC Working Paper #131. African Studies Centre Leiden (ASCL), Leiden, The Netherlands. https://openaccess.leidenuniv.nl/handle/1887/38674.

Alarape, A. (2009). "On the Road to Institutionalising Entrepreneurship Education in Nigerian Universities", *International Journal of Management Education*, 7(2), 81–86.

Anon (2009). "Globacom may acquire NITEL", *Daily Champion*, 16 September 2009. Last accessed 27 August 2015.

Archibong, C.A. (2010). "Entrepreneurship as a Critical and Missing Factor in Economic Development of Poor Nations: A Systematic Analysis of Factors of Production", *The IUP Journal of Business Strategies*, 7(1/2), 1–2.

Aruwa, S.A.S. (2006). *Entrepreneurial development, small and medium enterprises*. Kaduna: Entrepreneurship Academy Publishing.

Bond, P. & M. Manyanya. (2003). *Zimbabwe's Plunge: Exhausted Nationalism, Neoliberalism and the Search for Social Justice*. Harare, Pietermaritzburg and London: Weaver Press, University of KwaZulu-Natal Press and Merlin Press.

Braathen, E. (2004). "Institutions Matter: Engineers and Telecommunication Development in Mozambique and Zimbabwe". *Telematics and Informatics*, 21(1), 25–47.

Bratton, M. & E. Masunungure. (2011). *The Anatomy of Political Predation: Leaders, Elites and Coalitions in Zimbabwe, 1980–2010*. West Perth: Developmental Leadership Program.

Brett, E.A. (2005). "From Corporatism to Liberalisation in Zimbabwe Economic Policy Regimes and Political Crisis (1980–1997)". Working Paper 58 (Series 1). London: Crisis States Research Centre.

Bruton, G.D., Ahlstom, D. & K. Obloj. (2008). "Entrepreneurship in Emerging Economies: Where are we Today and Where should the Research Go in the Future", *Entrepreneurship Theory and Practice*, 32(1), 1042–2587.

Carter, S. & W. Wilton. (2006a). "Enterprise Culture: Necessary in Promoting Enterprise; Lessons from Enterprise Development in Zimbabwe". *Journal of Enterprising Culture*, 14(3), 177–198. Doi: 10.1142/S021849580600012X.

Carter, S & W. Wilton. (2006b). "Don't Blame the Entrepreneur, Blame Government: The Centrality of Government in Enterprise Development. Lessons from Enterprise Failure in Zimbabwe". *Journal of Enterprising Culture*, 14(1), 65–84.

Cheater, A.P. (1984). *Idioms of Accumulation: Rural Development and Class Formation among Freeholders in Zimbabwe*. Gweru: Mambo Press.

Chikweche, T. & R. Fletcher. (2011). "Branding at the Base of Pyramid: A Zimbabwean Perspective". *Marketing Intelligence & Planning*, 29(3), 247–263.

Chivasa, S. (2014). Entrepreneurship culture among SMEs in Zimbabwe: A case of Bulawayo SMEs. *International Journal of Economic, Commerce and Management*, 11(9), 1–13.

Curwen P. & J. Whalley. (2011). "The Restructuring of African Mobile Telecommunications Provision and the Prospects for Economic Development", *info*, 12 (2), 53–71.

Curwen P. & J. Whalley. (2008). "Structural Change in Latin American and African Mobile Telecommunications Markets", *Telecommunications Policy*, 32(5), 349–363.

Daniels, L. (2003). Factors that influence the expansion of the microenterprise sector: results from three national surveys in Zimbabwe. *Journal of International Development*, 15(6), 675–692.

Davies, R. (2004). "Memories of Underdevelopment: A Personal Interpretation of Zimbabwe's Economic Decline". In: B. Raftopoulos & T. Savage (eds), *Zimbabwe: Injustice and Political Reconciliation*, Cape Town: Institute for Justice and Reconciliation, 19–41.

Dawson, M., & Kelsall, T. (2012). Anti-Developmental Patrimonialism in Zimbabwe. *Journal of Contemporary African Studies*, 30(1), 49–66.

Devarajan, S., Easterly, W. & H. Pack. (2001). "Is Investment in Africa Too High or Too Low? Macro- and Micro-Evidence". *Journal of African Economies*, 10 (supplement 2), 81–108.

*Doing Business* (2016). "Measuring Regulatory Quality and Efficiency". 13th Edition. Washington DC: The World Bank. Retrieved from: http://www.doingbusiness.org/~/media/GIAWB/Doing%20Business/Documents/Annual-Reports/English/DB16-Full-Report.pdf.

Dolan, K. (*Forbes*, 18 November 2015). "Africa's 50 Richest 2015: South African Tycoons Overtake Nigerians amid Economic Weakness". Retrieved from: http://www.forbes.com/sites/kerryadolan/2015/11/18/africas-50-richest-2015-south-african-tycoons-overtake-nigerians-amid-economic-weakness/.

Edoho, M. (2015). "Entrepreneurship and Socioeconomic Development", *African Journal of Economic and Management Studies*, 6(2), 127–147. Doi: http://dx.doi.org/10.1108/AJEMS-03-2013-0030.

Efem, N. (2008). "Benin: Glo Launches Network in Country Today", *All Africa*, 5 June. Last accessed 27 August 2015.

Forrest, T.G. (1994). *The Advance of African Capital: The Growth of Nigerian Private Enterprise*. University of Virginia Press.

Gillwald, A. & M. Mureithi. (2011). "Regulatory Intervention or Disruptive Competition? Lessons from East Africa on the End of International Mobile Roaming Charges", *info*, 13(3), 32–46.

Globacom (n.d.). "Globacom, Nigeria's Second-Largest Mobile Phone Network". Globacom Limited, Mike Adenuga Towers, 1, Mike Adenuga Close, Off Adeola Odeku Street, Victoria Island, Lagos. Nigeria. http://www.gloworld.com/ng/about-us/.

*Global Witness* (2002). "Branching Out: Zimbabwe's Resource Colonialism in Democratic Republic of Congo". London: Global Witness.

Goredema, C. (2003). "Zimbabwe". In: P. Gastrow (ed.), *Penetrating State and Business Organised Crime in Southern Africa*, London: Institute for Strategic Studies. http://www.iss.co.za/pubs/Monographs/No89/Chap1.htm, last accessed 26 July 2010.

Goodstein, J.D. & S.R. Velamuri. (2009). "States, Power, Legitimacy, and Maintaining Institutional Control: The Battle for Private Sector Telecommunication Services in Zimbabwe". *Organization Studies*, 30(5): 489–508.

Government of Zimbabwe (2007a). Indigenisation and Economic Empowerment Act, [Chapter 14:33] 2007.

Government of Zimbabwe (2007b). Mid-Year Monetary Policy Statement issued in Terms of the Reserve Bank of Zimbabwe Act, 1 October, 2007.

Government of Zimbabwe (2009). Statement on the 2009 Budget, Government of Zimbabwe, the Ministry of Finance, 17 March, 2009.

Government of Zimbabwe (2010). The 2010 National Budget Statement, Government of Zimbabwe, Ministry of Finance, 2 December 2009.

Government of Zimbabwe (2011a). Monetary Policy Statement issued in Terms of the Reserve Bank of Zimbabwe Act. January, 2011.

Government of Zimbabwe (2011b). Supplement to the Monetary Policy Statement issued in Terms of the Reserve Bank of Zimbabwe Act, July 2011.

Government of Zimbabwe (2011c). Mid-Term Fiscal Policy Review Statement, July 2011.

Gu, J. (2009). "China's Private Enterprises in Africa and the Implications for African Development". *European Journal of Development Research*, *21*(4), 570–587.

Handley, A. (2008). *Business and the State in Africa: Economic Policy-Making in the Neo-Liberal Era*. Cambridge: Cambridge University Press.

Hoffman, D. (2006). "South African Cellular Wars in Nigeria". *International Journal of Emerging Markets*, 1(1) 84–95.

*Horizon* (1992). "How Zanu (PF) Built a Capitalist Empire". Harare: *Horizon Magazine*.

Iliffe, J. (1983). *Emergence of African Capitalism*. London: The MacMillan Press.

Inegbenebor, A.U. (2006). Financing Small and Medium Industries in Nigeria-Case Study of the Small and Medium Industries Equity Investment Scheme (SMIEIS): Empirical Research Findings. *Journal of Financial Management & Analysis*, 19(1), 71–80.

Inegbenebor, A.U. (2006). You can be an entrepreneur. In A.U. Inegbenebor (ed). *The fundamentals of entrepreneurship*. (1st Ed), pp. 1–14, Lagos: Malthouse Press Limited.

Inititative for Global Development, 5 May 2011. Retrieved from: http://www.igdleaders.org/wp-content/uploads/New-Report-Showcases-Growth-of-Sub-Saharan-African-Multinational-Corporations.pdf

Inyang, B.J. & R.O. Enuoh. (2009). "Entrepreneurial Competencies: The Missing Links to Successful Entrepreneurship in Nigeria". *International Business Research*, 2(2), 62–71.

Jackson, R.H. & C.G. Rosberg. (1984). "Personal Rule: Theory and Practice in Africa", *Comparative Politics* 16, No. 4: 421–42.

Jagun A., Heeks R. & J. Whalley. (2008). "The Impact of Mobile Telephony on Developing Country Micro-Enterprises: A Nigerian Case Study", *Information Technology & International Development*, 4(4), 47–65.

Janssens-Bevernage, A. (2002). Capacity-building for private-sector development, The Southern African Enterprise Network (SAEN). Discussion Paper 38 (Maastricht: ECDPM).

Jones, J. (2010). "'Nothing is Straight in Zimbabwe': The Rise of the Kukiya-kiya Economy 2000–2008", *Journal of Southern African Studies*, 36(2), 285–299.

Justice for Agriculture. (2002). "Confirmed VIPs allocations". Harare: JAG. http://www.zimbabwesituation. com/VIP_farm_allocations.pdf. Last accessed 5 May 2015.

Karabag, S. & C. Berggren. (2011). "Mobile Communications in Turkey: From First Mover Advantages to Management Capabilities", *info*, 13(2), 72–84.

Keluro, Caesar (*Business News*, 8 November 2011) "Mike Adenuga. An Entrepreneur with the Nine Lives". http://businessnews.com.ng/2011/11/08/mike-adenuga-an-entrepreneur-with-the-nine-lives/. Accessed 7 July 2015.

Kraus, J. (2002). "Capital, Power and Business Associations in the African Political Economy: A Tale of Two Countries, Ghana and Nigeria". *The Journal of Modern African Studies*, *40*(3), 395–436.

Kuada, J. (2015) "Entrepreneurship in Africa – A Classificatory Framework and a Research Agenda", *African Journal of Economic and Management Studies*, 6(2), 148–163. Doi: http://dx.doi.org/10.1108/AJEMS-10-2014-0076.

Levy, B. (2010). "Development Trajectories: An Evolutionary Approach to Integrating Governance and Growth", *Economic Premise 15*. Washington, DC: World Bank.

Lindvert, M., Yazdanfar, D. & H. Boter. (2015). "Perceptions of Financial Sources among Women Entrepreneurs in Tanzania", African *Journal of Economic and Management Studies*, 6(2), 197–218.

Madichie, N. (2016). "The Business of Saving Lives in Sub-Saharan Africa (SSA). A Social Imperative? Insights from 'The Global Soap Project'", *Journal of Enterprising Communities: People and Places in the Global Economy*,10(3), 321–342.

Madichie, N. (2011a). "A Preliminary Assessment of Middle East Investments in Sub-Saharan Africa: Insights from the Mobile Telecoms Sector". *Thunderbird International Business Review*, 53(1), 79–92.

Madichie, N. (2011b). "Setting an Agenda for Women Entrepreneurship in Nigeria: A Commentary on Faseke's Journey through Time for 'The Nigerian Woman'", *Gender in Management: An International Journal*, 26(3), 212–219.

Madichie, N. (2010). "Putting Melville on the World Stage – Let's Hear it from Lize Kruger, CEO of Life on 3rd", *Enterprising Matters*. Official magazine of the Institute of Small Business and Entrepreneurship. Online at: http://www.isbe.org.uk/lifeonthird.

Madichie, N. (2009). "Breaking the Glass Ceiling in Nigeria: A Review of Women Entrepreneurship", *Journal of African Business*, 10(1), 51–66.

Madichie, N. (2007). "Nigerian Restaurants in London: Bridging the Experiential Perception/Expectation Gap", *International Journal of Business and Globalisation*, 1(2), 258–271.

Madichie, N. & A. Katwalo. (2008a). "Entrepreneurial and Cultural Dynamics: A Gender Kaleidoscope of Ugandan Microenterprise", *International Journal of Entrepreneurship and Small Business*. 5(3/4), 337–348.

Madichie, N. & A. Nkamnebe, A. (2008b). "Cultural Determinants of Entrepreneurial Emergence in a Typical Sub-Sahara African Context", *Journal of Enterprising Communities: People and Places in the Global Economy*, 2(4), 285–299.

Magure, B. (2012). Foreign investment, black economic empowerment and militarised patronage politics in Zimbabwe. *Journal of Contemporary African Studies*, 30(1), 67–82.

Majumdar, S. (2011). "Do Cross-Subsidies Hinder Telecommunications Market Entry?" *Info*, 13(2), 85–96.

Makanyeza, C., & Dzvuke, G. (2015). The influence of innovation on the performance of small and medium enterprises in Zimbabwe. *Journal of African Business*, 16(1–2), 198–214.

Maphosa, F. (1998). "Towards the Sociology of Zimbabwean Indigenous Entrepreneurship", *Zambezia*, 25(2), 173–190.

Marsden, K. (1990), "African entrepreneurs: pioneers of development", International Finance Corporation Discussion Paper No. 9, World Bank, Washington, DC.

McCormick, D. (1999). "African Enterprise Clusters and Industrialization: Theory and Reality". *World Development*, 27(9), 1531–1551.

McDade, B.E. & A. Spring. (2005). "The 'New Generation of African Entrepreneurs': Networking to Change the Climate for Business and Private Sector-Led Development", *Entrepreneurship & Regional Development*, 17(1), 17–42, doi:10.1080/0898562042000310714.

Meagher, K. (2006). "Social Capital, Social Liabilities, and Political Capital: Social Networks and Informal Manufacturing in Nigeria", *African Affairs*, 105(421), 553–582.

Moyo, J.N. (1992). "State Politics and Social Domination in Zimbabwe", *The Journal of Modern African Studies*, 30(2), 305–330.

Mpofu, K.C. (2015). "Building Networks for Success of SMEs in Africa", *A Guide to Commonwealth Markets*. Published by Globaltrader in association with the British Chambers of Commerce and the Institute of Export (IOE).

Munslow, B. (1980). "Zimbabwe's Emerging African Bourgeoisie", *Review of African Political Economy*, 7(19): 63–69. http://dx.doi.org/10.1080/03056248008703441.

Ncube, G., & Gomez, G. (2011). Local economic development and migrant remittances in rural Zimbabwe. *ISS Working Paper Series/General Series*, 523, 1–26.

Nest, M. (2001). "Ambitions, Profits and Loss: Zimbabwean Economic Involvement in the Democratic Republic of the Congo", *African Affairs*, 100: 469–490.

Nicholas, S.M. (1994). "The State and the Development of African Capitalism in Zimbabwe". In: B.J. Berman & C. Leys (eds), *African Capitalists in African Development*. Boulder CA: Lynne Rienner Publishers.

Nigeria Investment Promotion Commission (2004). *Overview of small and medium scale enterprises in Nigeria*. An Information Booklet, Abuja.

Noko, J. (2011). "Dollarization: The Case of Zimbabwe", *Cato Journal*, 31(2), 339–365.

Nyamwanza, T., Mavhiki, S., Mapetere, D., & Nyamwanza, L. (2014). An Analysis of SMEs' Attitudes and Practices Toward Tax Compliance in Zimbabwe. *SAGE Open*, 4(3), 2158244014542776.

Obamuyi, T.M. (2009). "Credit Delivery and Sustainability of Micro-Credit Schemes in Nigeria", *Journal of Enterprising Communities: People and Places in the Global Economy*, 3(1), 71–83.

Ojong, C.M. (2005). Starting a new business. In S.N. Udo (ed). *Entrepreneurial development: principles and practice*. pp. 43–45, Calabar: Wusen Press.

Ostergaard, T. (1994). "The Role of the National Bourgeoisie in National Development: The Case of the Textile and Clothing Industries in Zimbabwe". In: B.J. Berman & C. Leys (eds), *African Capitalists in African Development*, Boulder, CA: Lynne Rienner, 115–137.

Osuagwu, P. (*Nigerian Vanguard*, 3 January 2016). "Nigeria: Mike Adenuga, Jnr: The Triumph of African Enterprise". Retrieved from: http://allafrica.com/stories/201601042669.html. Accessed 7 July 2016.

Otieno, G. (2009). *Baseline Study of Anti-Corruption at an Institutional Level in Zimbabwe*. Harare: Multi-donor Trust Fund.

Oxford Business Group (22 April 2016). "Nigeria's Shifting Telecoms Landscape". Retrieved from: http://www.oxfordbusinessgroup.com/news/nigeria%E2%80%99s-shifting-telecoms-landscape.

Oxford Business Group (24 April 2015). "A Handful of Mobile Operators Dominate Nigeria's Rapidly Expanding Telecoms Sector". Retrieved from: http://www.oxfordbusinessgroup.com/news/nigeria%E2%80%99s-shifting-telecoms-landscape.

Pache, A. & F. Santos. (2010). "When Worlds Collide: The Internal Dynamics of Organizational Responses to Conflicting Institutional Demands", *Academy of Management Review*, 35(3): 455–476.

Partnership Africa Canada. (2010). *Diamonds and Clubs the Militarized Control of Diamonds and Power in Zimbabwe*. Ottawa: Partnership Africa Canada.

Pedersen, P.O. (1992). Entrepreneurs and managers in Zimbabwes district service centres. *Entrepreneurship & Regional Development*, 4(1), 57–72.

Raftopoulos, B. (2005). "The Zimbabwean Crisis and the Challenges for the Left". Public Lecture, 23 June, University of Kwa-Zulu Natal.

Raftopoulos, B. (1996). "Fighting for Control: The Indigenization Debate in Zimbabwe", *Southern Africa Report*, 11(4), 3–7.

Raftopoulos, B. (2000). "The State, NGOs and Democratisation". In: S. Moyo, J. Makumbe & B. Raftopoulos (eds), Harare: SAPES Books, 21–45.

Raftopoulos, B. & D. Compagnon. (2003). "Indigenization, the State Bourgeoisie and Neo-authoritarian Politics". In: S. Darnolf & L. Laakso (eds), *Twenty Years of Independence in Zimbabwe: From Liberation to Authoritarianism,* New York: Palgrave, 15–33.

Ramachandran, V. and Shah, M. K. (1999). Minority entrepreneurs and firm performance, Sub-Saharan Africa. Journal of Development Studies, 36 (2): 71–87.

Remmy, N. (2008). "E-Readiness: Nigeria Ranks 94", *Daily Champion*, 25 June 2008. Last accessed 14 September 2015.

Richardson, C.J. (2005). "The Loss of Property Rights and the Collapse of Zimbabwe", *Cato Journal*, 25(3), 541–565.

Sandbrook, R. (1985). *The* Politics of Africa's *Economic Stagnation*. Cambridge: Cambridge University Press.

Saunders, R. (2008). "Crisis, Capital, Compromise: Mining and Empowerment in Zimbabwe", *African Sociological Review*, 12(1), 67–89.

Seekings, J. & N. Nattrass. (2011). "State-Business Relations and Pro-Poor Growth in South Africa", *Journal of International Development*, 23(3), 338–357.

Sen, K. & D.W. te Velde. (2009). "State Business Relations and Economic Growth in Sub-Saharan Africa", *Journal of Development Studies*, 45(8), 1267–1283.

Singh, S., Simpson, R., Mordi, C. & C. Okafor. (2011). "Motivation to Become an Entrepreneur: A Study of Nigerian Women's Decisions", *African Journal of Economic and Management Studies*, 2(2), 202–219.

Smith, W.K. & M.W. Lewis. (2011). "Toward a Theory of Paradox: A Dynamic Equilibrium Model of Organizing", *Academy of Management Review*, 36(2): 381–403.

Stoneman, C. & L. Cliffe. (1989). *Zimbabwe: Politics, Economics and Society*. London: Pinter Publishers.

Sutherland, E. (2011). "International Mobile Roaming in the Arab States", *info*, 13(2), 35–52.

Tambudzai, Z. (2003). "Privatisation: A Review of the Zimbabwean Experience 1991–2002", *Africana Bulletin*, 51: 165–203.

Tangri, R. (1998). "Politics, Capital and the State in Sub-Saharan Africa", *Commonwealth & Comparative Politics*, *36*(2), 108–122.

Tangri, R.K. (1999). *The Politics of Patronage in Africa: Parastatals, Privatization, and Private Enterprise*. Asmara, Eritrea: Africa World Press.

The Confederation of Zimbabwe Industries (2010). *The Confederation of Zimbabwe Industries (CZI) 2010 Manufacturing Survey*. Harare, Zimbabwe.

UNDP (2008). *Comprehensive Economic Recovery in Zimbabwe: A Discussion Document*. Harare: UNDP.

United Nations (2001). "Report of the Panel of Experts on the Illegal Exploitation of Natural Resources and other Forms of Wealth of the Democratic Republic of the Congo". New York: United Nations.

Uzo, U. (2015) "Research in Motion/ BlackBerry: Managing Channel Conflicts in Nigeria". In: I. Adeleye, K. Ibeh, A. Kinoti & L. White. (eds) *The Changing Dynamics of International Business in Africa*. London: Palgrave, 205–219.

Velamuri, S.R. (2007). "Resisting Political Corruption: Econet Wireless Zimbabwe (Research Case Study)". SSRN Working Paper Series.

Velamuri, S.R. (2003). *Resisting Political Corruption: Econet Wireless Zimbabwe (Research Case Study)*. Shanghai: China Europe International Business School. Available at SSRN 1009452.

Venkataraman, J.D. (1997). "The Distinctive Domain of Entrepreneurship Research", *Advances in Entrepreneurship, Firm Emergence and Growth*, 3: 119–138. JAI Press.

Wild, V. (1997). *Profit not for Profit's Sake: History and Business Culture of African Entrepreneurs in Zimbabwe*. Harare: Baobab Books.

Wilton, W. (2015). Want to support enterprise development in developing countries? Think about the other salient factors. An investigation of Zimbabwe and Pacific Island countries. *International Journal of Entrepreneurship and Small Business*, 25(3), 282–295.

World Bank, The. (2010). *Africa Development Indicators 2010*. Washington, DC: World Bank.

Xavier, P. & D. Ypsilanti. (2011). "Geographically Segmented Regulation for Telecommunications: Lessons from Experience", *info*, 13(2), 3–18.

CHAPTER 9

# The Development of Entrepreneurship in Sudan

*Yagoub Ali Gangi and Hesham E. Mohammed*

## Introduction

Entrepreneurship is one of the important driving forces for an economy. It can generate job opportunities, invent technology, introduce new products, enhance economic growth and promote socio-economic development for countries (Gangi and Timan 2013; Gangi 2015). Countries with an improved entrepreneurial ecosystem and a high level of entrepreneurial activity tend to be economically developed and their people are socio-economically well off. Consequently, many developed countries throughout the globe have recognised the importance of entrepreneurship and made efforts in this regard, including allocating significant resources for its development. As part of these efforts, many studies have been carried out to identify the state of entrepreneurship in those countries and determine the main factors that contribute to their development. However, the case in developing countries is somehow different. Few countries have realised the importance of entrepreneurship for their economy. Therefore, few studies have been undertaken to examine the state of entrepreneurship development and its driving forces in those countries. As is the case in most developing countries, studies on entrepreneurship development in Sudan are rare. Moreover, Sudan is not covered by the Global Entrepreneurship Monitor (GEM) reports. As a result, there is no adequate information about entrepreneurial activities in Sudan and there is a literature gap in this field of study.

The little evidence available about the state of entrepreneurship in Sudan indicates that Sudan is entrepreneurially underdeveloped. A study undertaken by Gangi and Timan (2013) has indicated that the entrepreneurial environment is poor and suffers from various weaknesses. Moreover, the World Bank's Doing Business reports ranked Sudan at the bottom of the listed countries. Indeed, different studies undertaken by the World Bank reveal that entrepreneurial activities are very low compared to other countries in the region (World Bank 2015). The main objective of the present chapter is to explore the state of entrepreneurship in Sudan. Moreover, it aims to examine the role of national factors in shaping and constraining the entrepreneurship state in Sudan.

 | DOI 10.1163/9789004351615_010

### Background on the Sudanese Economy

Sudan is a lower-middle-income country with a gross domestic product (GDP) per capita income of about $US 1500 and, in 2015, a total population of 39 million, with an average annual population growth rate of about 3 per cent. This high population growth rate has resulted in a relatively young population and a high proportion of the labour force being of a productive working age. An average of about 55 per cent of the total population are between the ages of 15 and 64 years, and creating enough jobs for them is a major challenge (African Economic Outlook 2015). Moreover, about 66 per cent of the total population lives in rural areas with little access to quality education and health services. Thus, a large proportion of Sudanese suffer from illiteracy, poverty, unemployment, high mortality at birth and low life expectancy. These factors have resulted in Sudan been ranked very low in terms of human development indicators. Furthermore, Sudan economy is characterised by public sector domination of the productive sector, leaving limited room for the private sector to expand. Even the slim private sector is largely dominated by informal sectors, which remains the most important source of production and employment (Country Watch 2015).

The main characteristic of the Sudanese economy is that it depends largely on the agricultural sector and it can be described as an agricultural economy and largely driven by natural resources extraction. Historically, and for a long period, agriculture has been the main source of economic activity in Sudan. It used to contribute more than 50 per cent of GDP, more than 90 per cent of foreign currency and provided employment opportunities for more than 80 per cent of the population. However, at the beginning of the twenty-first century, the situation has changed, with the exploitation of petrol and Sudan embarking on the export of crude oil. The contribution of agriculture to GDP has gradually fallen to around 35 per cent by the end of 2010. During the period 2000 to 2010, the oil sector drove much of Sudan's GDP growth and the economy boomed on the back of rising oil production and high oil prices. Thus, petrol became the main source of foreign currency and its contribution equated to over 70 per cent of total value of exports. But after South Sudan's secession in 2011, Sudan lost most of its oil fields. Since then, it has struggled to stabilise its economy and compensate for the loss of foreign exchange earnings. As a result of this shock, GDP growth dropped from an average of 6 per cent before 2011 to less than 3 per cent in 2014, and the rate of inflation increased from an average of 10 per cent to 36.7 per cent for the same period.

Sudan has experienced a central economic planning system for most periods since its independence in 1956. This planning system has resulted in the

TABLE 9.1 *Macroeconomic indicators*

| Indicator | 1990 | 2000 | 2006 | 2007 | 2008 | 2009 | 2010 | 2011 | 2012 | 2013 | 2014 |
|---|---|---|---|---|---|---|---|---|---|---|---|
| GDP (current price billion US$) | 12.4 | 12.2 | 35.8 | 45.8 | 54.8 | 53.1 | 65.6 | 67.5 | 62.3 | 66.4 | 73.8 |
| GDP growth | −5.5 | 6.3 | 10.1 | 11.5 | 7.8 | 3.2 | 3.5 | −2.0 | −2.2 | 3.3 | 3.1 |
| Inflation | 66.2 | 9.9 | 9.4 | 6.7 | 14.2 | 4.0 | 19.6 | 21.0 | 27.6 | 36.7 | 29.9 |
| Agriculture % | 40.6 | 42.2 | 29.8 | 26.7 | 25.8 | 26.3 | 24.6 | 25.4 | 28.8 | 29.2 | 29.2 |
| Industry % | 15.3 | 20.8 | 27.8 | 30.6 | 33.4 | 24.6 | 28.4 | 27.4 | 22.4 | 20.9 | 20.4 |
| Services % | 44.2 | 37.0 | 42.4 | 42.7 | 40.8 | 49.2 | 47.0 | 47.2 | 48.8 | 49.9 | 50.4 |

SOURCE: WORLD BANK 2016

emergence of a large public sector that dominates economic activities, leaving limited room for the private sector to evolve. Therefore, historically, the contribution of the private sector to Sudan's economy has been smaller than is the case in other developing countries. For example, the World Bank (2014) estimated the share of the private sector in non-hydrocarbon GDP to be 70–75 per cent for both Egypt and Tunisia, and its share in employment to be 60 per cent for Egypt and 80 per cent for Tunisia (Adly and Khatib 2014), whereas in Sudan the share of the private sector in GDP was estimated at an average of about 30 per cent during the three decades following Sudan's independence (World Bank 2014). However, this share has gradually increased since the mid-1990s, reaching an average of about 55 per cent during the period 2000–2010 (World Bank 2014). Recently, the contribution of the private sector to the national economy has significantly increased. According to the African Economic Outlook (2014), the private sector is the main source of employment in Sudan, providing about 75 per cent of jobs and about 70 per cent of foreign currency proceedings. This change in the private sector share can be attributed to the government's decision to embark on liberalisation policies in the mid-1990s, which opened the way for the emergence of a productive private sector.

Since Sudan's independence in 1956 until the mid-1990s, private sector economic activities have largely been dominated by individual activities rather than corporate activities. For example, in the traditional agricultural subsector, small-scale production activities are carried out by individuals on their own land using family members as labour. This practice is traced to the land tenure system in Sudan where agricultural land is distributed in small lots between villagers. Moreover, many rural residents lack the necessary entrepreneurial skills to undertake these activities at a larger scale. Individual economic activities are also applicable to retail trading, where individuals own and run small shops buying different commodities all over Sudan's villages. The main problem associated with such individual economic activities is that they operate at very limited scale and employ primitive technology that is characterised by low productivity.

Enterprise activities exist in the modern agriculture (mechanised and irrigated); manufacturing (food processing, clothes and furniture) and services (banking, insurance, export and import of goods, education, and health) sectors. These sectors consist largely of small firms employing a limited number of workers. Until the late 1980s, the majority of firms were publicly owned. However, after the liberalisation and privatisation policies of the 1990s, the situation has started to change. The United Nations Industrial Survey (UNIDO 2013) has found that 96 per cent of industrial firms are privately owned. Moreover, the enterprise sector as a whole consists largely of private limited liability companies and sole proprietorships. The number of common stocks companies is very limited and they operate mostly in banking and insurance services.

## The State of Entrepreneurship in Sudan

Generally, there is no precise data available on entrepreneurial investment projects or entrepreneurial activities in Sudan. The Global Entrepreneurship Monitor (GEM) survey, which provides data on entrepreneurial activities for many countries of the world, does not include Sudan. Also, the Central Bureau of Statistics (CBS) in Sudan does not publish data on entrepreneurial activities or any other relevant variables for this field of study. Finally, there has been no comprehensive survey that covers all aspects of entrepreneurship in Sudan.

To deal with this challenge, we used the available data from different sources to draw a picture of the actual situation of entrepreneurship in Sudan. First, we used the data on newly registered business, which is published by the Companies Registration Authority of the Ministry of Justice, as an indicator for entrepreneurial activities. There are, however, some reservations about these data as a measurement tool for entrepreneurial activities, because there are a considerable number of new firms that have been registered but have not yet begun business. A counter argument to these reservations is that registration of any new firm can be taken as an indicator of a new business idea and as an indicator of the intention of the firm's owner to transfer his business idea into actual business.

TABLE 9.2 *New business registered in Sudan (2005–2014)*

| Indicator | 2005 | 2006 | 2007 | 2008 | 2009 | 2010 | 2011 | 2012 | 2013 | 2014 |
|---|---|---|---|---|---|---|---|---|---|---|
| Limited liability companies | 494 | 761 | 960 | 962 | 1257 | 2400 | 1894 | 1761 | 2100 | 2527 |
| Sole proprietorship | 894 | 961 | 1160 | 1262 | 3936 | 4840 | 4867 | 5316 | 6375 | 4000 |
| Total firms | 1388 | 1722 | 2120 | 2224 | 5193 | 7240 | 6761 | 7077 | 8475 | 6527 |
| % growth in new firm | | 24 | 23 | 5 | 133 | 39 | −7 | 5 | 20 | −23 |

SOURCE: COMPANIES REGISTRATION AUTHORITY 2015

The data in Table 9.2 indicate the total number of newly registered limited liability or sole proprietorship companies in each year during the period 2005–2014. As the table depicts, there is a large variation in the number of newly registered firms in each year. For example, the number of newly registered companies of limited liability was only 494 in 2005, but increased in four years to 1,257 in 2009. The same pattern occurred for sole proprietorship firms, where the number of new registrations increased from 894 in 2005 to 3,936 firms in 2009. Thus, when adding the number of companies of limited liability to the number of companies under sole proprietorship we get the total number of newly registered firms, which indicates a rising trend over the same period. The highest number of births of new firms in terms of absolute number occurred in 2013, with a total of 8,475; but it fell to 6,527 firms in 2014. The highest percentage growth rate of newly registered firms was witnessed in 2009 and 2010 (133 per cent and 39 per cent respectively). This observation can be taken (with reservations) as an indicator for a dynamic phase in the development of private enterprises in Sudan during these two years, which represent the most prosperous years for Sudan's economy in its modern history. This is based on the assumption that the birth of new firms involves new business ideas that emerged from a creative and innovative process. In this vein, as more and more people create new business ideas and decide to turn them into actual businesses, the state of entrepreneurship will evolve. However, this alone should not be taken as sufficient evidence of a favourable environment for the founding of new firms or an indicator of a healthy entrepreneurial state, because many of these newly registered businesses may not start-up their business at all or they fail at an early stage. To clarify the state of entrepreneurship in Sudan, another set of data on micro-, small- and medium-sized enterprises was obtained from the World Bank database. This data is presented in Table 9.3 below.

Table 9.3 depicts the available data on the total number and density of micro-, small-, and medium-sized enterprises (MSMEs) in Sudan in comparison with a number of African countries. The selection of these countries is governed by the availability of data on these variables. As we observe from the table, the number and density of MSMEs in Sudan lags behind the selected countries. At the time when the density of these firms was only 0.7 in Sudan, it reached 87.4 in neighbouring Kenya and 74.6 in Tanzania. Even when we compare Sudan with the other selected countries, we find that it has the lowest number as well as the lowest density of the MSMEs. This reflects an underdeveloped state of entrepreneurship in Sudan in comparison with some other African countries.

This raises the questions, why is entrepreneurship in Sudan underdeveloped? And why does it always lag behind other countries in the region? Can this underdeveloped situation be traced to the poor entrepreneurial environment? Or can it be attributed to the lack of entrepreneurial skills in Sudan? Moreover, what are the factors that lead to the backwardness of the entrepreneurial environment in Sudan? To answer these questions, two publications by the World Bank on the state of entrepreneurship and the business environment will be reviewed.

The World Bank publishes the dataset on entrepreneurial environment for 189 economies in its Doing Business report. This dataset covers ten aspects of the lifecycle of a business: starting a business; dealing with construction permits; getting electricity; registering property; getting credit; protecting minority

TABLE 9.3 *Micro-, small-, and medium-sized enterprises in Sudan and other countries*

| | **Micro-, small-, and medium-sized enterprises** | |
|---|---|---|
| | **Total number** | **Per 1000 people (2000–2005)** |
| Sudan | 22,460 | 0.7 |
| Uganda | 160,453 | 6.2 |
| Kenya | 2,800,000 | 87.4 |
| Tanzania | 2,700,000 | 74.6 |
| Ghana | 25,679 | 1.2 |
| Algeria | 580,000 | 18.8 |
| Botswana | 14,986 | 3.8 |

SOURCE: WORLD BANK, WORLD DEVELOPMENT INDICATORS 2007

TABLE 9.4 *Sudan's ranking on aspects of doing business (2011–2016)*

| Topics | Rank in 2016 | Rank in 2011 | Change in ranking |
|---|---|---|---|
| Starting a business | 146 | 121 | -25 |
| Dealing with construction permits | 146 | 139 | -7 |
| Getting electricity | 102 | – | – |
| Registering property | 89 | 40 | -49 |
| Getting credit | 167 | 138 | -29 |
| Protecting minority investors | 166 | 154 | -12 |
| Paying taxes | 140 | 94 | -46 |
| Trading across borders | 184 | 143 | -41 |
| Enforcing contracts | 142 | 146 | 4 |
| Resolving insolvency/closing a business | 154 | 183 | .. |
| Ease of doing business | 159 | 154 | -5 |

SOURCE: WORLD BANK, DOING BUSINESS REPORT (2011: 196, 2016: 236)

investors; paying taxes; trading across borders; enforcing contracts; and resolving insolvency. All these indicators are summed up in one indicator known as "ease of doing business". The 189 countries are ranked in accordance with this value of "ease of doing business". We utilise this dataset in our analysis to examine the business environment in Sudan with regard to these ten topics.

Sudan ranks 159 out of 189 economies in the ease of doing business reports of 2016, moving down five places from the 2011 ranking of place 154. During a period of five years, Sudan failed to improve or to maintain its position on eight out of nine topics. In three of the eight indicators in the ranking, Sudan has significantly dropped by more than forty places. In the areas that Sudan's performance has worsened, the biggest drop was under the heading of registering the property, where it dropped from 40 in 2011 to 89 in 2016. The only area in which Sudan has succeeded to improve its ranking is enforcing contracts.

In addition to the Doing Business report, the World Bank carries out an Enterprise Survey study for different economies to examine the factors that shape the business environment in these countries. The Enterprise Survey for Sudan was conducted in 2014 by a team of experts from the World Bank. This survey aimed to fill the gap in information related to this sector. It covered the following sectors: manufacturing, services, and transportation and construction. Public utilities, government services, healthcare, and financial services sectors are not included in the sample. The areas covered in enterprise surveys include: infrastructure; trade; finance; regulations; taxes and business licensing; corruption; crime and informality; finance; innovation; labour; and perceptions about obstacles to doing business.

TABLE 9.5 *Summary of enterprise survey indicators*

| Indicator | Sudan | Sub-Saharan African countries | Lower-middle-income countries |
|---|---|---|---|
| Incidence of Graft Index | 10.1 | 20.4 | 20.2 |
| Days to obtain import license | 5.5 | 14.7 | 17.7 |
| Days to obtain construction-related permit | 6.1 | 47.3 | 54.4 |
| Days to obtain operating license | 4.7 | 19.5 | 28.1 |
| Internal finance for investment | 75.3 | 75.9 | 72.3 |
| Bank finance for investment | 2.4 | 9.7 | 12.1 |
| Trade credit financing for investment | 16.3 | 4.6 | 5.3 |
| Number of power outages in a typical month | 3.4 | 8.3 | 8.4 |
| Number of water shortages in a typical month | 0.2 | 1.8 | 4.1 |
| Average duration of water shortages (hours) | 0.3 | 2.6 | 2.2 |
| Average time to clear direct exports through customs | 8.6 | 10.6 | 8.7 |
| Average time to clear imports from customs (days) | 6.0 | 16.8 | 11.6 |
| Losses due to theft, robbery, vandalism, and arson against the firm (% of sales) | 0.5 | 1.4 | 0.9 |
| % of firms with internationally recognised quality certification | 7.0 | 15.1 | 15.5 |

SOURCE: WORLD BANK 2014

The estimated values of these indicators reflect that Sudan's infrastructure condition is poor; the Graft Index (measurement of corruption) rating is high; the financial services are weak; regulations, taxes and business licensing are inefficient; trade operations, innovation and technology are lagging behind. The spread of crime imposes some additional costs on firms (Word Bank 2014). This implies that the poor business environment in Sudan has played an important role in constraining the development of entrepreneurship in recent years. Nevertheless, the state of the business environment in Sudan is better than the average of the neighbouring sub-Saharan African countries in 2016.[1] Foreign investors are not as afraid to take risks as they are elsewhere in the region. This is one reason for the major inflow of a large amount of foreign direct investment into Sudan in recent years, and particularly during the period 2004 to 2008.

## Contextual Factors that Shape the Entrepreneurial State in Sudan

Entrepreneurial activities in any country are embedded in an environment and are influenced by interaction with its contextual factors. These factors can either promote or hinder the business environment and thus affect the entrepreneurial activities in a positive or negative way. Previous research in this field recognised the importance of contextual factors in creating a conducive business environment and, therefore, fostering the state of entrepreneurship development. The most important factors that are widely identified by the literature are economic, financial, political, administrative and regulatory, and finally cultural factors. These factors formulate the entrepreneurial environment and thus influence the willingness and ability of people to become entrepreneurs (Gnyawali and Fogel 1994). In what follows, these factors are discussed in the context of Sudan.

### Economic Factors

The economic environment is one of the most important factors that influences entrepreneurship development in different ways. Firstly, the

1 In 2016, the World Bank's Doing Business report shows that six of Sudan's ten neighbours were doing (much) worse: Chad ranked 183, the CAR 185, the DRC 184, Eritrea 189, South Sudan 187, and Libya 188 out of 189 countries. Only Ethiopia (146), Egypt (131), Uganda (122) and particularly Kenya (108) were doing better, although three of those experienced a deterioration of relative positions on the global scale during the last five years: Egypt from 94 in 2011 to 131, Ethiopia from 104 to 146 and Kenya from 98 to 108. Uganda's position was stable at rank 122 (World Bank 2011 and 2016).

macroeconomic stability of a country encourages investment in general and entrepreneurship development in particular, since it determines the profitability of investment projects. Moreover, good economic performance creates positive economic expectations and improves opportunities and perceptions, motivating individuals to engage in entrepreneurial activity. Therefore, any economic policies that improve economic performance and help establish a stable macroeconomic environment stimulate entrepreneurship. For example, a low-interest monetary policy and low tax rates may produce desirable outcomes such as an increase in economic activity and greater economic stability (Castaño et al. 2015). On the contrary, irrelevant economic policy may create economic instability (recession or inflation), and make it difficult for investors to predict the net return on their investment projects accurately; consequently, they become reluctant to invest. Under such circumstances, the state of entrepreneurship development is adversely affected. Secondly, per capita income levels and economic prosperity of the country plays a major role in the success of entrepreneurial ventures. For instance, a high per capita income involves high purchasing power of the residents of a country, and this increases the amount of opportunities for entrepreneurs in that country. Thirdly, other economic factors, such as the availability of natural resources, skilled labour, the state of a country's infrastructure and extent of economic growth and diversity of economic activities, have been found to influence entrepreneurship development (Gnyawali and Fogel 1994).

In Sudan, the impact of the economic environment in entrepreneurship development has been mixed. Its different elements have played a varying role in entrepreneurship development. Firstly, the economic conditions have passed through different stages of development. During the 1990s (before the petroleum extraction and export), the macroeconomic condition was generally characterised by instability, where the rates of inflation were high, the rates of economic growth and per capita income were relatively low. On the contrary, during the period between 2000 and 2011, the economic performance was characterised by relative stability, where rates of inflation were low, economic growth and per capita income had rapidly grown and exchange rates had continued to be stable (see Table 9.1). However, the period after 2011 can again be characterised by poor economic performance. The rate of inflation soared to about 37 per cent, the exchange rate deteriorated from 3 Sudanese pounds per US dollar in 2010 up to about 10 pounds in 2015, and economic growth dropped from an average of 6 per cent before 2011 to an average of 0.5 per cent after 2011. Table 9.6, presents a comparison between Sudan's economic performance and other African countries.

As can be seen from Table 9.6, Sudan is rich in natural resources (land area). The land area is about 1.8 million square kilometres, which ranks second

TABLE 9.6 *Economic indicators of selected African countries in 2014*

| Country | Population (thousands) | Land area (thousands of km²) | Population density (pop./km²) | GDP based on PPP valuation (USD million) | GDP per capita (PPP valuation, USD) | Annual real GDP growth (average over 2006–2014) |
|---|---|---|---|---|---|---|
| Chad | 13 211 | 1 284 | 10 | 29 851 | 2 260 | 4.7 |
| Congo | 4 559 | 342 | 13 | 28 090 | 6 162 | 4.8 |
| Congo, Dem. Rep. | 69 360 | 2 345 | 30 | 55 731 | 804 | 6.6 |
| Djibouti | 886 | 23 | 38 | 2 858 | 3 225 | 4.9 |
| Egypt | 83 387 | 1 001 | 83 | 945 388 | 11 337 | 4.3 |
| Eritrea | 6 536 | 118 | 56 | 7 855 | 1 202 | 1.8 |
| Ethiopia | 96 506 | 1 104 | 87 | 139 434 | 1 445 | 10.6 |
| Kenya | 45 546 | 580 | 78 | 134 711 | 2 958 | 6.5 |
| Libya | 6 253 | 1 760 | 4 | 103 267 | 16 514 | 3.2 |
| South Sudan | 11 739 | 644 | 18 | 23 306 | 1 985 | ... |
| Sudan | 38 764 | 1 879 | 21 | 159 510 | 4 115 | 4.1 |
| Africa | 1 136 526 | 30 066 | 38 | 5 432 451 | 4826 | 4.8 |

SOURCE: AFRICAN ECONOMIC OUTLOOK 2014.

among comparable countries. In terms of population, Sudan is not one of the most populated countries; it is ranked fifth in this group, and thus has relatively low population density compared to other countries in the group.

Based on this, we can argue that Sudan possesses the key raw materials of success, including a youthful population, natural resource endowments and some aspects of economic stability. These elements could have contributed positively to facilitating entrepreneurial activities in Sudan during the last three decades. However, there are some other economic aspects that undermined the evolution of entrepreneurship and thus contributed negatively to its future development. These included the instability of economic conditions, which has manifested itself in high rates of inflation and devaluation of exchange rates.

### Financial Factors

Finance plays an essential role in the development of entrepreneurship in any country. The most important constituent of any successful investment project is the suitable sources of finance for its operations. The ease with which a firm can raise the required finance with suitable conditions paves the way for success. Therefore, developed financial institutions provide payment services and facilitate the start-up of new businesses and consequently promote the state of entrepreneurship in the country. This is mainly because all entrepreneurs need developed financial institutions to provide sufficient finance for their projects.

Access to finance is claimed to be one of the main factors affecting the development of entrepreneurship in developing countries. The lack of finance in many developing countries is believed to be the most important challenge confronting entrepreneurs in Sudan. Bearing in mind the low per capita income in Sudan, most people have limited personal savings and lack the required capital to start their own business. Moreover, the government usually lacks the sufficient financial resources to provide loans to entrepreneurs. Thus, entrepreneurs have no other option than to seek external financing for their investment projects. One source of external finance is the commercial banks. However, this option is associated with many difficulties. One of these difficulties is related to entrepreneurs themselves; that is, many entrepreneurs are not regarded as creditworthy or do not have the necessary collateral to obtain finances for their projects. The second difficulty relates to the banking system in Sudan, which has a limited amount of capital. Moreover, most banks charge high interest rates due to the high risk associated with new business projects.

To tackle the problem related to the financing of small projects, the Central Bank of Sudan established a microfinance unit in 2007. The main objective of this unit is to provide flexible forms of finance for entrepreneurs who have a business idea and are looking for finance opportunities. Since its establishment, the microfinance unit has helped many entrepreneurs and contributed significantly to promoting entrepreneurship in Sudan. However, it has also experienced significant criticism. One of these criticisms relates to the amount of finance available, which, it is claimed, is very small and inadequate for covering the total costs of investment projects. Another criticism relates to the limited extent of its coverage. In addition, its services are limited to a small percentage of potential entrepreneurs.

### Political Factors

The political environment in any country plays an important role in encouraging or discouraging entrepreneurial processes. It determines the set of rules and policies that govern entrepreneurial activities, and the overall atmosphere in which firms can operate. This factor is generally comprised of many sub-factors, among which are: competition policy; taxation policy; employment law; patent law; and regulation of financial markets. In addition, it includes the political situation (e.g. government stability, corruption) and a country's relations with other states (David 2013; FitzRoy et al. 2012). In this regard, a good set of policies and a stable political situation can contribute to increasing the likelihood of formulating and starting-up a new business, and thus fostering entrepreneurship development.

As shown above, the political environment includes many factors and it is hard to review all of them here. To deal with this challenge, the authors interviewed political economist, Mohamed H. Ahmed about the impact of the political environment on entrepreneurship and business development in Sudan. This interview is summarised in the two paragraphs below.

Sudan, like any newly independent country, witnessed a humble start-up of businesses in its post-independence era in the 1950s. However, by the end of the decade, the political struggle over Sudan's economic orientation had become deeply disputed between the rival liberal and communist parties. Yet, the business sector was growing and benefiting from intact infrastructures and a sound civil service tradition that was left by British rule (1899–1956). In early 1969, however, Numeiri took power on behalf of the Communist Party. This dealt a heavy blow to the *laissez-faire* mood of the economy due to the nationalisation of the private sector, although the regime made a quick shift back to the free market ideology, following the logic of the Cold War swings, after Numeiri liquidated the communist leadership and hence worsened relations with the Soviet Union. But the damage had already been done to the business sector and there was capital flight from Sudan. In sum, the business formation has never moved away from being dominated by the service sector and the manufacturing sector remained humble.

Post 1989, there was a mushrooming of business registrations due to the growth of the service sector and encouragement from the government for the private sector to take the lead in many areas that used to be publicly financed as a result of the discovery of oil by 1998. The sudden bonanza that followed encouraged both internal and external entrepreneurs to seek opportunities in Sudan's economy, especially in oil related fields. That steady growth was helped by the stability of the foreign exchange rate and the flexibility of the investment laws, tailored to attract foreign investment. All this was taking place despite the problematic political relations of Sudan with many international players, primarily the US, which still considers Sudan to be a state that supports terrorism and, consequently, has maintained an economic blockade on the country since 1993. This US embargo, together with worsening relations with other influential countries, impacted on the international business sector in Sudan, not least in the form of the US Divestment Act, which punishes entities that venture in Sudan. This Western uneasiness with Sudan, coupled with the separation of South Sudan in 2011 and the subsequent loss of oil, reversed the trend of booming business in Sudan and hence discouraged international entrepreneurs and serious investment partners. However, the continued increase in the registration of new companies can be explained, cautiously, as a result of the advantages that one gets from loopholes in the investment laws if one has a registered company or because small, local services are not hard hit by the continued devaluation of the exchange rate of the Sudanese pound.

### Regulatory and Administrative Factors

Although the Heritage Foundation has not graded Sudan in its annual Index of Economic Freedom since 2000, an analysis of selected indicators is provided in its 2013 report. In the category of regulatory efficiency, the report on Sudan states, "Inconsistent enforcement of regulations and other institutional shortcomings often impede business activity and undermine economic development. Launching a business takes more than 30 days, and completing licensing requirements costs over twice the level of average annual income" (Heritage Foundation 2013: Sudan).

> One of the most significant obstacles facing investors is the high level of bureaucracy and complexity of the administrative procedures at both the federal and state levels. In spite of the existence of the unified Investment Encouragement Act 1999, amended in 2007, and the adoption of a single outlet policy by the Federal Ministry for Investment for registering a new business, the committee found that, in practice, an investor wanting to register a new business must complete 56 steps in most sectors, and 66 steps in the agricultural, animal, health services, mining, and hotel sectors. That is to say, instead of completing the registration of a new business in one outlet, the investor has to do it in 56 to 66 places.
>
> In cases where an investor has to amend his company statute to include a new type of investment, this process may take up to six months. If the investor is a foreigner, it might also take months to achieve security clearance in the home country.
>
> In spite of the existence of the Federal Investment Act, it has been found that a number of state and federal authorities possess some authority related to investment business, delegated to them by the Federal Investment Encouragement Act, which defeats the idea of a single outlet for completing registration procedures.

In addition to the above-mentioned obstacles, private investment is confronted with heavy taxes and custom duties and several other types of fees to be paid to different government authorities even before starting the business. The conflict over land ownership between federal, state authorities and citizens also contributes to this gloomy picture. One has to draw attention to the widespread corruption among many government officials who run the business of registration of new ventures.

### Cultural Factors

Culture is another important factor that explains cross-country differences in entrepreneurship development. Hofstede (1991) proposed that national culture has six dimensions that shape people's personality and behaviour. Four of these are believed to influence entrepreneurs' decision-making: power distance; individualism versus collectivism; uncertainty avoidance; and long-term orientation. Power distance is defined by Hofstede as the perception of the degree to which people accept unequal distribution of power among individuals in a given society. Individualism refers to the degree to which people prefer to act as individuals rather than as members of groups, whereas collectivism emphasises a strong social framework in which people expect others in their group to cater to them. Uncertainty avoidance is defined as the degree to which people in a country prefer structured over unstructured situations. Long-term orientation and short-term orientation refers to the importance given to the future, on the one hand, and to the past and present, on the other hand. In long-term orientation countries, the society encourages serious, long-lasting commitments. In short-term oriented countries, individuals are interested in protecting existing personal safety and stability.

As far as the impact of culture on entrepreneurship development is concerned, low power distance, individualism, low uncertainty avoidance, and long-term orientation are associated with entrepreneurial activities and innovation (Shane 1995; Thomas and Mueller 2000; Jones and Davis 2000). Low power distance cultures do not encourage people to work harder to gain more power in society. In a national culture that scores high on "collectivism", individuals' ability to achieve their dreams are hindered by their caring for others. Also, in cultures that score highly on uncertainty avoidance, people have an increased level of anxiety about uncertainty and ambiguity, which is a situation people usually find themselves in when they engage in an entrepreneurial activity. Long-term orientation in the business context is related to pragmatism. Although Hofstede's dimensions do not explain exactly what will happen in a certain situation, they can help us better predict what is likely to occur.

Unfortunately, Sudanese culture is dominated by "collectivism", high "uncertainty avoidance", "short-term orientation" and "low power distance". This is certainly the conclusion of Adam's (2016) study on the impact of culture on strategic decision-making in Sudan. Thus, the cultural aspect may be considered a barrier to Sudanese people engaging in entrepreneurial activities.

Risk aversion is common in Sudan. Consequently, many young people lack the confidence to establish their own business for fear of failure, and its severe legal and social consequences. Moreover, risk aversion causes many people to prefer secured rent-seeking jobs to entrepreneurial activities. This is reflected in the attitudes of many Sudanese families, who send their children to schools and universities to be educated and earn certificates in order to secure jobs in the public or the private sector. Moreover, this risk averse attitude causes some Sudanese investors to imitate others in their investment projects. Consequently, innovative entrepreneurs are often discouraged by others who imitate them (Gangi and Timan 2013).

## A Case Study of Two Firms

As shown in the previous section, the entrepreneurial environment in Sudan is very complicated and it is influenced by the interaction of many contradictory national factors. These factors represent both opportunities and challenges for entrepreneurship development. In this section, we try to understand how firms in Sudan have dealt with these challenges and opportunities. A case study of two firms is undertaken for this purpose. The selection of the firms is governed by data availability and permission of the firm owners.

### Dajin for Poultry Products

Dajin for Poultry Products was established in 2005 as a joint project between the Ministry of Agriculture and Livestock of Khartoum State and Mico Company for the Poultry Industry. The latter was a private company, founded in 2003 by a successful entrepreneur and veterinary physician, Sanosi Hassan Sanosi. Sanosi initiated the business idea and served as managing director of Dajin for about ten years. The company project was started with just four production houses, with a total production capacity of 700,000 birds per year. However, in less than ten years its production capacity multiplied by more than 14 times (from 0.7 million in 2005 to 10 million birds per year in 2015). In addition, its production units were integrated to include ten houses for mother chicks, a hatchery, a feed mill, a modern slaughterhouse and a rendering plant. Moreover, during the same period, all the necessary infrastructural facilities and the distribution channels equipment were established.

The main objectives of the company were: to promote poultry production and generate a substantial qualitative change in the poultry sector in Khartoum state through productivity enhancement and integration of different production cycles; to support the government policy of self-sufficiency in food production; to generate job opportunities and contribute to building the capacity of national labour by improving their skills in this profession; to encourage investment in the agricultural sector by utilising the available resources in productive activity; to increase the per capita consumption of chicken in Sudan and change the consumption behaviour of Sudanese society towards chicken; and to realising a reasonable profit for the owner of the company.

Having completed its ten-year strategic plan (2005–2015), Dajin has been described as one of the fastest growing companies in Sudan. By doing so, it succeeded in fulfilling a great achievement for both shareholders and the national economy. In the following section, we will summarise what Dajin has achieved during the last decade.

On the financial side, the company has succeeded in implementing its expansion plan with the minimum possible cost and sold all its products at a reasonable price for both producers and consumers. The company has raised a total profit of around $US 56 million during the last ten years for the shareholders. This profit enabled the company to pay back all its commitments to creditors on time. On the economic side, the company has stimulated the banking sector in Sudan by borrowing a total of $US 227 million for the project operation, creating around 600 direct jobs and ten times this number in indirect employment opportunities. Moreover, it contributed to the economic growth of the national economy by producing more than 50 million birds. Furthermore, the company has contributed to the government budget by paying taxes (of about one million dollars). On the technical side, the company has contributed to enhancing technological advancement in poultry industry by importing modern technology; establishing breeding houses with varying capacity ranged between 28 to 70 thousand birds; creating opportunities for technical training and research experiences for university students and other researchers. Finally, the company has provided a social contribution to the rural area, where the project is located, and to Sudanese society at large. To this end, the company has achieved the following: contributed to establishing a number of public service institutions, such as schools, medical centres and electricity stations; contributed to organising the residents of "Ahamda" villages (the project area) into a cooperative association and paying all expenses of the association's registration; contributed to government fundraising campaigns and contributed to Khartoum State's policy to improve the standard of living and reduce its costs by providing chicken at affordable prices.

An interview was carried out with the entrepreneur who established the company and served as a general manager for ten years. This interview indicated that, at the time of its establishment, the company was confronted with many challenges, the most important one being the difficulty of finding a suitable source of finance for its investment projects. This was mainly because the company was recently established and did not have adequate assets to provide collateral to the banks. The company solved this problem by cooperating with its partner, the government of Khartoum state, which provided a letter of guarantee that covered the total amount of its investment projects and extended it for five years. The letter enabled the company to get the required finance for all its operations. Another challenge that faced the company was the lack of the necessary infrastructure (for example, paved road, electricity supply) in the project area. Again, the company used its communication channels with the Khartoum state government to solve this problem. On the other hand, there were many factors that contributed positively to the development of the company. One of the most important factors was the economic and political stability that characterised the period between 2005 and 2010, which had witnessed a good economic performance and stable political situation, enabling the company to start-up and grow rapidly.

### KMK Company

Mr. Khalid Elhasan was a young engineer who graduated from the University of Khartoum in early 1990s. After graduation, Mr. Elhasan engaged in several small business activities, unlike most of his peers, who preferred rent-seeking activities and joined the public sector and private firms as employees to earn a fixed income.

After failing to establish a number of business activities, Elhasan set up a small company named KMK. The name is an abbreviation of his name and that of his partner. The company started business in 1998; its main business is selling electrical appliances to trade union members and middle-income groups. This kind of business already existed in Sudan, but KMK introduced payment by instalment and started to sell commodities on a credit basis. According to the company instalment policy, customers must repay the value of their purchase in 12 equal instalments. This kind of arrangement enabled employees with a limited fixed income to own the electrical equipment that they had dreamed of. Since the start of the business, the demand for KMK services and commodities has been high. Large numbers of trade union members rushed to the company and signed contracts to enjoy KMK services and facilities. The company achieved high annual profits during the first years. Indeed, their profitability was estimated to be around 300 per cent per annum.

KMK began business with a small number of employees; two of them were graduates of accounting, a third of economics and a few others were non-graduates. Elhasan was the general manager and the chairman of the board of directors, which was composed of Elhasan, his partner and two other names. The partner was a silent partner, providing financial support but with no part in the operations. After the expansion of the business, Elhasan began to feel that he was losing control. He talked to a friend who was a university business lecturer and asked him to help formulate a business plan and organise the company. However, Elhasan was too busy to follow through on the advice, because he was wrapped up in running the business as a one-man show. He was always complaining of the lack of competent assistants to help him run KMK.

In spite of the above-mentioned difficulties, the company performed well and made huge profits. Elhasan succeeded in getting the agency of a famous Chinese electrical appliances producer, which was a remarkable gain for the company. Driven by moral and strategic motivations, Elhasan decided to enter into importing and selling automobiles, vans and rickshaws to his customers. The vans and rikshaws are wanted for business purposes, i.e. transportation of others. The company also planned to sell these new commodities using the same mode of finance, in this case with 48 monthly instalments. However, this kind of new business was risky due to the ongoing deterioration of the value of the Sudanese currency, a situation in which the seller loses a large percentage of the repayment value of the commodity. KMK succeeded in overcoming this risk by inventing a new mode of finance for its car imports. The financing mode was a blend between a letter of credit with deferred payment and partnership with banks. The credit letter with deferred payment was covered by the local insurance companies. Since KMK was not in a position to secure local collateral, it convinced one of the Sudanese commercial banks to enter into partnership in this transaction. By involving the commercial bank in this business, KMK managed to avoid the risk of currency devaluation, since the bank financed the transaction in part by using the current accounts of its clients. Current accounts are interest free in an Islamic economy such as Sudan.

KMK imported more than 1000 automobiles, vans and rikshaws and delivered them to its customers. This move annoyed the automobiles agents in Sudan, who lobbied government officials and they managed to get a decree issued to confine the import of automobiles to official agents only. KMK decided to continue the fight in the market and succeeded in obtaining an agency contract from a major Korean automobile exporters to Sudan. A number of rival firms began to adopt the same business model as KMK, a matter that resulted in a major threat to the automobile agents. Again, the group of automobile agents secured the issuance of a decree that banned importing cars through letters of credit with deferred payment. KMK had already signed contracts with many parties to deliver large numbers of cars. Unfortunately, the company failed to meet its obligations and therefore found itself sued by its customers and, ultimately, liquidated.

## Case Study Analysis

The data obtained from the companies' documents and the interviews carried out with the general directors shows that both companies had been confronted with many obstacles. The difference between the two companies lies in the ways in which they tackled these challenges. For example, Mico had overcome the finance problem by seeking support from its partner, the government of Khartoum State. KMK decided to confront the finance problem alone or with a private sector partner, and that is why it failed. The lesson that can be learned from the experience of these companies is that collaboration between the public sector and the private sector to establish joint ventures would help to overcome those challenges generated by the complexity of the business world.

KMK invented a new mode of finance for its operations, i.e. a letter of credit with deferred payment and partnership with local commercial banks. This mode of finance enabled the company to offer credit sales to customers to be repaid in monthly instalments for up to 48 months, and thus the company managed to overcome the dilemma of the deteriorating local currency.

When the operations of company were of a limited scale, Mr. Elhasan succeeded in running the business and achieved sizeable profits. But when business expanded, Mr. Elhasan was overwhelmed by the amount of work due to his centralised decision-making style. Moreover, Mr. Elhasan had no training in business management, so he failed to address the importance of developing a business plan. It is also clear that the lack of competent managerial staff contributed to his failure.

The main reasons for KMK's failure can be attributed to failure of the company management to adapt to the external environment represented in the elements of competition and the political environment. The company could have developed some proactive strategies to deal with those elements instead of being retroactive.

## Conclusion

The objective of this chapter was to examine the current status of entrepreneurship development in Sudan and to investigate the role of national factors in shaping this status. Generally, in Sudan there is lack of precise data available on either the entrepreneurial investment projects or entrepreneurial activities. The World Bank reports that were consulted revealed that Sudan's infrastructure condition is poor; the rate of corruption is high; the financial services are weak; regulations, taxes and business licensing are also inefficient; trade operations, innovation and technology are lagging behind. Despite these conditions, the state of the business environment in Sudan was better than in many other countries in sub-Saharan Africa. However, the unfavourable business environment in Sudan has played an important role in constraining the development of entrepreneurship in recent times.

It has been clear from the presentation of the case studies that an entrepreneurial business has a high chance of succeeding if it allies with or is supported by a public sector entity. The future of entrepreneurial activities in Sudan depends largely on improvement of the political and economic conditions, which have resulted in high rates of inflation and devaluation of exchange rates. The government needs to revise and fine tune its regulatory and institutional measures to facilitate and expedite the procedures of starting new businesses. As far as the cultural barriers are concerned, we believe that training and development of potential entrepreneurs can result in changing their attitudes and equip them with the necessary skills to manage an investment project successfully.

The authors recommend that more in-depth research be conducted in the area of entrepreneurship development in Sudan, especially in light of the limited sources of data. Further research should focus in detail on revealing the relative importance of the different contextual factors and their impact on the entrepreneurship development in Sudan.

## References

Adam, Tarig S. (2016). "Impact of Culture on Strategic Decision Making: Exploring Culture and Strategic Decision Making Process in the Sudanese Context", Unpublished PhD Thesis, University of Khartoum, Sudan.

Adly, A., & L. Khatib. (2014). "Reforming the Entrepreneurship Ecosystem in Post-Revolutionary Egypt and Tunisia". *CDDRL Policy Briefs*.

African Economic Outlook (2014). *Sudan*. Retrieved from www.africaneconomicoutlook.org.

African Economic Outlook (2015). *Sudan*. Retrieved from www.africaneconomicoutlook.org.

Amos, A.O., Oluseye, O.O. & A.A. Bosede. (2015). "Influence of Contextual Factors on Entrepreneurial Intention of University Students: The Nigerian Experience", *Journal of South African Business Research*, 2015, DOI: 10.5171/2015.750622.

Castaño, M.S., Méndez, M.T. & M.Á. Galindo. (2015). "The Effect of Social, Cultural, and Economic Factors on Entrepreneurship", *Journal of Business Research*, 68(7), 1496–1500.

Country Watch. (2015). *Country Review: Sudan*. Retrieved from http://www.countrywatch.com.

David, F.R. (2013). *Strategic Management Concepts and Cases: A Competitive Advantage Approach*. Edinburgh Gate: Pearson Education Limited.

FitzRoy, P.T., Hulbert, J.M. & A. Ghobadian. (2012). *Strategic Management: The Challenge of Creating Value*. Abingdon: Routledge.

Gangi, Y.A. & E. Timan. (2013). "An Empirical Investigation of Entrepreneurial Environment in Sudan", *World Journal of Entrepreneurship Management and Sustainable Development*, 9(2/3), 168–177.

Gangi, Y.A. (2015). "The Role of Entrepreneurship Education to Achieve MDGs in Sudan", *International Journal of Sudan Research (IJSR)*, 5(1), 41–55.

Hayton, J.C., George, G. & S.A. Zahra. (2002). "National Culture and Entrepreneurship: A Review of Behavioural Research: Entrepreneurship", *Theory & Practice*, 26(4), 33–52.

Heritage Foundation (2013). *Index of Economic Freedom*. http://www.heritage.org/index/pdf/2013/countries/sudan.pdf.

Hofstede, G. (1991): *Cultures and Organization: Software of the Mind* London: McGraw-Hill.

Jones, G.K. & H.J. Davis. (2000). "National Culture and Innovation: Implications for Locating Global R&D Operations", *MIR: Management International Review*, 11–39.

Mack, J. & J. Pützschel. (2014). "The Influence of Contextual Factors on the Entrepreneurial Process: A Multiple-Case Study of Sustainability-oriented and Commercial Entrepreneurship in Central America". Unpublished MSc. dissertation, Umeå School of Business and Economics, Umea University.

Rusu, C. (2014). "Culture-moderator of the Relationship between Contextual Factors and Entrepreneurial Outcomes", *Managerial Challenges of the Contemporary Society*, 7 (1), 63–67.

Shane, S., Venkataraman, S. & I. MacMillan. (1995). "Cultural Differences in Innovation Championing Strategies", *Journal of Management*, 21(5), 931–952.

Steven, L. (2010). *Private Sector and Enterprise Development: Fostering Growth in the Middle East and North Africa*. Cheltenham: Edward Elgar.

Thomas, A.S. & S.L. Mueller. (2000). "A Case for Comparative Entrepreneurship: Assessing the Relevance of Culture", *Journal of International Business Studies*, 31(2), 287–301.

UNIDO (2013). *Industrial Development Report. Sustaining Employment Growth: The Role of Manufacturing and Structural Change*. Vienna: UNIDO.

World Bank (2006). *Sudan Review of Administrative Barriers of Investment*, World Bank, Washington, DC.

World Bank (2007). *World Development Indicators 2007*. Washington DC.

World Bank (2009). *Sudan Investment Climate Assessment*. World Bank, Washington, DC.

World Bank (2011). *Doing Business Report: Making a Difference for Entrepreneurs, Economy Profile: Sudan*, Washington, DC.

World Bank (2013). *The World Development Indicators*. Retrieved from http://data.worldbank.org/country/sudan.

World Bank (2015). *Doing Business Report: Doing Business in a More Transparent World, Economy Profile: Sudan*, Washington, DC.

World Bank (2016). *Doing Business Report: Measuring Regulatory Quality and Efficiency Economic Profile: Sudan*, Washington, DC.

CHAPTER 10

# Challenges to Entrepreneurship Development in Tanzania

*Nsubili Isaga and Albogast Musabila*

## Introduction

Entrepreneurship is widely considered an important factor in the search for development, competitiveness and sustainable success. Like many other developing countries, Tanzania has recognised the importance of entrepreneurship for economic development and poverty alleviation. Historically, Tanzania, after its independence, chose the path of socialism and self-reliance for national development. Along this path, almost all means of production and exchange were put under the direct control of the State. As a result, major businesses were nationalised and the government, through its parastatals, owned almost all the activities and investments that had previously been in the private sector. However, the nationalisation of the private sector led to poor economic results and to a number of macro-economic imbalances and, consequently, to an economic crisis that lasted for over a decade (Kanaan 2000). This crisis signalled a need for a movement towards a market economy. In the 1990s, the significance of the private sector to economic growth became very clear and was widely recognised; available data suggests that about a third of the Gross Domestic Product (GDP) originates from the SME sector (URT 2003). Since then, a number of policies and programmes have been undertaken to strengthen and widen the role of the private sector in economic development. At the national level, Vision 2025 – National Strategy for Growth and Poverty Reduction (NSGPR) was established, a programme which emphasises the significance of the private sector as the engine of economic growth in Tanzania (URT 2003). Unfortunately, despite the existence of various programmes, the outcomes of these efforts have generally yielded poor results with only a few SMEs managing to expand and develop. Most of the SMEs have remained at the micro level (Kinunda-Rutashobya and Olomi 1999; Olomi 2001). This phenomenon in Africa has been referred to as the "missing middle" (the lack of medium-sized enterprises, as SMEs can be categorised as micro, small and medium-sized firms) and this continues to be a long-term concern for African policymakers (Agyapong 2010).

 | DOI 10.1163/9789004351615_011

Through a review of previous research regarding business development in Tanzania, we found that most of the studies regard firm performance as being significantly affected by external factors and firm characteristics. As a response to such findings, several initiatives and programmes in Tanzania are focusing on solving environmental problems, such as providing government assistance, examining the role of banks, and providing infrastructure and competition, while ignoring the individual running the firm. Though some of the issues addressed in these studies have changed, the performance of the SME sector has not yet been impressive. This suggests the need to further investigate the factors that influence SME growth from different angles. Owing to the crucial role played by individuals, several studies worldwide have acknowledged the importance of entrepreneurs for the development of SMEs. Accordingly, Kuratko and Hodgetts (2001) have proposed that the effectiveness of programmes aimed at the development of SMEs depends on a thorough understanding of the individual owner-managers. This is because the majority of SMEs are owned and managed by a single entrepreneur; thus, the entrepreneur is the one who makes important decisions concerning products, markets, motivation of employees, expansion plans and other strategic decisions concerning the firm (Von Gelderen et al. 2000). Thus, this leads to the possibility that a large proportion of the difference in performance among SMEs can be explained by the individual entrepreneurs (Shane 2007). The purpose of this paper is to analyse the challenges affecting entrepreneurship development in Tanzania. A qualitative study comprising of three case studies on Tanzanian SMEs has been conducted with the aspiration to describe the drivers of being entrepreneurs, drivers for SME development and challenges affecting their business performance.

## Literature Review

### *Brief Overview of Entrepreneurship*

The important role of entrepreneurs in economic growth is well documented. However, the precise meaning of the word entrepreneur is not clear (Amit, Glosten and Muller 2003; Kobia and Sikalieh 2010). The problem of the identification of an entrepreneur has been caused by the fact that there is still no generally accepted definition of entrepreneurship (Chell, Haworth and Brearley 1991; Kobia and Sikalieh 2010). The lack of an agreed definition has led to a variety of opinions regarding its meaning (Shane and Baron 2008). Indeed, various scholars have defined the terms entrepreneur and entrepreneurship differently. In the next section, an overview will be given of the development of the terms entrepreneur and entrepreneurship.

### *Who is an Entrepreneur?*

The term entrepreneur comes from the French verb *entreprendre*, which means to undertake (Hebert and Link 1989). The first economist who is believed to have recognised the role of the entrepreneur was Richard Cantillon (around 1730; Kirby 2003). According to Cantillon, the entrepreneur is an individual who assumes a risk by buying at a certain price and selling at an uncertain price and bears the risk caused by price fluctuations in the market, with the difference being a profit or loss (Bridge, O'Neill, and Martin 2009). Cantillon saw the role of the entrepreneur as lying in the creation of entrepreneurial income through operating under conditions of uncertainty.

Later, Knight (1921) refined the Cantillon idea by distinguishing between the risk, which is insurable and the risk which is not insurable (uncertainty). He related insurable risk to recurring events whose relative frequency is known from experience, whereas uncertainty relates to unique events whose probability can only be subjectively estimated (Hebert and Link 1989). According to Knight (1921), uncertainty is the basic element and starting point when defining an entrepreneur. On this point, Knight (1921) considers an entrepreneur as a calculated risk-taker and the recipient of pure profit, where profit is seen as the reward for bearing the costs of uncertainty.

Schumpeter (1934) had a different approach and emphasised the role of innovation. Clearly, Schumpeter was the first author to draw attention to the central role of an entrepreneur in the innovation process. According to Schumpeter, the entrepreneur is an innovator who implements change within markets as a result of carrying out new combinations. In his theory of economic development, the entrepreneur does not invent things but exploits them by carrying out new combinations such as the introduction of new products or processes, identification of new export markets or sources of supply, or creation of new types of organisation (Carrasco and Perez 2008). Other scholars (e.g. Kirzner 1979) came up with other definitions of an entrepreneur. Kirzner (1985) considers an entrepreneur as someone who perceives profit opportunities and initiates action to fill currently unsatisfied needs. The author argues that the entrepreneurial process is always competitive and that an entrepreneur has nothing but his alertness (Kirzner 1979). For Kirzner, the role of the entrepreneur is to achieve the kind of adjustment necessary to move economic markets towards the equilibrium state.

### *Definition of Entrepreneurship*

From the above definitions, it seems clearly that there is no agreed definition of an entrepreneur. As a consequence, there is also vagueness about a functional definition of entrepreneurship (Kuratko and Hodgetts 2001). Entrepreneurship scholars have proposed a variety of definitions of the term, some of which share no common attributes at all (see Table 10.1)

TABLE 10.1 *Selected definitions of entrepreneurship*

| Authors | Definition |
|---|---|
| Cantillon (1755) | Entrepreneurship is an act of assuming risk, by buying at a certain price and selling at an uncertain price, bearing the risk caused by price fluctuations in the market. |
| Knight (1921) | Entrepreneurship is the ability to deal with risk and uncertainty |
| Schumpeter (1934) | Entrepreneurship is seen as making new combinations, which include the introduction of new goods, new methods of production, opening of new markets, new sources of supply and new organisations. |
| Kirzner (1979) | Entrepreneurship is the ability to perceive new opportunities. |
| Casson (1982) | Entrepreneurship encompasses decisions and judgments about the coordination of scarce resources. |
| Drucker (1985) | Entrepreneurship is the act of innovation that involves endowing existing resources with new wealth producing capacity. |
| Stevenson, Roberts and Groesbeck (1985) | Entrepreneurship is the pursuit of an opportunity without concern for current resources or capabilities. |
| Low and Macmillan (1988) | Entrepreneurship is the creation of a new business. |
| Katz and Gartner (1988) | Entrepreneurship is the creation of an organisation or process by which new organisations come into existence. |
| Sharma and Chrisman (1999) | Entrepreneurship encompasses acts of organisational creation, renewal or innovation that occur within or outside an existing organisation. |
| Kuratko and Hodgetts (2001) | Entrepreneurship is a process of innovation and new venture creation through four major dimensions, namely individual, organisational, environmental, and process. |

ADAPTED AND MODIFIED FROM HITT ET AL. (2002)

From this mass of definitions, it is apparent that entrepreneurship is interdisciplinary in nature. And, given its nature, various theories or approaches can be used to gain better understanding of this concept (Kuratko and Hodgetts 2001). One way of understanding this concept is through the schools of thought from which entrepreneurship can be divided into specific activities (Cunningham and Lischeron 1991; Kuratko and Hodgetts 2001). The entrepreneurship schools of thought provide a means of examining the diversity of viewpoints about entrepreneurship (Hebert and Link 1989; Kuratko and Hodgetts 2001). These schools of thought illustrate what an entrepreneur does and what functions and processes are key (Kuratko and Hodgetts 2001).

### *Definition of SMEs*

Like entrepreneurship, there is no single, uniformly accepted definition of SMEs (Storey 1994). Different countries define SMEs differently depending on their level of development. A study by USAID (1993) for example, found more than 50 different definitions. Although there are several definitions, a distinction can be made between quantitative and qualitative definitions. The former define SMEs based on quantitative characteristics, whereas the latter define SMEs based on qualitative characteristics. Within these two types, the quantitative definition is commonly used for defining SMEs, and often the definition is based on the number of employees, sales revenues/turnover, total assets and capital invested in machinery. The first three criteria are most widely used in defining SMEs. In support of this argument, USAID (1993) shows that the majority of countries use the number of employees or total assets to define SMEs. Accordingly, in the context of Tanzania, SME is a term used to refer to micro, small and medium-sized enterprises in non-farming activities, which include manufacturing, mining, commerce and services (URT 2003). Furthermore, the number of employees and capital invested in machinery are the two criteria used to define SMEs in Tanzania. Subsequently, a micro enterprise is defined as a firm with fewer than five employees, whereas a small firm is a firm with 5 to 49 employees and a medium-sized enterprise is a firm with 50 to 99 employees. Any firm with 100 employees or more is regarded as a large enterprise (see Table 10.2). In the case where an enterprise falls under more than one category, the level of investment would be the deciding factor.

### *Definition of the Entrepreneur in this Study*

There is no single uniformly accepted definition of the term Entrepreneur. In this study, the terms entrepreneur and owner-manager are used

TABLE 10.2 *SMEs in Tanzania*

| Category | Number of employees | Capital invested in machinery (Tshs) |
|---|---|---|
| Micro enterprises | 1–4 | Up to 5 million |
| Small enterprises | 5–49 | 5–200 million |
| Medium-sized enterprises | 50–99 | 200–800 million |
| Large enterprises | 100 and more | Above 800 million |

SOURCE: (URT 2003)

interchangeably to define a person who both owns the firm and takes overall responsibility for the strategic and operational direction of the business.

### Growth and Entrepreneurship

Several researchers have revealed growth to be an essential part of entrepreneurship, thus making the relationship between growth and entrepreneurship relevant. This link is very important, especially when the theory of the firm is considered, in which both entrepreneurship and growth play important roles. For example, Davidsson, Delmar, and Wiklund (2002) look more deeply into this relationship and identify the aspects of growth which form part of entrepreneurship and those which do not. Specifically, they argue that if entrepreneurship is defined as the creation or emergence of a new firm then growth is not formally part of the definition of entrepreneurship. But as most of these start-ups remain very small for their entire existence, it is wise to include aspects of early growth in the entrepreneurship definition (Davidsson, Achtenhagen, and Naldi 2007). It is further suggested that if entrepreneurship is defined as the creation of new economic activities and the like, then firm growth is an aspect of entrepreneurship which can be achieved through the introduction of new products and services. However, if growth is achieved through the acquisition of activities, which were already run by businesses, then growth is not an aspect of entrepreneurship (Davidsson, Delmar and Wiklund 2002). From these elaborations, it is then obvious that growth is an aspect of entrepreneurship if the term is understood as the creation of new economic activities.

## The Concept of SMEs Growth

In discussing firm growth, it is important to firstly define the term. Growth refers to a change in size or magnitude from one period of time to another (Wiklund 1998). Furthermore, when it comes to the growth of a firm, the term growth has two meanings: it sometimes merely denotes a change in amount and, at other times, implies an increase in size or improvement in quality (Penrose 1959). Just as researchers have often noted the heterogeneity of entrepreneurship theories, they also assert that there is no single theory which can explain firm growth. Due to this dilemma, a large number of theories have been developed to explain aspects of SMEs growth. These theories can be distinguished according to the underlying assumptions they make about the growth process (Dobbs and Hamilton 2007).

For instance, O'Farrell and Hitchens (1988) are among the authors who have reviewed theories of small firm growth. They identified four main groups of theories: the static equilibrium approach, the stochastic model, the strategic management approach, and the stages model. The recent review of SMEs growth conducted by Dobbs and Hamilton (2007) classified the available approaches to the study of small business growth into six groups: stochastic, descriptive, evolutionary, resource-based, learning, and deterministic.

It can be argued that each of these theories consists of logical concepts and assumptions, but most of them consistently share the same theoretical perspective. For example, the commonly mentioned theory is that of a stages model which is based on showing several stages through which most organisations pass. A few examples include the three-stage models (Smith, Mitchell and Summer 1985), the four-stage models (Quinn and Cameron 1983) and the five-stage models (Greiner 1972; Galbraith 1982; Churchill and Lewis 1983; Miller and Friesen 1984; Scott and Bruce 1987). These multistage models use various organisational characteristics to explain organisational growth and development. Collectively, these models suggest that the organisation may progress sequentially through major steps of development (e.g. birth, start-up, survival, growth and maturity). For instance, Masurel and Van Montfort (2006) focused their attention on analysing the differences between the subsequent stages in the life cycles of SMEs in the professional service sector. Their results reveal that firms do change over the course of their lifecycles from start-up to maturity.

It has been observed that most of the theories that have theoretical firms as a point of departure have rarely proved to be accurate in the real sense of the word and, as such, they have added confusion in terms of understanding small firm growth (Ardichvili et al. 1998). Furthermore, none of these theories was created for the specific purpose of analysing firm growth (Delmar and Wiklund 2008; Davidsson and Wiklund 2000). For instance, most of the theories do not indicate how and when growth should be studied and, as a result, their applicability to firm growth is questionable (Delmar 2000). This argument also corresponds to that of Gibb and Davies (1990) who assert that existing theories are inadequate when used as a basis for developing policy. Thus, despite the growing volume of applied research, our knowledge still lacks a body of theory capable of explaining firm growth (Dobbs and Hamilton 2007).

The inability of the existing theories in explaining firm growth has led researchers to look for a different approach (Davidsson and Wiklund 2000). One of the common approaches is to utilise some of the theories grounded in real world firm conceptualisation, called empirical firm theories, by Seth and Thomas (1994). For example, Ardichvili et al. (1998) classified empirical growth studies into two groups, namely: factors of growth studies and growth process studies. The former can be labelled as a deterministic approach, and the latter as an evolutionary approach. Davidsson and Wiklund (2006) categorised empirical growth studies into four groups, based on their underlying assumptions. Three groups belong to the deterministic approach while one group belongs to the process approach. Between these two approaches, the deterministic approach has gained popularity in entrepreneurship research. This approach focuses on identifying the set of explanatory variables relating to people, the firm and its industry that can explain firm growth (Dobbs and Hamilton 2007).

### Determinants of SMEs Growth

The surveyed literature regarding the determinants of SMEs growth has shown that the factors that influence SMEs growth can be divided into internal and external factors (Dobbs and Hamilton 2007). External factors are those factors, which are outside the entrepreneur's control. On the other hand, internal factors relate directly to the entrepreneur and to specific firm characteristics.

### Empirical Research on SMEs Growth

A number of studies have attempted to develop and test different factors that influence the performance of SMEs. For example, Davidsson (1991) developed a model of small firm performance in which the actual growth is seen to be the function of ability, need and opportunity. His findings suggest that need, ability and opportunity can explain variation in the growth rates among small firms. Likewise, Storey (1994) made a substantial contribution in this area by reviewing previous studies on small firm performance and constructed a theoretical framework to describe different types of factors that might influence the performance of small firms. He later concluded that there are three key influences upon the performance rate in small firms. These include: characteristics of the entrepreneurs and their access to resources, specific firm characteristics and types of strategy associated with growth. Similarly, Hall (1995) identified seven factors that may determine firm performance. These factors include the personal characteristics of the owner, the availability of outside assistance, motivation, strategic management, marketing policy, financial management, and market characteristics

### *Challenges Faced by SMEs*

Despite this acknowledged importance and SME contribution to economic growth, SMEs across the world and in Tanzania in particular, are still faced with numerous challenges that inhibit their business survival and performance. In support of this, previous studies (e.g. Muhammad et al. 2010; Foon et al. 2006) have identified various challenges facing SMEs in the World. These include low productivity, lack of managerial capabilities and financing, technology, heavy regulatory burden, and lack of access to formal business. According to Naicker (2006), problems experienced by SMEs can be categorised according to the nature and stage in which SMEs are currently in. Those constraints can be categorised as formal, informal, economic and others across different stages. The framework which identifies SME development trends based on an analysis of 35 empirical studies on constraints facing SME development in transition countries, found that more fundamental barriers in early stages are related to legal issues while more specific constraints related to human resources, and skill development characterise at later stages. Furthermore, researchers found that three formal constraints, taxes, policy instability and legal regulations, form a barrier for business development throughout the stages. This confirms a previous study conducted by Benzing, Chu, and Kara (2009) in Turkey, which found that the most serious problem facing entrepreneurs is confusion and complex tax system. In the same way, studies conducted in Africa argued that the principal challenges facing SMEs include difficulty in accessing start-up capital, stringent credit conditionality, high interest rates on credit, inadequate government support for SMEs, the added expenses of corruption and bribery, a weak economy, limited access to financial capital, an inability to hire reliable employees, and too much competition (Gray, Cooley, and Lutabingwa 1997; Ivy 1997; Kiggundu 2002; Benzing, Chu, and Callanan 2005; Chu, Benzing, and

McGee 2007). It has, however, been observed that insufficient capital is still the major bottleneck faced by the SME operators (Lader, 1996; Abor and Quartey 2010). According to a World Bank study, about 90 per cent of small enterprises surveyed stated that credit was a major constraint to new investment (Parker et al. 1995). Levy (1993) also found that there is limited access to financial resources available to smaller enterprises compared to larger organisations and this results in their low growth and development. This is largely contributed to the fact that SMEs have limited access to capital markets partly due to the perception of higher risk, informational barriers, the higher costs of intermediation for smaller firms, the high interest rates, collateral requirements and the cumbersome processes have often been mentioned as the main impediments to SMEs (Biekpe 2004). Similarly, Orser et al. (2000) noted that unavailability or lack of information about alternative sources of finances and inability of SMEs to evaluate financing option were some of the major problems facing the SMEs.

Apart from SME funding and access to finance, the GEM Reports (2001–2010) noted that South African SMEs suffer from poor management skills, which is a result of a lack of adequate training and education. In addition, Tushabonwe-Kazooba (2006) revealed that poor record-keeping and lack of basic business management experience and skills are major contributors to failure of small business. In fact, Ogunjiuba (2004) observed that several small-scale enterprise operators are highly proficient in their technical field but are less well experienced in managerial competence. This may be part of the reasons for the longevity in their backwardness. Mbugua et al. (2013) found that (in)adequacy of availability of finances, good or poor business management skills, good or poor marketing and entrepreneurial attributes of the owner managers were statistically significant in determining growth or lack of growth of these enterprises.

In Tanzania, SMEs are faced with unique problems including heavy costs of compliance resulting from their size. Other constraints include insufficient working premises and limited access to finance. In addition, Business Development Services, namely services related to entrepreneurship, business training, marketing, technology development, and information are underdeveloped and not readily available (URT 2002). On the other hand, SME operators lack information as well as appreciation for such services and can hardly afford to pay for the services. As a result, operators of the sector have rather low skills. Also, there is no umbrella association for SMEs. At the same time, the institutions and associations supporting SMEs are weak, fragmented and uncoordinated partly due to lack of clear guidance and policy for the development of the sector (URT 2002).

## Methodology

This exploratory study focused on micro and small wood furniture manufacturers in Tanzania. The exploratory case studies were conducted in Dar es Salaam city and involved three owner-managers. The choice of the sector was based on their predominance in the micro and small manufacturing sector. Furthermore, this sector is not very import-dependent because most of the raw materials used are found in Tanzanian forests (Harding et al. 2002). Dar es Salaam City was selected because it is the largest commercial city in Tanzania, with more than 3 million people and most of the SMEs in this region. The three firms used for this study were purposely chosen on the author's judgement of how well the firm related to the topic in question. Three criteria were used in trying to find suitable interviewees by the author's own judgement. These criteria are: the respondent has to be an owner-manager, the firm is considered to be successful, the awareness of the respondent in the area under study. In this study, we define a successful business as one that has been able to increase its firms' assets and sales since its establishment.

The main source of primary data was in-depth interviews with three owner-managers of wood furniture manufacturing. The interview guide consisted of the following set of questions: owner-manager's personal demographic information, reasons behind establishment of the current business, firm specific factors, drivers for the firm's success and challenges affecting business performance. The interviews lasted between two to three hours. Data analysis was qualitative, consisting mainly of making summaries and tables according to key issues and themes.

## Findings

### *Personal Demographic Information of Owner-managers*

As shown in Table 10.1, the age of entrepreneurs range from 31 to 44 years. One owner-manager is a primary school leaver, one is a secondary school leaver, and one is a degree holder in Forestry Management. Moreover, the findings indicate that all owner-managers sampled have attended vocational training (carpentry education), offered by various colleges in Tanzania. Owner-managers in the case show a wide range of experiences. Two owner-managers had entrepreneurial experience prior to starting their current business. Likewise, all of them had managerial and industrial experience prior to starting their current business. All the owner-managers interviewed in the study are married

TABLE 10.3 *Owner-managers: Key characteristics*

| Characteristics | Detail | Number |
|---|---|---|
| Owner-manager's age | 33 | 1 |
| | 35 | 1 |
| | 44 | 1 |
| Education level | Primary school | 1 |
| | O-level secondary school | 1 |
| | A level secondary school | 0 |
| | Bachelor Degree | 1 |
| SME category | Micro enterprises | 1 |
| | Small enterprises | 2 |
| Number of employees | 1–4 | 1 |
| | 5–10 | 2 |

and have children. All three wood furniture enterprises sampled were in the micro- and small-size category and employ between four and ten workers (see Table 10.3).

All firms sampled were established more than ten years ago. With regard to their legal framework, the results revealed that all SMEs interviewed operate as limited liability companies.

The three owner-managers are running their business by themselves, working full-time in the business, and are the primary decision makers in their own business.

### *Motivation for Starting a Business*

The motivation for the interviewed owner-managers to start a business varied from need for independence, to make a living, to increasing personal income. One respondent felt that he enjoyed working better in his own business than working for somebody else. Another owner-manager had been pushed to starting a business because it was the only way he could survive. On the other hand, another respondent started a business because he was dissatisfied with the salary he was getting from his previous employment. These motivating factors are not dissimilar to those given by researchers in both developed and developing economies (Mitchell 2004; Swierczek and Thai 2003; Kirkwood 2009; Isaga, Masurel, and Kees 2015). For example, Respondent Juma explains the motivation for starting a current business.

*Juma is a graduate who comes from the Songea region in Tanzania. While studying, Juma also worked as a part-time employee in his uncle's carpentry business. After finishing his Bachelor's degree, Juma got employed with a banking firm for five years before starting his current business. During the interview, Juma started to say that the main reason for starting his current business was the desire to be independent and to do the work he wanted to do most. Juma further noted that having been involved in the wood furniture business from the early age of ten to 23, he knows what the business environment is in that industry. Juma was convinced that before entering into that business he needed to investigate why foreign wood products are cheaper than local products and to raise some capital for his potential businesses. After his research, Juma decided to look for a paid job so that he could raise some money before starting his current business. While working at the bank, Juma managed to buy some wood works machines and save some money for starting his current business. Juma started his business while he was still working with the bank. However, organising and managing the firm next to his job in the bank became increasingly complicated and after three months he decided to quit the paid job and started working full time on his current business. Currently, the firm produces wood furniture and it is situated in a busy area in Dar es Salaam. The firm has an open workshop including a number of heavy sawing machines. The company also saws wood and parts for other furniture producers, as a paid service. The firm has also opened two showrooms in Dar es Salaam. The firm currently has fifteen workers. Three out of the fifteen have fixed employment contracts. His goal is now to expand the business and lay the groundwork for exporting the products.*

### *Drivers for SME Development*

Based on the in-depth interview among owner-managers of the three wood furniture businesses it became clear that their firms had grown in some way since their start-up. In fact, there was a significant increase in number of employees, sales turnover, production, the value of the business and number of sawing machines.

> My business is growing, expanding to be more precise. It has been eleven years since I started out and I already own two workshops and one show room.

*Hamisi started his business in Dar es Salaam in 2001 as a sole proprietor with a retail shop selling a variety of items. He moved to self-employment after completing secondary school education. After making a reasonable profit, in 2005, Hamisi decided to move into the furniture business because the money in circulation in the furniture industry was higher than in the retail shop. He further argued that when you sell one wood furniture product the profit you make is far better than the profit you could be making in a retail shop for a month. The furniture business started to expand after winning a tender to supply office furniture and students' desks to ten primary schools. The profit obtained from the tender was partly injected in the business and some was used to buy 20 acres of trees. He also employed his wife as an assistant manager and he employed one full-time employee. Since 2010, despite some ups and downs, the demand for his products has been increasing significantly. With the loan, profits and savings, the owner managed to buy three large machines and five small hand machines and moved to a larger premise. The machines enabled him to produce furniture faster, and of higher quality than his local competitors. On the other hand, the larger premise enabled him to accommodate the expanded stock and machines.*

In summary, the research shows that the firms interviewed had grown or developed in some way, and that there was a significant increase in the number of employees and firms' assets from their start-up. Significantly, the findings also show that most of those employed were on permanent contracts. There are also signs that as the business develops, owner-managers make improvements in the benefits they put in place for employees, and increasingly they recognise the value to the business of putting these benefits in place.

Moreover, self-determination, creativity, passion and respect for business were at least mentioned by all owner-managers interviewed as major driver for their success. Other success factors include the desire to fulfill family responsibilities, having more customers and trust.

### *Challenges Affecting Their Business Performance*

There are a number of challenges that affect the development of the wood furniture business in Tanzania. From the interviews, lack of access to finance, international competition and cheap imports, a problematic business environment, unreliable power supply and poor infrastructure were perceived as major factors affecting the performance of wood furniture enterprises in Tanzania.

With regard to the financial constraints, the respondents further expressed their deep concern about the difficult terms and stringent credit conditions of formal credits of the financial institutions in Tanzania. These constraints include high interest rates, prohibitive requirements of collateral, short or zero grace period and short repayment periods. Moreover, another respondent argued that there are so many stringent procedures to be adhered to in order to obtain bank finance. Nevertheless, all interviewees felt that the best approach to finance their business was through internal financing. They all have a strong desire to avoid external financing whenever possible.

> I have seen how external financing affected my Uncle's business and I don't want to lose control of my firm or be burdened with the risk of debt or lose my house and put all my family in pressure because of the debt. I am comfortable to fund my firm's expansion through internal funds.

Previous studies (Gray, Cooley, and Lutabingwa 1997; Ivy 1997; Kiggundu 2002; Benzing, Chu, and Callanan 2005; Chu, Benzing, and McGee 2007) have also noted the lack of access to external finance to be a major constraint to SMEs.

Furthermore, each owner-manager who was interviewed mentioned at least one problem associated with imported furniture.

> "And because of the imported furniture it is more difficult to get orders from the government offices. Most government agencies prefer imported furniture." The owner wonders why the government is buying imported instead of local products – "people from the government usually say that they will buy furniture from Tanzania but I have never seen them actually buying local furniture."

The effect of societal norms and practices regarding low-level trust between small SME owner-managers and customers in business operations were also cited to be among the challenges facing owner-managers. For example, the owner-managers were of the opinion that Chinese products that are exported to Africa are of low quality and lack durability. But he wonders why Tanzanian clients buy this lower quality Chinese furniture at a much higher price. From this finding, it is obvious that owner-managers of furniture enterprises in Tanzania faced challenges related to the imported wood products. This is in line with the study conducted by Urban and Naidoo (2012) who both found that the key challenges facing SMEs in most developing countries is meeting local and global competition from well-established businesses.

Furthermore, the survival and performance of the SMEs may also be constrained by environmental challenges such as an unfriendly business environment, government's legal and regulatory framework and developments in the wider economy. Regarding the business environment, the owner-managers were of the opinion that the business environment is not conducive for them to run their business successfully. In fact, the owner-managers blamed the government for not playing its part on making an enabling environment to entrepreneurs. To them, they find the government to be more of a bottleneck than a support agency to entrepreneurship development in Tanzania. One of the respondents further noted that

- "Most of the time when government officers come here, they are coming for their official issues. For example, an official from the municipality is interested in business registration or tax collection, a representative from the Ministry of Natural Resources is interested in inspecting the wood."
- "I never see government officers coming here to talk or ask how the business is going or what problems I am facing."
- "several times we have complained to the Tanzanian government about the high interest rate which is charged by commercial banks and asked the government to establish a venture capital agency, which will enable the majority of us to secure external finance at reasonable rates but in vain."

Moreover, owner-managers who have been interviewed had difficulties in accessing modern equipment, appropriate technologies, and access to the international market.

## Conclusion and Recommendations

The purpose of this paper was to investigate the challenges affecting entrepreneurship development in Tanzania. A qualitative study comprising of three case studies on Tanzanian SMEs was conducted with the aspiration to describe the drivers of being entrepreneurs, drivers for SME development, and challenges affecting their business performance. The findings suggest that the motivation for the interviewed owner-managers to start a business varied from their need for independence, to make a living, to increasing personal income. The findings also suggested that lack of access to finance, international competition, and cheap imports, a problematic business environment, unreliable power supply, and poor infrastructure were the major factors affecting the performance of wood furniture enterprises in Tanzania. Based on the findings, the following recommendations can be put forward to SME owner-managers and government and other agencies that assist SME development in Tanzania

- ***Owner-managers***

To minimise some of the challenges experienced by owner-managers of SMES, as revealed by this study, owner-managers should participate in networking discussions where they can share their experiences on business success and the challenges they are facing to run their businesses. Furthermore, SMEs are recommended to attend entrepreneurship and financial management training so as to enhance their competencies.

- ***Government***

The business environment needs to be one that will foster the growth of SMEs including the wood furniture business. However, the policymakers need to understand the business environment, which should be conducive to SMEs. Based on the findings, some of the issues that need to be addressed include the legal and regulatory framework, cheap imports and financial incentives to SMEs. Regarding the cheap imports the government should concentrate on creating policy and regulations that will promote products that are produced locally and encourage small firms to grow. The government should also develop a financial scheme that protects SMEs from high interest rates.

- ***Stakeholders***

This study noted that some non-governmental organisations are doing a commendable job in promoting SMEs. However, most of these organisations are rather weak, concentrated in urban areas and uncoordinated. This calls for linkages of the institutions supporting SMEs.

## References

Abor, J. & P. Quartey. (2010). "Issues in SME development in Ghana and South Africa", *International Research Journal of Finance and Economics*, 39(6), 215–228.

Agyapong, D. (2010). "Micro, Small and Medium Enterprises' Activities, Income Level and Poverty Reduction in Ghana: A Synthesis of Related Literature", *International Journal of Business and Management*, 5(12), 196.

Amit, R., Glosten, L. & E. Muller. (2003). "Challenges to Theory Development in Entrepreneurship Research", *Journal of Management Studies*, 30(5), 815–833.

Ardichvili, A., Cardoza, R.N., Harmon, B. & S. Vadakath. (1998). "Towards a Theory of New Venture Growth". In: P.D. Reynolds, W. Bygrave, M. Carter, S. Manigart, C. Mason, D. Meyer & K. Shaver (eds), *Frontiers of Entrepreneurship Research*, Wellesley, MA: Babson College.

Benzing, C., Chu, H.M. & G. Callanan. (2005). "A Regional Comparison of the Motivation and Problems of Vietnamese Entrepreneurs", *Journal of Developmental Entrepreneurship*, 10(01), 3–27.

Benzing, C.M., Chu, H. & O. Kara. (2009). "Entrepreneurs in Turkey: A Factor Analysis of Motivations, Success Factors, and Problems", *Journal of Small Business Management*, 47 (1), 58–91.

Biekpe, N. (2004). "Financing Small Business in Sub-Saharan Africa: Review of Some Key Credit Lending Models and Impact of Venture Capital", *Journal of African Business*, 5(1), 29–44.

Bridge, S., O'Neill, K. & F. Martin. (2009). *Understanding Enterprise: Entrepreneurship and Small Business*. Hampshire: Palgrave Macmillan.

Cantillon, R. (1755). Essay on the nature of general commerce. Henry Higgs, trans. London: Macmllan.

Carrasco, F.R.C. & M.T.A. Perez. (2008). "Innovation as a Source of Entrepreneurial Opportunities", *Revista de Economia Mundial*, (19), 135–156.

Casson, M. (1982). *The Entrepreneur: An Economic Theory*. Rowman & Littlefield.

Chell, E., Haworth, J. & S. Brearley. (1991). *The Entrepreneurial Personality: Concepts, Cases, and Categories*. London: Routledge.

Chu, H.M., Benzing, C. & C. McGee. (2007). "Ghanaian and Kenyan Entrepreneurs: A Comparative Analysis of Their Motivations, Success Characteristics, and Problems", *Journal of Developmental Entrepreneurship*, 12 (3), 295–322.

Churchill, N.C. & V.L. Lewis. (1983). "The Five Stages of Small Business Growth", *Harvard Business Review*, 61(3), 30–35.

Cunningham, J.B. & J. Lischeron. (1991). "Defining Entrepreneurship", *Journal of Small Business Management*, 29(1), 45–61.

Davidsson, P. (1991), "Continued Entrepreneurship – Ability, Need, and Opportunity As Determinants of Small Firm Growth," Journal of Business Venturing, 6(6), 405–29.

Davidsson, P. & J. Wiklund. (2006). "Conceptual and Empirical Challenges in the Study of Firm Growth". In: P. Davidsson, F. Delmar & J. Wiklund (eds), *Entrepreneurship and the Growth of Firms*, Cheltenham: Edward Elgar Publishing, 39–61.

Davidsson, P. & J. Wiklund. (2000). "Conceptual and Empirical Challenges in the Study of Firm Growth". In: D.L. Sexton & H. Landström (eds), *The Blackwell Handbook of Entrepreneurship*, Oxford: Blackwell, 26–44.

Davidsson, P., Achtenhagen, L. & L. Naldi. (2007). "What Do We Know About Small Firm Growth?" In: Simon Parker (ed.), *The Life Cycle of Entrepreneurial Ventures*, New York: Springer 361–398.

Davidsson, P., Delmar, F. & J. Wiklund. (2002). "Entrepreneurship as Growth; Growth as Entrepreneurship". In: M.A. Hitt, R.D. Ireland, S. Camp & D. Sexton (eds), *Strategic Entrepreneurship: Creating a New Mindset*, Blackwell: Oxford, 328–342.

Delmar, F. (2000). "The Psychology of the Entrepreneur" In: S. Carter & D. Jones-Evans (eds), *Enterprise and Small Business, Principles and Practice Policy*, Upper Saddle River, NJ: Prentice Hall.

Delmar, F. & J. Wiklund. (2008). "The Effect of Small Business Managers of Growth Motivation on Firm Growth: A Longitudinal Study", *Entrepreneurship Theory and Practice*, 32(3), 437–457.

Dobbs, M. & R.T. Hamilton. (2007). "Small Business Growth: Recent Evidence and New Directions", *International Journal of Entrepreneurial Behaviour and Research*, 13(5), 296–322.

Drucker, P.F. (1985). *Innovation and Entrepreneurship Practices and Principles*. New York, Harper and Row.

Foon, L.S. & S. Eu-Gene. (2006). "The Changing of Education in the Globalized World". *Proceedings of Persidangan Kebangsaan IKS 2006*, Kuala Lumpur: Universiti Utara Malaysia.

Galbraith, J.R. (1982). "The Stages of Growth", *Journal of Business Strategy*, 3(4), 70–79.

Gibb, A., and Davies, L.G. (1990), "In pursuit of frameworks for the development of growth models of the small business," International Small Business Journal, 9, 15–31.

Gray, K.R., Cooley, W. & J. Lutabingwa. (1997). "Small-scale Manufacturing in Kenya", *Journal of Small Business Management*, 1, 66–72.

Greiner, L.E. (1972). "Evolution and Revolution as Organizations Grow", *Harvard Business Review*, 50, 37–46.

Hall, G. (1995), "Surviving and Prospering in the small firm sector," London Routledge.

Harding, A., Söderbom, M. & F. Teal. (2002). *The Tanzanian Manufacturing Enterprise Survey*, Centre for the Study of African Economies (CSAE) University of Oxford, Oxford.

Hebert, F.R. & N.A. Link. (1989). "In Search of the Meaning of Entrepreneurship", *Small Business Economics*, 1(1), 39–49.

Hitt, M.A., Camp, S.M., Ireland, R.D. & D.L. Sexton. (2002). *Strategic Entrepreneurship: Creating a New Mindset*. Oxford: Blackwell Publishers.

Isaga, N., Masurel, E. & K. van Montfort. (2015). "Owner-manager Motives and the Growth of SMEs in Developing Countries: Evidence from the Furniture Industry in Tanzania", *Journal of Entrepreneurship in Emerging Economies*, 7(3), 190–211.

Ivy, R.L. 1997. "Entrepreneurial Strategies and Problems in Post-Communist Europe: A Survey of SMEs in Slovakia", *Journal of Small Business Management*, 93–97.

Kanaan, O. (2000). "Tanzania's Experience with Trade Liberalization", *Finance and Development*, 37(2), 30–33.

Katz, J. & W.B. Gartner. (1988). "Properties of Emerging Organizations", *Academy of Management Review*, 13(3), 429–441.

Kiggundu, M.N. (2002). "Entrepreneurs and Entrepreneurship in Africa: What is Known and What Needs to be Done", *Journal of Developmental Entrepreneurship*, 7 (3), 239–258.

Kinunda-Rutashobya, L. & D.R. Olomi. (1999). *African Entrepreneurship and Small Business Development*, Dar es Salaam: DUP Ltd.

Kirby, A.D. (2003). *Entrepreneurship*. Maidenhead: McGraw-Hill Education.

Kirkwood, J. (2009). "Motivational Factors in a Push-Pull Theory of Entrepreneurship", *Gender in Management: An International Journal*, 24(5), 346–364.

Kirzner, I. (1985) *Discovery and the Capitalist Process*. Chicago, IL: University of Chicago Press.

Kirzner, I.M. (1979) *Perception, Opportunity and Profit*. Chicago, IL: University of Chicago Press.

Kirzner, I.M. (2009). "The Alert and Creative Entrepreneur: A Clarification", *Small Business Economics*, 32(2), 145–152.

Knight, F. (1921). *Risk, Uncertainty and Profit*. New York: Houghton Mifflin.

Kobia, M. & D. Sikalieh. (2010). "Towards a Search for the Meaning of Entrepreneurship", *Journal of European Industrial Training*, 34(2), 110–127.

Kristiansen, S., Kimeme, J.A., Mbwambo, A.H. & W. Fathul. (2005). "Information Flows and Adaptation in Tanzanian Cottage Industries", *Entrepreneurship and Regional Development*, 17(5), 365–388.

Kuratko, D.F. & M.R. Hodgetts. (2001). *Entrepreneurship: A Contemporary Approach*, Orlando, FL: The Dryden Press, Harcourt Brace College Publishers.

Lader, P. (1996). "The Public/Private Partnership", *Springs Spring*, 35(2), 41–44.

Levy, B. (1993). 'Obstacles to Developing Indigenous Small and Medium Enterprises: An Empirical Assessment', The World Bank Economic Review, 7(1), pp. 65–83.

Low, M.B. & I.C. MacMillan. (1988). "Entrepreneurship: Past Research and Future Challenges", *Journal of Management*, 14(2), 139–161.

Masurel, E. & K. van Montfort. (2006). "Life Cycle Characteristics of Small Professional Service Firms", *Journal of Small Business Management*, 44(3), 461–473.

Mbugua, J.K., Mbugua, S.N., Wangoi, M., Ogada, J.O. & J.N. Kariuki. (2013). "Factors Affecting the Growth of Micro and Small Enterprises: A Case of Tailoring and Dressmaking Enterprises in Eldoret", *International Journal of Business and Social Science*, 4(5), 285–293.

Miller, D. & P.H. Friesen. (1984). "A Longitudinal Study of Corporate Life Cycle", *Management Science*, 30(10), 1161–1183.

Mitchell, B.C. (2004). "Motives of Entrepreneurs: A Case Study of South Africa", *The Journal of Entrepreneurship*, 13 (2), 167–183.

Muhammad, M.Z., Char, A.K., bin Yasoa, M.R. & Z. Hassan. (2010). "Small and Medium Enterprises (SMEs) Competing in the Global Business Environment: A Case of Malaysia", *International Business Research*, 3(1), 66.

Naicker N.I. (2006). "Factors Contributing to Women being successful in the SMME Sector". A mini dissertation submitted in partial fulfilment of the requirements a Master's in Business Administration in the Faculty of Management at the University of Johannesburg.

Nchimbi, M.I. (2002). "Gender and Entrepreneurship in Tanzania: A Comparative Analysis of Male-Female's Start-up Motivation, Individual Characteristics and Perceptions of Business Success", PhD dissertation, University of Dar es Salaam, Tanzania.

O'Farrell, P.N. & D. Hitchens. (1988). "Alternative Theories of Small Firm Growth: A Critical Review", *Environment and Planning A*, 20 1365–1383.

Ogunjiuba, K.K. (2004). "Credit Availability to Small Scale Enterprises in Nigeria: Important of New Capital Base for Banks-Background and Issues". Retrieved from www.Business.com.

Olomi, D.R. (2001). "Entrepreneurial Motivation in Developing Country Context: Incidence, Antecedents and Consequences of Growth-Seeking Behaviour among Tanzanian Owner-managers", PhD dissertation, University of Dar es Salaam, Tanzania.

Orser, B.J., Hogarth-Scott, S. & A.L. Riding. (2000). "Performance, Firm Size, and Management Problem Solving", *Journal of Small Business Management*, 38(4), 42.

Parker, R., Riopelle, R. & W. Steel. (1995). "Small Enterprises Adjusting to Liberalization in Five African Countries", World Bank Discussion Paper, No. 271, African Technical Department Series, The World Bank, Washington DC.

Penrose, E.T. (1959). *The Theory of the Growth of the Firm*. New York: Blackwell.

Quinn, R.E. & K. Cameron. (1983). "Organizational Life Cycles and Shifting Criteria of Effectiveness: Some Preliminary Evidence", *Management Science*, 29(1), 33–51.

Schumpeter, J.A. (1934). *The Theory of Economic Development*, Cambridge, MA: Harvard University Press.

Scott, M. & R. Bruce. (1987). "Five Stages of Growth in Small Business", *Long Range Planning*, 20(3), 45–52.

Seth, A. & H. Thomas. (1994). "Theories of the Firm: Implications for Strategy Research", *Journal of Management Studies*, 31(2), 165–191.

Shane, S. (2007). "A general theory of entrepreneurship: The individual-Opportunity Nexus". Aldershot: Edward Elgar.

Shane, S.A. & R.A. Baron. (2008). *Entrepreneurship: A Process Perspective*. Mason, OH: Thomson/South-Western.

Sharma, P. & J.J. Chrisman. (1999). "Toward a Reconciliation of the Definitional Issues in the Field of Corporate Entrepreneurship", *Entrepreneurship Theory and Practice*, 23(3): 11–27.

Smith, K., Mitchell, T. & C. Summer. (1985). "Top-Level Management Priorities in Different Stages of the Organization Life Cycle", *Academy of Management Journal*, 28(4), 799–820.

Stevenson H.H., Roberts M.J. & H.I. Groesbeck. (1985). *New Business Ventures and the Entrepreneur*, Homewood, IL: Irwin.

Storey, D.J. (1994). *Understanding the Small Business Sector*, Routledge: London.

Swierczek, F. & T.H. Thai. (2003). "Motivation, Entrepreneurship, and Performance of SMEs in Vietnam", *Journal of Enterprising Culture*, vol. 11, no. 1, 47–68.

Tushabonwe-Kazooba, C. (2006). "Causes of Small Business Failure in Uganda: A Case Study from Bushenyi and Mbarara Towns", *African Studies Quarterly*, 8(4).

Urban, B. & R. Naidoo. (2012). "Business Sustainability: Empirical Evidence on Operational Skills in SMEs in South Africa", *Journal of Small Business and Enterprise Development*, 19(1), 146–163.

URT. (2003). "Small and Medium Enterprise (SME) Development Policy", Ministry of Industry and Trade, [online], Available: http://www.tanzania.go.tz/pdf/smepolicy.pdf. Accessed in January 2016.

URT. (2008). "Business Survey Tanzania", Ministry of Finance and Economic Affairs, National Bureau of Statistics (Dar es Salaam).

URT. (2002). "Small and Medium Enterprises Development Policy", Ministry of Industries and Trade, Government Printer, Dar es Salaam, 3, 4, 7–9.

USAID. (1993). "The Evaluation of Small Enterprise Programs and Projects: Issues and Community Development", *Evaluation Special Study*, 13, 1–12.

Von Gelderen, M., Frese, M. & R. Thurik. (2000). "Strategies, Uncertainty and Performance of Small Business Startups". *Small Business Economics*, 15(3), 165–181.

Wambugu, M.C. (2002). "Trade Liberalization and Entrepreneurship: Responses to Constraints and Opportunities by Micro and Small Garment Producers in Nairobi", MA Thesis, University of Nairobi.

Wiklund, J. (1998). "Small Firm Growth and Performance: Entrepreneurship and Beyond", PhD dissertation, Jönköping International Business School, Jönköping.

CHAPTER 11

# Institutional and Contextual Factors Effects on Entrepreneurship in Cameroon: The Case of the Transport Sector

*Françoise Okah-Efogo and Crescence Marie-France Okah-Atenga*

## Introduction

In Africa, whatever the considered age group, there are more entrepreneurs in the early stages of entrepreneurship than anywhere else in the world (Global Entrepreneurship Monitor (GEM) Report 2014). According to the GEM survey (2014), 55.57 per cent of the population between 18–64 years expresses entrepreneurial intentions in Cameroon. Similarly, 37.4 per cent of the same age population is in the early course of their business activity. Between 2014 and 2015, total entrepreneurial activity has decreased in Cameroon (from 37.4 per cent to 25.4 per cent of all adults). Nonetheless, 61.1 per cent of the respondents think that entrepreneurship is a good career choice (GEM Report 2015). Furthermore, SMEs contribute to gross domestic product (GDP) at a level of 36 per cent.

According to the same surveys and to Okah Efogo and Timba (2015), more than 50 per cent of entrepreneurship activities are opportunity-driven. Moreover, financing problems are the second factor hindering entrepreneurship, behind technology transfer issues. Yet, most articles and books published on entrepreneurship focus mainly on developed countries. This study participates in bridging the gap. In this perspective, it has three purposes: namely, to identify the institutional and contextual factors that represent barriers and/or opportunities for entrepreneurship in theory; to assess their potential impact in the specific context of Cameroon; and to propose strategies to alleviate constraints based on the experience of some enterprises.

Specifically, this study is based on the case of three Cameroonian companies in the transport sector. To avoid negative publicity for these companies, we will call them company 1, company 2, and company 3. These companies have operated in Cameroon for 18 years, 17 years and 11 years, respectively. Their activities cover, respectively, the Centre, East, Littoral, North,[1] South, South-West

1 Broader definition: Adamawa, Extreme-North and North.

 | DOI 10.1163/9789004351615_012

and North-West regions. The different destinations allow for the capturing of cultural specificities and diversity in Cameroon, generally called "small Africa" (Tchawa 2012; Henry 2008).

The choice of this sector is based on several facts. Firstly, the report TRANSTAT (2014) from the Ministry of Transport states that this sector plays an important role and has had an increasing contribution to the GDP between 2009 and 2013 (33.33 per cent). But demographic growth and the resulting movements of populations from villages to towns or from one region to another, for economic purposes, induce the need for a better supply of transport services in terms of quantity and quality.

Secondly, between 2006 and 2016, 466 persons (357 for the French version and 109 for the English version, Cameroon is bilingual) expressed their opinion on the quality of transport in Cameroon through an online survey on the Cameroonian Ministry of Transport website (last accessed on 2 May 2016). More than 60 per cent of them declare that the quality of transport is poor. This perception is corroborated in the TRANSTAT report, which shows that most of the vehicles operating in Cameroon are ten to 20 years old (75 per cent of new registrations, 83.4 per cent of re-registrations; Ministry of Transport 2014: 58). Despite the age of the vehicles, the number of accidents has decreased. The National Statistical Institute reports an increase in transport prices of 14.2 per cent in July 2014.

Nevertheless, some enterprises offering transport services can be seen as success stories, given their long life span (more than 15 years). Therefore, a study on transport firms could help to shed light on barriers and opportunities relating to entrepreneurship in Cameroon, to understand the managerial choices of entrepreneurs, and to highlight the influence of culture through passengers' behaviour.

Such a study is of both scientific and contextual interest. At the contextual level, the study highlights the institutional and cultural factors that influence the development of enterprises in Cameroon. The goal is to identify weaknesses in the system of entrepreneurship promotion and to propose solutions that would improve the creation and survival of enterprises given the fact that they are important tools against poverty through job creation. On the scientific plan, the case studies enrich the literature on entrepreneurship in Africa, especially regarding the impact of institutional and contextual factors.

The specifics of the Cameroonian business context are taken from a documentary analysis. The main documents are legal documents (laws and other legislation), periodic reports from national and international agencies

(Ministry of Transport, GEM and others) and other publications. The case study part is based on a semi-directive survey addressed to managers of the three selected companies.

The remainder of this chapter is organised as follows: a brief introduction is followed by a look at the actual entrepreneurship context in Cameroon. We then underline the main opportunities and barriers and subsequently discuss the case of three transport companies. The chapter closes with a summary of our findings.

The results should reveal that if the regulatory changes have simplified creation of enterprises in the transport sector, it remains that other factors including road infrastructure, financial needs, and the behaviour of different actors linked to the Cameroonian culture are likely to hinder entrepreneurship growth and survival.

## Global Environment of Entrepreneurship Development in Cameroon

This section begins with a brief review of the influence of institutions and context on the propensity to undertake and on the effects of entrepreneurship. This helps to identify the main institutional elements to evaluate the attractiveness of the Cameroonian context for entrepreneurship in general, and more specifically in the transport sector. Hence, the section ends with a description of the institutional context of entrepreneurship in Cameroon.

### *A Brief Theoretical Review on Institutions, Context, and Entrepreneurship*

Since the work of Porter (1985), the environment of an enterprise has been identified as an important component of the performance of a company and specifically its competitiveness. This idea is also echoed by more recent authors (Niyonsaba 2013). With particular reference to the transport sector, Didier & Prud'homme (2007) note in their report that the activity is linked, among other things, to the physical, economic and institutional organization of the country. Economic theory of enterprise defines environment as all external forces that act and react in favour of or against the activity and health of a company. The usual taxonomy distinguishes three types of environments: the macro-environment, the meso-environment, and the microenvironment. A less common classification can be represented by the following figure (Figure 11.1):

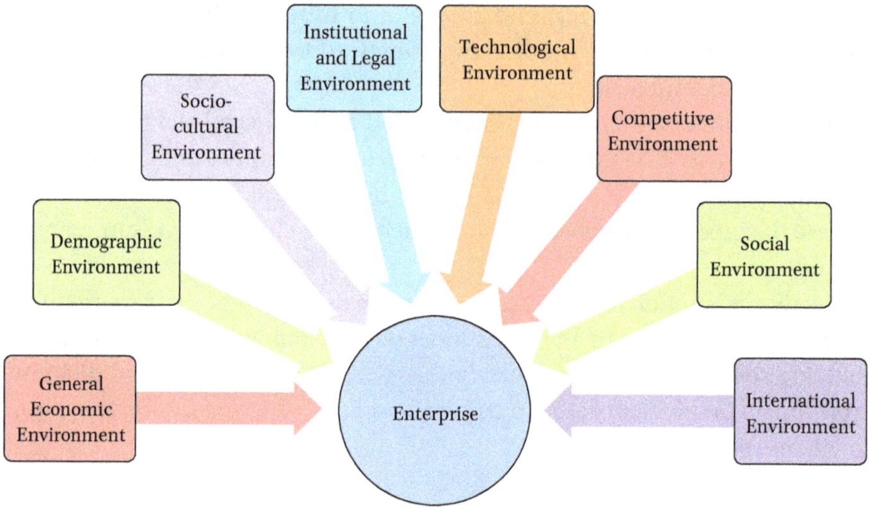


FIGURE 11.1 *Environment elements of enterprises*
SOURCE: BRESSY AND KONKUYT (2014)

The environment elements of enterprise may be constraints or opportunities that are binding influences on entrepreneurship. Concerning the sociocultural environment, it is closely linked to the context and refers to lifestyles, moral and aesthetic values, and others that affect customers' economic needs and behaviour. The institutional environment is the framework that established all the rules to which the company must comply (tax regulations, commercial, social, etc.).

Theoretically, the beginnings of an institutional theory of entrepreneurship can be found in the work of Baumol (1990). He rejects the hypothesis that an invisible hand would ensure markets' efficient functioning. He demonstrates that instruments leading to optimal entrepreneurship, i.e. innovative, sustainable, and productive entrepreneurship, are very concrete steps. Precisely, government actions should lead to an incentive-rich institutional environment. This task is realised through the establishment of rules of law, implementation of tax arrangements, and the like. Baumol adds that institutions are the best levers for entrepreneurship development because they can be profoundly and rapidly changed (Pacitto et al. 2014). If the allocative effect of institutions on entrepreneurial activities has been validated by empirical studies (see for example the work of Sobel, 2008), Williamson (2000) qualifies this theory by showing through a classification (Table 11.1) that institutions cannot be changed as quickly as suggested by Baumol (1990).

Following Williamson (2000), Hwang and Powell (2005) spell out the ways and means for changing institutions. They identify three institutional change

TABLE 11.1 *Speed of institutions replacement*

| Type of institutions | Time for change |
|---|---|
| Embeddedness: informal institutions, customs, traditions, norms, religion | 100 to 1000 years |
| Institutional environment: formal rules of the game – esp. property (polity, judiciary, bureaucracy) | 10 to 100 years |
| Governance: play of the game – esp. contracts (aligning governance structure with transactions) | 1 to 10 years |
| Resource allocation and employment (prices and quantities; incentive alignment) | Continuous |

SOURCE: WILLIAMSON (2000: 596–600)

processes. The first process involves extending the jurisdiction of a court. The second process is the creation or adoption of standards by a professional or technical group. The third method is the development of formal rules to assist some groups of workers/activities.

Casson (1991) has contributed to the institutional theory of entrepreneurship. He emphasises the important role of the entrepreneurial environment and especially the impact of family networks. In the same vein, Marchesnay and Julien (2011) point out that territorial specificities, quality of infrastructure, and quality of state intervention to mobilise resources and supplement them with appropriate support are important for entrepreneurship.

According to Boettke and Coyne (2009: 139), "institutions are the formal and informal rules governing human behavior (*see North (1990, 1991)*). Examples of formal rules include codified legal and political structures, as well as written rules such as constitutions. [...] Informal rules include culture, norms, conventions, and mores not backed by formal law, but by social custom" (Boettke and Coyne, 2009: 139).

They add, following Shirley (2005, 2008) who defined institutional theory of entrepreneurship as including culture, informal rules, and formal institutions. Moreover, for them, institutions represent the most important factor before entrepreneurial resources and technology. This statement proves true both in the Schumpeterian hypothesis of entrepreneurship as well as in the Kirznerian assumption of entrepreneurship (Kirzner 1999).

Empirically, Campbell (2007) says that the institutionalised environment is measured through the regulatory role played by the state, the role of industry, the role of NGOs, the role of associations, the role of the normative environment, and the role of communication with stakeholders. Many studies highlight the transmission channels of the effect of institutions on entrepreneurship. They show that when the economic structure of institutions changes (globalisation, advent of new technologies, demographics, global competition, etc.), expected benefits from entrepreneurial opportunities change too (Acs and Audretsch 2001; Audretsch and Thurik 2001; Verheul et al. 2001). Specifically, economic freedom, good currency, an appropriate regulation of credit, well-defined property rights, legal system, and stable laws attract and encourage productive entrepreneurship (Harper 2003; Bjornskov and Foss 2006; Nyström 2008). In Africa, and particularly in Cameroon, some studies confirm the importance of the entrepreneurship environment (Niyonsaba 2013; Berrios 2013). By contrast, government presence (intervention) should be minimal (Bjornskov and Foss 2006; Nyström 2008).

Finally, institutions, theoretically, have a role to play in entrepreneurship. They provide incentives for orientation of entrepreneurship towards innovative and productive activities instead of unproductive and evasive activities. Nevertheless, they can also hinder the emergence of a productive entrepreneurship, hence the importance to change them. However, government presence should be limited.

The next section builds on this literature and proposes a review of Cameroon's institutional environment.

### *An Illustration of Theoretical Highlights in the Cameroonian Context*

Two levels of analysis are implemented in this section. The first level concerns the entire entrepreneurial activity in Cameroon. The second level focuses exclusively on the transport sector.

#### a) Cameroon's Entrepreneurial Institutional Context

In Cameroon, entrepreneurship is governed by a number of institutions and regulations. At the supranational level, there is a set of rules to ensure the harmonisation of business law in 17 African countries, including Cameroon (OHADA). At the national level, the institutional context has been marked by dynamism since the late 1990s. Nevertheless, rankings of international organisations present a mixed figure of the Cameroonian business environment (GEM Report 2015; World Bank Group 2015).

Figures 11.2 and 11.3 illustrate the evaluation of Cameroon's entrepreneurial context. Figure 11.2 suggests that efforts have been made in terms of electricity supply, construction permits, and starting a business (more than 50/100). Cameroon's efforts are deemed insufficient in relation to, for example, access

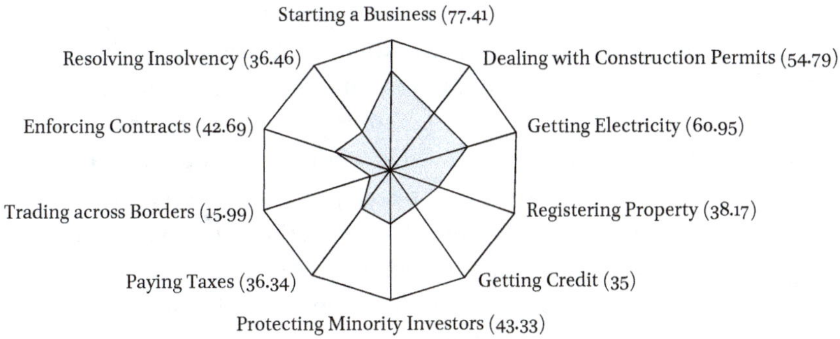


FIGURE 11.2 *Cameroonian business environment*
SOURCE: WORLD BANK GROUP (2015: 9)

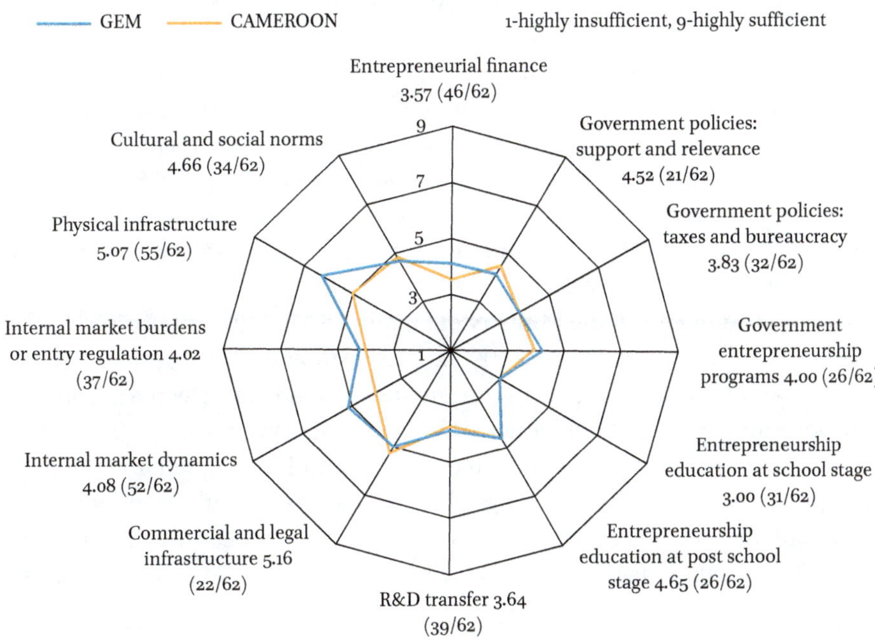


FIGURE 11.3 *Cameroonian business environment* – GEM
SOURCE: GLOBAL ENTREPRENEURSHIP MONITOR (2016: 63)

to credit, resolving insolvency problems, and payment of taxes. In figure 11.3, it appears that the Cameroonian government has made efforts with regard to physical infrastructure, entrepreneurship education, commercial and legal infrastructure, and policy support and relevance. In those aspects, the score is fairly good (more than 4.5/9).

Between 2000 and 2016, many regulatory texts were voted on, adopted, and promulgated, while others were repealed. Notably, in April 2002, the investment charter was enacted with orientations, among others, to promote "[...] entrepreneurship as a rating engine of Cameroon's creative potential, a prerequisite for creating viable and competitive enterprises and a decisive factor for a lasting solution to unemployment and poverty";[2] to facilitate and promote investment and exports in line with the entrepreneurial potential and "the establishment of attractive and incentives tax for investment, that would take into account, firstly, the specificity of the taxation of production equipment and, secondly, the requirements of competitiveness in exports". This charter, revised in 2004 (Law n°2004-20, Ordinance n°09-001), repeals Ordinance n°90-001 of 29 January 1990 establishing the regime of the free zone in Cameroon, ratified by Act n°90-023 of 10 August 1990 and Ordinance n°90-007 of 8 November 1990 relating to the investment Code in Cameroon. It defines an investor (art. 3) as "[...] any moral or physic Cameroonian or foreign legal resident or non-resident, who acquires an asset for its activity in anticipation of a return."

This charter clearly defines the state's role (Ch. 3, Section 1, art. 8). Precisely, "State manages the nation, guarantees the right to justice and security to people and their property. [...] The State enacts laws and regulations, provides oversight, facilitation and regulation of social and economic activities, development of basic infrastructure and information, training, safety, and the substitution for market failures."

On 8 December 2004, the Ministry of Small and Medium Enterprises, Social Economy and Handicraft (MINPMEESA) was established by Presidential Decree N°2004/320 organising the government, as amended by Decree n°2011/408 of 9 December 2011 and supplemented by Decree n°2013/169 of 27 May 2013. In 2010, Law n°2010/001 of 13 April 2010 on the promotion of small and medium enterprises in Cameroon was adopted. This Law has recently been amended and supplemented by Law n°2015/010 of 16 July 2015. This Law defines the concepts of very small business,[3] small business,[4] and medium business.[5] It also

2 Cameroonian texts about laws and regulations can be found for instance in International Business Publications (Inc), Cameroon, Investment, Trade Laws and Regulations Handbook. Volume 1: Strategic Information and Regulations. This source provides annual updates.

3 A very small business is a business that employs less than five persons and whose annual turnover excluding VAT does not exceed fifteen (15) million CFA francs.

4 A small business is a business that employs between six and 20 persons and whose annual turnover excluding VAT exceeds fifteen (15) million CFA francs, and does not exceed 250 million CFA francs.

5 A medium business is an enterprise employing between 21 and one hundred persons and whose annual turnover excluding VAT exceeds 100 million CFA francs and does not exceed one billion CFA francs.

specifies the conditions necessary to benefit from incentives to entrepreneurship. In particular, any company with capital held by at least by 51 per cent of Cameroonians can claim the benefits associated with promoting entrepreneurship (Law n°2015/010 of 16 July 2015, art.2 (new), al. 5).

To the institutional apparel described above we add: the Law on the General Tax Code in Cameroon; the finance laws that have rendered obsolete some measures of the last investment code or have taken special measures to promote certain investments or reinvestments of companies; Law n°2010/020 (adopted December 21, 2010) on the organisation of leasing in Cameroon; the creation of an SME bank in June 2011; the creation of the award subcontracting and partnership following the Decree n°002/PM of 15 February 2012 on the promotion of subcontracting for partnership contracts and contracts negotiated under other investment incentives schemes; the Act establishing the Agency for Investment Promotion as executing agency of the government policy on investment promotion; Decree n°2013/092 of 3 April 2013 establishing the agency for the promotion of SMEs (APME) under the technical supervision of the Ministry of SMEs and the financial supervision of the Ministry of Finance; Law n°2013/004 of 18 April 2013 laying down the incentives for private investment in the Republic of Cameroon.

If entrepreneurship in the transport services sector must comply with this global institutional framework, the fact remains that there are specific laws and regulations for this particular sector.

### b) Cameroon's Entrepreneurial Institutional Context for the Transport Sector

In the transport services sector, different acts have the strength of law and fix the formal rules of the game. At the national level, there is Law n°2001/015 of 23 July 2001 to lay down conditions governing the activities of road carriers and transport agents. It repeals and replaces the Law n°90/030 of 10 august 1990 governing the same sector. There is also Decree n°2004/0607/PM of March 17 to lay down conditions for the practice of the professions of road carrier and road transporter and the Decree n°2015/4209/PM of November 24 laying down the procedures for the exercise of certain powers transferred by the State to municipalities or urban communities in the organisation and management of urban public transport. The Law n°2015/018 of 31 December 2015 on commercial activity in Cameroon, which repealed and replaced the Law of 1990 relating to the same matter, can be added to this legal framework.

At the sub-regional level, the OHADA regulation (Council of Ministers of the Organisation for the Harmonisation of Business Law in Africa) and CEMAC are significant. Regarding OHADA, the Uniform Act on General Commercial Law, which has been revised in 2010, and the Uniform Act relating to Commercial

Companies and Economic Interest Group (AUDSCGIE), which has been revised in 2014, apply to commercial activities, among which transport services traders and auxiliary transporters activities. With regard to the CEMAC regulation, member countries have passed laws to harmonise certain aspects of trade in transport services in general, and land transport in particular. Table 11.2 below presents the major sub-regional texts. These texts are regulations. They must apply entirely to all countries in the region (cf. art 41 of CEMAC act).

With this clarification, it should be noted that, according to article 2 of the Cameroonian Law of 23 July 2001, a road carrier is any individual or corporate body involved in conveying persons or goods by road as a business, using one or more vehicles which he owns or hires. In accordance with the same article, the transport agent is any individual or corporate body who is engaged in an activity that contributes to transporting persons and goods. There are several activities in the field of transport agents, like the management of a road transport terminal, running of a loading and off-loading operation at a road transport terminal, moving and delivery of parcels, and the bunking and debunking of goods (more details in Decree n°2004/0607/PM of 17 March 2004; art.2).

The Law of 2001 also determines who has the right to exercise road transport activities and/or transport agent activities. Any individual or corporate body may exercise these activities, if s/he has the legal capacity to trade. Foreigners can also carry out that activity if, in their own country, Cameroonians can do the same (principle of reciprocity). Finally, the analysis of this subsection seems to support the idea that institutions can play an undeniable

TABLE 11.2 *Sub-regional texts applying to the transport sector*

| | |
|---|---|
| Transport Services | 1. Regulation N°9/00/CEMAC-067-CM-04 of 20 July 2000 adopting the Integrated and Priority Road System in CEMAC<br>2. Regulation N°4/01-UEAC-089-CM-06 adopting the revised Community Code of the road (03/08/2001)<br>3. Regulation N°2/99/UEAC-CM-654 regulating the transport of dangerous goods by road in UDEAC/CEMAC<br>4. Community Regulation on conditions for the exercise of maritime professions and auxiliary transport professions (1998)<br>5. Regulation N°15/03-UEAC-612-CM-11 adopting the regulation on conditions of access to the profession of Interstate General Cargo Road Carrier (12/12/2003) |

SOURCE: CEMAC: PORTAIL DE LA CEMAC (WWW.CEMAC.INT)

incentive role, especially since the bulk of entrepreneurship in Cameroon is opportunity-driven (Okah-Efogo and Timba 2015; GEM 2015). Rules can then be modified to create opportunities in priority and productive markets. As an instrument of economic growth and regional integration, the transport services sector is one of the priority sectors in Cameroon. The next section focuses on institutional barriers that must be lifted to promote entrepreneurship in the transport sector.

## Contextual Opportunities and Barriers in the Transport Sector

This section is based on the laws and regulations in force and aims to evaluate opportunities and barriers to entrepreneurship in the transport sector. It also refers to the results of interviews with three road carriers companies to illustrate some of the underlined points.

### *Contextual Opportunities*

Opportunities offered by the Cameroonian context are primarily related to the dynamism of the legal and regulatory framework that shapes investment and promotion of SMEs. Indeed, SMEs are considered one of the engines of economic growth and increasing importance is given to them in sectoral development strategies. Since 2000, a number of texts have been accepted by Government to improve the investment climate in Cameroon and especially to promote the development and survival of SMEs. Those efforts are acknowledged by reports that evaluate the entrepreneurship environment in Cameroon (GEM 2015; World Bank Group 2015). Nonetheless, there is more to be done.

Another opportunity lies in the liberty of the exercise of commercial activities in Cameroon. Indeed, the Cameroonian constitution has placed no restrictions on the possibility of a person to engage in a commercial activity. If one refers to the old Law n°90/031 of 10 August 1990 on trading activity in Cameroon, it is clear from its provisions that any natural or corporate body may freely engage in business in Cameroon. In this sense, article 6 of that Act argued that "commercial enterprises duly established in Cameroon freely determine their political [sic] production, distribution and marketing, in compliance with laws and regulations." Similarly, Article 12 of the Act adds that "the prices of goods and services are freely determined by competition on the market subject to restrictions [...] hitting certain anti-competitive practices." The Law of 1990, however, raised some restrictions regarding foreign persons and protection of consumers. In order to conduct business, foreigners must obtain a licence. As for consumers, they benefited from protection measures against professionals.

Law n°2015/018 of 31 December 2015 relating to trade activity in Cameroon repealed the 1990 Law. But this new law maintained the principle of freedom in the exercise of trade activities in Cameroon as well as restrictions on foreigners. It also strengthened consumer protection. It follows that access to a profession such as road carriers or transport agents is greatly facilitated by the rules.[6] Moreover, a road carrier or transport agent business is likely to generate a profit for whoever engages in it.

Another opportunity lies in the campaign of road renovation and road building. It should be noted that Cameroon is renovating its road network in order to overcome the lack of and poor condition of its roads. For this purpose, the government created the Road Funds, which role was initially designed to fund protection national road heritage programs, prevention programs, and safety and road maintenance programs. In 2004, a Law extended the terms of this facility to the field of financing the rehabilitation and remodeling of roads. The Road Fund derives its resources from, among others, road tolls and from other resources that collect and transfer funds under the responsibility of the Highway Revenue Enhancement Program (tolls, penalties and axle tax). To achieve its mission, it works in synergy with donors and the Ministry of Public Works. Following this collaboration, many achievements have been made in the road sector.

As an illustration, it appears from the results of the implementation of the 2014 budget of the Ministry of Public Works, that 249 km of roads have been rehabilitated in the national territory.[7] The same document shows that since January 2014, 114 km of new roads have been built. Moreover, several motorway construction projects were set up by the government, including the Yaounde-Douala and Yaounde-Nsimalen highways. The project of asphalting the Kumba-Mamfe road was established and asphalting roads that open up the Cameroon production basins and borders with neighbouring countries (corridors Douala-Bangui, Douala-Ndjamena, Bamenda-Enugu, Sangmélima-Djoum-Congo frontier) have been pursued.

Finally, institutional dynamism, freedom to engage in entrepreneurship, emergence of new roads, and rehabilitation of old ones should open up the market by creating a need to transport people and goods in new areas. This

6 There is a specific law for the protection of consumers, namely the Law n°2011/012 of 6 May 2011 relating to consumer protection in Cameroon. It repealed the Law of 1990 that existed on the matter.

7 Fonds Routier report (2014: 7).

need for transport services could be filled by the creation of new transport enterprises and/or extension of existing business activities in the field.

*Contextual Barriers in the Transport Sector*

This sub-section presents the diverse institutional and contextual barriers to entrepreneurship in the transport sector.

a) Administrative Requirements for Road Carriers Activities

To pursue the occupation of road transport operator, an entrepreneur has to obtain a road carriers' licence from the Transport Minister and a blue card. The road carriers' licence is personal, so it cannot be lent, transferred, or rented. This means that, if the holder dies, any individual taking over the business must get his/her own licence. The blue card permits its holder to use a vehicle for business. This document can be demanded during roadside checks.

The road carriers' licence contains important information. For example, the passenger transport licence specifies the areas and/or the routes in which transportation is authorised (art.7). According to the decree of 17 March 2004, there are two kinds of road carriers' licences: ordinary licences and special licences. There are four categories of ordinary licences:

- → Category I: granted for urban and peri-urban transport services with a seating capacity of a maximum of ten seats, including the driver's seat;
- → Category II: granted for intercity passenger bus services with a seating capacity of a minimum of eleven seats;
- → Category III: granted for freight transport services with a gross vehicle weight of more than 3.5 tons;
- → Category IV: granted for mixed transport services with a gross vehicle weight equal to or less than 3.5 tons.

There are three categories of special licences:

- → Category S1: granted for urban bus transport;
- → Category S2: granted for urban transport service by motor cycle taxi in peri-urban and rural areas;
- → Category S3: granted for funeral transport service.

In accordance with the provisions of articles 13 and 14 of Decree n° 2015/4209/PM of 24 November, the granting of category I ordinary licences, special licences (categories S1 and S2) and relating blue cards, is now the responsibility of urban communities and municipalities.

The granting of a licence is subject to an application file. According to article 6 of a decree of 2004, the file must include:

- → A stamped application form, a sample of which shall be provided by the transport service;
- → A certified true copy of the identity card of the applicant or the manager of the corporate body;
- → A certificate of nationality for foreign persons (subject to the reciprocity principle);
- → An updated copy of articles of association, if the applicant is a corporate body;
- → A receipt attesting to payment of the fee corresponding to the category of the licence applied for.

The applicant must add proof of his/her technical and financial capacity. S/he must also show a certificate of non-conviction. The rates of fees applicable for the issue of road transport licences are determined by article 10 of the decree of 2004, following Table 11.3 below:

Before granting a licence, the administration will check on the applicant's character and that s/he possesses the necessary technical and financial capacity. With regards to character, the administration will check the criminal record of the applicant. Examination is favourable when the applicant or the manager of the company has not been subject to a sentence banning him/her from practicing a public profession.

An individual fulfils the technical capacity requirement when s/he is the permanent manager of the transport activity in question and holds the necessary professional qualifications (art. 8 of decree of 2004). This file certifies that an applicant has knowledge in the field of management issues, road transport regulations, labour regulations, and road safety rules. If an applicant does not

TABLE 11.3 *Categories of road transport licences fees*

| Categories of licence | Rate of fees |
|---|---|
| Category I, Categories S2 et S3 | 7,500 FCFA |
| Category II, III and IV, Category S1 | 15,000 FCFA |

SOURCE: DECREE N°2004/0607/PM OF 17 MARCH 2004 (ART. 10)

have this document, s/he must show proof of at least five years of practical experience in a managerial position within a transport company.

In terms of financial capacity, an applicant must prove that s/he possesses vehicles or show proof that s/he owns equity capital and reserves amounting to 1.5 million FCFA for a license in category II or 10 million FCFA for a licence in categories III or S1. After the granting of the road carrier's licence, the Transport Administration must register the document in its database.

Beyond the administrative documents required and proof of sufficient financial and technical resources, it should be noted that the decision to issue a licence is subjective, insofar as the competent authority evaluates the request based on transportation needs in the national territory. This is clear from article 8 of the 2001 Act and suggests that a licence may be refused if it is to allow somebody to carry out transport activities in a geographical area where there is no demand for such a service. It is therefore a way of directing road transport activities to areas that have insufficient transport services. Hence, there is more chance of getting a licence if an entrepreneur wants to organise transport in remote areas where road carriers are scarce.

b) Administrative Prerequisites for Transport Agent Activities

According to article 12 of the decree of 2004, road transport agent activity shall fall into two classes: transport agents for urban and intercity passengers and freight transport agents. In the first class are activities such as urban/intercity road passenger terminal or travel managers in urban and/or intercity transport terminals. In the second class are activities like road freight terminal managers, bulking agents, or movers.

Access to the business of transport agent is subjected to the issue of an authorisation by the Ministry of Transport. Subsequently, the authorisation is registered by the administration. It is important to note that authorisation is personal, so it cannot be transferred to another person. In addition, authorisation contains important information, such as the route or the zone where transportation is authorised. Any person who wants to become a road transport agent must submit a file comprising:

→ A stamped application;
→ A certified copy of the national identity card of the applicant or the manager if the applicant is a corporate body;
→ A certificate of nationality for foreigners;
→ A certificate of non-conviction (it is important to establish that the applicant is of good character);
→ A receipt attesting to the payment of the required fees.

The 2004 decree requires persons who want to manage road transport terminals to submit other documents; specifically:

- → A certified copy of an ownership certificate, a lease contract for the site or a management concession agreement;
- → A site development plan comprising a parking lot for vehicles waiting to be loaded, a boarding lobby, one or more counters, a travellers lounge, a rest room for drivers, administrative offices, public toilets, a fence, a security gate, and a water point.

The applicant must also submit certified copies of the vehicles licences and the public transport licence of vehicles that will be used in the terminal, if s/he wishes to operate in a private road terminal.

It is important to note that the issue of authorisation is subject to payment of fees, the rate of which is fixed by article 15 of the decree of 2004 (Table 11.4).

c) Other Constraints Linked to Transport Activities

Vehicles that are used in the transportation of goods or persons are subject to checks during the trip. In such a situation, the driver must present a number of administrative documents, including personal documents (driving licence) and the contract that the driver of the vehicle sets has, and documents related to transportation, including the consignment note in the case of freight transport and a road slip in the case of passenger transport. The consignment is a

TABLE 11.4 *Rates of fees depending on categories of authorisation*

| Categories of authorisations | Rate of fees in FCFA |
|---|---|
| Authorisation to manage urban road transport terminal | 100,000 |
| Authorisation to manage an intercity passenger transport terminal | 200,000 |
| Authorisation to manage travels within urban or intercity transport terminals | 50,000 |
| Authorisation to manage a road freight terminal | 500,000 |
| Authorisation for road freight transport operators | 500,000 |
| Authorisation for bulking agent | 100,000 |
| Authorisation for parcel service operator | 50,000 |
| Authorisation for mover | 100,000 |

SOURCE: DECREE N°2004/0607/PM OF 17 MARCH 2004 (ART. 12)

mandatory document for carriage of goods. This is, according to article 2c of the Act of July 2001, a road contract between the shipper of the goods and the public road carrier. The road slip is a document that embodies the list of passengers transported by the carrier in its vehicle.

The driver must also submit documents relating to the vehicle, including the blue card, the technical inspection, the licence, the insurance policy, and the vehicle registration. During his trips, the driver must observe traffic rules, including speed limits, limitations on cargo weight or the authorised number of persons transported by vehicle type. Similarly, s/he must fulfill certain expenses such as tolls, and fees charged for the consignment and for the road slip. The entrepreneur must ensure the maintenance of the vehicle, show adequate hygiene and sanitation, and adequate operational quality of the machine. Indeed, the 2001 Act requires vehicles used for the transport of persons or goods to meet certain minimum safety standards.

In this regard, the three companies we interviewed all indicated that they were generally asked for the national identity card of the driver and users, the driving licence of the driver, and the complete record of the vehicle. As for expenses related to vehicle maintenance, the transport companies assess the maintenance expenditure to be over 500,000 FCFA per month. Respondents also note that for each trip, with an average of 60 trips per month per vehicle,[8] we should add toll charges, fuel costs, driver and conveyor meal as well as "travelling expenses". So, there is significant financial need for the survival of a transport company.

#### d) Sanctions Linked to Failure

Illegally carrying on the business of road carriers or transport agent is an offence against the Law of 2001. According to article 13 of this Law, illegal practices that can be punished are: engaging in the business of road carriers or transport agent without the prior granting of a licence or an authorisation; operating with a hired, lent, ceded or transferred licence or authorisation; using a private vehicle for the transportation of persons or goods for commercial purposes; and doing interurban or international transportation of goods or persons without mandatory consignment note or waybill. It is the responsibility of sworn officials of the service of the Transport Ministry to record the offences in a report.[9] After this, the document is transferred to the legal department and the Ministry of Transport.

8 It means, on average, two travels by bus a day for a month of 30 days in Company 1, three bus trips daily for Company 2 and one bus trip daily for Company 3.

9 However, the legal department and judicial police officers, with wide powers, can also do it.

It is important to note that any persons illegally carrying on the business of road carriers or transport agent shall be punished with imprisonment of up to six months or with a fine of between 500,000 and 5 million FCFA, or both. In the case of a repeat offence, the penalties may be doubled. It should be noted that these penalties relate to individuals; the punishment of corporate bodies seems to have been overlooked in the Law of 2001.

In addition, any persons who violate the provisions of the Law of 2001 and its implementation instruments may be subject to an administrative punishment, such as the suspension of the use of a licence or authorisation for a period not exceeding one year. The administration can order the withdrawal of a licence or authorisation under certain conditions resulting from article 15 of the Law of 2001. This generally occurs when the court orders the liquidation of the holder or following repeat offending that has previously resulted in the temporary suspension of a licence.

#### e) Road Infrastructure

Road infrastructures also constitute a serious impediment to trade in long-distance transport operations. This has been confirmed by the interviewed companies who, in response to the question: *according to you what is the impact of road quality on your activity?* declare that the roads are bad and considerably reduce cars' speed and the number of trips. Better quality roads affect destination choices positively. This is confirmed by the respondents who, answering the question: *why do you choose those destinations?* point out the quality of roads and the availability of customers.

According to the Fonds Routier (Road Fund) Report of 2014, the national road network in Cameroon covers about 121,424 km, of which 21,973 km constitute the priority network and nearly 100,241 km is a rural network. Regarding the characteristics of the road network, it emerges from the report that, in relation to the priority national network, 6,110 km of roads are paved and 15,863 km of roads are unpaved.[10] 80 per cent of traffic is on the priority network.[11] The road network of Cameroon is insufficient; hence, the Growth and Employment Strategy Paper (GESP) calls for an increase in the extent of tarred roads in Cameroon to 8,500 km,[12] to be among the objectives to be achieved by the government in 2020.

---

10 Fonds Routier report (2014: 24).

11 Ibid.: 24.

12 Ibid.: 7. In 2000, the road network spanned 50,000 km, including 4048 km of paved road; 18,016 km of classified gravel road and 27,936 km of rural road (Ministry of Public Works, Road network in 2000/2001, Publication of the Directorate of Roads).

### f) Corruption

Corruption can be defined as the misuse of a function. It is passive when someone is open to being bought through offers, promises, donations, presents or anything of value to perform or to abstain from an act. It is active when a person pays for the complacency of a professional. Several articles of the Cameroonian Penal Code set out the sanctions for such practices, such as Sections 134 and 161, which target official corruption, or Section 312, which relates to employee corruption.

Corruption is a constraint for road carriers. Concretely, corruption may be used by a road carrier to speed up administrative investigations into his/her case or to escape the effects of the Law, especially in relation to offences against laws and regulations. A report by the National Anti-Corruption Commission (NACC) on the fight against corruption in Cameroon, published in 2013, reveals the existence of corruption in the road transport sector. Indeed, it is clear from this report that road carriers engage in corruption when faced with a check by the authorities and they find themselves without the necessary documents (outdated technical visit, absence of driving licence, etc.). Besides the fact that this practice endangers the safety of conveyed persons or transported things, it also results in shortfalls for the state.

Another example of corruption was revealed following a mission conducted by the Monitoring and Evaluation Committee of the NACC in November 2013 at selected weighing stations. Here it was noted that protection of the road "is undermined by officials and other servants of weighing stations that have established a real fraud network involving a chain of stakeholders whose most prominent are: business leaders, smugglers, employees in these companies, the heads of weighing stations, operators of computers and the law enforcement forces weighing stations".[13] As an illustration, it has been observed at Mandjou weighing station that the computer was manipulated to produce fraudulent outcomes.[14]

To overcome these findings, the Road Fund noted in its report in 2014 that it was necessary to set up automated toll stations in 14 tolls positions with revenues less than the amount of traffic carried on the axes they cover (Table 11.5):[15]

13 CONAC, Rapport sur l'état de la lutte contre la corruption au Cameroun (2013: 45).

14 Ibid.: 45.

15 The project is in progress. Cf. Fonds Routier Report (2014: 47).

TABLE 11.5 *Axes identified to need automated toll stations*

| Positions | Axes |
|---|---|
| Mbankomo (Pilot Post) | Yaoundé – Mbankomo |
| Tiko | Douala – Mutenguene |
| Edea | Edéa-Douala – Edéa |
| Mbanga | Douala – Mbanga |
| Manjo | Mbanga – Manjo |
| Mboumnyebel | Edéa – Mboumnyebel |
| Nsimalen | Yaoundé – Mbalmayo |
| Nkometou | Yaoundé – Obala |
| Bafia | Obala – Bafia |
| Bayangam | Bangangté – Bafoussam |
| Foumbot | Bafoussam – Foumbot |
| Bandja | Bafang – Bafoussam |
| Matazem | Bafoussam – Bamenda |
| Dschang | Dschang – Bamougoum |

SOURCE: FONDS ROUTIER (2014: 47)

### g) Prices to be Paid to the Administration, Fuel Prices and Consumer Income

A final constraint is due to the combination of three elements, namely, fees to be paid to the administration, fuel prices, and the purchasing power of customers.

Regarding the first point, it should be noted that fees for transport services are, in principle, traded OTC ("over-the-counter"). Very often, they are set unilaterally by the road carrier. Given this state of affairs, the Ministry of Trade, after negotiations with the transport unions, fixes a maximum tariff that the carrier must not exceed when setting its prices. This intervention is in the form of an Order. In 1990, for example, an order was issued to achieve this goal. Prices have been revised upwards by Order n°0006/MINCOMMERCE of 8 March 2005 harmonising urban transport fares for taxis and intercity buses and coaches throughout the country. Recently, this 2005 Order was revised, with a new Order of 9 July 2014, and the maximum price was increased. Generally, the maximum tariffs established by the Minister reflect the price of fuel (petrol, diesel). The higher tariffs adopted in 2014 were due to increased fuel prices.

Finally, it should be noted that the public transport prices must also consider the customer purchasing power. Indeed, customers choose the carrier depending on their financial capacity. But in a country where the guaranteed minimum wage (minimum wage) amounts to 36,270 FCFA per month (or the equivalent to €55 in 2016), with per capita gross domestic product (GDP) equal to $US 1,405, prices in the transport sector may not exceed a certain limit. With regard to this issue, the interviewed companies declare that their prices are cheap (Company 1), realistic (Company 2) or reasonable (Company 3).

## Lessons from Three Cameroonian Case Studies in the Transport Sector

This section intends presents respondents from three transport service firms active in Cameroon for more than ten years. All of the companies started with SME status, in accordance with the definition of MINPMEESA presented above. Today, according to their own statements, they are big businesses and, in this section, they present their experiences with regard to perceptions of rules and laws, difficulties encountered, and proposed solutions.

Regarding the relationship of these companies with the law and rules, Company 1 (established in 2005), Company 2 (established in 1998) and Company 3 (established in 1999) have all declared that they have the necessary licence, they respect speed limits, and the number of people permitted in their cars. Respondents also proved their knowledge of required documents as well as penalties for non-submission of this paperwork. They do not complain about the formal institutional framework in the transport sector. This suggests that there have been concrete improvements that promote entrepreneurship in this sector.

The case studies corroborate the theoretical investigations regarding constraints. While the companies discussed the costs of entry into the market (more than 60 million FCFA, or €91,000 at the current exchange rate), the bad quality of roads, insufficient number of means of transportation, low access to finance, low profitability of the business (Company 2), competition from illegal road carriers (Company 1), harassment from authorities (Company 3) and the attitude of users were all mentioned. Yet, it seems that the abundance of taxes to be paid and harassment by the authorities are their major problems.

The main solutions proposed are increasing customers and reducing taxes. Regarding the increase in the number of customers, the companies intend to achieve this through a marketing strategy based on the loyalty of existing customers and seeking new customers through the acquisition of new rolling stock (Company 1), the choice of shorter travel destinations, the use of advertising and the choice of high-density travel destinations guaranteeing a significant number of customers (Company 1; Company 2), and customers' segmentation (Company 3). Company 2 focuses on staff training and recruitment of qualified personnel able to effectively manage the company.

What, then, can we learn from these examples? Firstly, despite the constraints, a company can survive in this sector, and even grow and survive for more than ten years. Secondly, the regulatory and legal framework in this sector is dynamic enough to adapt to the new opportunities and constraints related to promoting SMEs. Thirdly, the rehabilitation of the road network and construction of new roads will open up new opportunities in this sector in Cameroon. Fourthly, innovation in services and the quality of these services are a corporate survival mechanism in this sector. Indeed, competition from other companies is a catalyst for companies to reinvent themselves and offer good quality services (departure on time, safety, reduced accidents, etc.).

## Summary and Recommendations

The goal of this paper was to identify institutional and contextual weaknesses in the system of entrepreneurship promotion in Cameroon and to propose solutions that would improve the creation and survival of enterprises, given the fact that they are important tools against poverty through job creation. We focused specifically on the transport services sector and the results of interviews with three transport services companies.

Our analysis shows that the regulatory and legal framework for entrepreneurship in general and transport in particular is dynamic. Following the third process identified by Hwang and Powell (2005), this framework continuously changes to adapt to new entrepreneurial needs in Cameroon. We also find, in line with the literature, that the Cameroonian institutional framework could reallocate entrepreneurship towards areas in need of transport services. We also found that infrastructure rehabilitation and construction will create new opportunities in the road carrier sector and provide incentives to invest in this area of activities. Companies can indeed be innovative and propose good quality services to deal with competition from other companies. However, the companies working in this sector suggest that the problem of illegal road carriers, corruption, and the problem of numerous taxes should be urgently addressed.

## References

Acs, Z.J. & D.B. Audretsch (2001). *The Emergence of the Entrepreneurial Society*. Stockholm: Swedish Foundation for Small Business Research.

Audretsch, D.B. & A.R. Thurik (2001). "Capitalism and Democracy in the 21st Century: From the Managed to the Entrepreneurial Economy". In: D.C. Mueller & U. Cantner (eds): *Capitalism and Democracy in the 21st Century*. Heidelberg: Physica-Verlag, 23–40.

Baumol, W.J. (1990). "Entrepreneurship: Productive, Unproductive and Destructive", *Journal of Political Economy* 98(5), 893–921.

Berrios, Mario (2013). "The Enabling Environment for Sustainable Enterprises in Cameroon". ILO Report. November. http://www.ilo.org/wcmsp5/groups/public/---ed_emp/---emp_ent/---ifp_seed/documents/publication/wcms_230287.pdf.

Bjornskov, C. & N. Foss (2006). *"Economic Freedom and Entrepreneurial Activity: Some Cross-Country Evidence"*. Working Paper, Copenhagen Business School.

Boettke, P.J. & C.J. Coyne (2009). "Context Matters: Institutions and Entrepreneurship". In: G. Bressy & C. Konkuyt, *Foundations and Trends in Entrepreneurship*, 136–209.

Bressy G. & C. Konkuyt. (2014). *Management et Economie des Entreprises*. 11è édition. Editions Sirey, 500.

Campbell J.L. (2007). "Why Would Corporations Behave in Socially Responsible Ways? An Institutional Theory of Corporate Social Responsibility", *The Academy of Management Review* 32(3), 946–967.

Casson, M. (1991). *Global Research Strategy and International Competitiveness*. Oxford: Blackwell.

CEMAC, Portail de la CEMAC (www.cemac.int) (last accessed 2016).

Didier M. & R. Prud'homme. (2007). *Infrastructures de transport, mobilité et croissance*. Rapport. La Documentation Française.

Fonds Routier (2014). *Annual Report*. www.fondsroutiercameroun.org/www.fondsroutier.cm.

GEM (2014). *Global Entrepreneurship Monitor*. http://www.gemconsortium.org/.

GEM (2015). *Global Entrepreneurship Monitor*. http://www.gemconsortium.org/.

GEM (2016). *Global Entrepreneurship Monitor*. http://www.gemconsortium.org/.

Harper D.A. (2003). *Foundations of Entrepreneurship and Economic Development*, London and New York: Routledge, 276.

Henry, A. (2008). "Culture et gestion au Cameroun. Le respect des rituels, source d'une entente amicale". In: E. Davel, J.-P. Dupuis & J.-F. Chanlat (eds), *Gestion en contexte interculturel: approches, problématiques, pratiques et plongées*, Québec: Presses de l'Université Laval et Télé-université (UQAM).

Hwang H. & W.W. Powell. (2005). "Institutions and Entrepreneurship". In: Sharon A. Alvarez, Rajshree Agarwal & Olav Sorenson (eds.), *Handbook of Entrepreneurship Research: Disciplinary Prospectives*. International Handbook Series on Entrepreneurship, vol 2. New York: Springer, 201–232.

International Business Publications, Inc (2015) (Annual Updates). *Cameroon, Investment, Trade Laws and Regulations Handbook. Volume 1: Strategic Information and Regulations*. Int'l Business Pubns. USA. 292.

Julien, P.A. & M. Marchesnay. (2011). *L'Entreprenieurat*. Paris: Economica.

Kirzner, I. (1999). "Creativity and/or Alertness: A Reconsideration of the Schumpeterian Entrepreneur", *Review of Austrian Economics* 11, 5–17.

Ministry of Transport (2014). TRANSTAT Report. Republic of Cameroon.

Niyonsaba S.E. (2013). "How Does Investment Climate and Business Environment Impact Firms' Efficiency in a Post-Conflict Setting? Evidence from Democratic Republic of Congo", *International Journal of Business and Management*, 8(10), 169–184.

North, D.C. (1990). *Institutions, Institutional Change and Economic Performance*. New York: Cambridge University Press.

North, D.C. (1991). "Institutions", *Journal of Economic Perspectives* 5(1), 97–112.

Nyström, K. (2008). "The Institutions of Economic Freedom and Entrepreneurship: Evidence from Panel Data", *Public Choice* 136(3–4), 269–282.

Okah-Efogo, F. & G.T. Timba. (2015). "Female Entrepreneurship and Growth in Cameroon", *African Journal of Economic and Management Studies*, 6(1), 107–119.

Pacitto, J.C., Arlotto, J., Fabiani, T. & P. Jourdan. (2014). *Cultures nationales et actions entrepreneuriales. Une nouvelle perspective pour la recherche en entrepreneuriat*. In 12ème Congrès International Francophone en Entrepreunariat.

Porter, M.E. (1985). *The Competitive Advantage: Creating and Sustaining Superior Performance*. New York: Free Press. (Republished with a new introduction, 1998.).

Shirley, M.M. (2005). "Institutions and Development". In: C. Menard & M.M. Shirley (eds), *Handbook of New Institutional Economics*. The Netherlands: Springer, 611–638.

Shirley, M.M. (2008). *Institutions and Development*. Cheltenham: Edward Elgar Publishing.

Sobel, R. (2008). "Testing Baumol: Institutional Quality and the Productivity of Entrepreneurship", *Journal of Business Venturing* 23(6), 641–655.

Tchawa P. (2012). "Le Cameroun. Une 'Afrique en miniature'?", *Cahiers D'Outre-mer*, N°259 Juillet–Septembre, 319–338.

Verheul, I., Wennekers, S., Audretsch, D.B. & A. Roy Thurik. (2001). "An Eclectic Theory of Entrepreneurship". *Tinbergen Institute Discussion Paper* 2001-030/3, Tinbergen Institute.

Williamson, O.E. (2000). "The New Institutional Economics: Taking Stock, Looking Ahead", *Journal of Economic Literature* 38, 595–613.

World Bank Group. (2015). *Doing Business 2016: Measuring Regulatory Quality and Efficiency* (Vol. 13). World Bank Publications, http://www.doingbusiness.org/reports/global-reports/doing-business-2016.

# PART 3

## *Entrepreneurship and Sectoral Considerations or Determinants*

CHAPTER 12

# Dangote Cement: The Challenges of Pan-African Expansion

*Akinyinka Akinyoade and Chibuike Uche*

## Introduction

Dangote Cement is the largest company quoted on the Nigerian Stock Exchange. In 2016, it accounted for 32 per cent of the equities capitalisation in the Exchange.[1] The company was founded by Aliko Dangote, who has an entrepreneurial pedigree. Aliko Dangote was born in 1957. Incidentally, it was in the same year that the Nigerian Cement Company (NCC), the first cement production company in Nigeria, commenced operations (Akinyoade and Uche 2016). His father, Mohammed Dangote, was a business associate of Alhassan Dantata, who was the richest African during the colonial era (Forrest 1994: 215). His mother, Mariya Sanusi Dantata, was the eldest daughter of one of Alhassan Dantata's sons, Sanusi Dantata, a major groundnut merchant in Kano. After the death of Mohammed Dangote in 1963, Aliko was brought up by his maternal grandfather, Sanusi Dantata. As a child, Aliko showed keen interest in entrepreneurship. As a primary school student, he sold candies (sweets) for profit (Anyansi-Archibong and Anyansi 2014: 276). Through his association with his maternal grandfather, Dangote quickly learnt that in Nigeria, "politics and business are closely related" (Fayemiwo and Neal 2013).

Dangote started his career by working as a store manager for his grandfather. In 1976, he established his own business specialising in cement and commodity trading. This was done with a loan of N500,000.00 from his grandfather. This business venture proved to be extremely profitable, making it possible for him to pay back the loan within three months (Ogbor, 2009: 276). This period coincided with the era of rapid growth in cement demand in Nigeria. This growth was fuelled by the reconstruction needs of the country as a consequence of the Nigerian Civil War (1967–1970) and the decision of the government to host the Second World Black and African Festival of Arts and Culture (FESTAC) in

1 *This Day*, 9 March 2016, downloaded from <https://www.thisdaylive.com/index.php/2016/03/09/dangote-group-controls-43-of-nigerian-stock-market/> on 17 February 2017.

 | DOI 10.1163/9789004351615_013

1977 (Cf. Kulla 1976). Widespread corruption, however, ensured that the entire cement importation process became riddled with fraud (See Federal Republic of Nigeria 1976: 12; Forrest 1992: 57).

In 1977, Aliko Dangote moved to Lagos, where he continued his rapidly growing trading business and, by the early 1980s, Dangote had become the largest importer of sugar in Nigeria (Forrest 1994: 215).

Although Dangote was making money from the importation of various commodities he never lost sight of the fact that, given the population of the country and the abundance of natural resources, localising the production of some of the imported commodities could be more profitable for his company and also more beneficial to the Nigerian government.[2] This was particularly true for cement. Its low cost and high bulk nature made it an extremely promising industry for local production. Cement production is, however, capital intensive (Pan African Capital Research PLC 2011). Investors therefore require some degree of political and economic stability in a country before making huge investments in such an industry (Ugoh 1966).

Although foreign investors were enthusiastic about investing in the Nigerian cement industry in the 1960s, this waned in the 1970s, especially after the indigenisation Decrees of 1972 and 1977 were promulgated. The Shagari administration (1979–2003) subsequently reversed the indigenisation policy (Onwuka 1992: 80). Despite this policy reversal, multinational companies still chose to exercise caution when it came to establishing new cement plants. The result was that, between 1980 and 2000, no new cement company was established in Nigeria (Mojekwu et al. 2012). Despite this, cement demand in the country continued to increase, resulting in the importation of more cement into the country. In 1990, for instance, 23 per cent of the 3.9 million metric tons of cement consumed in the country was imported, while by 2000, 59.3 per cent of the 5.6 million metric tons of cement consumed in the country was imported. This created huge opportunities for bulk cement importation and bagging in the country. Arguably because of his close links to the government, Dangote became the major player in this industry. At its peak, Dangote controlled 46 per cent of the bulk cement market in Nigeria (Ohimain 2014).

When the Nigerian government decided to privatise its loss-making cement companies, during the regime of President Obasanjo, Dangote acquired a 65.96 per cent stake in the Benue Cement Company "as part of the group's

2 See *World Stage Newsonline*, "Dangote Cement to complete plants across Africa this year" 12 January 2014), downloaded from http://www.m.worldstagegroup.com/readnews.php?&id=13084&active=news (3 August, 2014).

strategic decision to move from cement importation to local production."[3] The Obasanjo administration subsequently adopted a backward integration policy for the cement industry. The objective of this policy was to promote local cement production and phase out cement importation. While foreign cement companies like Lafarge adopted a cautious approach to expanding their local cement production, Dangote did not. The result was that Dangote's company dramatically increased its cement production capacity in Nigeria from 0.9 million metric tonnes (Mta) in 2000 to 28.2 Mta per annum in 2015. In other words, Dangote, who was not a cement producer in Nigeria before the year 2000, rapidly rose to become the dominant player in 2015 when he controlled 71.7 per cent of Nigeria's total cement production capacity (Akinyoade and Uche 2016: 6). Given the fact that "cement prices in Africa are still the highest in the world, averaging around 200 percent higher than any other region" (White 2015), it is perhaps not surprising that Dangote rapidly became the richest man in Africa.

It was, arguably, his rapid success in cement production in Nigeria and the high price of the commodity across the African continent that made Dangote set his eyes on expanding his cement operations to the rest of Africa. In 2010, for instance, the company announced its intention to invest $3.9 billion in cement production in 13 African countries outside of Nigeria. This strategy was defended, at least in part, on the grounds of African nationalism and unity:

> Our investments are justified because African governments and private sector combined are reportedly investing an estimated $72 billion a year in a new infrastructure across the continent. We are further encouraged in our expansion activities because of the favourable investment policies put in place by the Governments of these African countries, which recognize that in the final analysis, it is only Africans themselves that can salvage the economic fortunes of the continent.
>
> Dangote Cement Plc. Annual Report, 2010: 13

This paper explores the expansion of Dangote Cement into other African countries. It shows how diverse forces have affected the investment of Dangote in some of these African countries. Although both the Economic Community of West African States (ECOWAS) and the African Union (AU, formerly the Organisation for African Unity, OAU) are supposed to help promote such intra-continental business expansion, the reality is more complex. While the advent of Dangote Cement into other African countries has helped promote

3 See official website of Dangote, downloaded from <http://dangote.com/Investorrelations/quotedcompanies/operationsdangotecement.aspx> on 17 February 2017.

competition, its investments and strategies in some of these African countries have been questioned. This paper also further demonstrates that adverse economic developments in Dangote Cement's home country is now beginning to affect the company's Pan African expansionist bid. Specifically, the recently deteriorating economic situation in Nigeria, which has resulted in the scarcity of foreign exchange, has forced Dangote to scale down its ambitious Pan African expansion plan.[4]

To achieve its aim, this paper is divided into four parts. Part one explores the environment for intra-continental business expansion in Africa in the context of the existing regional and sub-regional economic cooperation agreements. Part two critiques the various challenges Dangote has faced in expanding his business operations within the West African sub-region, while Part three explores Dangote's business expansion in the entire continent and in the context of Africa-wide economic cooperation agreements. Part four concludes the paper.

## Regional Cooperation and the Environment for Pan-African Business Expansion

Theoretically, African businesses should derive some benefits when it comes to intra-continental expansion. This is because of the existence of multiple regional bodies aimed at promoting economic cooperation amongst member states. In the case of Dangote Cement, for instance, Nigeria – its home country – is a member of both ECOWAS and the AU. In reality, the situation is more complex as the rules governing such bodies rarely mention business establishments. Although the general subject of economic cooperation is always captured in the rules of such regional bodies, experience has shown that economic cooperation among neighbours in a continent that has the highest concentration of poor countries in the world can sometimes be complicated (Uche 2001: 30). This is partly because it is easy for parties external to the region to maintain influence with some member states through aid and economic diplomacy. The result is that the possibility of African multinational businesses

4 According to the company's Group Chief Executive Officer, Onne van der Weijde, "[w]e will focus our efforts and our capital expenditure on improvements in 2017, rather than building and expanding. That's because the currency situation has made it difficult to source enough dollars to fund the expansion in the timescale we had originally envisaged, where we would have about 75 Mta capacity by 2020" (2016 Dangote Cement Annual Report: 55).

operating in other African countries having any meaningful advantage over non-African multinational businesses also operating in Africa is impeded.

The above dynamics clearly impact on Dangote's ambition to build a Pan-African cement multinational business. Within the West African sub-region, for instance, Nigeria played a pivotal role in the formation of ECOWAS in 1975. Despite its name, the real reason why Nigeria championed the establishment of ECOWAS was to limit the influence of France in the sub-region. This was because the country was unhappy with the support France provided to Biafra during the Nigerian Civil War through some of its proxy states in the region (Bach 1983: 607). This agenda naturally drew opposition from France. The result is that francophone African states belong to both ECOWAS and an increasingly strong francophone West African body that has now transformed into the West African Economic and Monetary Union (WAEMU). WAEMU member countries are by far the most economically integrated group in West Africa. They share a common currency and have a common central bank. All this has been made possible by the backing of the French Treasury. It is this relationship with the French Treasury that has ensured currency stability and convertibility in the region (Uche 2011: 21–23). The same, however, cannot be said of the other countries in ECOWAS. This perhaps explains why all attempts, to date, to actualise an effective ECOWAS-wide economic integration scheme have not been very successful (but see: Dietz, Lange & Rau 2016).

Although Nigeria played a major role in the founding of ECOWAS and is by far the largest economy in the region, it was unwilling to support the poorer countries of the continent with its enormous oil wealth. It has, for instance, been argued that one reason for the failure of the West African Clearing House, which was established to facilitate ECOWAS-wide trade, was Nigeria's refusal to channel its oil sales to other West African countries through the body (Cf. Uche 2001: 23). This explains, at least in part, why the francophone countries in West Africa have been more willing to cooperate within WAEMU, with the support of France, than within ECOWAS.

The result is that most ECOWAS initiatives aimed at achieving economic cooperation and integration within the sub-region have met with little success. A clear example is the attempt by ECOWAS to establish a single currency. Although talks about a single currency started in 1987, when the ECOWAS Monetary Cooperation Agreement was signed, there has been little progress towards attainment of the said goal. There is also little chance that any meaningful progress will be made in the near future in this regard. This is partly because it is unlikely that the francophone West African countries will abandon their current monetary arrangements with France, which acts both as a hegemon and an agency of restraint, for an ECOWAS-wide monetary agreement that has no hegemon and/or agency of restraint. This is compounded by the fact that francophone West African countries have the most stable and internationally acceptable currency (CFA Franc) in West Africa.

Another area where ECOWAS has been trying to promote cooperation is with respect to the establishment of the ECOWAS Trade Liberalisation Scheme (ETLS) and the Common External Tariffs. Articles 2 of the 1975 ECOWAS Treaty specifically listed the objectives of the organisation to include the:

> elimination as between the member states of customs duties and other charges of equivalent effect in respect of the importation and exportation of goods; the abolition of quantitative and administrative restrictions on trade among member states [...] [and] the establishment of a common customs tariff and a common commercial policy towards third world countries.

Consequently, ECOWAS decided to establish the ETLS in 1979. It was not until 1990, however, after three postponements, that the scheme was finally established. It was agreed at the time that it was to be implemented in three phases.[5]

Some progress has since been made in this direction. The liberalisation of trade in unprocessed goods and traditional handicrafts has commenced and, in 2013, ECOWAS adopted a common external tariff (CET) for goods coming into the region (GIZ, Undated:). In practice however, the entire scheme is riddled with problems and its enforcement has proved very difficult. This has been explained thus:

> Political commitments on regional integration programmes have not yet been translated into policy and regulatory reforms [...] The share of intra-regional trade has remained low, in part because such long-standing commitments like the ETLS are extremely complex to implement [...]. In spite of the numerous benefits accruing from the ETLS, the scheme has been marred by obvious lack of legal backing at the national level, hence the charging of full duties by custom authorities in disregard of the regional laws and policies. As it is now, ETLS does not provide any

5 The phases are: (1) an immediate and full liberalisation of trade in unprocessed goods and traditional handicrafts (2) phased liberalisation of trade in industrial products, with the phasing reflecting the differences in the levels of development of three categories of ECOWAS member states, and; (3) gradual establishment of a common external tariff (CET) (ECOWAS 2013: 2).

> mechanism where traders in the region who have been molested or extorted could establish any redress just as it is in the EU.
>
> ECOWAS 2013: 7

Widespread corruption in the region is also another impediment to the implementation of the ETLS. According to ECOWAS:

> The lack of a credible legal redress mechanism has even empowered corruption along several border routes as border officials continue to erect illegal road blocks and harass traders at such points. This presents increasing barriers to the free movement of goods along the trade corridor [...]. Even when a product is registered and all information provided, crossing the border can be difficult as additional payments often accrue from the activities of corrupt officials. In the application of import bans, Nigerian customs officials make no distinction between ECOWAS and third-country originating products. This is in contradiction with the ETLS, which specifically determines that originating goods should not be subject to quantitative restrictions (Ibid.: 7–8).

At the continental level, the economic cooperation scheme has also not fared better. When the Organisation of African Unity was established in 1963, for instance, economic cooperation was listed as one of the areas where member states should coordinate and harmonise their general policies (OAU Charter 1963: Section 2). Despite the above, it was not until 17 years after its establishment (1980) that the OAU produced an economic blueprint for Africa. This was contained in the Final Act of Lagos and the Lagos Plan of Action. Under the Final Act of Lagos, for instance, the Heads of States reaffirmed their commitment to establish an African Economic Community by the Year 2000. The main essence of this strategy was to ensure the economic, social and cultural integration of Africa (Section 2a). On the other hand, under the Lagos Plan of Action, African leaders resolved to adopt a regional approach towards the development of the African continent, "based primarily on collective self-reliance" (Paragraph 1).[6]

Before the ink on the agreements could dry, it became clear that several African countries lacked the political will, and perhaps the economic ability, to operationalise the recommendations contained in both Plans. This was especially so given the fact that, at the time, most of the African countries were

6 See also Bujra (1982: i); Achenhou (1983: 6).

undergoing various degrees of economic difficulties. This was based, at least in part, on the fall in commodity prices – the mainstay of several of the concerned African countries.

It was as a consequence of this that, shortly after the adoption of the Lagos Plan of Action and the Final Lagos Plan, many OAU member countries sought the assistance of the World Bank in tackling the economic crisis in their various countries. A subsequent World Bank Report ("Accelerated Development in Sub-Saharan Africa") sharply criticised the Lagos Plan of Action. It specifically argued that the Plan failed to emphasise the need for public sector reform as an important ingredient of economic development. The Report also further criticised the Plan for placing little emphasis on the importance of private sector participation in the promotion of economic development. It then went on to recommend that African states should decrease their role in the economy and social welfare programmes through mechanisms such as privatisation, liberaliszation and the promotion of market forces as determinants of economic activity. Contrary to the position contained in the Lagos Plan of Action, the World Bank reiterated the need for the increased integration of African economies into the international economy.[7] Given the precarious state of most African economies at the time, it was not surprising that the World Bank's views triumphed (See Organisation of African Unity 1998: 2). The subsequent adoption of the International Monetary Fund imposed Structural Adjustment Programmes, based on principles similar to those propounded by the World Bank, became a major setback for the possibility of establishing an Africa-wide regional economic cooperation programme at the expense of the economic interests of non-member states of OAU. Under the above scenario, foreign multinational companies continued to dominate the African business landscape (Heilman and Lucas 1997; Elkan 1988).

A landmark factor that impacted on the development of African entrepreneurship and the advancement of African multinational businesses across Africa was the end of Apartheid in 1994 and the subsequent admission of South Africa into the African Union. Although South Africa was considered as a rogue state and excluded from the AU as a consequence of its apartheid policies, it was still the largest and most advanced economy in Africa at the time (Nkuhlu 2003; Cornwell 2002). It is instructive that South Africa was able to achieve the above economic feat under neo-liberal market conditions. This was despite the limitations imposed by its Apartheid policies. It was,

7 For an analyses of these criticisms, see: Makgetlaneng (2003); Achenhou (1983); Amin (1982); Bujra (1982).

however, as a consequence of the increasing difficulties of doing business in an increasingly isolated country that South African businesses supported the ending of the Apartheid programme. Along these lines, it has been asserted that:

> During the 1970s and the 1980s South African companies, at a time when their profits were declining in South Africa, also faced resistance from a rising working class in South Africa as well as from newly independent countries in the Southern African region. They realised how dependent they are on the region and set out to overcome this resistance. That they have achieved this through legitimising the South African state is undeniable […]. [It has been] argued that South African capital spurred on the movement towards a negotiated transition to end apartheid for securing its own long term interests in South Africa and through this, its interests in the region as a whole not just for quick financial gain but for ensuring long-term stability in the region for capital accumulation.
>
> TAAL 2014: 2

It is also important to note that South Africa ended its Apartheid system shortly after the collapse of the Soviet Union, which for a long time was the shining star of state-controlled economies. This further entrenched the general belief in neo-liberalism at the time (Daniel et al. 2003). The above scenario contributed to the fact that, despite the end of Apartheid and the installation of majority rule in South Africa, the ruling African National Congress was reluctant to tamper with the structure of South African private companies and the neoliberal economic policies that facilitated their success. In fact, the South African government, especially under President Mbeki, cooperated with South African businesses in order to facilitate their expansion across Africa. It was this cooperation that led to the establishment of the New Partnership for African Development (NEPAD) (Ezeoha and Uche 2005: 11).

The main reason for the establishment of NEPAD was to create a conducive environment for the advancement of South African capital across Africa (Ibid.: 6). Based on the above objective, it was not surprising that the NEPAD document adopted a neo-liberal economic approach that emphasises the supremacy of market forces and the promotion of free competition within the continent. In other words, to support and encourage the above objectives, the NEPAD agenda stresses the promotion of good governance (Habib 2009: 149).

Given the overbearing role of South Africa in its formation, it is not surprising that the NEPAD Programme has sometimes generated mistrust amongst

African leaders. Muammar Ghadafi of Libya once described it as a "a neo-colonial plan designed to please colonialists and racists"[8] and Daniel Arap Moi of Kenya accused South Africa of "rushing ahead with NEPAD without explaining the programme to the rest of Africa" (Ayittey 2010: 98). Despite the above criticisms, South African companies, through the spearhead of NEPAD, rapidly advanced their interests across the continent. Notable among such South African companies were: MTN, Shoprite, Standard Bank and Vodacom (Taal 2014: 24; Daniel et al. 2003: 378–379). Their operations in some of the host African nations have, however, not always been smooth (Cf. Malan 2005). Dangote Cement is following in the footsteps of these South African multinational businesses. Within West Africa, and in the context of the ECOWAS, however, Dangote Cement is a trailblazer.

## Dangote Cement and the Challenges of ECOWAS Expansion

Dangote has never hidden his ambition to exploit the ECOWAS agreement in order to extend his business operations across West Africa. In 2011, for instance, while addressing the Lagos Chamber of Commerce and Industry, Aliko Dangote complained that, although the ECOWAS Trade Liberalisation Treaty contained provisions that were aimed at developing and promoting trade within the West African sub-region, the objectives of establishing the regional body have yet to be attained.[9]

It was in the same year that Dangote Cement commenced its operations in Ghana by importing and bagging bulk cement at its terminal in Tema. Until recently, all the bulk cement Dangote imported into Ghana came from outside Nigeria. According to the company's 2016 Annual Report, it was not until the "second half of 2016 we began exporting cement from Nigeria to Ghana, reducing our need to import Far Eastern cement and generating useful foreign currency sales. By the end of the year we had exported 0.2Mt of cement to Ghana, out of total sales there of 1.1Mt" (Dangote Cement Annual Report 2016: 11).

Dangote Cement's importation into Ghana has, however, increasingly been met with stiff opposition from local cement manufacturers. This is perhaps not surprising, especially given the relatively small size of the market and its oligopolistic nature. It is, for instance, estimated that prior to the advent of

8 *Africa Confidential*, 2002, 43: 14, 12 July. "Part of the Union", p. 7, downloaded from <http://www.africa-confidential.com/article/id/637/Part_of_the_union> on 10 March 2017.

9 Vanguard, 27 May 2011, downloaded from <http://www.vanguardngr.com/2011/05/dangote-urges-ecowas-to-dismantle-trade-barriers/> on 10 March 2017.

Dangote Cement into the Ghana market, the country had an annual cement demand of approximately 5.5 million tonnes and a local production capacity of 7.6 million tonnes (3.2 million tonnes by Diamond Cement and 4.4 million tonnes by Ghana Cement, GHACEM).[10]

Based on the above market structure, it is not surprising that local cement companies in the country have consistently called on the Ghana government to protect the local cement industry by banning the importation of Dangote Cement into the country. According to Mr. Tati Rama Rao, General Manager of Diamond Cement Ghana, DANGOTE enjoys a 30 per cent subsidy under Nigeria's Export Expansion Grant Scheme (EEG) for cement exports from that country, while also benefiting from ECOWAS' zero per cent tax through its ECOWAS land border (Aflao). He further argued that while Ghana was allowing Dangote imports under the ECOWAS trade protocol, Nigeria was restricting imports of the product from other countries including ECOWAS states. He therefore argued that Dangote is exploiting the ETLS and the subsidies the company gets from the Nigerian government to dump cement in the country to the detriment of local producers. It is such subsidies that explain why Dangote Cement is cheaper in Ghana than in Nigeria, where it is produced.[11] Dangote Cement has, however, debunked the above allegations arguing that the company's entry into the Ghanaian market had brought healthy competition. According to the Media Relations Manager of Dangote Cement Ghana, Etornam Komla Buami:

> [O]ur coming onto the market has brought lots of competition which is healthy for the economy and the end user is benefiting […]. I can tell you on authority that we are not under-pricing; you need to understand that every other cement manufacturing company imports clinker and other additives so it is not only Dangote that is importing some bit of items for their manufacturing as well.[12]

Despite the above opposition to Dangote Cement in Ghana, the company is already planning for its future in the country. It recently announced plans to

10 *Ghana Business News*, 10 February 2016, downloaded from <https://www.ghanabusinessnews.com/2016/02/10/cement-manufacturers-cry-foul/> on 3 March 2017.

11 See *Daily Guide*, 20 October 2016, downloaded from <http://dailyguideafrica.com/stop-dangote-cement-imports-manufacturers-tell-govt/> on 3 March 2017.

12 "Gov't must respond to Nigeria's unfair trade practices – Cement manufacturers" (12 October 2016), downloaded from <http://citifmonline.com/2016/10/12/govt-must-respond-to-nigerias-unfair-trade-practices-cement-manufacturers/> on 10 March 2017.

"build a 1.5 Mta clinker grinding plant, in Takoradi, to capitalise on the fact that Ghana is likely to enforce a ban on the importation of bulk cement" (Dangote Cement Annual Report 2016: 68).

In Sierra Leone, Dangote Cement is currently completing building work on its 0.7 Mta import facility. This project, which was severely delayed by the Ebola outbreak, is set to commence operations later this year (Ibid.: 11). Dangote's main competitor in Sierra Leone will be Sierra Leone Cement Corp (Leocem), a subsidiary of Heidelberg Cement. In Liberia, Dangote also plans to build a 0.75MTAClinker grinding facility.[13] Since Liberia does not have limestone, Dangote Cement plans to import the clinkers from Nigeria or elsewhere.

The only English-speaking West African country where Dangote's attempt to establish a cement production plant was allegedly refused was in the Gambia. It has been suggested that

> the idea was meant to protect the local cement factory, GACEM owned by a Gambian business tycoon, Amadou Samba, who is believed to be the right hand man of [the ex-] Gambian leader, Yahya Jammeh […]. However, Dangote Cement is still available in the country for sale by agents who are partnering with his numerous factories across the continent.[14]

The report that Dangote was refused a licence to set up a factory in Gambia has, however, been denied by the Gambian authorities, who insist that since the country does not have limestone, there is no question of Dangote setting up a cement company there.[15]

The incursion of Dangote Cement into the francophone West African countries has proved more difficult. Dangote's biggest plant in the region is in Senegal. This is not surprising given the fact that the country has a strategic limestone reserve of 300 million tonnes. With a dearth of limestone reserves in many of Senegal's neighbouring countries, Dangote Cement views its investments in the country in terms of both the local and the export market.

---

13 See Table 12.1.

14 GAMBIA – Gambia Denies Dangote License to Open Cement Factory (Undated), downloaded from, <http://www.intercem.com/Intercem-Markets/News/ArtMID/683/ArticleID/55/GAMBIA-Gambia-Denies-Dangote-License-to-Open-Cement-Factory> on 3 March 2017. See also *Africa Review*,16 December 2015, downloaded from http://www.africareview.com/business-finance/Gambia-denies-Dangote-firm-licence/979184-2999538-60fefaz/index.html on 10 March 2017.

15 Gambia minister refutes reports on Dangote licence, http://www.cemnet.com/News/story/158607/gambia-minister-refutes-reports-on-dangote-licence.html Published: 18 February 2016

Establishing a plant in the country was however not easy. Although its 1.5 Mta integrated plant in Pout, located about 29km from Dakar, was supposed to come into operation in 2012, it was bogged down with lawsuits about land and arbitration about competition. On the contentious issue of the land title of its plant, the company's 2012 Annual Report noted:

> Title to the land on which part of the Group's plant in Senegal is located is still in dispute and therefore the plant was not able to commence operations in 2012, as had been hoped. Furthermore, an interim Administrative Order was served by the local authorities to cease construction work until the land issues are resolved. The Group believes the closure order was unlawful and unnecessary, given the plant's potential to create jobs and prosperity in the local area. The Group remains committed to achieving an acceptable resolution of the land dispute. Once such a resolution has been achieved, the commissioning process can begin in earnest and the plant could be operational and producing cement within weeks (18–19).[16]

The advent of Dangote Cement into the Senegal was also opposed by the dominant cement production company at the time, Sococim (a subsidiary of Vicat, a French Multinational Company), which had 65 per cent of the local market share. Ciments du Sahel controlled the remaining market in the country. This dispute eventually resulted in Sococim taking the Government of Senegal to the regional arbitration court based in Ivory Coast.

Sococim claimed that the plant represented a "distortion of competition" in a country where the market is already saturated. It also argued that an environmental impact study that was crucial to granting of permits to operate was not done. Specifically, the water-cooling technology involved in the $630 million Dangote plant would require a daily withdrawal of 4,500 cubic litres of groundwater, which would impact negatively on the fresh water security of the arid country. If production was allowed to begin, it would become more difficult to halt. Furthermore, the conditions granted to Dangote to install a plant meant that he would totally control the cement market up to the point he (Dangote) could set any price he wanted. The French president, Francois Holland, was reported to have intervened via a letter to the Senegalese President, Macky Sall,

16 During the plant construction phase, Senegalese courts were recorded to have ruled that the plant encroached on a sacred forest owned by the descendants of Cheikh Amadou Bamba, a Sufi Muslim mystic and religious leader, revered by millions of Senegalese. It was reported that construction was only allowed to recommence when Dangote offered the family a persuasive $12.6 million in compensation.

so as to "raise awareness of the difficulties faced by Sococim." Sall's response was that "the rule of law and the Senegalese courts" must be allowed to decide whether the project could go ahead.[17] All the issues were eventually resolved and the plant was completed and commissioned in December 2014.

By the end of 2016, Dangote Cement had taken control of about 25 per cent of the 4Mt cement market in Senegal. The company "achieved this rapid success by selling superior 42.5-grade cement at a price competitive with other manufacturers' 32.5-grade products. Since then, other producers have upgraded to 42.5-grade and cut the price of their 32.5-grade products in response" (Dangote Cement Annual Report 2016: 60). The company is also currently exploring the possibility of building a second plant in Senegal, which will aim at supplying clinkers to a proposed grinding plant in neighbouring Mali, a country without any limestone. The company also plans to build a 3.0 Mta grinding facility in the Port of Abidjan (Ivory Coast). Since the country does not have limestone, clinkers will be supplied to this factory from Nigeria (Ibid.: 68).

Another Francophone ECOWAS country where Dangote plans to establish a manufacturing plant is Niger. Although the country has abundant limestone, it has traditionally depended on cement importation from several countries, including Nigeria. In fact, the country currently has one cement plant, Société Nigérienne de Cimenterie, with a production capacity of 0.04Mt/yr.[18] Dangote plans to take advantage of the country's abundant limestone to build a 1.5 Mta cement factory in the country before the end of the decade. Dangote's expansionist ambitions are, however, not limited to West Africa. As will be seen in the next section, the company has also been able to expand its cement business to other parts of Africa amidst challenges.[19]

---

17 "African tycoon draws Nigeria, France into 'cement war' in Senegal", https://www.thenews.com.pk/archive/amp/492548-african-tycoon-draws-nigeria-france-into-%E2%80%98cement-war%E2%80%99-in-senegal.

18 Dangote to build 1.5Mt/yr cement plant in Niger (23 October 2013), downloaded from <http://www.globalcement.com/news/itemlist/tag/Niger> on 3 March 2017.

19 Dangote's views about the challenges of doing business in Africa have been summarised thus: "More than anything else [...] there needs to be more concerted action around strengthening institutions. This is one of the areas that we are lagging behind. Institutions are very, very important. Obviously nobody will go and invest in a place where there is no rule of law." He is also outspoken on the issue of regional integration. African trade is currently estimated to be lower than 15 per cent representing enormous untapped potential. Despite a myriad of pan-African conferences and agreements, aimed at addressing this challenge, Dangote believes "there is a lot of talk about integration but really not much action is taken. Unless governments address these issues, I think presidents have just been there [conferences] to waste taxpayers' money" (*African Business*, October 2015: 18).

## Dangote Cement and the Challenges of Pan-African Expansion

Although Cameroon is not part of the ECOWAS bloc, it has a common border with Nigeria. It is therefore not surprising that this is one of the African markets where Dangote Cement is active. In 2015, for instance, the company established a 1.5 Mta grinding facility in Doula. With this investment, Dangote Cement became "the first new entrant in Cameroon's cement market in 40 years" (Dangote Cement Annual Report 2015: 24). Since Cameroon does not have limestone, clinkers to this facility are currently being imported from the Far East. Dangote Cement, however, plans that, in future, it will import such clinkers from Nigeria. The entrance of Dangote Cement into Cameroon changed the dynamics of the cement market in the country. Prior to 2015, the market was essentially a monopoly that was dominated by a local subsidiary of Lafarge, the French multinational cement company. In 2016, for instance, Dangote sold nearly 1.1Mt of cement, a 90 per cent increase on the 0.6Mt sold in 2015. This translated to 43 per cent of the country's total cement consumption of 2.5 Mta (Dangote Cement Annual Report 2016: 58).

Aside from the above investment, the smuggling of Dangote Cement into Cameroon from Nigeria is also thriving, despite the ban on cement importation into Cameroon. This has resulted in lower cement prices in Cameroon. It has been reported, for instance, that such smuggled cement is usually transported on motor bikes in "collusion with local customs officers in charge of monitoring a porous, 150-km long border."[20] This is perhaps not surprising, especially given that, since the economic crisis in Nigeria and the attendant scarcity of foreign exchange, economic agents have resorted to smuggling goods into Nigeria's francophone neighbouring countries. This is seen as an easy way of earning CFA Francs, which are easily convertible into any of the major currencies in the world.

Aside from Cameroon, Dangote's business interests outside ECOWAS focus mainly on real cement production, rather than bulk cement importation and bagging or clinker importation and grinding. This explains the concentration of Dangote Cement operations outside ECOWAS, primarily in countries that have limestone. In 2015, for instance, Dangote opened its 3 Mta cement production plant in Mtwara Tanzania, which is 400 km from the capital Dar es Salaam. Specifically, the country's proven limestone reserves have been put at 500 million tonnes, enough to keep the Dangote plant in business for 149

20 Business in Cameroon, 6 February 2017, downloaded from http://www.businessincameroon.com/law/0602-6870-smuggling-of-dangote-cement-results-in-price-drop-in-northern-cameroon> on 10 March 2017.

years.[21] Prior to the establishment of Dangote Cement in Tanzania, the country "had approximately 4.5 Mta of capacity shared between six incumbents, mostly operating integrated Factories" (Dangote Cement Annual Report 2015: 41). At inception, therefore, Dangote Cement became the largest cement company in the country.

In November 2016, one year after the commencement of production, the Dangote plant stopped production. The immediate reason cited for the suspension of production was the persistent increase in the cost of fuel used in powering the plant. Prior to the suspension of production, the company's CEO, Harpeet Duggal, had lamented that the company was spending approximately $4 million on six million litres of diesel monthly to power its cement factory and that "promises to supply it with natural gas, which is produced in a nearby gas field, failed to materialize" (Nsehe 2016). This is particularly important given the fact that the abundance of natural gas around the area where Dangote's plant is located was a strategic factor in the decision to locate the cement plant in the area.

Although the previous government, led by former President Jakaya Kikwete, had promised Dangote cheaper prices for natural gas, the Tanzania Petroleum Development Corporation (TPDC) under the government of the new President John Magufuli was said to have refused to honour the agreement on the grounds that it was too generous. In April 2016, for instance, President Magufuli relieved Juliet Kairuki of her post as the Executive Director of the Tanzania Investment Center. She was alleged to have been pivotal in securing some of the incentives for Dangote Industries Tanzania. According to the TPDC, Dangote Cement factory asked for gas supply at below market prices, equivalent to the price of raw natural gas from producing wells. It is therefore not possible for the TPDC to agree to the demands of Dangote Cement (Alli 2016). Some have suggested, however, that this dispute actually goes beyond the price of gas. According to a Member of Parliament from Mtwara, what "complicates matters is the fact that it seems some powerful politicians who served in the past administration have strong, vested interests in the Dangote Cement. It is possible that they form part of the local shareholding in the project."[22]

The dispute between Dangote and the Government of Tanzania over the price of gas has now been resolved. The impact of this closure on the activities

---

21 Dangote Cement in Tanzania, http://www.dangotecement.com/operations/tanzania/ accessed 17 February 2017.

22 *The Citizen*, "Which way Dangote Cement?" http://www.thecitizen.co.tz/News/Which-way-Dangote-Cement-/1840340-3469754-dn3sab/index.html Wednesday, November 30, 2016; accessed February 17, 2017.

of Dangote Cement in Tanzania was recently explained by the Chief Executive Officer of Dangote Cement, Mr. Onne van der Weijde:

> It was a mixed year in Tanzania. We started well and despite being the furthest cement plant from the main market in Dar es Salaam, we quickly gained more than 20 per cent share. But a few months later we had a temporary closure for some technical issues and that cost us some sales. At the same time, we were negotiating a gas supply agreement and I'm pleased to say we managed to resolve that issue satisfactorily. The lack of an agreement on gas supply had forced us to use diesel gensets before that because there isn't enough grid power in the area to keep the plant running, and that affected margins in Tanzania quite badly. Now we have reached an agreement on gas supply we can swap the diesel gensets for much cheaper gas turbines that will immediately bring the plant into profitability after they are commissioned at the end of the second quarter of 2017.
>
> Dangote Cement Annual Report 2016: 54–55

Another African country that has abundant limestone reserves and that Dangote Cement has invested in is Congo. The strategy here is to replace imported cement with locally produced cement. This is because, although the country currently has an annual cement demand capacity of 2.4 Mta, it is still heavily dependent on imported cement. In fact, before the advent of Dangote Cement, "the country had limited production capacity, from sub-scale plants, and most demand was satisfied by imported cement" (Ibid.: 59). Specifically, the local cement companies in the country are Forspak, which has a 0.3 Mta works at Dolisie, Niari, and Sonoc, which runs a 0.3 Mta plant at Loutété, Bouenza.[23] In pursuit of the aforementioned strategy, Dangote Cement recently completed a 1.5 Mta cement production facility that began clinker production in February 2017. This instantly made Dangote Cement the biggest cement manufacturing company in the country. It is also hoped that, in future, Dangote will be able to export cement to neighboring Democratic Republic of Congo.

In 2015, Dangote Cement also opened a 2.5 Mta cement production facility in Ethiopia. Unlike in several African countries, cement production in Ethiopia is very competitive. Before the advent of Dangote, there were four large cement companies in the country with production capacities ranging from 1.2

23 See, "DR Congo: New plant online in December 2016," 29 September 2016, downloaded from http://www.cemnet.com/News/story/157694/dr-congo-new-plant-online-in-december-2016.html> on 10 March 2017.

to 2.5 Mta. These included Derba MIDROC, Mugher, Messebo, and National. After the establishment of Dangote, Habesha, with a production capacity of 1.4 Mta has also become operational (FDRE Ministry of Industry 2015: 28–29). Cement production competition in Ethiopia has arguably been aided by the fact that most of the cement companies in the country are able to take advantage of Ethiopia's well-developed electricity grid.

Despite Ethiopia's efficient energy infrastructure and the size and newness of Dangote's factory in the country, the company's operations in Ethiopia have not always been smooth. The recent political crisis in the country has negatively impacted the company. At Ada Berga in Oromia Region, the company's plant was recently torched by protesters in the backdrop of the demise of 55 people, trampled to death in a stampede triggered during clashes between police and demonstrators during a religious festival (Adesanya 2016).[24] Despite these problems, the company currently controls about 24 per cent of the market share in the Ethiopia (Dangote Cement Annual Report 2016: 59).

In Kenya, Dangote plans to build an integrated factory, which is expected to commence operations in 2019. However, there is currently stiff opposition to this plan. The genesis of this plant and the opposition to it has been summarised thus:

> A proposal by Aliko Dangote [...] to build a multi-billion cement factory in Kenya is facing fierce opposition from local businessmen, amid fears that he could dominate the Kenyan cement industry. In September 2013, while on a visit to Kenya, Mr Dangote said his company – Dangote Cement – was planning to establish a 35 billion two-million-tonne-a-year cement plant factory in Kitui [...]. Mr Dangote's announcement immediately sent shockwaves across the local cement sector, which is already contending with excess capacity and the influx of cheaper cement from Egypt, India, China and Pakistan. Many commentators reacted by foretelling that Dangote Cement would intensify the price war in the cement business as it strives to grab a market share from local firms who are fighting to defend their stakes in the increasingly competitive environment [...] In order to prevent such a scenario, highly connected local and international businessmen are reportedly marshalling their forces for a ferocious battle against Mr. Dangote, including calls for inhibitory legislation to disrupt the project.[25]

24 http://www.cemnet.com/News/story/160239/ethiopia-protesters-start-fires-at-dangote-plant.html Published: 05 October 2016.

25 *Business Review*, 18 January 2015, downloaded from <http://www.constructionkenya.com/3011/dangote-faces-opposition-in-kenya/> on 3 March 2017.

In the Second quarter of 2015, Dangote Cement opened a 1.5 Mta cement processing plant in Ndola, which is 271 km from Lusaka. The cement industry in Zambia currently has a production capacity of about 3.5 Mta. Dangote Cement is the country's biggest cement producer and currently controls about 40 per cent of the cement market in the country (Dangote Cement Annual Report 2016: 62). It is perhaps testament to Dangote's growing political clout in Africa that the commissioning of the Dangote Plant in Zambia was witnessed by President Edgar Lungu of Zambia, Jakaya Kikwete, the former President of Tanzania, Prime Minister Hailemariam Desalegn of Ethiopia and President Paul Biya of Cameroon, as well as Vice President Yemi Osinbajo of Nigeria (Cf. Dangote Cement Annual Report 2015: 9).

Also, Dangote's operations in Zambia have not always been smooth. In 2014, for instance, Zambia's labour minister, Fackson Shamenda, said a Nigerian executive seconded to the Zambian unit of Dangote Cement tried to bribe him. Shamenda, who did not specify what was offered by the executive, said he rejected it because he had critical labour issues to sort out with the company and did not want to be compromised. "He told me that it was a tradition in their culture to give someone a token of appreciation. Maybe his idea was that I turn a blind eye to what is happening at Dangote." Specifically, Shamenda said Dangote Cement should offer workers at the company permanent employment and allow them to join unions. "There is no union and according to the reports I have received those who have attempted to join unions have had their contracts terminated," Dangote Cement, however, denied these claims of corruption and bribery and described the allegations as "malicious misinformation."[26] Dangote subsequently sued the Minister for defamation. After Shamenda failed to put up a defence, the court entered a judgement in default of appearance and ordered Shamenda to pay special damages to the sum of K112,042.84 to Dangote Industries Zambia (DIZ). DIZ subsequently applied for the matter to be settled out of court.[27]

Dangote also has investments in South Africa, a country that has blazed the trail in intra-continental investments in Africa. It is therefore not surprising that South Africa has a very competitive cement industry, with 19 cement plants, seven of which are owned by Pretoria Portland Cement Company (PPC). Other major players in the cement industry in South Africa include Natal Portland

26 *Reuters*, 16 September 2014. Downloaded from <http://www.reuters.com/article/us-zambia-dangote-corruption-idUSKBN0HB1L720140916> on 10 March 2017.

27 *Lusaka Times*, 15 May 2015, downloaded from <https://www.lusakatimes.com/2015/05/15/lusaka-high-court-orders-labour-minister-fackson-shamenda-to-pay-dangote-for-defamation/> on 10 March 2017.

Cement, Afrisam and Lafarge.[28] Despite the existence of numerous players in the cement industry, cases of collusion have been identified and punished in the past by the International Trade Administration Commission of South Africa. "After finding out the existence of cement cartels, the commission imposed fines of US$9.21m on Afrisam while Lafarge got US$11.07 m between 2011 and 2012."[29]

Arguably, because of the level of development and complexity of the South African cement market, Dangote entered the market by acquiring controlling shares in an existing cement company in the country. In 2010, for instance, Dangote Industries Limited (DIL), paid R779 million to increase its stake in Sephaku Cement South Africa, from 19.76 per cent to 64 per cent. The transaction "is the largest ever foreign direct investment (FDI) by an African company into South Africa."[30] In November 2015, Sephaku Cement was renamed Dangote Cement. The company decided, however, to retain its Sephaku branding in the country (Dangote Cement Annual Report 2015: 39). Dangote Cement currently has two production plants located in Aganang and Delmas, both near Johannesburg. The Aganang plant is a 1.8 Mta integrated plant, while the Delmas plant is a 1.5 Mta grinding plant.

Despite the fact that South Africa has several cement production facilities, the country has always had space for cement importation. Generally, such imports come from Pakistan, India and China. In 2014, however, a consortium of cement manufacturers in South Africa, which included Afrisam, Lafarge, NPC Cimpor and PPC Limited petitioned the International Trade Administration Commission of South Africa to complain that the Portland Cement being imported from Pakistan was being dumped in South Africa to the detriment of local cement companies.[31] This culminated in the imposition of import dumping duties on such imported cement. This development was welcomed by Dangote Cement in South Africa; according to its 2016 Annual Report:

28 *Global Cement*, 11 December 2014, downloaded from <http://www.globalcement.com/magazine/articles/894-the-cement-industries-of-southern-africa> on 10 March 2017.

29 *Construction Review Online*, 3 September 2015, downloaded from <https://constructionreviewonline.com/2015/09/pakistani-cement-firm-sues-south-africas-itac/> on 10 March 2017.

30 *Vanguard*, 1 November 2010, downloaded from <http://www.vanguardngr.com/2010/11/dangote-acquires-64-stake-in-south-african-cement-firm/> on 10 March 2010. See also "Dangote acquires 64% stake in South African cement firm" (undated), downloaded from <https://www.proshareng.com/news/Investors-NewsBeat/Dangote-acquires-64Percent-stake-in-South-African-cement-firm/12421> on 3 March 2017.

31 See *Dawn*, 24 August 2014, downloaded from https://www.dawn.com/news/1127310> on 10 March 2017.

> Cement imports declined significantly in 2016 after new duties were imposed to prevent dumping by foreign exporters. We estimate total imports to have been 430kt for the full year, which is significantly lower than the 820kt imported in 2015. This has obviously created opportunities for substitution with local cement (61).

From the above analysis, it is clear that Dangote Cement has been able to rapidly expand its cement production capacity across Africa within a relatively short period. The company, which has more than doubled production capacity since 2013, stated in April 2016 that "it may increase cement capacity by a further 77 percent by the end of 2019."[32] Dangote Cement's ability to rapidly expand its business across Africa was aided in the past by the availability of capital; specifically, most of the capital invested came from Nigeria, Dangote Cement's home country. As previously mentioned, Dangote Cement is by far the largest company quoted on the Nigeria Stock Exchange. "With the Nigeria Naira-US Dollar exchange rate devalued by over 50% since the start of 2016 and the Nigerian economy bracing itself for a recession, it seems unlikely that Dangote Cement could do anything else than slow down its expansion plans given how much of its revenue comes from within Nigeria."[33] It is therefore not surprising that the company's aggressive expansion timetable has now been revised. "Foreign-exchange constraints in Nigeria have prompted the company to reconsider the pace of its expansion."[34]

## Conclusion

Irrespective of the slowdown in its pan-African expansionist agenda, Dangote Cement remains one of the most remarkable business success stories in Africa. It is important to note that the company commenced cement production in 2000, when it acquired Beneue Cement, which, at the time, had a production capacity of 0.9 Mta. Today, the company has a total production capacity of 45.75 Mta scattered across ten African countries.[35] Perhaps more important

32 *Bloomberg*, 28 July 2016. Downloaded from https://www.bloomberg.com/news/articles/2016-07-28/dangote-cement-signals-slower-pace-of-expansion-as-profit-falls>on10March 2017.

33 *Global Cement*, 3 August 2016, downloaded from <http://www.globalcement.com/news/item/5158-dangote-cement-slows-its-pace-of-expansion> on 9 March 2017.

34 *Bloomberg* (26 July 2016), downloaded from https://www.bloomberg.com/news/articles/2016-07-28/dangote-cement-signals-slower-pace-of-expansion-as-profit-falls> on 9 March 2017.

35 Table 12.1.

TABLE 12.1 *Dangote's cement production plants in Africa (commissioned and planned)*

| # | Country | Year | Location | Process | Planned Mta | Operating Mta |
|---|---|---|---|---|---|---|
| 1 | Nigeria | 2007 | Gboko | Integrated | 4 | 4 |
| | Nigeria | 2008 | Obajana | Integrated | 13,25 | 13,25 |
| | Nigeria | 2012 | Ibese | Integrated | 12 | 12 |
| | Nigeria | Planned | Itori | Integrated | Not stated | N/A |
| | Nigeria | Planned | Okpella | Integrated | Not stated | N/A |
| 2 | South Africa | 2008 | Aganang | Integrated | 1,8 | 1,8 |
| | South Africa | 2008 | Mpumalanga | Grinding | 1,5 | 1,5 |
| 3 | Ghana | 2011 | Tema | Bagging | 1 | 1 |
| | Ghana | Planned | Takoradi | Grinding | 1,5 | N/A |
| 4 | Senegal | 2014 | Pout | Integrated | 1,5 | 1,5 |
| 5 | Cameroon | 2015 | Douala | Grinding | 1,5 | 1,5 |
| 6 | Ethiopia | 2015 | Mugher | Integrated | 2,5 | 2,5 |
| 7 | Tanzania | 2015 | Mtwara | Integrated | 3 | 3 |
| 8 | Zambia | 2015 | Ndola | Integrated | 1,5 | 1,5 |
| 9 | Congo | 2016 | Mfila | Integrated | 1,5 | 1,5 |
| 10 | Sierra Leone | 2017 | Freetown | Bagging | 0,7 | 0,7 |
| 11 | Kenya | 2019* | Kitui | Integrated | 1,5 | N/A |
| 12 | Mali | 2019* | | Grinding | 1,5 | N/A |
| 13 | Niger | 2020* | Nigeria border | Production | 1,5 | N/A |
| 14 | Cote d'Ivoire | Planned | Abidjan | Grinding | 1,5 | N/A |
| 15 | Liberia | Planned | Monrovia | Grinding | 0,75 | N/A |
| 16 | Zimbabwe | Planned | | Integrated | 1,5 | N/A |
| | Total | | | | | 45,75 |

SOURCE: COMPILED FROM DANGOTE CEMENT WEBSITE. HTTP://DANGOTE.COM/OURBRANDS/CEMENT.ASPX#AFRICA
Note: * - estimated year of commencement of operations

is the fact that Dangote Cement is now the largest cement company in Africa. The rapid rise of Dangote Cement in Africa is evidence of the underdeveloped nature of the cement industry in Africa. Despite the high bulk – low cost nature of cement and the availability of limestone in several countries in the continent, cement importation thrived in several African countries. Cement prices in Africa also remained the highest in the world. At the very least, the advent of Dangote into the cement market in Africa is helping to increase competition and reduce prices. Perhaps more important is the fact that local limestone is now increasingly being used in cement production to the detriment of imported cement. Unlike many of the other cement multinationals that have dominated the African cement landscape, Dangote has been willing to invest heavily in local cement production across Africa, despite the obvious political and economic risks. It is perhaps this experience that made Aliko Dangote conclude that "only Africans can develop Africa."[36] If this is so, then the time has come for African countries to take regional economic integration more seriously. At the very least, this will help reduce obstacles to intra-African business investments.

## References

Achenhou, A. (1983). "South South Cooperation, the Lagos Plan of Action and Africa's Independence", *Africa Development*, vol. 8, 5–19.

Adesanya, F. (2016). "Protesters Destroy Dangote Cement Factory in Ethiopia", http://www.informationng.com/2016/10/dangote-cement-factory-in-ethiopia.html October 4, 2016.

*African Business* (Various issues).

Akinyoade, A. & C. Uche. (2016), "Dangote Cement: An African Success Story?". African Studies Centre Leiden Working Paper 131/2016.

Alli, F. (2016). "Tanzania in Talks with Dangote Cement Over Gas Price", 8 December, http://www.vanguardngr.com/2016/12/tanzania-talks-dangote-cement-gas-price/ accessed 17 February 2017.

Amin, S. (1982). "A Critique of the World Bank Report Entitled Accelerated Development in Sub Saharan Africa", *Africa Development*, vol. 7, 23–42.

Anyansi-Achibong, C. & P. Anyansi. (2014). "African Entrepreneurs and their Philanthropies: Motivations, Challenges and Impact". In: M. Taylor, R. Strom & D. Renz (eds), *Handbook of Research on Entrepreneurs' Engagement in Philanthropy: Perspectives*, Cheltenham: Edward Elgar Publishing Limited.

Ayittey, G. (2010). "The United States of Africa: A Revisit", *ANNALS AAPSS*, 632: 86–102.

Bach, D. (1983). "The Politics of West African Economic Co-operation: CEAO and ECOWAS", *The Journal of Modern African Studies*, vol. 21, Issue 4, 605–623.

Bujra, A. (1982). "Editorial Note", *Africa Development*, vol. 7, I–VI.

Cornwell, R. (2002). "The New Partnership for Africa's Development: Last Chance for Africa?" In: H. Melber, R. Cornwell, J. Gathaka & S. Wanjala. (2002), "The New

36 *Vanguard*, 11 October 2015. Downloaded from <http://www.vanguardngr.com/2015/10/dangote-to-build-cement-plants-in-18-african-countries/> on 10 March 2017.

Partnership for Africa's Development: African Perspectives", *Nordic Africa Institute Discussion Paper Number 16.*

Dangote Cement (Various Years) Annual Report and Accounts.

Daniel, J., Naidoo, V. & S. Naidu. (2003). "The South Africans Have Arrived: Post Apartheid Corporate Expansion into Africa". In: J. Daniel, A. Habib & R. Southall, (eds), *State of the Nation: South Africa 2003–2004,* Cape Town, HSRC Press.

Deutsche Gesellschaft für Internationale Zusammenarbeit (GIZ) GmbH (Undated), "The Common External Tariff (CET): Structure, Benefits, Challenges and the Way Forward of the CET", downloaded from <http://www.ecowas.int/wpcontent/uploads/2016/06/CET_Factsheet_EN.pdf> on 10 March 2017.

Dietz, T., Lange, P. & M.-L. Rau.(2016). Scoping Report "Improving the perspective for regional trade and investment in West Africa: the key to food security, economic development and stability in the region". See: http://ecdpm.org/wp-content/uploads/Improving-Perspective-Regional-Trade-Investment-West-Africa-July-2016.pdf.

ECOWAS (2013). The ECOWAS Trade Liberalisation Scheme: Genesis, Conditions and Appraisal, ECOWAS Vanguard, Volume 2, Issue 3, 1–10.

Elkan, W. (1988). Entrepreneurs and entrepreneurship in Africa, *World Bank Research Observer* 3, 171–188.

Ezeoha, A. & C. Uche. (2005). "South Africa, NEPAD and the African Renaissance (with Abel Ezeoha)", *Africa Studies Centre Working Paper Number 65/2005* (Leiden, Africa Studies Centre).

Fayemiwo, A. & M. Neal (2013). *Aliko Mohammad Dangote: The Biography of the Richest Black Person in the World,* Houston, TX: Strategic Book Publishing.

FDRE Ministry of Industry (2015). Ethiopian Cement Industry Development Strategy 2015–2025, downloaded from <http://www.icapitalafrica.net/uploads/6/9/9/6/69965091/ethiopian_cement_industry_development_strategy_2015-2025.pdf> on 3 March 2017.

Federal Republic of Nigeria. (1976). Report of the Tribunal of Enquiry into the Importation of Cement, Lagos, Federal Ministry of Information, Printing Division.

Forrest, T. (1992). *Politics and Economic Development in Nigeria,* Boulder, CO: Westview Press.

Forrest, T. (1994). *The Advance of African Capital: The Growth of Nigerian Private Enterprise,* Edinburgh: Edinburgh University Press.

Habib, A. (2009), "South Africa's Foreign Policy: Hegemonic Aspirations, Neoliberal Orientations and Global Transformation", *South African Journal of International Affairs,* 16, 143–159.

Heilman, B. & J. Lucas (1997). "A Social Movement for African Capitalism? A Comparison of Business Associations in Two African Cities", *African Studies Review* 40, 141–171.

Kulla, M. (1976). "The Politics of Culture: The Case of FESTAC", *Ufahamu: A Journal of African Studies* 7, 166–192.

Makgetlaneng, S. (2003), *Continental Political Governance and Regional Integration: From the Lagos Plan of Action to the New Partnership of Africa's Development*, Africa, Institute of South Africa.

Malan, D. (2005). "Corporate Citizens, Colonialists, Tourists or Activists? Ethical Challenges Facing South African Corporations in Africa", *Journal of Corporate Citizenship* 18, 49–60.

Mojekwu, J., Ademola Idowu, A. & O. Oluseyi Sode. (2012). "Analysis of the Contribution of Imported and Locally Manufactured Cement to the Growth of Gross Domestic Product (GDP) of Nigeria (1986–2011)", *African Journal of Business Management* 7, 360–371.

Nkuhlu, W. (2003). "South Africa and the New Partnership for Africa's Development (NEPAD)", *Paper Presented at the University of Stellenbosch* (4 September 2003).

Nsehe, M (2016). "Africa's Richest Man Faces Challenges In Tanzania; Shuts Down Cement Plant", *Forbes*, 2 December 2016, http://www.forbes.com/sites/mfonobongnsehe/2016/12/02/africas-richest-man-faces-challenges-in-tanzania-shuts-down-cement-plant/#53a1aa0a4270 accessed 16 February 2017.

Ogbor, J. (2009). *Entrepreneurship in Sub-Saharan Africa: A Strategic Management Perspective*, Bloomington, IN: Authorhouse.

Ohimain, E. (2014). "The Success of the Backward Integration Policy in the Nigerian Cement Sector", *International Journal of Materials Science and Applications* 3, 70–78.

Onwuka, R. (1992). *A Political Economy of the Control of Transnational Corporations*, Owerri: International Universities Press.

The Organisation for African Unity (1980). *The Lagos Plan of Action.*

The Organisation of African Unity (1980). *The Final Act of Lagos.*

*The Organisation of African Unity Charter* (25 May 1963).

The Organisation of African Unity (1998), *The OAU: 35 Years in the Service of Africa*, Essex: World of Information.

Pan African Capital Plc. (2011). *Nigerian Cement Industry: A Review of Opportunities and Recurrent Price Hike*, Lagos: Pan African Capital plc.

Taal, M. (2014). "South African Multinational Corporations in Africa – Trends in 2013/2014, A report by the Labour Research Service (November)", downloaded from <http://www.fes-southafrica.org/media/MNC%20Trend%20Report%20%20FES%20draft%202014.pdf> on 15 February 2017.

Uche, C. (2001). "The Politics of Monetary Sector Cooperation Among the Economic Community of West African States Members". *World Bank Policy Research Working Paper Number 2647*, Washington D.C.: World Bank.

Uche, C. (2011). "The European Union and Monetary Integration in West Africa", *Centre for European Integration Studies (ZEI) Discussion Paper C 206/2011*, Bonn: Centre for European Integration Studies.

Ugoh, S. (1966). "The Nigerian Cement Industry", *Nigerian Journal of Economic and Social Studies* 8, 97–112.

White, L. (2015). "The Case of Cement". In: T. McNamee, M. Pearson & W. Boer (eds), *Africans Investing in Africa: Understanding Business and Trade, Sector by Sector*, Hampshire: Palgrave Macmillan.

CHAPTER 13

# Culture as a Facilitator and a Barrier to Entrepreneurship Development in Uganda

*Jane N.O. Khayesi, Arthur Sserwanga and Rebecca Kiconco*

## Introduction

There has been substantial scholarly interest in culture as an institution that affects human life, including entrepreneurship (George and Zahra 2002; Hayton, George, and Zahra 2002). Most of this research, however, focuses on Western and Eastern countries, with limited research on the relationship between culture and entrepreneurship in Africa. For instance, a search of business and management literature on 23 May 2016 using the key terms "culture" and "entrepreneurship" in the ISI Web of Science database yielded 654 articles, of which, only ten focused directly on Africa. There remains ambivalence about the contribution of culture to entrepreneurship development in African countries. While, on the one hand, there are stories of successful entrepreneurial efforts, on the other hand, there are tales of failure attributed to cultural factors. Furthermore, the different strands of research on culture and entrepreneurship development in Africa remain scattered and have not been consolidated into an easily accessible resource. This chapter aims to fill this gap in knowledge by synthesising and discussing available evidence showing how the cultural factor facilitates and/or constrains entrepreneurship development in Uganda.

Following the introduction, the next section discusses what the existing evidence reveals about the situation of entrepreneurship development in Uganda. Specifically, we discuss the efforts of governmental and non-governmental initiatives and programmes in entrepreneurship development in Uganda. We then discuss culture as an institution, examining its facilitative and constraining role in entrepreneurship development in Uganda. This section assesses culture-related opportunities and difficulties encountered by Ugandan entrepreneurs in the development of their businesses. Based on research conducted by Khayesi and George (2011), the third section provides a case illustration of culture's facilitating and constraining effect on entrepreneurship development in Uganda. This illustration is based on empirical evidence gathered by Khayesi and George (2011) on the contextual effect of socio-culture on entrepreneurs' resource assembly efforts through their social ties among micro-, small-, and

 | DOI 10.1163/9789004351615_014

medium-sized entrepreneurs in Uganda. The chapter then concludes with a discussion of policy, research, and practical recommendations for entrepreneurship development in Africa based on the preceding sections.

## The Situation of Entrepreneurship Development in Uganda

The 2014 Global Entrepreneurship Monitor's (GEM) data ranks Uganda second in the world in terms of Total Early-stage Entrepreneurial Activity (TEA), and first in the world in terms of new and established business ownership rates (Singer, Amorós, and Moska 2015). Taken together, these facts have earned Uganda the title of *the most entrepreneurial country of the world*, with approximately 28 per cent of the adult population owning a new business and 36per cent of the adult population owning an established business. One may wonder, in a country where approximately 20 per cent of the population live in poverty (Uganda 2014), how does such a country become the world's most entrepreneurial country?

While it might be speculated that the 28 per cent of adult Ugandans might have gone into business as a last resort, clearly the 36 per cent who are already established must have a reason for surviving in business. In fact, Uganda relies heavily on small- and medium sized enterprises (SMEs) as job creators and income generators for its economy (Uganda Investment Authority 2008). This warrants an examination of entrepreneurship development in Uganda with a focus on facilitative and/or constraining factors. Both governmental and non-governmental institutions play different roles in putting in place policies, initiatives, and programmes to facilitate entrepreneurship development in Uganda. We hereby examine these roles and institutions in depth.

### *Government Role*

The government's effort at entrepreneurship development mainly takes the form of putting in place and enforcing, as far as possible, policies and programmes that support micro-, small-, and medium-sized enterprises in Uganda. We examine these policies and programmes in this section.

### *Government Policy*

Generally, Ugandan national experts agree that national policies outlined in policy documents such as the Poverty Eradication Action Plan (PEAP) are supportive of entrepreneurship in Uganda (Namatovu et al. 2011). Over the past three decades, the Government of Uganda has maintained a policy divesting itself from doing business. Instead, entrepreneurship has been left mainly to the private sector. Nevertheless, the government of Uganda has encouraged entrepreneurship through its policies aimed at reducing predatory taxation, for instance removing implicit taxation on exports, liberalising the foreign exchange rate, supporting industrialisation, and improving the financial system, and opening sectors, which were previously a monopoly of government (Walter et al., 2003). These policies facilitate the participation of entrepreneurs in international trade.

The government has continued to maintain low inflation as one of its macro-economic policies. Coordinated prudent fiscal and monetary policy management have been employed to contain inflation. By maintaining low inflation, the government provides a stable investment climate that attracts entrepreneurial start-ups and enables existing ones to grow (Kasaija 2015; Kiwanuka 2014).

Government policy has also targeted financial inclusion and deepening. One of the challenges faced by entrepreneurs in developing countries is lack of access to credit. The emergence of new mobile telephone technology and agency banking are key drivers of improved financial inclusion. Government has put in place policies and laws that accommodate alternative banking approaches like mobile banking, agent banking, bank assurance, and Islamic Banking. These new financial approaches will ease the credit accessibility barriers faced by business start-ups and small- and medium-sized enterprises (Kasaija 2015; Kiwanuka 2014).

The government has enacted the Public-Private Partnerships (PPPs) policy, as an important option for delivering public infrastructure projects and services. PPPs provide entrepreneurs with new business start-up or growth opportunities. Entrepreneurs can exploit innovative business opportunities offered by government. The entrepreneurs together with government will be in a good position to exploit resources and advantages that either party could hardly explore single-handed. The Public-Private Partnerships are creating a new era of doing business with government (Kasaija 2015; Kiwanuka 2014; Walter et al., 2003).

In addition to national and regional initiatives, the government of Uganda has put in place policies aimed at improving the participation of Ugandan entrepreneurs in international trade. Such policies promote participation in international trade through inter-regional organisations and agreements like the East African Community (EAC), the New Partnership for Africa's Development (NEPAD), SMART partnership dialogue, the African Growth and Opportunity Act (AGOA), and Everything But Arms (EBA) (Walter et al., 2003).

Despite efforts to put encouraging policies in place, it is important to highlight that Uganda still has a long way to go with respect to a taxation system favourable to micro, small and medium enterprises. Additionally, some of the Ugandan national experts perceive the regulatory and administrative bureaucracy as limiting entrepreneurship (Ibid. 2003).

### *Government Programmes*

Over time, the Government of Uganda has established a number of organisations and initiatives to provide specific support to entrepreneurs in the hope of facilitating entrepreneurship development. These programmes include (Uganda Investment Authority, 2008):

- UNIDO *Master Craftsman Programme* providing skills upgrading and advisory services in partnership with Uganda Small Scale Industries Association, Northern Uganda Manufacturers' Association, Nakawa Vocational Training Institute, Uganda Leather Allied Industries Association, Uganda Gatsby Trust, and Textile Development Agency.
- *Business Uganda Development Scheme* working with the *Private Sector Foundation* to support technology and know-how acquisition.
- *The Jua Kali Initiative* under the Ministry of Tourism, Trade and Industry through facility centres such as Luzira and Soroti Industrial Business Parks enabling the growth of micro-, small- and medium-scale manufacturing businesses owned by local artisans.
- *Microfinance Outreach Plan* strengthening financial services and systems, particularly the microfinance industry.
- *The Warehouse Receipt System* through the Common Fund for Commodities and the Ministry of Tourism, Trade and Industry facilitating the improvement of marketing products for farmers and small-scale traders.
- Other government programmes and initiatives include The Uganda Investment Authority, Uganda Registration Services Bureau, Enterprise Uganda, and the Presidential Investors Round Table (Kasaija 2015; Namatovu et al., 2011; Walter et al., 2003).

To improve the performance of these programmes and initiatives, the government has recently embarked on several actions such as the transformation of The Uganda Investment Authority and the Uganda Registration Services Bureau into one-stop centres to efficiently facilitate investors and quicken business registration. The plans for online company registration are complete and some services can now be completed on the internet. These measures have reduced the burden of multiple data requirements for business start-ups, by use of information collected at business registration for taxation and licensing. The Uganda Investment Authority has continued to build infrastructure to ensure serviced industrial and business parks have water, roads, and power. Specific attention has been placed on improving the Luzira, Soroti, and Namanve Industrial Business Parks to make them operational (Kasaija 2015; Kiwanuka 2014; Namatovu et al., 2011).

Additionally, the government is rolling-out the National Land Information System from six zones to 21 land offices, thereby significantly reducing the time and cost of undertaking land transactions, and enhancing the security of land registration. This will reduce fraud and corruption related to transfer and titling of land, which will, in turn, ensure that entrepreneurs have secure collateral to enable them obtain credit from financial institutions. The government also launched the *Energy for Rural Transformation* programme that has supported rural electrification (Walter et al., 2003). Infrastructure facilities such as electricity have been known to facilitate income generation and business development particularly in rural areas (Kooijman-Van Dijk 2012; Kooijman-Van Dijk and Clancy 2010; Schillebeeckx et al., 2012). Other key interventions meant to improve regional integration under the East African Community include implementation of the Customs Union, the Common Market, and the Monetary Union protocol. East African Community partner states are now undertaking common infrastructure investments and reducing non-tariff barriers. By removing road blocks, weigh bridges, and multiple bonds, the number of days it takes for a container to move from Mombasa to Kampala has been reduced from 18 to a maximum of four, and to Kigali from 22 to a maximum of seven. A Single Entry East African Tourist Visa, and Common Payment system has also been introduced (Kasaija 2015; Kiwanuka 2014). These arrangements not only widen Uganda's export market in the region, but also reduce the cost of doing business within Uganda and the expanded East African Region thus enhancing entrepreneurship in Uganda.

Despite the government's efforts to introduce new programmes and reform existing ones, these programmes are viewed generally as unsatisfactory due to implementation challenges (Namatovu et al., 2011; Walter et al., 2003). To overcome such challenges, there is a need for the government to improve and increase specific services for Ugandan entrepreneurs, especially start-ups in the small- and medium enterprises sector. Such services could include increased financial support for entrepreneurs, improved export promotion programmes, and increased scope of existing programmes to take care of the recent business environment dynamics (Walter et al., 2003).

### *Private and Non-governmental Role*

Besides government policies and programmes, Ugandan entrepreneurs benefit from parastatal, private, and non-governmental institutions that offer services ranging from business development, information, and advice, financial support, and other services. These institutions take the form of microfinance deposit-taking institutions (MDIs), savings and credit cooperatives (SACCOs), and banks, business associations, international organisations, and self-organising groups. While most of these institutions are headquartered in the capital city Kampala, they do have branches that operate in various parts of the country.

A number of organisations offer multiple services. The services offered by these organisations facilitate entrepreneurship development. An illustration of the parastatal, private, and non-governmental services offered by some of the organisations towards entrepreneurship development in Uganda is provided in Table 13.1.

## Role of Culture in Entrepreneurship Development

Culture plays a key role in influencing and shaping different aspects of society, including organisational phenomena and practices. For this reason, management and entrepreneurship scholars continue to study different aspects of culture in order to establish its effect on organisational practices. For more than three decades, culture has remained central to organisation studies and entrepreneurship research (Giorgi, Lockwood, and Glynn 2015; Hayton, George, and Zahra 2002).

Culture has been defined as shared beliefs, values, and behaviours that shape socio-economic, technical and political institutions (Hayton, George, and Zahra 2002). Culture distinguishes a group of people or society from others through different behaviours (Giorgi, Lockwood, and Glynn 2015). These differences in behaviours may then help to explain differential outcomes among organisations based on culture. Culture can be both facilitative as well as constraining to entrepreneurship development through its effect on organisational outcomes. While different authors have suggested different categorisations of cultural dimensions, Hofstede's (1980) dimensions of power-distance, uncertainty avoidance, individualism-collectivism, and masculinity-femininity remain the most widely used dimensions in entrepreneurship research.

The way one perceives social obligations is a societal influence and can be attributed to culture (Janoff-Bulman and Leggatt 2002; Oyserman, Sakamoto, and Lauffer 1998). Societal differences have generally been attributed to individualistic and collective orientations (Hansen 2003). Collective societies and cultures tend to be group-oriented, emphasise attending to the needs of other people, discourage personal control (Hansen 2003; Janoff-Bulman and Leggatt 2002), and emphasise success through the fulfilment of duties and obligations towards one's group (Oyserman, Sakamoto, and Lauffer 1998). Individualistic societies and cultures, on the other hand, emphasise independence, personal control, personal recognition, and achievement (Hansen 2003; Janoff-Bulman and Leggatt 2002), and success through the development and attainment of one's own goals (Oyserman, Sakamoto and Lauffer 1998).

In the next section, we use results from a study by Khayesi and George (2011) to explain and illustrate culture's facilitative and constraining effect on entrepreneurship development in Uganda. The results presented here are based on a study on the effect of the socio-cultural context on resource accumulation among entrepreneurs in Uganda. Specifically, this study examines the role of collectivism through the variable of communal orientation.

### *An Example of the Effect of Collectivism and Communal Orientation on Resource Accumulation among Entrepreneurs in Uganda*

The norm of collectivism requires that a social or economic actor gives precedence to the needs of others such as an extended family or other members of the community (Hofstede 1980; Maznevski et al., 2002). In collectivist communities, able and wealthier individuals are expected to help or provide for less able members of society. In the case of entrepreneurship, whereas such help may provide skills and resources that can contribute towards firm growth and development of the recipients, it may also deduct resources from entrepreneurial firms through the fulfilment of social obligations (Kiggundu 2002). When this happens, the firm may experience constraints in its growth.

A study conducted by Khayesi and George (2011) examined the effect of communal orientation on resource accumulation in Uganda. Communal orientation is revealed in controlled behaviour emanating from external forces to an individual that make him/her feel bound to others to the extent of committing time, effort, and resources to meet the needs of others (Janoff-Bulman and Leggatt 2002). Social obligations pressure an individual to comply with others' requests (Barrett et al. 2004). Social obligations may be viewed as burdens in some societies, and desirable and necessary in other societies (Janoff-Bulman and Leggatt 2002). Social obligations take such forms as providing financial assistance for funerals or the needs of family or community members in distress (Hansen 2003). The study by Khayesi and George (2011) interviewed 242 entrepreneurs in Kampala, Uganda. The entrepreneurs had micro-, small- and medium-sized garment and information and technology businesses. They responded to questions on their communal orientation, which was measured using a scale. They were asked to rate four statements related to communal orientation, for example, "I often go out of my way to help other people". The study also collected information on the amount of money the entrepreneurs had received and the amount of money they had spent on different social obligations. A statistical analysis revealed that entrepreneurs with high communal

TABLE 13.1 *Parastatals, private and non-governmental services to enhance entrepreneurship development in Uganda*

| Service | Description | Key institution(s) | Sample organisations |
|---|---|---|---|
| Business development services | Business training and skills/capacity building | Educational institutions, banks, business networks, NGOs | Stanbic Bank Uganda Limited (capacity building through its partner institutions), Business Uganda Development Scheme (Private Sector Foundation), Uganda Women Entrepreneurs Association Limited, Aclaim Africa, British Council, Kyambogo University, Makerere University Business School, Uganda Institute of Information and Communications Technology, Uganda Investment Authority, FIT Uganda, Uganda Network of Businesses, African Centre for Trade and Development, Textile Development Agency/UNIDO, Uganda Industrial Research Institute, International Labour Organization, Uganda Manufacturers' Association, Uganda Manufacturer's Association |
| | Market research, and R&D | Educational institutions, research institutions, NGOs | Kyambogo University, Makerere University Business School, Uganda Institute of Information and Communications Technology, FIT Uganda, Business Clinics Services Limited, African Centre for Trade and Development, Textile Development Agency/UNIDO, Uganda Industrial Research Institute |
| Information and advisory services | Business counselling and consultancy | Private organisations, Educational institutions, | GroFin, Uganda Women Entrepreneurs Association Limited, Makerere University Business School, FIT Uganda, Textile Development Agency/UNIDO, Uganda Manufacturers' Association |
| | Provision of business information | Private and international organisations, Business/trade Associations | GroFin, British Council, Makerere University Business School, Uganda Investment Authority, Uganda Small Scale Industries Association, Uganda Manufacturer's Association, Uganda Network of |

| | | | |
|---|---|---|---|
| | | | Businesses, International Labour Organization, Uganda Manufacturer's Association |
| | Business mentorship | Private organisations and trade associations | Uganda Women Entrepreneurs Association Limited, |
| Financial support | Provision of business loans and grants | Banks, Savings and Credit Cooperatives (SACCOs), Microfinance institutions, international organisations | Equity Bank Uganda Ltd., Centenary Rural Development Bank, Bank of Africa Uganda Limited, Stanbic Bank Uganda Limited, DFCU Bank, National Bank of Commerce, Standard Chartered Bank, Finance Trust, Pride Microfinance, Uganda Agency for Development, BRAC Uganda, Vision Fund, Micro Credit for Development and Transformation, Rural Credit Finance Company Ltd., GroFin, United States African Development Foundation, Business Uganda Development Scheme (Private Sector Foundation), Wazalendo SACCO, Uganda Women Entrepreneurs Association Limited |
| | Provision of banking services such as deposit (current and savings) accounts | Banks, and Savings and Credit Cooperatives | Equity Bank Uganda Ltd., Centenary Rural Development Bank, Finance Trust, Diamond Trust Bank, Stanbic Bank Uganda Limited, National Bank of Commerce, Standard Chartered Bank, Bank of Africa Uganda Limited, Wazalendo SACCO |
| Other services | Representation and advocacy | Trade associations and networks | Uganda Small-Scale Industries Association, Uganda Manufacturer's Association, Uganda Network of Businesses |

SOURCE: COMPILED BY AUTHORS BASED ON AUTHORS' KNOWLEDGE, NTALAKA (2013–2014) AND UGANDA INVESTMENT AUTHORITY (2008)

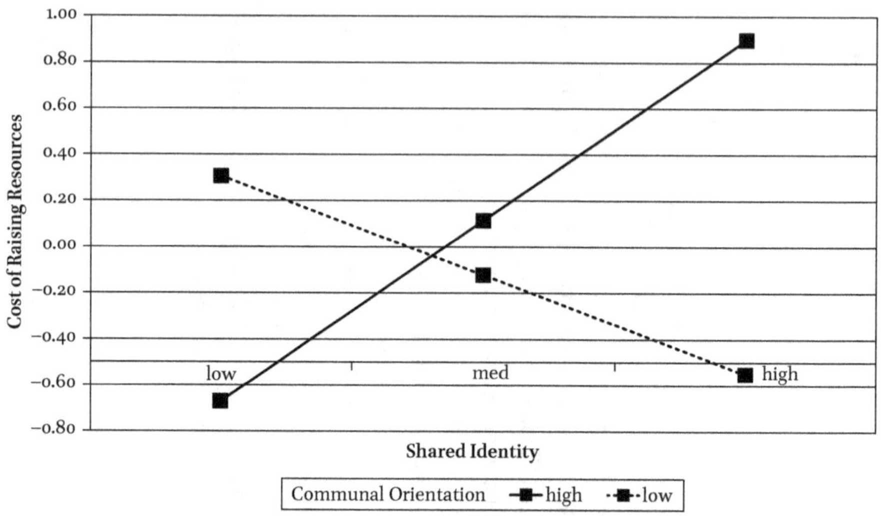


FIGURE 13.1 *Moderation of the effect of shared identity on cost of raising resources by communal orientation*
SOURCE: KHAYESI AND GEORGE (2011: 485)

orientation had higher social obligations compared to those with low communal orientation. The results also revealed that high communal orientation resulted in increased costs of resource accumulation (see Fig. 13.1).

The findings of the above study are supported by other studies. For example, Hansen's (2003) study on Ivorian firms confirms this view by revealing that there are negative effects on the firm, such as poor employee performance, where social obligations come before one's job and business. Pedersen and McCormick (1999) also identify social obligations as a hindrance to firm resource accumulation in Africa. Dondo and Ngumo (1998) argue that communal and collective values in the African society do not promote individualistic wealth creation and resource deployment activities. With specific reference to Kenya, these authors observe that the communal spirit, once a good quality of the Kenyan culture, has become a millstone around the necks of aspiring entrepreneurs. This is because the community expects entrepreneurs to share their business financial resources with members of the community and this may inhibit entrepreneurial development.

### *Life Experience of a Practicing Entrepreneur*

This section presents the life experience of an entrepreneur from Uganda. He is a male called Joho (not his real name). He is a successful Ugandan entrepreneur who has operated a hostel business in Kampala for over ten years. The hostel comprises 75 accommodation rooms and one study room. Additionally, he has rental houses, a hotel and is involved in real estate and farming. He was motivated to start a hostel business due to a high demand for student accommodation. With the emergence of new universities around Kampala, Joho took advantage of an opportunity to build a hostel since he had land near Makerere University Business School and Kyambogo University.

A total of 1.2 billion Uganda shillings was needed to construct the hostel. Although Joho sold his family land in a village far away from Kampala and invested the money into the hostel construction, this money was not enough to complete the project. He therefore sought a bank loan in order to complete the construction.

Joho's business has drawn on professional and social networks for such activities as conducting a feasibility study, constructing the hostels, securing a bank loan, and securing tenants. On the one hand, his business networks enabled him learn of the opportunity of getting a bank loan and advice on conducting a feasibility study that helped him establish the viability of the business. His family networks, on the other hand, have been instrumental in business idea development, providing business advice on various aspects of the business, advertising the business through their networks, and keeping a close eye on those who are employed to work in the business (Box 1). Joho clearly states that he does not use family members in the day-to-day management of the business. Rather, he has employed staff members (cleaners, security guards, etc.) who are "not necessarily relatives."

### BOX 1: ROLE OF BUSINESS AND FAMILY NETWORKS IN JOHO'S BUSINESS

***Interviewer: How did you get know about the opportunity of getting a bank loan?***

JOHO: Through business networks; also through social capital. Most of the people I was interacting with had the knowledge of the opportunities with the banking institutions. They advised me that if I could work out a feasibility study to establish the viability of this enterprise, then I could go for a loan and put it up and be able to pay and that is what we did. We carried out a feasibility study which was very supportive of the idea and after that we went to the bank, and presented our project proposal. They found it viable and they financed it.

***Interviewer: Do you have any family members who contribute to the business in terms of operations, marketing, labour capital, and any other aspects?***

JOHO: Yes, we have family members who contributed to the idea of developing the project and we looked at the market opportunities. We looked at what needs to be in place in order to attract clients and after that advice and sharing ideas of how this business could run then we went forward for it.

***Interviewer: Can you give some examples***

JOHO: One example is, for instance, when we, at one time, reached a point where the earnings form the project were not enough to meet the costs of running the business and also costs of loan in terms of interest and payment of principal. I think they advised that we could (1) liquidate some of the idle assets we had to pay the bank, (2) to use other buildings/houses for which we had to remove tenants who were paying monthly and also convert them into students accommodation because they were near Kyambogo university. That way, we would be able to pay and everybody was agreeable to that and I thought that was a very great contribution from the family members. Also, how to manage, for instance, one challenge we had was collecting of the fees by paying cash, but eventually some members proposed that we could use the banks to receive the payments from students instead of the staff of the business to be the ones to receive the money. We had some challenges, money was disappearing and some [clients] were not paying but since we introduced the idea of paying in the bank, it has helped quite a lot and it streamlined the financial management of the organisation

They have also through their networks convinced some people to send their children there to stay in the hostel. So, it has been a concerted effect in running the project.

***Interviewer: How about in operations of the business, do you have any family members?***

JOHO: No, in management of the day to day, we have employed a few staff to do it. We have cleaners, we have people who provide security guards, they are employed and not necessarily relatives.

In relation to contributions from family members, Joho's clearly states that he does "not have any negative interference from relatives from this business." He, however, adds that he has "had positive contributions from friends from outside the family especially with respect to financial management, public relations, the things that we need to put in place that attract the clients, future development plans."

An analysis of Joho's case as well as the research by Khayesi and George (2011) reveals the importance of institutions (North 1990) in facilitating and constraining entrepreneurship development. In the cases in question, both government and culture as institutions have played key roles in entrepreneurship development in Uganda. Culture, for instance, has facilitated Joho's business through contributions from family mainly in terms of advice, idea development, initial land for the business, and keeping an eye on Joho's business. Though hailing from and living in a collectivist society, Joho has not experienced any negative interventions from his family. This could be due, in part, to the fact that he has limited the involvement of his family in the day-to-day management of the business. This, in a way, has reduced family involvement and the consequent constraints that come with it; for instance, the inability to sanction poor performance by a relative and work not being biased by obligations from kin members as in the case of Cote d'Ivoire (Hansen 2003). Indeed, for entrepreneurs to reduce negative effects of networks, Khayesi and George (2011: 487) have recommended, among other things, that they "expand their networks beyond their communities." This could be one of the contributing factors to Joho's success in entrepreneurship and limitation of negative influences from kin. In another study, Khayesi, George, and Antonakis (2014) found that the cost of raising resources (mainly in the form of obligations imposed on entrepreneurs) increased when entrepreneurs relied heavily on family networks (thus increasing their shared identity). One way that Joho has dealt with this problem is to rely on his business networks for financial matters, thus reducing shared identity among his networks. Reduced family involvement and a reduction of shared identity in the network by expanding beyond his community may help explain the limited negative influence of family on Joho's business and thus his success.

Regarding finances, the government as an institution has played a key role in Joho's business through policies that make it possible for banks to lend to entrepreneurs. As North (1990) puts it, institutions are crucial in determining the "rules of the game in a society." With government policies that support bank lending to entrepreneurs, Joho's uncertainty is greatly reduced when his business networks point out to him what he needs to do in order to receive a loan from the bank. As pointed out in the second section, the government still has some way to go with regards to implementing programmes that support entrepreneurship development in Uganda. Failure to implement suggested programmes appears to be one of the constraints of entrepreneurship development in Uganda.

## Conclusion

The evidence presented from the empirical study and case illustration reveals the dynamics of social aspects of entrepreneurship in Africa. Entrepreneurs are expected to contribute to the well-being of their social networks. The social networks are also expected to contribute to the work of entrepreneurs. The empirical study cited shows that entrepreneurs with high communal orientation incur higher cost to raise resources and also spend more on meeting social obligations than those with low communal orientation. However, entrepreneurs who configure their networks to involve members beyond their immediate families, benefit immensely from reduced negative contributions associated with culture-related social capital. This, coupled with the availability of entrepreneurship support facilities, may partly explain Joho's entrepreneurial success. Using Joho's example, this chapter recommends that entrepreneurs in Uganda as well as those from other resource-constrained economies configure their networks wisely in order for their businesses to benefit. Entrepreneurs should aim at involving network members who will contribute positively to their businesses in terms of ideas and other resources.

Whereas this chapter has provided some insights into culture and entrepreneurship in Uganda, there is still more that we do not yet know. A viable strategy to take this research further is to conduct a comprehensive review of the existing literature on entrepreneurship and culture in Uganda and Africa to get a better picture of the issues that have been addressed. Such a review will identify areas that require further research or aspects that need to be revisited.

## References

Barrett, D.W., Wosinska, W., Butner, J., Petrova, P., Gornik-Durose, M. & R.B. Cialdini. (2004). "Individual Differences in the Motivation to Comply Across Cultures: The Impact of Social Obligation", *Personality and Individual Differences*, 37, 19–31.

Dondo, A. & M. Ngumo. (1998). "Africa: Kenya". In: Alison Morrison (ed.), *Entrepreneurship: An International Perspective*. Oxford: Butterworth Heinemann.

George, G. & S.A. Zahra. (2002). "Culture and its Consequences for Entrepreneurship", *Entrepreneurship Theory and Practice*, 26(4), 5–8.

Giorgi, S., Lockwood, C. & M.A. Glynn. (2015). "The Many Faces of Culture: Making Sense of 30 Years of Research on Culture in Organization Studies". *The Academy of Management Annals*, 9(1), 1–54.

Hansen, C.D. (2003). "Cultural Myths in Stories about HRD: Analyzing the Cross-Cultural Transfer of American Models to Germany and the Cote d'Ivoire", *International Journal of Training and Development*, 7(1), 16–30.

Hayton, J., George, G. & S.A. Zahra. (2002). "National Culture and Entrepreneurship: A Review of Behavioural Research", *Entrepreneurship Theory and Practice*, 26(4), 33–52.

Hofstede, G. (1980). *Culture's Consequences: International Differences in Work-related Values*. Beverly Hills, CA: Sage Publications.

Janoff-Bulman, R. & H.K. Leggatt. (2002). "Culture and Social Obligation: When 'Shoulds' are Perceived as 'Wants'". *Journal of Research in Personality*, 36, 260–270.

Kasaija, M. (2015). "Budget Speech: Financial year 2015/16". Retrieved from http://www.statehouse.go.ug/media/speeches/2015/06/11/uganda-budget-20152016.

Khayesi, J. & G. George. (2011). "When Does the Socio-Cultural Context Matter? Communal Orientation and Entrepreneurs' Resource Accumulation Efforts in Africa", *Journal of Occupational and Organizational Psychology*, 84(3), 471–492.

Khayesi, J., George, G. & J. Antonakis. (2014). "Kinship in Entrepreneur Networks: Performance Effects of Resource Assembly in Africa", *Entrepreneurship Theory and Practice*, 38(6), 1323–1342.

Kiggundu, M.N. (2002). "Entrepreneurs and Entrepreneurship in Africa: What is Known and What Needs to be Done", *Journal of Developmental Entrepreneurship*, 7(3), 239–258.

Kiwanuka, M. (2014). "Budget Speech: Financial Year 2014/15". Retrieved from http://www.statehouse.go.ug/media/news/2014/06/12/budget-speech-financial-year-201415-delivered-meeting-4th-session-9th-parliame.

Kooijman-Van Dijk, A.L. (2012). "The Role of Energy in Creating Opportunities for Income Generation in the Indian Himalayas", *Energy Policy*, 41, 529–536. doi:10.1016/j.enpol.2011.11.013.

Kooijman-Van Dijk, A.L. & J. Clancy. (2010). "Impacts of Electricity Access to Rural Enterprises in Bolivia, Tanzania and Vietnam", *Energy for Sustainable Development*, 14(1), 14–21. doi:http://dx.doi.org/10.1016/j.esd.2009.12.004.

Maznevski, M.L., DiStefano, J.J., Gomez, C.B., Noorderhaven, N.G. & Wu Pei-Chuan. (2002). "Cultural Dimensions at the Individual Level of Analysis: The Cultural Orientations Framework", *International Journal of Cross-Cultural Management*, 2(3), 275–295.

Namatovu, R., Balunywa, W., Kyejjusa, S. & S. Dawa. (2011). "Global Entrepreneurship Monitor: GEM Uganda 2010 Executive Report". Retrieved from http://www.gemconsortium.org/report.

North, D.C. (1990). *Institutions, Institutional Change, and Economic Performance*. Cambridge: Cambridge University Press.

Ntalaka, R. (ed.) (2013–2014). *The Uganda Microfinance Directory 2013/2014* (6th Edition). Retrieved from http://www.amfiu.org.ug/images/docs/carol/Directory2013.pdf.

Oyserman, D., Sakamoto, I. & A. Lauffer. (1998). "Cultural Accommodation: Hybridity and the Framing of Social Obligation", *Journal of Personality and Social Psychology*, 74(6), 1606–1618.

Pedersen, P.O. & D. McCormick. (1999). "African Business Systems in a Globalising World", *The Journal of Modern African Studies*, 37(1), 109–135.

Schillebeeckx, S., Parikh, P., Bansal, R. & G. George. (2012). "An Integrated Framework for Rural Electrification: Adopting a User-Centric Approach to Business Model Development", *Energy Policy*, 48, 687–697.

Singer, S., Amoros, J.E. & D. Moska. (2015). *Global Entrepreneurship Monitor 2014*. Report. Retrieved from http://www.gemconsortium.org/report.

Uganda. (2014). *Poverty Status Report 2014: Structural Change and Poverty Reduction in Uganda*. Government of Uganda, Ministry of Finance, Planning and Economic Development. Retrieved from http://library.health.go.ug/publications/health-workforce/human-resource-development/poverty-status-report-2014.

Uganda Investment Authority. 2008. *Small and Medium Enterprises (SME) Business Guide*. Uganda Investment Authority. Retrieved from http://www.iceida.is/media/pdf/SME_GUIDE_FINAL_COPY.pdf.

Walter, T., Balunywa, W., Rosa, P., Sserwanga, A., Barabas, S. & R. Namatovu. (2003). *Global Entrepreneurship Monitor Uganda 2003 Report*. Retrieved from http://www.gemconsortium.org/report.

CHAPTER 14

# African Women Large-Scale Entrepreneurs: Cases from Angola, Nigeria and Ghana

*Miriam Siun, Akinyinka Akinyoade and Ewurabena Quaye*

## Introduction

This paper critically examines the road to prosperity for three African women entrepreneurs of large-scale businesses within male-dominated fields of portfolio – investments, oil production and construction. Angolan Isabel Dos Santos, Nigeria's Folorunsho Alakija and Ghana's Dr. Theresa Oppong-Beeko are highly ranked among the wealthiest women in Africa. In fact, Dos Santos and Alakija are positioned as number eight and number thirteen in terms of personal wealth on the continent irrespective of gender, as contained on the African section of Forbes' annual list of the world's billionaires.[1] Dos Santos, Alakija and Dr Oppong-Beeko have firmly established themselves and their companies in their respective industries, despite the challenges women face to enter these spaces. In some quarters, their individual trajectories to wealth calls meritocracy into question, as claims of patrimonialism and corruption is sometimes used to taint their accomplishments. This necessitates further studies on the obstacles for African women to become large-scale entrepreneurs without personal connections to influential people/high profile leadership. In conclusion, this paper warns against uncritical praise of success stories on the basis of gender and takes a class-based approach to the study of women and entrepreneurship in Africa.

In the mid-to-late twentieth century, Africa was afflicted with political and economic turmoil that made the continent unattractive to both domestic and foreign investors. Failure of most of its countries in attracting foreign investment, coupled with capital flight as domestic savers sought investment opportunities in more stable economies abroad further dampened the economic outlook (Mbaku, 2013). But by the turn of the century, economic and governance reforms brought about positive changes, bringing the African continent back on the road to recovery. As many as thirty-six governments in sub-Saharan Africa have significantly improved their economies' regulatory environments,

1 See 2016 online edition – http://www.forbes.com/billionaires/list/#version:realtime.

 | DOI 10.1163/9789004351615_015

leading to increased trade and investment (Mbaku 2013). In the past decade, multinational corporations have set up businesses and invested heavily across the continent. And there is also a concomitant increase in numbers of African business moguls, managing large enterprises with ever-increasing and improving intra-African network of subsidiaries and trading, generating jobs, contributing to decline in poverty levels and increase in national economic productivity. Several Africans now feature in the Forbes annually published list of billionaires.

The emergence of Aliko Dangote of Nigeria on Forbes' list of billionaires, particularly as the richest black man, has spurred interest in knowing the rich in Africa, examining the sources and extent of their wealth. Forbes' list is interesting in that it goes beyond the cliché of listing billionaires' acquisition of wealth on the basis of corrupt practices, but as entrepreneurs.[2] In more recent times, the breaking down of such annual billionaire list has also yielded information on ranking of rich African women. Prominent in this list are Isabel Dos Santos and Folorunsho Alakija whose businesses span international networks. Theresa Oppong-Beeko is added based on the "nationally concentrated" but highly successful business venture. In this chapter we examine the level of wealth of these three African women entrepreneurs, and the pattern of their wealth acquisition.

It has been observed that the majority of women in developing economies are in micro enterprises with limited potential for growth, and a pattern still exists that the bigger a firm, the less likely it is to be headed by a woman. But very recently, the ILO (2016) estimates that women entrepreneurs account for about one-third of all businesses in the formal economy worldwide. The emergence of a growing community of women entrepreneurs is a significant economic and social development, which has profound implications for reshaping the modern global economy. Much of the available data on women entrepreneurs comes from studies in developed economies. In the transitioning economies, investigations of the motivations and aspirations of women entrepreneurs in Africa's formal sector have been relatively limited, and where present, the focus is mostly on the informal sector. This paper attempts to shed light on female entrepreneurs in the formal sector.

2 Forbes tracks the wealth of African citizens who reside on the continent. Individual net worth are calculated using stock prices and currency exchange rates from the close of business on Friday, 7 November. To value privately-held businesses, Forbes "couples estimates of revenues or profits with prevailing price-to-sales or price-to-earnings ratios for similar public companies."

Some questions arise as this study sets out to document and assess the level, extent, trends and patterns of sources of wealth of selected African women entrepreneurs of large scale businesses with turnover running into millions of dollars. Who are these African women entrepreneurs? Where are they active? What motivates their entrepreneurship? What unique challenges do these women face, and how are they overcoming them? This paper does not set out to give an in-depth analyses of the sources of wealth of the selected women. Rather, light is shed on the level of wealth and the entrepreneurial motivation of three African women who own and run large-scale businesses.

Having a deeper understanding of women's entrepreneurship for large-scale businesses requires an examination whether women suffer disadvantages arising explicitly from their gender on their trajectory to prosperity. In general, major barriers facing women entrepreneurs are access to credit, managerial skills and cultural barriers such as prevention from access to formal education (Palmerlee 2002). Not only that women-controlled businesses are often small, women's participation in official trade missions is usually quite minimal (OECD). The low participation or representation of women in management of large scale enterprises have been explained by the argument that because male counterparts do not face the same pressures of trade-offs between business and family responsibilities, males can make a greater time commitment to their businesses. For women entrepreneurs in particular, personal considerations appear to override economic considerations in the business expansion decision (Roomi and Parrott 2008; Cliff 1998). While some studies have demonstrated the link between family responsibility pressures and lower growth patterns among women-owned firms, other studies have also shown the vital importance of a supportive family environment for a successful woman entrepreneur (Powell and Eddleston 2013; Sandberg 2003; Loscocco 1991).

Motivations for starting a business can vary almost infinitely, but a basic distinction is made between so-called "necessity" and "opportunity" factors by Quartey et al. (2014), building on differentiation provided by Mumuni et al. (2013). Basically, necessity entrepreneurs go for entrepreneurship due to lack of choice while opportunity entrepreneurs arise due to quest for independence (see also: Aidis et al. 2006; Maritz 2004; Perunović 2005). Adom and Williams (2012) also discovered that women informal entrepreneurs are predominantly necessity-driven while men are principally intentional (opportunity driven) participants in informal entrepreneurship. However, over time, some women change from the state of being out-of-necessity entrepreneurs to become more opportunity-driven entrepreneurs.

Comparative studies assessed by Quartey et al. (2014) suggest that women are motivated to a higher degree than equally qualified men to become entrepreneurs for family-related lifestyle reasons; and that women are less motivated than men by wealth creation and advancement reasons. The empirical analysis of a survey of entrepreneurs in Swaziland confirmed the importance of start-up capital for sales. Women entrepreneurs have smaller start-up capital and are less likely to fund it from the formal sector than their male counterparts (Brixiová and Kangoye 2016; Aliata et al. 2013). While this may further explain why there are more women entrepreneurs of small businesses, it also sign-posts space for policy interventions to strengthen women's accessibility to credit for larger businesses. However, feminist scholars are increasingly critical of the prevailing discourse within women and entrepreneurship studies, and arguing for social change and not only remedial policy-initiatives e.g. efforts to increase access to finances (see Ahl 2004, 2006; Calas et al. 2009; Vossenberg 2013).

Much of the literature on women and entrepreneurship approaches the topic from a liberal feminist point of view, i.e. that men and women are equal, but that discrimination effects the latter. This has seemingly led to studies focusing on identifying various constraints for successful entrepreneurship (see e.g. UNIDO 2001), but also studies on individual success stories in order to provide policy-recommendations (see UNECA 2007). This study also focuses on the individuals. However, the intention is not to diminish the effects of structural constraints by highlighting individual characteristics, instead, it is to show how privilege changes the way gender impacts entrepreneurship. A structural approach is particularly important to consider in relation to the three women in this study because of corruption allegations, which leads to questions regarding their business acumen. Questionable business practices notwithstanding, these women provide an entry point to a presently understudied area within gender and entrepreneurship in Africa, namely the functioning of gender amongst elites. In the following section, Isabel Dos Santos, Folorunsho Alakija, and Theresa Oppong-Beeko are examined according to their level of wealth, types of business ventures, and entrepreneurial motivations.

## Isabel Dos Santos, Angola

Isabel Dos Santos is Africa's richest woman (and the 8th richest African), currently aged 43 years, whose real time net worth as of 11 July 2016 is $3.4 billion. She holds a Bachelor of Arts/Science, King's College.[3] In 2015 she was named

3 http://www.forbes.com/profile/isabel-dos-santos/?list=africa-billionaires (accessed 1 August 2016).

one of the most influential women in the world for her success as a businesswoman (BBC 2015). Her business career dates back to 1997, when at age 24 years, she invested in a small restaurant in Luanda called "Miami Beach". There are no exact figures of the sum of her investment, which is rumored to have been a small amount, but seemingly paved the way for a continued interest in investments, which are the source of her wealth. Her present fortune mainly comes from investments in key sectors in the Angolan economy: diamonds, oil, cement but also telecom and banking, with acquisitions in far-a-field Portugal (Dolan 2013).

Angola is one of the world's largest diamond producers, which, for example in 2014, generated revenue of US$1.6 billion, according to provisional figures from the country's Ministry of Geology and Mines (macauhub 2015). Diamond export is the second largest source of revenue for Angola after oil. The industry was initially monopolised by the state-owned company Endiama. However in 1999 Endiama agreed to form a joint-venture diamond trading company together with the companies Group Goldberg, Leviev Wellox and Trans Africa Investment Services (TAIS – a Gibraltar-based holding company in which she was the largest shareholder with 75 per cent together with her mother Tatiana Kukanova; De Morais 2015). Isabel Dos Santos' share in Ascorp amounted to 24.5 per cent, which at the time was generating millions of dollars monthly (Dolan 2013). However, the diamond sector in Angola has been marked with international scrutiny due to violence in the Lundas part of the country where the gems are being extracted (De Morais 2015). The "blood diamond" controversies seemingly led Dos Santos to transfer all of her shares in TAIS to her mother in 2004 and the company changed its name to Iaxonh Limited (Ibid.). Dos Santos later moved on to telecommunications, which proved highly lucrative.

The Angolan telecommunications sector was under state monopoly, as Angola Telecom, until 2000 when the Commission of the Council of Ministries "conceded to Unitel the license to exploit, in all national territory, the complementary service of mobile cell phone GSM." Dos Santos was part of the founders of Unitel and acquired 25 per cent of the company, which since its entry into the Angolan market has generated revenues of $2 billion annually, leading to estimates of Dos Santos' share being worth $1 billion (Dolan 2013). Interestingly, in 2014 Dos Santos was reported in a bid to takeover Portuguese company Portugal Telecom for $1.5 billion through her Lisbon-based holding company Terra Peregrin-Participacoes SGPS SA (Lima 2014). Portugal Telecom had earlier purchased 25 per cent of Unitel for $16.2 million in 2000; Isabel Dos Santos' bid for the company signposted a desire not only to increase her shares within Unitel, but also to spread business ventures abroad. She later withdrew her bid due to a ruling by the Portuguese Securities Market Commission (CMVM), which required her to raise her offer (Reis 2014). In the abovementioned cases we observed that Dos Santos buys shares in other companies through holding companies based outside of Angola. This strategy has been used to acquire stakes in the Angolan oil-sector as well, which has raised questions of legality.

The oil sector is controlled by state enterprise Sociedade Nacional de Combustíveis (Sonangol), which is in charge of concessions for oil exploration. Revenue from crude oil export amounts to 93–95 per cent of the country's exports, and 80 per cent of the GDP (Ovadia 2012). In the same way as the telecom sector opened up for private companies, access to the oil sector was written into law in 1978 through the General Petroleum Activities Law, which permits Sonangol to conduct joint explorations with foreign companies (Ibid.). Galp Energia is Portugal's largest oil and gas company worth an estimate of €9.5 billion (Maka Angola 2016). Sonangol owns Galp shares through Esperanza Holding BV, a company that was registered at the Dutch Chamber of Commerce (Handelsregisterhistorie) as belonging to Sonangol in 2005,[4] but also has an indirect stake through 15 per cent ownership of Amorim Energia (Pamuk 2012). However, in 2006 Esperanza Holding BV signed a contract with Exem Africa Limited, another holding company based in the British Virgin Islands. According to Maka Angola, "the contract specifies that Sonangol is the sole source of funds that will be invested in Galp in the name of both parties," and that Exem, which belongs to Dos Santos, receives 40 per cent of the Galp shares acquired by Esperanza Holding (Maka Angola 2016). In June 2016, given her track record in business, Isabel Dos Santos was appointed head of Sonangol to turn around the company's fortunes. This company, despite being responsible for half of Angola's gross domestic product (GDP) had hitherto been unproductive and ran in an opaque manner (Allen 2016).

In the Global Entrepreneurship Summit 2014 in Marrakech, Dos Santos spoke on the usefulness for foreign companies interested to invest in Africa to have a knowledgeable local partner.[5] One of the key factors in her success has been to fill that role. All of the aforementioned business ventures have been formed through the opening of previously state-owned enterprises for private investment. One of Dos Santos' biggest business partners has been Portugal's richest man, Américo Amorim. Dos Santos owns 45 per cent of Amorim Energia,[6] which in turn holds 33.34 per cent of Galp, implying an additional

4 See shareholder structure list on the company's website. Available: <http://www.galpenergia.com/EN/Investidor/AccaoGalpEnergia/Paginas/EstruturaAccionista.aspx>.

5 Global Entrepreneurship Summit 2014. Interview with Isabel dos Santos, 20 November 2014, https://www.youtube.com/watch?v=KkTForvCSz4.

6 An energy company part of the Amorim Group, Amorim's multinational company.

indirect stake in Galp. The Dos Santos – Amorim partnership has therefore meant that in as much as Dos Santos has been the local partner when Amorim has invested in Angola, the reverse has also taken place. In 2012 Dos Santos' investments in Portugal were reportedly worth €785.5 million. In the same year, she became the main shareholder of ZON Multimedia, a Portuguese media conglomerate, and also increased her shares in Banco BPI for €46.7 million (Costa 2012). What becomes apparent is thus that the partial privatisation of Angolan parastatals, alongside having connections to major investors has been crucial in Dos Santos business activities.

Messiant (2001) argues that the previously Marxist-oriented regime of Angola has gradually moved towards a political economy on the basis of capitalism and clientelism. Indeed, since the mid-1990s, the government has increasingly liberalised the economy, and introduced new legislation, which aimed to attract foreign capital.[7] The Angolan Industrial Development Plan for 1998–2000 clearly indicated a desire to decrease state-ownership, by approving the privatisation of one quarter of previously state-owned companies (Europa 2003). This shift is visible in the legal reforms in the most lucrative sectors of the national economy, which has been implemented before the 1990s, but also in the way that "[F]or almost half a century, rival social groups had competing ideas of Angola, of what the country was, should aspire to become […] and the unprecedented oil boom…meant that only the MPLA party elites ideas of Angola would hold sway" (De Oliveira 2016).

As previously discussed, the transactional history in the acquisition of Galp shares by Dos Santos with funding from Sonangol has drawn scrutiny into the legitimacy of her wealth. Dos Santos familial ties to the ruling party the People's Movement for the Liberation of Angola (MPLA) by being the daughter of the president is widely regarded to be the key to her success. When asked about the role her father has played in her success, Dos Santos replied: "I think that Angola is merit driven. So what I have achieved there I think it has been through merit. I have also started working a very long time ago […] over two decades ago. The success that I have today is not something that came overnight, it is not something that came, over the last five years, it's something that took two decades to build" (BBC 2015). Spring (2009) concluded that factors that can be attributed to women's success as large-scale entrepreneurs depend on "entry requirements of capital, education, [and] networks." Isabel Dos Santos' emphasis on merit constructs her success as an example of entrepreneurial exceptionalism, whilst her social status afforded her the necessary factors

7 The country was still experiencing civil war at that time. See Billon (2001) for a discussion on the role played by Angola's resources and foreign investment in sustaining the war.

to become the mogul she is today. For instance, Dos Santos has a degree in engineering from King's College London, and such an education can easily be financed when one comes from a wealthy family. Critics of Dos Santos, such as Angolan activist Rafael Marques de Morais, often point to her enormous wealth in contrast to the weak development of Angola (De Morais 2015).

Whether private-sector led development has generated improvements in the lives of poor people in Angola remains up for debate. Angola ranks 149 out of 188 in the human development index (HDI Report 2015), and is often referred to as "the world's richest poor country" (Power 2012). Efforts to incorporate the local population into the country's economic growth have been made through legislation to ensure "Angolanização" (that is, local content in terms of labour force, and goods and services) within the key sectors of the economy (Ovadia 2012). In the same study, it was found that private companies often try to circumvent the policy by hiring expatriates to the international divisions of their companies, and that employed Angolans often are either white or of mixed background, thus indicating employment disparities along racial lines despite local content legislation (Ibid.: 406).

Gender is another important dimension to consider in relation to inclusive development. At the New York Forum Africa 2013, Dos Santos spoke candidly about the challenges for women to succeed as large-scale entrepreneurs:

> Being a woman and going into the business sphere or investment sphere is a big challenge. Many women from whatever continent they're from – they know what I'm talking about. Not all doors are open to you. You don't often find the same treatment and you kind of have to prove yourself a little. But then again when you come from Africa, then there's like double jeopardy; you're a woman and you're African. And on top of it if you're young then you have no credibility.[8]

In another interview she again emphasised that the challenge for women is not to be business women, as many small-scale companies are run by women, but for women to reach "the next stage, more complex businesses, businesses that requires structuring that sometimes are not available to women, such as financial structuring. That's our big challenge."[9] Studies have confirmed that, African men are indeed dominant as large-scale entrepreneurs, while women are the majority of small-scale entrepreneurs (see Spring and McDade 1998).

8 Global Entrepreneurship Summit – Interview with Dos Santos, 2014. https://www.youtube.com/watch?v=KkTForvCSz4 accessed 17 November 2016.

9 Ibid.

Another study concluded that middle- and upper class women succeed well as middle- and large-scale entrepreneurs (Spring 2009). The reason for their success is access to key factors to expand businesses: education, capital and a wide network. The challenge which Dos Santos spoke of can therefore be reformulated to become more specific: the big challenge is for women from *lower* socio-economic backgrounds to become large-scale entrepreneurs. If we now examine Africa's second richest woman Folorunsho Alakija, we can confirm that her social status before she entered the oil sector was instrumental in opening up the possibility for her to become a large-scale entrepreneur.

### Folorunsho Alakija, Nigeria

Folorunsho Alakija is the 13th richest African, and Africa's second richest woman, worth $1.7 billion, and now at age 65, according to Forbes' 2016 listing.[10] Alakija follows Dos Santos on Forbes' list of Africa's wealthiest women. However, estimates made by Ventures Africa's analysts indicate that the value of her combined assets are $7.3 billion. Their rationale is that the proposed sale of shares in OML 127 owned by Brazilian Petrobas for $1.5 – 2.5 billion, increases the value of Alakija's 60 per cent ownership to $7.3 billion (Ventures Africa 2013). If these tentative estimates of her increased wealth are accurate, that would make her the richest woman in Africa as she would surpass Dos Santos. Nevertheless, Alakija is undoubtedly Nigeria's richest woman.

Her career started as a secretary at International Merchant Bank (IMB) Nigeria in the 1970s, not of her own volition, but because her father chose that as her career path (CNN 2012). She rose through the ranks to the position of executive secretary, upwards to being the Head of Corporate Affairs at the bank, which was followed two years later by a position at the Financial Treasury Department. Although Alakija had been afforded the task to trade and invest with the Bank's money, she nonetheless found herself surpassed by others when it came to further promotions, which made her quit the bank and start her own business.

In 1985 Alakija launched "Supreme Stitches" a fashion brand, which propelled her into success as a designer, and won a national award for Fashion Designer of the Year (Sambira 2015). Though her brand became a household name, it primarily catered to up-scale clientele. Alakija's entry into fashion industry came after having studied fashion in the United Kingdom. This decision, she argues was because she did not want to merely employ people, she wanted

10 See http://www.forbes.com/profile/folorunsho-alakija/?list=africa-billionaires.

to know the industry for herself in order to do it "professionally", spurred by personal motivation and a commitment to excellence and success in all of her endeavours (CNN 2012). Her education overseas was easily facilitated since she already came from a wealthy family. One would argue that capital is not only important in order to invest into one's business, but also to invest in acquiring the necessary know-how for the designated sector. Coming from the upper strata of society thus made her entry into the business world comparatively easier than had she come from a poorer background. Notwithstanding, it was her own observation of textile market trends in the mid-80s in Nigeria, with increasing interest in Nigerian designs, which propelled her to tap into the domestic fashion market. Therefore, it is imperative to juxtapose access to funding with entrepreneurial skill. Alakija's wealthy background does not take away from the fact that she made wise business decisions; it merely provided the necessary foundations to start her career as an entrepreneur.

The success of Supreme Stitches provided Alakija with the capital and connections, which pushed her success even further. Access to funding and having personal connections to high profile leadership in Nigeria have been other key factors leading to her success. Joseph (1987) argued that Nigeria is a prebendal society, where upward mobility often is contingent on access to elites as "an individual procures [...] as a reward for loyal service to a lord or ruler" (see also: Lewis 1996). In the case of Alakija, she herself attributed her entry into the oil business to Supreme Stitches as she in a CNN interview stated that it helped her gain access to a wide range of people, which later led to "a call from a friend". Therein, she found out that "this friend of ours had business associates who wanted to purchase crude oil" leading her to apply for oil fields (CNN 2012). Alakija entered the oil industry in the 1990s during the rule of military president Ibrahim Babangida, an outcome of her personal connection to Babangida through his wife Maryam, as she was her tailor. In 1996 she signed a deal with Texaco (which later became Chevron) and founded Famfa oil. In October 2016, Alakija publicly alluded to how she got an oil block in 1993, but it took 15 years for her company to strike oil in commercial quantity.[11] Her wealth has steadily grown since then and propelled her to the position as the fourth wealthiest person in Nigeria. Alakija recently sought to distance herself and her business from links to government when she asserted that the Obasanjo government frustrated the growth of her oil business in the heels of striking oil in commercial quantity. In the same public forum, this assertion was countered by former

11 *Daily Vanguard*, 30 October 2016, I made you a billionaire, Obasanjo tells Folorunsho Alakija, http://www.vanguardngr.com/2016/10/made-billionaire-obasanjo-tells-folorunsho-alakija/.

President Obasanjo (of Nigeria), where he stated "that Mrs Folorunsho Alakija, Africa's richest woman by Forbes reckoning, was among the 25 billionaires he made during his tenure as President." (See *Daily Vanguard*, 30 October 2016).

But after striking oil in 2008, Alakija diversified business ventures. In 2008, she started the Rose of Sharon foundation (RoSF), a non-governmental organisation dedicated to empowering widows and orphans by targeting their need for financial independence and education.[12] Access to start-up capital is one of the main barriers for women desiring to become entrepreneurs (Spring 2009). Alakija sees micro-finance as the solution to this problem:

> I'm sure you've seen a lot of women succeed in their various businesses. The only problem is that they do not have enough access to funding, so we have to find solutions for that. A clear example is the Grameen Bank (in Bangladesh). That is a bank where only women have taken the most advantage; 90–95 per cent of clients are women, in 35,000 villages. So they now have a source of funding and have been able to feed their families from that. We should borrow ideas like that within our continent to help women to get funding to be able to provide for their families.[13]

One of the means of harnessing the entrepreneurial potential of women is to increase access to funding and the RoSF's "Women Empowerment Programme" has been modeled on the Grameen Bank.

Micro-credit schemes were initially lauded as the panacea to lifting people out of poverty in the international development policy circles. However, this approach has some flaws as it is argued that the large numbers of women as loan-takers (Alakija's indicator of success) does not necessarily mean that their lives have improved. Indeed, while there are women who do succeed to utilise micro-finance loans to start small-businesses, many women have fallen victim to high interest rates and seen their situations become worse than they were before the loan. Micro-credit schemes have had disastrous effects in South Africa, which serves as a warning to uncritically introduce micro-finance in other African countries (Bateman 2014a). Furthermore, a study found that "no clear evidence yet exists that microfinance programs have positive impacts" (Duvendack et al. 2011). Considering the negative impacts of micro-finance in other cases and the critique of the Grameen Bank model specifically

12 The Rose of Sharon Foundation <theroseofsharonfoundation.org> Accessed: 30 April 2016.

13 MIT Africa Innovate Summit 2014. *Meet Madam Folorunsho Alakija*, https://www.youtube.com/watch?v=wZVH-mfxp5I.

(see Bateman 2014b), the likelihood of the RoSF's initiative to diverge from that trend seems unlikely.

Based on interviews where Alakija speaks on women's empowerment and her foundation, it is clear that she wants to portray an image as a facilitator of increased gender equality for women in Nigeria. However, as the abovementioned studies show, micro-credit can be a problematic means towards a good cause. Nonetheless, the corporate social responsibility programmes of Famfa Oil with their partner Agbami seem more beneficial. For instance, the Agbami Social Investments Programme offers scholarships for Nigerian undergraduate students in the field of Medicine and Engineering.[14] Secondary education has been found to be one key difference between female informal business owners and formal larger-scale business owners, where the latter in most cases have tertiary education as well (Spring 2009). A UNECA study (2007) study found that most women large-scale entrepreneurs had strong educational backgrounds within the science disciplines, and maths in particular.

The third case in this study, Dr. Theresa Oppong Beeko from Ghana is a prime example of the importance of education in order to develop the necessary knowledge in succeeding as a large-scale entrepreneur.

## Dr. Theresa Oppong-Beeko, Ghana

Ghana's wealthiest 80 individuals and families have a combined fortune of $29.3 billion, representing some 6.4 per cent of the nation's GDP, providing direct employment to over 150,000 Ghanaians. In this list of Ghana's wealthy people are three male billionaires – who together account for a total wealth of $3.96 billion – and five women multimillionaires who control a total of $1.62 billion. These women include Gifty Lamptey (4th richest Ghanaian woman and 69th richest Ghanaian), who with a net worth of $135 million is the largest individual shareholder in SIDALCO, one of West Africa's largest fertiliser distributors. Another is Kate Quartey-Papafio (third richest Ghanaian woman and 48th richest Ghanaian) net worth $250 Million, who is the founder and Chief Executive Officer of Reroy Cables Limited one of the leading manufacturers of electrical cables and telecom cables and conductors in Ghana, with significant links to the international market, exporting mostly to countries in the Economic Community of West African States. There is Theresa Oppong-Beeko (second richest Ghanaian woman and 24th richest Ghanaian), worth $420 Million, who

14 Famfa Oil <http://www.famfa.com/corporate-social-responsibility/> Accessed: 30 April 2016.

is into Real estate under the umbrella of Manet Group (owns commercial office properties, over 2,000 apartments, a 48-room niche hotel, as well as the Manet Towers at Airport City in Accra). Patricia Poku-Diaby is Ghana's richest woman, and 8th richest Ghanaian, owning three quarters of a billion dollars. She was initially into management of her family's business (trading and transportation), after which she established Plot Enterprise Group in Côte d'Ivoire which includes Plot Commodities (deals in cotton and cocoa, registered with the Dubai Metal and Commodities Centre in Dubai and the Cocoa Merchants Association of America), Plot Enterprise in Côte d'Ivoire (trading of cocoa, cashew nut and wood products) and Plot Enterprise Ghana (a cocoa processing company).[15]

Female entrepreneurs in Ghana's rich list appear to be in businesses that have a minimal link to government patronage. This is a large departure from the government corruption-to-wealth explanations largely ascribed to sources of wealth of some very rich Africans. Dr. Theresa Oppong-Beeko is the founder and chief executive officer of Manet Group Incorporated, and one of the richest and most influential women in Ghana. Although her wealth ranks behind that of Dos Santos and Alakija, a part of the lower rungs of Oppong-Beeko's ladder to wealth has to some extent been attributed to unexplained connections with high profile political leadership. It is documented that after completing her first degree in humanities she started her first business venture in fishing at the age of 25, which ended with her having a debt equivalent to $2.5 million at such a young age.[16] Interestingly, this remains the glaringly unexplained part of her trajectory to wealth. All documentary sources allude to this debt, yet, none proffered explanation on the source of this big loan, the concessions she might have had in repayment or debt forgiveness when the investment in fish business went sour, and whether it was eventually repaid, at what rate of interest (which is generally documented as astronomically high in Ghana). It begs the question whether a gap in banking regulation was utilised; or, did she receive some sort of support from government at high levels just at a time when Ghana was emerging from tough economic doldrums in the 80s? These questions remain unanswered, which in a way puts her foundation wealth in the category of the kinds of probable political links that Alakija and Dos Santos benefitted from. Hence the choice of the second wealthiest female in Ghana for analyses in this chapter.

---

15 Top 10 richest Ghanaians listed and described in blog: Talking Drums, 2015, Top 10 Richest Ghanaians, http://talkingdrums.com/en/2015/08/29/546/ Published 29 August 2015.

16 Goodman AMC, Theresa Oppong-Beeko, $420 Million President, The Manet Group, https://goodmanamc.blogspot.nl/p/blog-page_10.html accessed 18 November 2016.

Oppong-Beeko holds a Bachelor of Arts Honours Degree in Sociology and Political Science and a Master's degree in Business Administration (Marketing) both from the University of Ghana, Legon. No public documentation exists about her connections to high profile political leadership but her trajectory to prosperity warrants an examination of how she has managed to succeed in the backdrop of the fact that she decided to return to the University of Ghana at Legon to acquire a Master's degree in Business Administration (where she was declared Best Marketing Student in 1990) following the failed $2.5 million business venture. After graduation she established Manet Housing Limited in 1994, pursuing her dream of entering the constructing market. In the wider sense, Manet Construction Limited is primarily a civil engineering company that has specialised in the construction of urban roads and other related infrastructure such as drains, culverts, and high-rise edifice around the nation's capital, Accra.

In 1998, Theresa Oppong Beeko further established Manet Hotels Limited, located as a beach Resort at Ada (east of Accra, towards the Volta Region), which was developed into a three-star 48-room hotel that caters niche tourism of Aqua sport and marlin fishing. This would metamorphose into Manet Paradise and Beach resort. The Manet Group comprises Manet Housing (real estate development firm), Manet Beach Paradise (a three star Hotel Resort), Manet Construction Limited (a Civil Engineering Company) and Manet Towers Limited (to provide and manage office accommodation, signified in the Twin Tower office edifice at the Airport City in Accra, Ghana). The Manet Group also includes the Manet Cottage annex, the Manet Gardens and the Manet Ville. In the backdrop of being the second largest Real Estate Development Company in Ghana's construction sector, a lot of accolades have been bestowed on Theresa Oppong-Beeko, notable among these are: Manet's recognition for the Overall property award for 2012 at the 5th Ghana Property Awards; Theresa Oppong-Beeko in 2013 as Africa's most influential woman in business and government (overall winner for Africa in the industries category); recognition as a philanthropist for being the Highest Individual Donor to the society, in July 2004, by the Ghana Society for The Blind's Golden Jubilee Celebrations (1951–2001); an exemplary realtor, accorded as Property Personality of the Year (2007) and the Gold Star Award for Exemplary Leadership in provision of shelter for low income earners in West Africa; Property Personality of the Year 2010 (Ghana Property Express); Ghana's Indigenous Woman Entrepreneur of the Year (2010).

The housing construction industry in Ghana has been described as notoriously tricky to finance, and compounded by gender barriers in a still male-dominated business. She famously publicly refused to be drawn into oil exploration or crude oil drilling license business by declaring her comfort zone remains the building sector, particularly by saying "I'm into accommodation and I will be there to provide it," through extensive local knowledge and understanding of Ghana's market's needs and staying sensitive to the demands of the Ghanaian population for real estate development and the hospitality industry in Ghana. Oppong-Beeko does not rule out international expansion of her business as she declared: "I cannot fully predict the effects the Manet Group will have on the Ghanaian economy but I am certain, nonetheless, that we will extend the scope of our business well beyond the borders of Ghana."

Recently obtained data from the Global Entrepreneurship Monitoring (GEM) survey in Ghana show relatively high levels of entrepreneurial activities among women compared to their male counterparts—a condition which is an exception across all the GEM countries. Within the context of limited employment and other opportunities in the labour market, the development of entrepreneurial activity is seen as playing a key role in Ghana's economic growth (Quartey et al. 2014). But female-controlled businesses in Ghana often tend to be micro and small enterprises (MSEs) largely concentrated in the informal sector. Societal views on culture, religion, and childcare, and levels of education and development have serious implications for attitudes and opinions that weigh heavily against women entering the business world. Despite these challenges, the 2010 GEM survey revealed that in Ghana, women are more entrepreneurial than men. Entrepreneurship is to an extent a preferred career path for women as it is seen to have the potential to offer flexibility and independence that typical employment does not (Dzisi 2008). Despite women's dominance in entrepreneurial activities in Ghana, women still face significant obstacles. In addition, the challenges of men and women's entrepreneurship in Ghana cannot be separated from those of the informal sector in particular and the private sector development in general. Consequently, the policy response needs not to narrowly focus on promoting female entrepreneurship but to broadly resolve the constraints affecting the informal sector or entrepreneurship in general.

## Conclusion

There is a lot of literature on entrepreneurship, but little is known about the forms and characteristics of female entrepreneurship in transition economies in general or African countries in particular. This study has attempted to fill this gap. All three women discussed in this chapter have undoubtedly been successful in their respective business ventures. However, their life stories show that their success as women entrepreneurs should not be framed as entrepreneurial exceptionalism, as none of them went from rags-to-riches (although very little is known about the background of Oppong-Beeko). The privilege, which facilitated these women's success can be seen as an unfair advantage to some, but is a valuable insight that confirms what other studies have shown; namely, in order for women to succeed as entrepreneurs, they need access to funding, education and networks. Indeed, given the comparative privileges that all three women had in comparison to women coming from lower strata of society, one may arguably conclude that Spring's (2009) argument is valid that women who own formal sector businesses should be considered "mainstream business people" and that the category of "women entrepreneurs" is rather misleading because the women possess the same agency (if not more, as in the case of Dos Santos) as male counterparts.

The cases presented in this chapter confirm how crucial the initial social statuses of these three women have been to their success. Isabel Dos Santos had access to solid education, networks and funding. But it is argued that Dos Santos' benefitting from access to ownership of Angolan parastatals that were privatised, alongside having connections to major investors (such as Portugal's richest man, Américo Amorim) has been crucial in Dos Santos business gave her the necessary leverage for success in business. Alakija's path to her current wealth was laid out by her establishment of Supreme Stiches, which later gave her the necessary connections for procurement of oil licenses. She publicly denied having privileges from "government of the day"; but rebuttal given by former President Obasanjo strongly pointed to her being one of the highly favoured by government. How this favour was given and how it became a catalyst for Alakija's appearance on Forbes list.[17] In Theresa Oppong-Beeko's case, there is no clear answer as to what kinds of political favours she received when she laid the foundation blocks of her businesses. However, one may hypothesise that she has had influential backing considering the business climate during which she first got indebted to the tune of millions of dollars and came out unscathed unlike other individuals at the time. One thing that remain clear is that the growth of the three women's businesses and personal wealth has been sustained. As a potential force for economic growth, women entrepreneurs in large-scale sector are nonetheless a pioneering community, increasingly well-educated and well primed for their role as entrepreneurs, as they continue to demonstrate excellent results and growth prospects.

17 *Daily Vanguard*, 30 October 2016, "I made you a billionaire, Obasanjo tells Folorunsho Alakija", http://www.vanguardngr.com/2016/10/made-billionaire-obasanjo-tells-folorunsho-alakija/.

## References

Adom, K. & C.C. Williams. (2012). "Evaluating the Motives of Informal Entrepreneurs in Koforidua, Ghana", *Journal of Developmental Entrepreneurship* vol. 17, No. 1, 1–17.

*African Energy*. (2015). "Angola: Isabel dos Santos Expands Empire", http://www.africa-energy.com/article/angola-isabel-dos-santos-expands-empire accessed 20 September 2016.

Ahl, H. (2004). *The Scientific Reproduction of Gender Inequality: A Discourse Analysis of Research Texts on Women Entrepreneurship*. Copenhagen: Copenhagen Business School.

Ahl, H. (2006). "Why Research on Women Entrepreneurs Needs New Directions". *Entrepreneurship Theory and Practice*, 30: 595–621.

Aidis, R.F.W., Smallbone, D. & N. Isakova. (2006). "Female Entrepreneurship in Transition Economies: The Case of Lithuania and Ukraine", *Feminist Economics*, 13(2), 157–183.

Aliata, M.I., Baba, I. & B.A. Patrick. (2013). "Women in Entrepreneurship as a Means to Sustainable Livelihood in Ghana: A Study of the Upper West Region", *African Journal of Social Sciences*, vol. 3: 3 (2013) 160–171.

Allen, K. (2016). "Cult of Dos Santos and the State of Angola", BBC News Luanda, http://www.bbc.com/news/world-africa-36520290, accessed 20 June 2016.

Bateman, M. (2014a). "South Africa's Post-apartheid Microcredit-driven Calamity", *Law, Democracy and Development*, 18, 92–135.

Bateman, M. (2014b). "The Rise and Fall of Muhammad Yunus and the Microcredit Model". International Development Studies, Working Paper Series #001 January 2014.

*BBC* (2015). "Isabel dos Santos: "Education is Our Gap in Angola", *BBC Business* 27 November 2015, http://www.bbc.com/news/business-34944631 accessed 20 September 2016.

*BBC* (2015). "Isabel dos Santos: "What I Have Achieved is Through Merit", *BBC Focus on Africa* 27 November, http://www.bbc.co.uk/programmes/p039d88t, accessed 26 September 2016.

Brixiová, Z. & T. Kangoye. (2016). "Gender and Constraints to Entrepreneurship in Africa: New Evidence from Swaziland", *Journal of Business Venturing Insights*, volume 5, June 2016, 1–8.

Calas, M., Smircich, L. & K. Bourne. (2009). "Extending the Boundaries: Reframing Entrepreneurship as Social Change through Feminist Perspectives", *Academy of Management Review*, 34(3), 552–569.

Centre for Economic and Leadership Development (n.d.). *Theresa Oppong Beeko*. http://celdng.org/theresa-oppong-beeko/, accessed 29 September 2016.

Cliff, J.E. (1998). "Does One Size Fit All? Exploring the Relationship Between Attitudes Towards Growth, Gender, and Business Size", *Journal of Business Venturing*, vol. 13(6), November 1998, 523–542, http://dx.doi.org/10.1016/S0883-9026(97)00071-2.

*CNN* (2012). "African Voices: Folorunsho Alakija", *CNN African Voices* 16 February 2012, https://www.youtube.com/watch?v=V2OufVawofE, accessed 10 June 2016.

Costa, B. (2012). "Angola: Isabel Dos Santos Reinforces her Presence in Portuguese Firms", *Portugal Daily View*, 9 May 2012, http://www.portugaldailyview.com/whats-new/isabel-dos-santos-reinforces-her-presence-in-portuguese-firms, accessed 20 September 2016.

De Morais, R.M. (2015). *Blood Diamonds: Corruption and Torture in Angola*. Lisboa: Tinta da China.

De Oliveira, R.S. (2016). "The Struggle for the State and the Politics of Belonging in Contemporary Angola, 1975–2015", *Journal of Social Dynamics*, vol. 42, issue 1.

Dolan, K.A. (2013). "Daddy's Girl: How An African "Princess" Banked $3 Billion In A Country Living On $2 A Day", *Forbes*, 2 September 2013. http://www.forbes.com/sites/kerryadolan/2013/08/14/how-isabel-dos-santos-took-the-short-route-to-become-africas-richest-woman/#2d461bcd79fe, accessed 20 September 2016.

Duvendack, M., Palmer-Jones, R., Copestake, J.G., Hooper, L., Loke, Y. & N. Rao. (2011). *What is the Evidence of the Impact of Microfinance on the Well-being of Poor People?* EPPICentre, Social Science Research Unit, Institute of Education, University of London.

Dzisi, S. (2008). "Women Entrepreneurs in Small and Medium Enterprises (SMEs) in Ghana", PhD dissertation, Swinburne University of Technology.

Europa Publications (2003). *Angola*. Regional Surveys of the World. Africa South of the Sahara 2003. 32nd Edition, 33–59.

Famfa Oil. (n.d.). "Corporate Social Responsibility", http://www.famfa.com/corporate-social-responsibility/, accessed 30 April 2016.

*Forbes*. (2016). "Folorunsho Alakija", http://www.forbes.com/profile/folorunsho-alakija/, accessed 30 April 2016.

*Forbes*. (2016). "Isabel dos Santos", http://www.forbes.com/profile/isabel-dos-santos/, accessed 11 July 2016.

Global Entrepreneurship Summit 5th Edition (2014). Interview with Isabel dos Santos, 20 November 2014, https://www.youtube.com/watch?v=KkTForvCSz4, accessed 29 September 2016.

Joseph, R. (1987). *Democracy and Prebendalism in Nigeria*. New York: Cambridge, 56.

Le Billon, P. (2001). "Angola's Political Economy of War: The Role of Oil and Diamonds, 1975–2000", *African Affairs*, vol. 100 (398), 55–80.

Lewis, P. (1996). "From Prebendalism to Predation: The Political Economy of Decline in Nigeria". *The Journal of Modern African Studies*, 34(01), 79–103.

Lima, J. (2014). "Angolan President's Daughter Bids to Buy Portugal Telecom", *Bloomberg Technology*, 9 November 2014, http://www.bloomberg.com/news/articles/2014-11-09/angola-s-isabel-dos-santos-makes-bid-for-portugal-telecom-sgps, accessed 20 September 2016.

Loscocco, K.A., Robinson, J., Hall, R.H. & J.K. Allen. (1991). "Gender and Small Business Success: An Inquiry into Women's Relative Disadvantage", *Social Forces* (1991), 70 (1): 65–85. doi: 10.1093/sf/70.1.65.

*Macauhub*. (2015). "Angola mines 10 million carats of diamonds in 2014", *macauhub Home* 12 February 2015, http://www.macauhub.com.mo/en/2015/02/12/angola-mines-10-million-carats-of-diamonds-in-2014/, accessed 20 September 2016.

Maka, A. (2016). Republished by Rafael Marques on 31 May 2016. "Angola: Africa's Richest Woman's Assets were Paid by State Money and Public Funds", *Daily Maverick*, http://www.dailymaverick.co.za/article/2016-05-31-angola-africas-richest-womans-assets-were-paid-by-state-money-and-public-funds/#.V-FB1-J9670, accessed 20 September 2016.

Maritz, A. (2004). "New Zealand Necessity Entrepreneurs", *International Journal of Entrepreneurship and Small Business*, 1(3–4), 255–264.

Mbaku, J.M. (2013). "Providing a Foundation for Wealth Creation and Development in Africa: The Role of the Rule of Law", *Brook Journal of International Law*, 2012–2013, vol. 38:3, 959–1051.

Messiant, C. (2001). "The Eduardo Dos Santos Foundation: Or, How Angola's Regime is Taking over Civil Society", *African Affairs*, 100 (399): 287–309.

MIT Africa Innovate Summit (2014). "Meet Madam Folorunsho Alakija", https://www.youtube.com/watch?v=wZVH-mfxp5I, accessed 29 September 2016.

Mumuni, I.A., Insah, B., & A.P. Bowan. (2013). "Women in Entrepreneurship as a Means to Sustainable Livelihood in Ghana: A Study of the Upper West Region", *African Journal of Social Sciences*, 3(3), 160–171.

New York Forum Africa (2013). "Interview with Isabel dos Santos", https://www.youtube.com/watch?v=7bYNMOcn1VQ, accessed 29 September 2016.

Organisation for Economic Cooperation and Development (OECD). (1998). "Women Entrepreneurs in Small and Medium Enterprises", *OECD Proceedings*, 151.

Ovadia, J.S. (2012). "The Dual Nature of Local Content in Angola's Oil and Gas Industry: Development vs. Elite Accumulation", *Journal of Contemporary African Studies*, 30 (3), 395–417.

Palmerlee, A.W. (2002). "*Creating a Level Playing Field for Women, Remarks to the Global Women's Summit*", Barcelona, Spain, 11 July 2002, http://2001-2009.state.gov/g/wi/11894.htm, accessed 20 September 2016.

Pamuk, H. (2012). "Sonangol in Talks to Buy More of Portugal's Galp", *Reuters Africa*, 13 March 2012, http://af.reuters.com/article/investingNews/idAFJOE82C03S20120313, accessed 20 June 2016.

Perunović, Z. (2005). *Introducing Opportunity-Based Entrepreneurship in a Transition Economy*. Michigan: Policy Brief 39, The William Davidson Institute, University of Michigan.

Powell, G.N. & K.A. Eddleston. (2013). "Linking Family-to-Business Enrichment and Support to Entrepreneurial Success: Do Female and Male Entrepreneurs Experience Different Outcomes?" *Journal of Business Venturing*, 28 (2), March 2013, 261–280, http://dx.doi.org/10.1016/j.jbusvent.2012.02.007.

Power, M. (2012). "Angola 2025: The Future of the "World's Richest Poor Country" as Seen through a Chinese Rear View Mirror", *Antipode*, 44(3), 993–1014.

Quartey, P., Owusu, G. & S. Bawakyillenuo. (2014). *Are Ghana's Women More Entrepreneurial Than its Men?* Washington, DC: Brookings Institute, http://www.brookings.edu/blogs/africa-in-focus/posts/2014/08/19-ghanaian-women-entrepreneurs-owusu-quartey-bawakyillenuo, accessed 29 September 2016.

Reis, A. (2014). "Africa's Richest Woman to Stick to Portugal Telecom SGPS Bid", *Bloomberg Technology*, 4 December 2014, http://www.bloomberg.com/news/articles/2014-12-04/africa-s-richest-woman-to-stick-to-portugal-telecom-sgps-offer accessed 20 September 2016.

Roomi, M.A. & G. Parrott. (2008). "Barriers to Development and Progression of Women Entrepreneurs in Pakistan", *Journal of Entrepreneurship*, May, 17 (1): 59–72.

Sambira, J. (2015). "Investing in Women's Employment Essential for Economic Growth", *Africa Renewal*, April, 29 (1): 8, United Nations Department of Public Information, http://www.un.org/africarenewal/sites/www.un.org.africarenewal/files/Africa_Renewal_April_2015_en_0.pdf, accessed 17 November 2016.

Sandberg, K.W. (2003). "An Exploratory Study of Women in Micro Enterprises: Gender Related Differences", *Journal of Small Business and Enterprise Development*, 10 (4): 408–417.

Spring, A. (2009). "African Women in the Entrepreneurial Landscape: Reconsidering the Formal and Informal Sectors", *Journal of African Business*, 10:11–30.

Spring, A. & B. McDade. (1998). "Entrepreneurship in Africa: Traditional and Contemporary Paradigms". In: A. Spring & B. McDade (eds), *African Entrepreneurship: Theory and reality*, University Press of Florida, 1–34.

The Rose of Sharon Foundation, http://theroseofsharonfoundation.org/, accessed: 30 April 2016.

UNDP. (2015). *Angola*. Briefing note for countries on the 2015 Human Development Report, Human Development Report 2015. UNDP.

UNECA (2007). *Lessons from Success Stories of African Women Entrepreneurs*. Economic Commission for Africa. Addis Abeba, Ethiopia.

UNIDO (2001), "Women Entrepreneurship Development in Selected African Countries", *PSD Technical Working Papers Series*, Working Paper No. 7.

*Ventures Africa* (2013). "How Africa's Richest Woman Folorunsho Alakija Grew From $3.3 BN to $7.3 BN", 11 October 2013, http://venturesafrica.com/africas-richest-woman-folorunsho-alakija-grew-3-3bn-7-3bn/ accessed 29 September 2016.

Vossenberg, S. (2013). "Women Entrepreneurship Promotion in Developing Countries: What Explains the Gender Gap and How to Close It?". Working Paper No. 2013/08.

CHAPTER 15

# Financial Barriers and How to Overcome Them: The Case of Women Entrepreneurs in Tanzania

*Marta Lindvert*

## Introduction

Women-owned businesses all over the world contribute significantly to innovation, employment, and wealth creation in their respective economies. Even though women represent one of the fastest growing groups of entrepreneurs worldwide, and despite their growing importance as drivers of development, they are understudied and we know relatively little about them (Brush et al. 2006, 2009). The lack of research on women entrepreneurs is well documented (De Bruin et al. 2006, 2007; Brush and Cooper 2012). In particular, little attention has been given to the importance of women entrepreneurs in developing economies. This is troublesome, as entrepreneurship has the potential to play a key role in the development of any society, not least when involving women (Dijkgraaff 2007). Numerous studies have confirmed the economic value of entrepreneurship, and its importance for development is a widely accepted proposal (Schumpeter 1934; Landström 2000; Van Praag and Versloot 2007; Valliere and Peterson 2009; Bruton et al. 2013). At the same time, lack of access to capital and other resources is a severe barrier to the establishment of, and growth in, new ventures. Financial barriers are a constraint to any new and/or small business, but especially so in developing economies where the financial markets tend to be underdeveloped or dysfunctional (Morewagae et al. 1995).

When looking at women entrepreneurs, previous research shows that they face particularly high barriers in their search for capital and other resources (Amine and Staub 2009; Johnson 2004). Drawing on institutional theory, it is clear that women have to overcome barriers from both formal and informal institutions (Haile et al. 2012; Amine and Staub 2009). Since existing institutions in shifting ways and in different contexts create different preconditions for men and women to start and run their business, there is a need to understand entrepreneurship from a gender perspective (Spring 2009). Brush et al. (2009) argue that "motherhood" can be seen as a metaphor for the household

 | DOI 10.1163/9789004351615_016

and family context, an environment that has a bigger influence on women entrepreneurs compared to men. Women are also influenced by surrounding macro factors, such as expectations from society and cultural norms, and meso factors such as intermediate structures and institutions. (Brush et al. 2009). At the same time, it is important to remember that the group of women entrepreneur is by no means homogeneous. They differ in terms of education, experience, financial status, role, and control in the business, marital, and family situation and ethnic and religious background (Nchimbi and Chijoriga 2009).

The most frequently addressed obstacle for women entrepreneurs is lack of access to capital and discrimination in relation to loan applications (Morewagae et al. 1995; Satta 2003). Further, women in developing countries are often disadvantaged regarding property, marital rights, and inheritance laws. Without property ownership, it becomes difficult to show collateral in order to gain formal credit (SIDA 2009). Most women operate their ventures within the trade- and service sectors, and usually at a very small scale with low profits and with no, or very few employees (Pedersen 2001). This further decreases their access to formal finance, as these sectors, especially when unregistered, are seen as less important for economic development (Bennett 2010).

In this chapter, the focus is on resource acquisition among women entrepreneurs in Tanzania, where potential female entrepreneurs have almost no access to formal capital from the commercial bank sector. As a response to the financial gap between supply and demand, the microfinance sector has grown rapidly during the last couple of decades, and often specifically targets women entrepreneurs (D'Espallier et al. 2011; Mayoux 2001; Haile et al. 2012; Sigalla and Carney 2012) Other sources of capital are also widely used, such as savings and credit cooperatives (Johnson 2004). However, to a large extent, women entrepreneurs still rely on informal sources of capital, such as loans from family and friends (Olomi 2009).

Drawing on institutional theory, and based on a discussion of how formal and informal institutions create barriers and opportunities for women, the aim of this study is to discuss how women in Tanzania act in order to overcome financial barriers, as they start or develop their ventures. The chapter starts with a short introduction to the situation of entrepreneurship development in the Tanzanian context, followed by an overview of theory relevant for this study. Thereafter, stories from women entrepreneurs operating within the trade- and service sectors are presented. Data was collected during a field study, where semi-structured interviews were conducted. Lastly, findings are summarised and recommendations for practitioners and policymakers are presented.

## The Situation of Entrepreneurship Development in Tanzania

After being a German colony, and later a British protectorate under the League of Nations and later the United Nations flag, Tanganyika became independent in 1961. When uniting with Zanzibar in 1964, the Tanzanian republic was formed. During the decades after its independence, the country has undergone a number of political and economic eras, with profound effects on preconditions for the private sector and entrepreneurship (CIA 2015). Especially important for the development of the private sector were reforms following the economic crises of the 1970s and 1980s, when the government liberalised trade and implemented a vital transformation programme. This was urged and supported by the World Bank and the International Monetary Fund, and led to a liberalisation of practically all sectors of the economy. Gradually, the economic policy shifted from reliance on state-run enterprises to stimulation of foreign investments and local entrepreneurship (Olomi 2009). However, Tanzania is still one of the poorest countries in the world, and entrepreneurs face many challenges (Sigalla and Carney 2012). More than two thirds of the population (of currently 51 million people) live in rural areas, roads and communication systems are poor, and the education level is generally low. The population is very young, with 64 per cent under the age of 25, and average life expectancy is only 61 years. Like many other developing countries, Tanzania is struggling with a trade gap, foreign debt, and high inflation rates. The economy is depending on agriculture, accounting for more than 25 per cent of gross domestic product (GDP) and providing 85 per cent of exports. All land in Tanzania is owned by the government, which can be leased for up to 99 years (CIA World Fact Book, 2015).

During the last decades, the proportion of people who choose self-employment as a career has increased. The private sector is characterised by few large firms and a large segment of very small firms, where almost all (98 per cent) of firms are micro businesses, having less than five employees. Large firms stand for only 12 per cent of registered enterprises, but produce 38 per cent of GDP and have 20 per cent of the workforce. These are mainly subsidiaries or franchises of multinational companies, or state-owned firms, and tend to be capital intensive and strongly connected to industrialised countries. At the opposite end, micro and small businesses rely on the local environment for inputs and markets, are often more or less informal, and typically labour intensive (Olomi 2009; Bennett 2010).

The economy has shown significant growth rates during the last decades, and the GDP growth in 2009–2015 was as much as 6–7 per cent per year, where the tourism sector has played an important role (CIA World Fact Book, 2015; Sigalla and Carney 2012). The majority of micro and small businesses operate within trade (54 per cent) and services (34 per cent). As these ventures tend to be concentrated in a few lines of business, there is often a self-destructive competition. The majority of start-ups are financed by savings or grants from family or friends, and are typically run from the home of the founder or by the roadside (Olomi 2009).

Women operating their own businesses is not a new phenomenon, as women have always been involved in different kinds of entrepreneurship. However, the proportion of women-owned enterprises has increased during the last decades, mainly as a result of the structural adjustment programmes following the economic crisis in the 1970s and 1980s. The programmes led to lower purchasing power of salaried workers and fewer job opportunities. As women were more severely affected, and with greater responsibility to meet basic family needs, many women were pushed into self-employment (Nchimbi and Chijoriga 2009). Women are playing an increasingly important role within micro and small enterprise segments. In 1997, as many as 55 per cent of enterprises were owned by women (Olomi 2009). However, this should not be interpreted as an improvement of gender equality, but rather depends on the necessity for women to play a more active income generating role, as men, who traditionally have been the breadwinners, are facing reduced real salaries and employment opportunities. The majority of women-owned businesses operate within the trade- or service sectors. Women choose activities that harmonise with their traditional roles, run, to a higher degree, informal, home-based, micro firms and are dependent on the local market. Not surprisingly, their ventures are also the least profitable (Nchimbi and Chijoriga 2009; Pedersen 2001).

## Contextual Opportunities and Barriers

### *Institutional Preconditions*

Within social science, it has long been recognised that all economic activity is embedded in social structures (Granovetter 1985). The focus has often been on the micro level, where entrepreneurship has been interpreted based on actions of the individual (Welter and Smallbone 2011). It is also well known that social networks function as an important link between social and economic activities (Granovetter 1973, 1985). Today, there is a growing awareness that economic activity has to be interpreted based on a multitude of contextual factors. One way to distinguish different dimensions of context is by asking the questions of *who*, *where* and *when* entrepreneurship happens (Whetten 1989). The question of *who* reflects the impact of contexts on entrepreneurship and relates to who becomes entrepreneur and which ventures are created. The *where* refers to the different locations in which entrepreneurship occurs, which also affects the question of who, whereas the question of *when* relates to historical and temporal contexts and historical influences on the entrepreneurship of today (Whetten 1989). According to Welter (2011), it is necessary to interpret economic activity within its historical, temporal, institutional, spatial, and social contexts, as these different aspects of contexts provide individuals with opportunities, but also set boundaries for their actions. This means that the individual may experience the contextual preconditions as either an asset or liability, or maybe both at the same time (Welter 2011).

According to Scott (1995), institutions consist of structures and activities, which give stability and meaning to social behaviour. Institutions can, according to this definition, consist of cognitive, normative, or regulative structures and activities. The cognitive aspect focuses on social actor's acceptance of rules and routines, because these are taken for granted, while the regulative aspect focuses on how institutions limit and regulate behaviour. Institutions can also be seen as social orders or patterns. When these social patterns are chronically reproduced, they owe their survival to self-activating social processes; in other words, the patterns are institutionalised (Jeppersson 1991). Thus, institutionalisation is a mutual process, where actors create institutions through repetitive behaviour, but where the institutions also create the actors (Berger and Luckman 1966).

The institutional context consists of both formal and informal institutions, and is often referred to as *rules of the game* (North 1990). They both constitute the incentive system of a society and regulate the behaviour of the individual. Formal institutions refer to political and economy-related laws and regulations as well as the organisational framework for individual action. Informal institutions refer to codes of conduct, values, and norms, including uncodified attitudes embedded in a society. When institutions are stable and efficient, they can reduce uncertainty and risk for entrepreneurs, and lowers transaction costs associated with economic activity (North 1990). In any context, the development of entrepreneurship and the actions of entrepreneurs are influenced by the functions of formal institutions. The legal framework regulates market entry and exit as well as business development through contract and bankruptcy laws. Formal institutions with specific effect on women entrepreneurs relate to whether the constitution gives equal rights to men and women, and how family and social policies are constructed. Formal institutions are directly influenced by the state, but can also influence values and attitudes in a society as they declare the official norms (Welter and Smallbone 2011). Alongside these formal institutions, values, attitudes, and norms constitute informal institutions, which, just as formal institutions, provide individuals with opportunities or set boundaries for their actions. Attitudes and norms will state to what degree entrepreneurship is accepted or encouraged in the society, and if it is given a certain value. (Welter and Smallbone 2011).

Examples of informal institutions specifically affecting women entrepreneurs are related to religion and traditions, which form the status and standing of women in a society and influence their economic function. In more conservative societies, religious values often put restrictions on women, which can lead to conflicting economic and societal roles. Other cultural norms that affect women's preconditions as entrepreneurs are the general value a society gives to women employment and the value attributed to the family. It also relates to the role of extended family in the society, as this can facilitate the individual with resources, but also function as a constraint (Welter and Smallbone 2008). When studying women in a developing context, it is therefore important to understand how both formal and informal institutions work and how they affect women's abilities to get into venturing (Spring 2009; Johnson 2004; Haile et al. 2012). To summarise: formal institutions create opportunities for entrepreneurial action, but informal institutions decide how the collective and the individual perceive these opportunities.

### *Institutions and Resource Acquisition*

In developing countries, women entrepreneurs in general have to overcome severe funding obstacles, diminishing their potential in venturing (Ogunrinola 2011). Even though financial markets are weak in Tanzania, there are a number of financial actors who offer capital, even to very small firms (Olomi, Chijoriga, and Mori 2009). From an institutional perspective, financial actors can be divided into different categories, depending on their level of formality. At one end of the spectrum, there are highly formalised commercial banks, and at the other end are very informal loans or grants from family or friends (Lindvert et al. 2015). However, there is not always a clear distinction between formal and informal capital, as they both can cover a variety of institutions and mechanisms. One way to define informal capital, is that it provides capital or other resources without any control from the state, whereas formal capital is operating under governmental control mechanisms (Callier 1989).

In Tanzania, just like in many other African countries, the majority of women entrepreneurs have basically no access to finance from the commercial, regulated bank sector. To a large extent, this can be explained by the typical character of their businesses, as they are running micro enterprises, are typically labour intensive, and operating within the trade- and service sectors, but it also depends on the fact that women often lack property or other collateral (Ogunrinola 2011; Olomi 2009). From the perspective of the bank, these are perceived as high-risk clients and as they are seeking small amounts of capital they also require higher transaction costs (Satta 2003; Chittenden et al. 1996) . Far more important for women in Tanzania are the microfinance institutions (MFIs) that offer capital and other financial services (Ssendi and Anderson 2009; Sigalla and Carney 2012). Just like in other parts of the developing world, the MFIs are often international organisations, and reaching a relatively large number of clients. Many are also heavily donor-dependent, which is not surprising as they tend to specifically target the poor, most often women, and have social goals rather than striving for the highest profitability (Matin et al. 2002). The majority of MFIs choose to prioritise women clients, both because women are more exposed in poor areas, but also because women have proven to be more reliable clients with fewer defaults (D'Espallier et al. 2011). The fundamental idea within microfinance is to lower the risk involved in economic transactions, by letting clients form a loan group, where the social capital within the group functions as collateral towards the bank. Thus, access to capital is not depending on the individuals' ability to show collateral, instead, focus is on social capital, networks and the character of the client (Bhatt and Tang 1998).

Many of the financial actors offering micro loans started to operate at informal levels. During the last decades, the financial sector in Tanzania has undergone several reforms, which has led to the new situation that these actors, many of which were previously seen as informal, are now regulated and under governmental control (Piprek 2007; Bwana and Mwakujonga 2013). There have been, and are still, great variations between the different lending programmes, ranging from non-profit social actors to commercial and profit-driven MFIs. However, it is an important process for the whole sector to become regulated. A challenge for the microfinance institutions has been that they are operating in a comparatively new field. When striving to gain legitimacy, it is common that organisations within the same field become increasingly similar to each other (DiMaggio and Powell 1983). The formality of organisations tends to contribute to legitimacy, rather than just function as a formal structure for coordination and control. The survival of organisations thus depends on their ability to conform to given institutions and myths in their context. In order to gain legitimacy, they also have to be seen as legitimate within and outside the organisation. In order to be perceived as legitimate, and to handle external pressure, organisations often separate the formal structures from practical work activities. (Meyer and Rowan 1977). The microfinance sector is still in the process of gaining legitimacy through governmental regulation, and the actors are still in the process of conforming to each other. It is important for the MFIs to gain legitimacy from both clients, policymakers, and international donors and other actors. As the sector gains legitimacy, it also legitimates the venturing operations of the individual, who is taking micro loans. This is a good thing, especially for women entrepreneurs. At the same time, the sector is still partly immature, and clients are sometimes mistreated when formal structures are ignored by loan officers having their own agenda.

Another common way for women entrepreneurs in Tanzania to finance a business start-up is by using SACCOS, Savings and Credit Cooperatives. They function as voluntary cooperatives, where participants on a regular basis pool their savings, and together let the participants take loans for individual purposes. A main idea is to encourage individuals to save money, and thus enable later investments. SACCOS are either community based, where members live in the same area, or based on some other sort of common bond, such as sharing the same workplace or going to the same church (Bwana and Mwakujonga 2013). Similar to SACCOS are ROSCAS, Rotating Savings and Credit Associations, sometimes referred to as Rural Savings and Credit Associations, as they are more common in rural areas (Piprek 2007). Here, the members of the association contribute a fixed amount to a common pool on a regular basis. Every time the group meets, the pool is given to one of the members, and the order of members getting the pool can be decided in different ways, for example through lottery or negotiation (Callier 1989). Both SACCOS and ROSCAS are, to some extent, formal institutions, as they are under the control of authorities. At the same time, the core of their functions is built on trust and social capital between individuals, rather than on formal regulation.

The most important sources of capital for women entrepreneurs in Tanzania, come from those who are closely connected to the woman. In addition to savings, entrepreneurs use loans or grants from family and friends (Olomi 2009). This is not unique for developing countries, but a common strategy among new or small firms all over the world (Levie and Lerner 2009). In Tanzania, a negligibly small number of women entrepreneurs will grow to large, professional firms and meet the requirements of commercial banks. Instead, they remain strongly dependent on informal sources, which is also a socially and culturally accepted starting point for a new venture. The absolute majority continues to operate at a small scale, and thus remains dependent on informal linkages to family members, friends and other acquaintances (Adler and Kwon 2002). As the formal institutions are weak, and financial institutions fail to meet the needs of a large proportion of entrepreneurs, it is a natural effect that informal institutions play a more important role, as people are forced to rely on informal family bonds (Tsai 2000).

In sum, the institutional, cultural and contextual preconditions discussed above, shape and create opportunities and constraints for women who wish to develop as entrepreneurs. As women have the potential to play a crucial role for the economic growth of their society, it is important to remember that these preconditions do not only have an impact on individual decisions, but will impact on the development of the whole country.

## Stories of How Women Entrepreneurs Fail and Succeed When Reaching for Resources

In this section, stories from women who search for capital and other resources for their venturing are presented. These stories were collected during a field study in Morogoro, a town with approximately 200,000 inhabitants and located 200 km west of Dar es Salaam. A total of 21 semi-structured interviews were conducted with women who operated micro businesses, defined as having less than ten employees. They were operating within the service sector (for example, hairdressers, tailors, small hotels) or in trade (clothing shops, food stores, and similar business). They were all major owners and their ventures generated their main source of income.

According to Welter (2011), we are likely to better interpret the importance of context in a place where we are an outsider, rather than in a place we are familiar with, and thus take for granted. I believe that this was an advantage for me when conducting the field study and analysing data, as I was previously unfamiliar with the Tanzanian context. All interviews were conducted together with a local research assistant, which was valuable as she could help, not only to interpret the interviews, but also to explain what was going on in the context and to help me "read between the lines". Interviews were complemented with participant observation, and as I had the privilege to live with local families, I had a great opportunity to study informal institutions in the Tanzanian context.

### *High Barriers to Formal Capital*

As discussed above, there are high barriers for the studied group of entrepreneurs towards formal capital and none of the respondents in this study had ever used commercial bank loans. Most of them never even considered this as a serious alternative, as they were well aware of their own lack of collateral. Only one, Witness, who is running a restaurant and catering service, had actually tried to take bank loans, as she is working to expand her business. *"Yes, I've been going to the banks, but they want a house as collateral. Those who accept this [business] as collateral are those who only provide small loans, the micro banks. But banks, they ask for a house as collateral. [...] When you get a big loan, you can do many things."* Many women are not only hindered by lack of collateral, but also by their own feelings of fear and insecurity. Fatima, who owns a clothing shop, says that she wants to go to the bank, but that she *"does not know how it works."* Upendo, who runs a shop selling car spare parts, expresses that she is afraid of getting loans and does not want to be involved in any formal institutions. *"I have never taken any loan from any bank or institution. First of all, I don't dare going there [...] I am afraid."* And yet, despite feelings of insecurity towards the formal institutions, when asked, about half of the respondents express that they would prefer to take commercial bank loans. The major reasons are that banks offer bigger loans than the micro banks, and that loans are based on the capacity of the individual instead of the loan group.

***Micro Loans Create Opportunities, but also Frustration and Conflicts***

The micro finance institutions play an important role in providing capital, and the sector has grown rapidly in Tanzania during the last decades. It is a common starting point for women when entering entrepreneurship. Witness, who wanted commercial bank loans, acknowledges the importance of micro loans for her: *"I am totally depending on micro loans. For me, there are no other sources of capital."* She also points out the importance of loans, as the MFIs require regular meetings with their clients, where they get training. *"When I was taking that loan from PRIDE, they were educating people [in bookkeeping] before they get the loan. This is important for the business operations."* This also legitimates the business towards family as well as clients.

The typical process of micro loans is to start with a small amount, and gradually, as the business develops and the client proves to be reliable and trustworthy, builds up to bigger loan amounts. Nmzera, who is offering wedding catering services, explains: *"I started with a loan of 200,000 [TSH], and then I took 400,000. And then up to 800,000. This is how it works."* Before taking the first loan, she got two days of business training, and during the meetings for repayments, the training continued: *"You must have an exercise book and a pen, and they teach you how to go about with the money, and how to do this or that kind of business. It is good training, it helps you to run your business in a better way."* Even if the micro loans offer opportunities for business development, they also create conflicts and frustrations. Nmzera continues: *"It is very important that you know everyone in your loan group. Otherwise, there can be a problem. For example, if there is a new woman that you don't know and she fails to repay, you and the rest of the group will have to pay for her. So, you have to know everyone, and know where they are living, so that you can do follow up if someone fails."* Many of the loan clients are frustrated with the group function, but also because it is time consuming to meet for repayments and training. Sometimes meetings are every week, sometimes every second week, time which could be spent in the business or with family. Not surprisingly, the absolute majority of respondents would prefer individual loans.

Another serious situation is when family needs get too burdensome and the woman feels pressured to use some of the loan capital for other purposes than investing in the business. Philomena, a widow with the responsibility for her two children and two other young relatives, found herself using a large part of the loan for school fees. *"I just can't save any money. There are too many needs – school fees and bus fares to school for the children every day, and money for food and other needs at home* [...] *It is very difficult for me, and yet I am trying to repay the loan."*

### *Family – Providing Support or Demanding Support?*

Just like for any other group of entrepreneurs, own savings are important when setting up a venture. Savings are often combined with capital or other resources from family or friends. However, the importance of emotional support and encouragement should not be underestimated, and many of the respondents express how, for example, encouragement from their mother or husband helped them to take the first step towards entrepreneurship. Ebitha is selling make-up and women clothing and has two different stores. The major source of capital came from her own savings, but her husband has assisted with *"good advice and he paid rent for the first store."* She also values discussions with other women entrepreneurs, as they support each other with encouragement and advice.

For Witness, there has never been any support from family or friends when it comes to resource acquisition, quite the opposite. She is a widow, and in her household of seven people, she is the only one who brings an income which has to cover expenses for food, housing, and school fees for her son and her younger siblings. She says that she never borrowed money from family or friends, and that *"there is no one to rely on."* Grace, who is operating a beauty salon, is supported by her husband. He encouraged her to get started, and is also assisting with money sometimes. Yet, she feels strong pressure to provide for her extended family, and little money can be saved from her income. *"Unfortunately, most of my savings from last year was used for school fees for my younger brother."* She continues by explaining how her relatives put pressure on her to assist them with different things, as they have seen her costumers coming, and they know that she is making some money. For her, it has been important to get support from friends. One of them gave her a loan, and others assist with good advice: *"I discuss a lot with friends, like with the cosmetics, what the clients prefer, or how to run the business, or if I am thinking about making any changes. I often get good advice from them."* Trinity, who recently opened her clothing shop, is divorced and is solely responsible for four children. She has not taken any micro loans and found no support from family members. A close friend of hers gave her a loan, big enough to enable her to get started: *"It's a close friend, who has seen the way I was eager to start this. He thought that, 'if I just give her the loan, she can start this'."*

Upendo, the lady selling car spare parts, got her start-up capital from her mother. When her mother retired, she called on her children and gave them small amounts of money from what she had, which helped Upendo to enter business. Even though the business is profitable, she is struggling to meet all family needs. Her husband has been a drunkard for many years, which creates different problems for the family. She finds little support from social networks outside the family, but says that *"my children participate, especially my oldest son. They have got some role in my business."*

### *Formal Support is Needed*

Within the studied group of entrepreneurs, it is clear that the majority started their businesses out of necessity, because life is difficult and there are many family needs to meet. This does not mean that they lack ambitions or driving forces to develop their ventures to grow bigger. When asked about what they think is the best thing with being self-employed, most of them actually answer that they most of all enjoy the freedom and feeling of independence. As Witness said: *"You are free! And you meet with different people!"*

In the Tanzanian context, it is obvious that informal institutions still play a crucial role for these women, as they tend to rely on different kinds of resources and support from family and friends. However, the same informal institutions simultaneously put up barriers and hamper their potential to grow. Women are expected to take great responsibility for children's needs, and this is, of course, particularly challenging for those who are widows or divorced. As the Tanzanian culture is deeply family-oriented, women are also under pressure from extended family members.

Even though women who are using micro loans do acknowledge its benefits, and realise that these loans create opportunities for them to get into venturing, it also creates conflicts and frustration. The micro banks can be seen as a combination of formal and informal institutions, as they operate in a formal way and are under state authorities, and at the same time are founded on the client's ability to network and build trust to each other. This is the major reason why the majority of them would prefer individual loans and is striving for capital from formal institutions. When asked about what they think is needed for the development of women's entrepreneurship in Tanzania, the answers are almost identical. Virtually everyone requires formal support from the government. As Trinity said: *"The government should give women who are running a small business good loans with low interest, and then give them seminars on how to run their businesses."* Ebitha expressed both frustration and hope, as she concluded:

> It is important to improve the situation for women, especially with good loans. Women are capable of doing business, but we need education and loans. Many women are just staying at home, having nothing to do, and are just living bad lives [...] Even those who are married, they often get many problems from their husbands. So with good education and support, they can do something in their lives.

## Summary and Recommendations

In this chapter, preconditions for women entrepreneurs in Tanzania have been discussed, with a focus on barriers they are facing when acquiring capital and other resources. Drawing on institutional theory, the discussion was based on how formal and informal institutions create both opportunities and restrictions for women, but also on how women entrepreneurs actually manage to reach and use resources for their venturing. As stated by Welter (2011), the individual behaviour has to be interpreted in relation to contextual preconditions, and these can be experienced as both asset and liability, which definitely is the case among the studied entrepreneurs. With formal institutions being weak and underdeveloped in the Tanzanian context, where formal banks fail to provide services to women operating their businesses, informal institutions play a significant role. Yet, the majority of the women entrepreneurs ask for reliable, formal financial services and support, as they depreciate to rely on informal sources from family or friends. Results also show that the women tend to be very negative towards the loan group function, as they dislike the dependency on the collective group. As shown from the stories above, women in Tanzania struggle with a number of challenges when searching for capital, from both formal and informal levels. Still, they manage to find resources and develop their ventures, thanks to a combination of different methods. They often show high degrees of networking abilities, use of social capital and other types of informal solutions.

As women have the potential to fundamentally contribute to the development of the society, it is of urgent importance to support their venturing. As required by the respondents in this study, one of the crucial aspects for policymakers is to establish reliable loans with fair conditions. This needs to be combined with better education and training for women. The microfinance sector has given numerous women the opportunity to pursue entrepreneurial ideas, but needs to be further improved to better meet the needs of the individual loan taker. Even more important is to address gender related attitudes and discrimination in the society as a whole. As discussed above, women do not only face general financial challenges, but also challenges based on gender bias. This needs to be taken seriously, at family, community, national and international levels, in order to release women's full capacity and creativity.

## References


Adler, P.S. & S. Kwon. (2002). "Social Capital: Prospects for a New Concept", *Academy of Management Review,* Vol. 27(1), 17–40.

Amine, L.S. & K.M. Staub. (2009). "Women Entrepreneurs in Sub-Saharan Africa: An Institutional Theory Analysis from a Social Marketing Point of View", *Entrepreneurship and Regional Development,* Vol. 21(2), 183–211.

Bennett, J. (2010). "Informal Firms in Developing Countries: Entrepreneurial Stepping Stone or Consolation Prize?" *Small Business Economics,* Vol. 34(1), 53–63.

Berger, P. & T. Luckman. (1966). *The Social Construction of Reality.* Garden City, NY: Doubleday.

Bhatt, N. & S. Tang. (1998). "The Problem of Transaction Costs in Group-based Microlending: An Institutional Perspective", *World Development,* Vol. 26 (4), 623–637.

Brush, C., Carter, N., Gatewood, E., Greene, P. & M. Hart (eds). (2006). *Growth-oriented Women Entrepreneurs and their Businesses: A Global Research Perspective,* Edward Elgar: Cheltenham.

Brush, C., De Bruin, A. & F. Welter. (2009). "A Gender-aware Framework for Women's Entrepreneurship", *International Journal of Gender and Entrepreneurship,* vol. 1(1), 8–24.

Brush, C.G. & S.Y. Cooper. (2012). "Female Entrepreneurship and Economic Development: An International Perspective", *Entrepreneurship and Regional Development,* 24(1–2), 1–6.

Bruton, G.D., Ketchen, D.J. & R.D. Ireland. (2013). "Entrepreneurship as a Solution to Poverty", *Journal of Business Venturing*, vol. 28(6), 683–689.

Bwana, K.M. & J. Mwakujonga. (2013). "Issues in SACCOS Development in Kenya and Tanzania: The Historical and Development Perspectives", *Developing Country Studies*, vol. 3(5), 114–121.

Callier, P. (1989). "Informal Finance: The Rotating Saving and Credit Association – An Interpretation," *KYKLOS*, vol. 43(2), 273–276.

Chittenden, F., Hall, G. & P. Hutchinson. (1996). "Small Firm Growth, Access to Capital Markets and Financial Structure: Review of Issues and an Empirical Investigation", *Small Business Economics*, vol. 8(1), 59–67.

*CIA World Fact Book* (2015). Downloaded 2016-07-07 at https://www.cia.gov/library/publications/the-world-factbook/geos/tz.html.

De Bruin, A., Brush, A.C. & F. Welter. (2006). "Introduction to the Special Issue: Towards Building Cumulative Knowledge on Woman's Entrepreneurship", *Entrepreneurship Theory and Practice* 30(5), 585–593.

De Bruin, A., Brush, C.G. & F. Welter. (2007). "Advancing a Framework for Coherent Research on Women's Entrepreneurship", *Entrepreneurship Theory and Practice*, 31(3), 323–339.

D'Espallier, B., Guérin, I. & R. Mersland. (2011). "Women and Repayment in Microfinance: A Global Analysis", *World Development*, vol. 39(5), 758–772.

Dijkgraaff, E. (2007). "Women Entrepreneurs – A Challenge to a Gendered Economy". In: L.E. Lucas (ed.), *Unpacking Globalization – Markets, Gender and Work*. Plymouth: Lexington Books.

DiMaggio, P.J. & W.W. Powell. (1983). "The Iron Cage Revisited: Institutional Isomorphism and Collective Rationality in Organizational Fields", *American Sociological Review*, vol. 48(2), 147–160.

Granovetter, M. (1973). "The Strength of Weak Ties", *American Journal of Sociology*, vol. 78(6), 1360–1380.

Granovetter, M. (1985). "Economic Action and Social Structure: The Problem of Embeddedness", *American Journal of Sociology*, vol. 91(3), 481–510.

Haile, H.B., Bock, B. & H. Folmer. (2012). "Microfinance and Female Empowerment: Do Institutions Matter?" *Women's Studies International Forum*, vol. 35(4), 256–265.

Jeppersson, R.L. (1991). "Institutions, Institutional Effects, and Institutionalism". In: W.W. Powell & P.J. DiMaggio (eds), *The New Institutionalism in Organizational Analysis*. Chicago, IL: The University of Chicago Press.

Johnson, S. (2004). "Gender Norms in Financial Markets: Evidence from Kenya", *World Development*, vol. 32(8), 1355–1374.

Landström, H. (2000). *Entreprenörskapets rötter*, 2nd Edition, Lund: Studentlitteratur.

Levie, J. & M. Lerner. (2009). "Resource Mobilization and Performance in Family and Nonfamily Businesses in the United Kingdom", *Family Business Review*, vol. 22(1), 25–38.

Lindvert, M., Yazdanfar, D. & H. Boter. (2015). "Perceptions of Financial Sources among Women Entrepreneurs in Tanzania", *African Journal of Economic and Management Studies*, vol. 6(2), 197–218.

Matin, I., Hulme, D. & S. Rutherford. (2002). "Finance for the Poor: From Microcredit to Microfinancial Services", *Journal of International Development*, vol. 14(2), 273–294.

Mayoux, L. (2001). "Tackling the Down Side: Social Capital, Women's Empowerment and Micro-Finance in Cameroon", *Development and Change*, vol. 32(3), 435–464.

Meyer, J.W. & B. Rowan. (1977). "Institutionalized Organizations: Formal Structure as Myth and Ceremony", *American Journal of Sociology*, vol. 83(2), 340–363.

Morewagae, B.S., Seemule, M. & H. Rempel. (1995). "Access to Credit for Non-Formal Micro-Enterprises in Botswana", *Journal of Development Studies*, vol. 31(3), 481–504.

Nchimbi, M. & M.M. Chijoriga. (2009). "Gender and Entrepreneurship". In: D.R. Olomi (ed.), *African Entrepreneurship and Small Business Development*. Dar es Salaam: Otme Company Limited.

North, D.C. (1990). *Institutions, Institutional Change and Economic Performance*. New York: Cambridge University Press.

Ogunrinola, I.O. (2011). "Social Capital and Earnings Distribution among Female Micro-entrepreneurs in Rural Nigeria", *African Journal of Economic and Management Studies*, vol. 2(1), 94–113.

Olomi, D.R. (ed.) (2009). *African Entrepreneurship and Small Business Development*. Dar es Salaam: Otme Company Limited.

Olomi, D.R., Chijoriga, M.M. & N. Mori. (2009). "Micro-Finance". In: Olomi D.R. (ed.), *African Entrepreneurship and Small Business Development*. Dar es Salaam: Otme Company Limited.

Pedersen, P.O. (2001). "East African Microenterprises Negotiating Social Space – An Introduction". In: P.O. Alila & P.O. Pedersen (eds), *Negotiating Social Space – East African Micro Enterprises*. Asmara: Africa World Press.

Piprek, G. (2007). Linking with Savings and Credit Cooperatives (SACCOS) to Expand Financial Access in Rural Areas: A Case Study of CRDB Bank in Tanzania, working document, Rural Finance Group of the Food and Agriculture Organization (FAO) of the United Nations.

Satta, T.A. (2003). "Enterprise Characteristics and Constraints in Developing Countries: Evidence from a Sample of Tanzanian Micro and Small-scale Enterprises", *International Journal of Entrepreneurship and Innovation*, vol. 4(3), 175–184.

Schumpeter, J.A. (1934). *The Theory of Economic Development*. Boston, MA: Harvard University Press.

Scott, W.R. (1995). *Institutions and Organizations*. Thousand Oaks, CA: Sage Publications.

SIDA (2009). *Women's Economic Empowerment: Scope for Sida's Engagement*, SIDA working paper, publication series: Stockholm: Women's Economic Empowerment. 30 December.

Sigalla, R.J. & S. Carney. (2012). "Poverty Reduction through Entrepreneurship: Microcredit, Learning and Ambivalence amongst Women in Urban Tanzania", *International Journal of Educational Development*, vol. 32(4), 546–554.

Spring, A. (2009). "African Women in the Entrepreneurial Landscape: Reconsidering the Formal and Informal Sectors", *Journal of African Business*, vol. 10(1), 11–30.

Ssendi, L. & A.R. Anderson. (2009). "Tanzanian Enterprises and Micro Finance: The Role and Impact for Poor Rural Women", *The Journal of Entrepreneurship*, vol. 18(1), 1–19.

Tsai, W. (2000). "Social Capital, Strategic Relatedness and the Formation of Intraorganizational Linkages", *Strategic Management Journal*, vol. 21(9), 925–939.

Valliere, D. & R. Peterson. (2009). "Entrepreneurship and Economic Growth: Evidence from Emerging and Developed Countries", *Entrepreneurship and Regional Development*, vol. 21(5–6), 459–480.

Van Praag, C.M. & P.H. Versloot. (2007). "What is the Value of Entrepreneurship? A Review of Recent Research", *Small Business Economy*, vol. 29(4), 351–382.

Welter, F. (2011). "Contextualizing Entrepreneurship – Conceptual Challenges and Ways Forward", *Entrepreneurship Theory and Practice*, vol. 35(1), 165–184.

Welter, F. & D. Smallbone. (2008). "Women's Entrepreneurship from an Institutional Perspective; the Case of Uzbekistan", *International Entrepreneurship Management Journal*, vol. 4 (4), 505–520.

Welter, F. & D. Smallbone. (2011). "Institutional Perspectives on Entrepreneurial Behavior in Challenging Environments", *Journal of Small Business Management*, vol. 49(1), 107–125.

Whetten, D.A. (1989). "What Constitutes a Theoretical Contribution?" *Academy of Management Review*, vol. 14(4), 490–495.

CHAPTER 16

# Gentlemanly Capitalism and Entrepreneurial Management: Formation and Rise of Nigeria's Guaranty Trust Bank, 1990–2002

*Ayodeji Olukoju*

## Introduction

The establishment in 1929 of Nigeria's first indigenous bank, the Industrial and Commercial Bank (ICB) and its demise in 1930 (Newlyn and Rowan 1954; Hopkins 1966; Uche 2010: 473–474),[1] and the establishment in 1990 of the Guaranty Trust Bank (initially known as "GTB" and currently as "GTBank" – used interchangeably in this essay) provide two instances of insurgent banking in different epochs. However, the contrasting fortunes of the two enterprises – the ICB collapsed within a year while the GTBank became a leading indigenous bank within a decade – mask striking parallels in their emergence.

Firstly, both were insurgent pathfinders, challengers to an established order in the banking sector. The ICB was confronted (and overwhelmed) by the dominance of expatriate banks, which enjoyed the support of the British colonial government and expatriate business. For its part, GTBank emerged in a prevailing business environment characterised by stifling unethical business practices. Secondly, both banks were birthed in hostile and unstable macroeconomic environments: the Great Depression (1929–1933), on the one hand, and, on the other, the economic upheaval of the 1980s–1990s, aggravated by a dubious Structural Adjustment Programme (SAP) that devastated the Nigerian economy (Olukoshi 1994; Hamalai 1999; Umoren 2001). Thirdly, ICB and GTBank were founded in two non-democratic contexts: autocratic British colonial rule and draconian military rule from 1983 to 1999, respectively. It was

1 A version of this paper was presented at the Conference on "African Economic Development: Past, Present, and Future", Harvard University, 17–18 April 2015. I thank the conference participants for their insightful comments. I am indebted to Tayo Aderinokun, late co-founder of GTBank, for access to confidential source material and interviewees, to Paul Osifodunrin and Omon Osiki for excellent research assistance, and Chibuike Uche for some important reference material. This essay is dedicated to the memory of my late wife, Abosede Omowumi Olukoju, nee Olorunda (1961–2014).

 | DOI 10.1163/9789004351615_017

in the face of these odds that the two banks operated sixty years apart with divergent outcomes.

The literature on indigenous entrepreneurship in Nigeria[2] has established the high mortality rate of indigenous trading and banking enterprises during the colonial period up till the late 1940s (Forrest 1994; Harneit-Sievers 1996; Olukoju 2002, 2014). Most of these enterprises did not survive the death of their founders. Attempts to establish joint stock companies did not fare better. Of the 27 indigenous banks established between 1929 and 1959, only National Bank, Agbonmagbe Bank and the African Continental Bank, founded in 1933, 1945 and 1947, respectively, survived.[3] This has been attributed to the following factors.

First, the market environment, dominated by expatriate banks, was hostile to the survival of embryonic indigenous competition. Second, the indigenous banks were grossly under-capitalised. Third, the available funds were mismanaged, embezzled, and insider credit and loans were afforded to unviable businesses. Fourth, the promoters of the banks lacked the requisite professional experience and, in several instances, personal integrity (Newlyn and Rowan 1954: 97–98; Ndekwu 1994: 72; Uche 2010: 467, 473–474). "The so-called 'bankers'," Ndekwu (1994: 72) noted, "could not distinguish between capital and income. Most of the 'mushroom' bankers [...] were neither experienced in banking management nor did they prepare themselves for the banking business." We shall see later how promoters and managers of GTBank surmounted the aforementioned obstacles.

Founded in 1990, GTBank, currently one of the top five banks in Nigeria, is now well established in the other English-speaking countries of West Africa: The Gambia, Sierra Leone, Ghana and Liberia. Its formation and phenomenal expansion in the vortex of military rule, the Structural Adjustment Programme (SAP) and tottering financial institutions presents a new face/phase of Nigerian business that is multinational and competitive. Within a decade of its founding, GTBank recorded some remarkable accomplishments, unprecedented in the Nigerian context (Maklan and Knox 2009; Ogunbiyi 2010: 113–114). These "feats and firsts", as the bank tagged them, include the following: the first Nigerian bank to attain an AA-Fitch rating (2005); the first enterprise to attain the ISO 9001 rating; the first to be listed on the London Stock Exchange (2007); the first bank to adopt the Customer Relationship Management CRM approach in

2 In the context of this paper, entrepreneurs are defined as "persons who are ingenious and creative in finding ways that add to their own wealth, power, and prestige." See, Baumol (1990: 987).

3 Uche, 2010: 469 (Table 1), lists the banks.

its operations; the first West African bank to adopt a total banking solution via its GT Connect, a fully interactive self-service contact centre; the first Nigerian bank to record a profit before tax (PBT) of N1.01 billion (1996), N2 billion (2001) and over N10 billion (2006); and the first indigenous Nigerian bank to establish subsidiaries in other West African countries (The Gambia and Sierra Leone, 2002; Ghana, 2006; Liberia, 2009), in addition to one in London in 2008.

Based on research into the first twelve years of the bank, this paper reflects on a major problematique – the challenge of building credible and competitive financial institutions in colonial and post-independence Nigeria. GTBank's success contrasts with the fate of many family businesses and indigenous banks during (and since) the colonial period. The paper thus provides perspectives on transformations in Nigerian capitalism. It challenges the uncritical narrative in GTBank's official history (Ogunbiyi 2010),[4] and fills gaps in case studies of its development, all of which focus on the post-2002 history of the bank (Knox and Maklan 2005; Maklan and Knox 2009; Maklan, Antonetti and Knox 2014). It draws upon an extensive collection of documentary evidence – previously inaccessible private papers and minutes of meetings of GTBank's board of directors, and newspaper reports – and interviews with the promoters and foundation staff of the bank.[5] The paper re-appraises the roles of the key personalities in the formation and development of the bank. It also highlights how GTBank surmounted various challenges as its stock rose dramatically on the Nigerian economic landscape. Key to its success is the managerial entrepreneurship[6] of its co-founders, whose duumvirate leadership model epitomised the innovativeness of their enterprise. The formation and rise of GTBank exemplify three connected aspects of entrepreneurship as identified by two authors: "*what* happens when entrepreneurs act: *why* they act; and *how* they act." (Stevenson and Jarillo 1990:18).

The interest in GTBank is predicated on some of its unique features. Firstly, the role of friendship, shared career and professional experiences, marital ties and business partnership, as exemplified by the co-founders, Fola Adeola

4 This source lacks details on the founding of GTBank and omits the potentially crippling challenges of the bank discussed in this paper.

5 While this author interviewed all core GTBank Promoters, the author of the bank's commissioned history could not reach the co-founder, Fola Adeola (Ogunbiyi 2010: XVIII). The absence of such a critical stakeholder from the conversation created a significant gap in the narrative. This writer's interview with Adeola revealed, among other things that, contrary to the popular narrative, tension simmered below the surface in the much vaunted relationship between the two co-founders. The oral evidence used in this paper has yielded information unrecorded in documentary evidence and clarified certain issues.

6 See an illuminating analysis of this concept in Stevenson and Jarillo (1990).

and Tayo Aderinokun. Cain and Hopkins' study of the City of London and the driving force of "gentlemanly capitalism" highlighted this human factor in successful business partnerships. "By the 1890s," they noted, "the great merchant bankers not only shared a similar educational background with aristocrats and leading professionals but also were regularly intermarrying with the landed interest." (Cain and Hopkins 2002: 124) Secondly, the uniqueness of the corporate culture of the bank and the business strategies developed in the face of the peculiar challenges of the decade of its establishment. Thirdly, its unique duumvirate leadership model, which served it well in the first twelve years and ensured a smooth transition, has been replicated by two of its alumni in another bank.

## Friendship, Trust and Business Partnership: The Establishment of Guaranty Trust Bank

As is well established in the literature, GTBank was founded by two longstanding friends, who later became its foundation Managing Director (MD) and Deputy Managing Director (DMD), respectively. However, such a story line over-simplifies the process of the gestation and delivery of the bank. Oral evidence obtained from the principal actors confirmed that the idea of setting up the bank was mooted by Adeola, who shared the vision with his friend, Aderinokun. Victor Gbolade Osibodu, Akindele Akintoye and the frontline merchant and industrialist, Aliko Dangote, had, on different occasions, urged Adeola to consider forming a bank given his acknowledged expertise. Adeola and Aderinokun were joined by Osibodu and Akintoye at this early stage of envisioning the proposed bank. It was this quartet that finalised the shape of the bank.[7]

Akintoye reminisced that he hosted a crucial meeting that resolved two critical issues – whether the proposed bank would be a merchant or a commercial bank, and what name it should bear. "Guarantee Trust", coined by Adeola, was reframed as "Guaranty Trust" at Osibodu's insistence, in order to depict the ethos of the proposed bank. This would also produce the acronym "GTB", which would easily register with the banking public. However, against the expectations of Adeola and Aderinokun, the meeting decided to establish a commercial bank.

7 The discussion in this and the following paragraphs draws on interviews in Lagos with Adeola (14 October 2004), Aderinokun (26 September 2004), Osibodu (12 October 2004) and Akintoye (27 October 2004).

The relative ease with which these issues were resolved underscores the role of personal friendship, trust and shared background in business partnerships. Cain and Hopkins (2002: 122–123) noted that the City of London "depended as heavily upon networks of social intercourse as it did upon formal structures [...] [,] an intricate world where business, social life and political intrigue all overlapped." The GTBank experience paralleled the world of The City in the following ways.

First, the core Promoters – Adeola, Aderinokun and Bode Agusto – had been friends since attending high school at St. Gregory's College, Obalende, Lagos. Aderinokun married Agusto's sister, who had been Adeola's classmate at the Methodist Boys' High School, Lagos. Their paths later crossed in the job market. This shared background oiled the process leading to the success of the bank. Adeola aptly remarked that secondary school bonding "never extinguishes."[8]

A second bonding element was Adeola and Aderinokun's common professional development in the banking sector, in which they had risen to management level. After initially following different employment paths, they re-united at the Chase Merchant Bank (renamed Continental Merchant Bank). Aderinokun later moved to Prime Merchant Bank, but he quit after six months owing to disenchantment with the running of the bank. Significantly, it was at Prime that he met Aigboje Aig-Imoukhuede, whom he later recruited into GTBank.

A thorny issue, about which we have no details, is the power-sharing agreement between Adeola and Aderinokun at the bank's inception. But some inferences can be drawn from anecdotes and remarks made by both men during separate interviews. While Adeola laid claim to the office of Managing Director (MD) as the originator of the idea, Aderinokun, who had borne the brunt of the groundwork for the take-off of the proposed bank, thought he was more deserving of it. A compromise was for both men to become Executive Directors (ED) of the bank at inception. Eventually, Adeola emerged as MD, but agreed to share every other benefit equally with Aderinokun, who became Deputy Managing Director. Their remarkable partnership was pivotal to the stability and growth of the bank.

The partnership was a blend of two contrasting personalities. Adeola was the more boisterous, endowed with excellent communication and networking skills, while Aderinokun was more subdued and inclined to focus on details and tie loose ends. Their twelve years of partnership, which proved critical to the overall success of the enterprise, was described as follows: "Adeola was

---

8 Adeola, interview cited. Cain and Hopkins (2002: 124) also alluded to how the London Stock Exchange was "run by former public schoolboys in a club-like atmosphere and ruled by gentlemanly codes of behaviour."

the public face of GTB, Aderinokun was the engine house." (Famakinwa 2004) Such complementarity of character and disposition produced the synergy that drove the GTB machine up to 2002.

The aforementioned informal social networks and shared professional experiences laid the foundation of trust[9] critical to the formation of GTBank. This is made clearer in the following examination of the formation and consolidation of the bank.

## Recruiting Investors and Getting a Banking Licence

The birthing of the GTB entailed raising funds, securing an operating licence from the government, recruiting staff, and acquiring office accommodation. Between February 1989 and July 1990, the core promoters held 28 meetings, according to records kept by Akin Akintoye.[10] Recruiting likely investors was a major task as the promoters were men of ideas without the financial resources to raise the huge deposit of N20 million ($US 2.5 million) required by the Central Bank of Nigeria (CBN). In keeping with the resolve to maintain high ethical standards from the start, the promoters decided to enlist only investors whose sources of income could be ascertained to be untainted. An initial list of 150 persons, mainly professionals, was screened. A final shortlist of 42 names survived the exercise and formal invitations were forwarded to the prospective investors to pay up their shares within a stated time limit.

Direct and indirect approaches were made to prospective investors. GTBank promoters refused to conform to the norm of getting a retired military or paramilitary officer, or a notable politician to serve on the Board of Directors to facilitate the acquisition of a banking licence. Adeola, for example, attracted Adetokunbo Adesanya, a lawyer with some knowledge of banking, with whom he shared an intellectual interest in philosophy, and Ifeyinwa Nwakwesi, a medical doctor and entrepreneur, whom he had dealt with as a customer at Chase Merchant Bank. She claimed to have known from the outset that the venture

9 Cain and Hopkins (2002: 121), citing Gann and Duignan (1978: 69), stated that the Crown Agents "operated via an informal, even secretive, network of financial institutions in the City 'on the basis of trust of a kind that could only exist in a society where private business and public administration were linked by informal ties of school, class and clubland'."

10 Tayo Aderinokun Papers (TAP), Akintoye to MD, First Marina Trust, 7 August 1990, in File "G.T.B. – Application and Approval for Banking Licence". All letters exchanged in 1989 and 1990 cited below are in this file, in the possession of Tayo Aderinokun. Akintoye was the *de facto* Secretary to the inaugural board of GTB.

was going to be successful since "all the fundamentals were there [...] and Fola and Tayo knew exactly what they were going to do with the Bank."[11] Nwakwesi's recruitment satisfied the requirements of affirmative action – gender balance and "federal character" (representation of different parts of Nigeria).

Yet, a few politicians got in. For example, Muhammed K. Jada from Adamawa State was recruited by Akin Kekere-Ekun, MD of Habib Bank. Kekere-Ekun had been approached by Adeola to recruit persons of integrity within his political network from Northern Nigeria. Ironically, Jada made the final list but Kekere-Ekun did not.[12] Mosobalaje Oyawoye, Nigeria's first Professor of Geology, who later became the second Chairman of the Board of Directors, was also invited by proxy. Though he had served as Chairman of the Kaduna Refinery Limited and in a few other public capacities, he got in as a representative of a serving official who could not invest in such an enterprise while still in public service.[13] The foundation Chairman, Chief J.K. Agbaje, was the first Nigerian Executive Director of the leading bank in Nigeria, Standard Bank (later nationalised as First Bank).[14] He was recruited for the strategic purpose of facilitating the procurement of the banking licence by lending his credibility and deploying his influence as a highly respected retired banker. Adeola acknowledged at Agbaje's retirement party, without elaboration, that he was "instrumental in obtaining a banking licence for the bank."[15] Osibodu, like Aderinokun, was a friend of Chief Agbaje's son, whom he persuaded to help recruit his father.[16] The process of applying for the banking licence and getting investors to pay up was coordinated by Aderinokun, then MD of First Marina Trust, who corresponded with the proposed investors at each stage of the exercise. A critical stage in the process was a formal interview at the CBN on 7 December 1989. The promoters adequately prepared the bank's representatives for the interview, emphasising its six "unique selling points."[17]

The first was the dispersion of ownership: it was not "any one man's Bank". Second, unlike many other new-generation banks, it had a "strong technical base". Fourteen of its 41 promoters were serving or retired senior bankers. Third, its operations would be technology driven to raise bank services in Nigeria to

11 Dr. (Mrs) I.I. Nwakwesi, interviewed on 12 January 2005.

12 Alhaji M.K. Jada, interviewed on 8 October 2004.

13 Professor M.O. Oyawoye, interviewed on 21 September 2004.

14 Guaranty Trust Bank Library, Lagos (GTBL), Minutes of Board Meeting, 12 April 1995, Min. 10.5.

15 GTBL, Minutes of Board Meeting, 12 April 1995, Min. 10.5.

16 Osibodu, interview cited.

17 TAP, Aderinokun to Select Group of Promoters, 28 November 1989, enc. "Guaranty Trust Bank: Briefing for CBN Interview – Core Points to Stress".

international standards. Fourth, the subscribers were "men and women of proven integrity and high professional standards." Among them were legal and medical practitioners, entrepreneurs and bankers. Fifth, the proposed bank would assist in meeting government's objectives, especially promoting small and medium scale enterprises. Finally, the bank's branch expansion programme would cover Kano, Rivers, Anambra, Imo, and Oyo States.[18]

In March 1990, the promoters were requested to pay the sum of N20 million, the proposed bank's equity capital with the Central Bank of Nigeria (CBN), so that the Honourable Minister of Finance and Economic Development could present the application for consideration by the Federal Executive Council. Prospective investors paid between N500,000 and N1 million apiece, depending on their means. At the end of the day, those who paid N500,000 were allotted 2.5 per cent shares, while those who contributed N1 million got 5 per cent, the highest possible allotment.

Musing on initial investors' commitment of large sums of money to a 35-year old banker, Adeola recalled his apprehension much later, when considering what might have been if the venture had failed. He likened his situation to that of a survivor of a fatal accident who, realising his near-death experience, started shivering with fear. He acknowledged that it was the fear of failure that drove his team to success.[19]

In the final analysis, the sum of N20 million required for the incorporation and licensing of the Bank was paid up by the investors. Chief Agbaje also played a pivotal role in steering the application through the CBN. He brought enormous prestige and credibility to the GTB team, and opened doors at the CBN.

However, Adeola and Aderinokun, still in their mid-30s, were saddled with processing documents from door to door at the CBN.[20] They had an unassailable edge in their well thought out, convincing and "superior business plan." The charismatic Adeola was a notable asset, described by his co-founder as "a very good persuader, [...] a good orator who could convince anybody."

The ability of the promoters to follow due process rather than resort to short-cuts impressed the CBN officials and the State Security Service (SSS), who screened all applicants for banking licences. The promoters took the unprecedented step of producing all investors for screening. "The SSS," Aderinokun

18 As GTB held on to niche banking for almost a decade after its take-off, it appears that the promoters conveniently jettisoned their original plan for expansion into the hinterland or merely stated what they felt the CBN would like to hear.

19 Adeola, interviewed on 14 October 2004.

20 Aderinokun, interviewed on 26 September 2004, for quotes and the discussion in this and the following paragraphs.

recalled, "had never seen something like that." This was unlike the practice of seeking to save investors the rigour of screening by inducing the officers in charge to do the screening by proxy. After scaling the CBN hurdle, the application went for approval by the Minister of Finance. The process was drawn out and arduous, but the promoters harnessed their social capital instead of bribing officials. Aderinokun recalled a visit to the Permanent Secretary of the Ministry of Finance when Adeola, a fellow Muslim, upon hearing of their host's bereavement, spontaneously recited some Quranic verses in prayers for the deceased. Such empathy elicited the goodwill of officials involved in the licensing process. One of the Bank's investors and a future Director facilitated approval by the Minister, who was the godfather to one of her children.[21] In all, everyone contributed to the success of the application.

But the process was far from smooth. "How we acquired the banking licence," Adeola recalled, "is itself [the subject of] a book. [...] There were processes, there were human beings that we met. [...] There were people we visited at 1.00am [who had given us] [...] an 8.00p.m. appointment," which they had not kept. Such "big men" would then appear and simply dismiss the young bankers with the expression (in Yoruba): "*Ile ti su ... se wa tun wa l'ola*?" (meaning: "It's late, hope you'll call again tomorrow"?). Getting a banking licence at the time, he stated, "is something to write for a play for people to see." The young promoters learnt the virtue of patience, which served them well in later life.[22]

Finally, on 5 July 1990, the banking licence was issued to the promoters of GTB, completing a process that began in May 1989. Next, approval was obtained for membership of the Board of Directors and Management Team from the CBN and the Ministry of Finance and Economic Development.[23] The seven persons that served on the inaugural Board of Directors were selected on the basis of certain criteria: professional integrity; banking or business experience; commitment to the ideals of a well-managed organisation; equitable representation of shareholders' interests; and representation of the different parts of the country. The inaugural Board comprised J.K. Agbaje, Muhammed Jada, Mosobalaje Oyawoye, Victor Osibodu, Ifeyinwa Nwakwesi, Fola Adeola (MD), and Tayo Aderinokun (Deputy MD).[24] Finally, on 2 August 1990, the GTB promoters were formally notified in writing that they had been issued licence No 000058, dated 1 August 1990, signed by the Minister of Finance.[25]

21 Nwakwesi, interview cited.
22 Adeola, interview cited.
23 TAP, Aderinokun to Promoters, 6 July 1990.
24 TAP, Aderinokun to Promoters, 11 July 1990.
25 TAP, E.P.O. Edeogho (for Hon. Minister) to Promoters of GTB, 2 August 1990.

The licence secured, shares were allotted on the basis of one million naira for 5 per cent equity and half a million naira for half that percentage. They were classified into two: Class A shares were ordinary shares owned by those that may be called "pure investors", while Class B entitled their owners ("the core or professional investors") to determine who became MD and Deputy MD of the bank.[26] This classification was to protect the fledgling bank from falling into the hands of those who might misuse their control to the detriment of the organisation.

## Creating GTB Culture: The Recruitment and Training of Staff

Concurrent with the process of obtaining a banking licence, plans were being made for the formal launch of GTBank. This involved three tasks: recruitment and training of competent staff; securing a suitable location for the bank; and articulating the governing ethos of the bank.[27]

Given the age bracket of the two key promoters, only persons within and below their age bracket (mid-30s) were recruited. Young persons were expected to grow with the organisation. Head-hunting, rather than job advertisements, was undertaken. Banks where Adeola and Aderinokun had worked were fertile hunting grounds. All prospective staff underwent the sifting process leading to recruitment.

Only university graduates were engaged. It was felt that while there could be outstanding products of polytechnics, only a few such institutions were of suitable quality.[28] All fresh employees underwent four months of rigorous training. Graduates of all disciplines were given a chance to pass through the mill. Thus, Chika Mbonu and Titi Osuntoki were graduates of civil engineering (though the former had also qualified as an accountant), Kafilat Araoye had a first degree in History and a Master's in Personnel Management; Tokunbo Talabi majored in Physical Therapy before obtaining an MBA; Aigboje Aig-Imoukhuede and Jide Ogundare were lawyers; Femi Pedro, a professional banker, had studied Economics; while Mosun Olusoga, Herbert Wigwe, Segun Agbaje and

26 The classification was attested by Osibodu, Akintoye and Aderinokun, interviews cited. See also, GTBL, Minutes of Board Meeting, 6 April 1994, Min. 5.2, MD's answer to Oyawoye's question.

27 The discussion in this and the following paragraphs is based upon interviews with Adeola, Aderinokun and Kafilat Araoye (interviewed on 29 September 2004).

28 Adeola, himself a polytechnic graduate but with a professional qualification in Accountancy and a Master's degree, endorsed this policy. Interview cited.

Dolapo Ogunmekan were qualified accountants. As Professor Oyawoye noted, GTB was willing to engage anyone with a "brain that could be trained."[29] The training was conducted by senior staff and external consultants, and anchored by Bode Agusto. The training was both generic and specific. The former gave everyone a broad knowledge of the industry while the latter gave individuals a grounding in specific tasks or skills.

One aspect of the training was the evolution of a vision and mission for the Bank. Sadiq Bello recalled that foundation staff were young idealists committed to building a unique organisation that would be a pride to the black race.[30] Pedro reminisced that Adeola,

> had no doubt in his mind that he wanted to build an institution unrivalled by any other [...] in the world. And that was the preaching right from day one – total quality, first class; integrity not in doubt; character, doing things right and well; service, excellent! Fola was so particular about customer service that if a customer [...] reported you to the MD you would lose your job.[31]

"Everything about GTB was well thought out from the beginning," another foundation staff affirmed, "including the vision and even the building (of the Plaza). GTB came on the basis of breaking from the past by doing things differently, but with the best practices."[32] All foundation staff shared the vision of the founders that GTBank was going to be different in terms of its ethical approach to business, the conduct of interpersonal relations and the quality of its service delivery. Those were critical pillars of the edifice that emerged from the planning and deliberations of the initial formative months in response to the prevailing conditions in the larger society.

First, GTBank emerged in a milieu of widespread corruption and unethical practices in the Nigerian economy and society at large, and the banking industry in particular. Adeola stated that he learnt from the way that sharp business practices caused the downfall of his previous employer. "I saw a bank destroyed by unethical practices," Adeola recalled, "and if I didn't learn how to run a bank, I came out of Continental knowing fully how not to run a bank.

29 Oyawoye, interview cited.

30 Sadiq Bello, interviewed on 29 September 2004. The reference to 'race' is not to imply that racism drove the GTBank project.

31 Femi Pedro, interviewed on 16 December 2004.

32 Chika Mbonu, interviewed on 13 January 2005.

I guess the choice that would be left is how to run one and on which model."[33] Hence, the emphasis on ethics derived from that sad experience. Second, the bank resolved to evolve its peculiar culture different from the norm in the industry. Specifically, it enshrined a culture of informality in a formal work environment. Staff of all ranks were to relate with one another on first name terms, a revolutionary step given the dominant culture of deference to age in the larger society. Informality removed barriers to the kind of interaction necessary for the work at hand. It also fostered the mentoring of younger or junior employees.[34] The practice has been entrenched in the bank and copied by virtually all other Nigerian banks.

Adeola and Aderinokun were pivotal to the success of these foundation-laying efforts. In a departure from the rigid formality of older organisations, they did not reserve any special car park or elevator for themselves. Their personal example of punctuality and hard work made it impossible for their subordinates to do otherwise. Talabi recalled that Aderinokun always arrived before anyone else and did a considerable amount of work even before formal office hours.[35] Such was the impact of exemplary leadership that staff saw themselves as "disciples" of "Fola and Tayo" as the MD and Deputy MD were addressed. Bello explained that "they were able to carry everyone along. It was more like they had this idea, you bought into it, and at the end of the day, it was [...] like the disciples were the ones who became more convinced about it."[36] Pedro stated that Adeola was "the most visionary person" he had ever met, who was able to translate his dreams into reality.[37]

One significant outcome of the interaction of the staff was a high degree of bonding among them. It was relatively easy to get along informally and to work long hours without complaint. In any case, as they all shared the vision of creating a unique organisation, the motivation was quite high. Yet, discipline was maintained within the ranks. As Adeola stated, though he was on first name terms with everyone else, no subordinate abused the informality.[38] Everyone did their work and was prepared to make the extra effort. To be sure, for most of them, the pay was good; a notable exception was Dolapo Ogunmekan, who had to take up the GTB job in spite of the lower remuneration it offered.[39]

33 Adeola, interview cited.
34 Bello, interview cited.
35 Tokunbo Talabi, interviewed on 25 November 2004.
36 Bello, interview cited.
37 Pedro, interview cited.
38 Adeola, interview cited.
39 Dolapo Ogunmekan, interviewed on 4 October 2004.

This indicates that it was more than the pay packet that galvanised the staff. Their commitment to work was often tested and the relationship was not without strains since workers were driven to achieve targets. As Ogundare asserted, targets at GTB had always been "cast in stone."[40] Hence, Adeola did not spare anyone in spite of the camaraderie. Mosun Olusoga recalled instances when she received hard knocks from the MD and naturally passed the treatment down the ladder.[41] In sum, the staff had varied experiences of long working hours, hard work, an informal work atmosphere, relative autonomy as each person knew what to do, minimal supervision, mutual trust, and the tendency to look out for the others.

One major experience of all staff, which became the norm, was the idea of job rotation. As soon as the mandatory period of training was over, staff were assigned their duties and reposted to other assignments within two years. This ensured that GTBank was not held to ransom if an "expert" suddenly became incapacitated. Moreover, the founders expected everyone to know a little of everything. Reflecting on this practice, Agbaje, who later succeeded Aderinokun as MD, pointed out that banking "is not a rocket science and it is a little simpler than what people think it to be. The easiest way to learn banking is by doing it."[42] This was illustrated by, among others, Aig-Imoukhuede, who was first posted to the Consumer Banking Group, where four others reported to him, before being moved to the Treasury. In due course, in spite of his background in Law, he occupied the vital positions of Treasurer and Financial Controller of the Bank.[43] Araoye pointed out that heads of units were not moved until they had trained substitutes who will take over from them. This made for mentoring, an essential part of the GTB work ethic.[44]

Given the commitment of the founding fathers of the GTB to building a unique organisation, a deliberate attempt was made to fashion a "GTB Culture". The core components of this culture may be identified as integrity, diligence and excellent service delivery, encapsulated in the concept of Total Quality Management (TQM). Although TQM was not invented by the bank, it was entrenched as one of its core principles. It entailed, in Adeola's words, "getting it

---

40 Jide Ogundare, interviewed on 3 October 2004.

41 Mosun Olusoga, interviewed on 6 October 2004.

42 Segun Agbaje, interviewed on 26 September 2004. Agbaje was himself a pioneering staff member, who was instrumental in the recruitment of his father as the first Chairman of the Board of Directors (1990–1995).

43 Aig-Imoukhuede, interview cited.

44 Araoye, interview cited.

right the first time." He also said: "If you do it well, you will do well."[45] This was to be a way of life within and beyond the organisation: it included how staff answered their phone calls, how they behaved in traffic, and how they wrote their letters. In short, the idea was to create role models for society. Asked how he would characterise the GTB work ethic, Aderinokun summed it up as follows: "It is a mixture of many cultures. Sometimes we work like the Chinese, like soldiers for long hours; sometimes we work like Americans, very driven by profits; sometimes like English people, trying to do things properly. What has emerged here is a mixture of global cultures."[46]

The evolving GTB culture, forged in the crucible of the training programmes and the work environment, was formally codified in the Bank's Vision and Mission Statement. The Vision, after much tinkering, was expressed thus: "We are a team driven to deliver the utmost in customer services. We are synonymous with building excellence and superior financial performance in Nigeria; and creating role models for society." The bank's Mission Statement was equally striking: "We are a first-class financial services provider possessing the urge to win at all times, consistently adding value to all stakeholders." These high ideals underpinned GTBank's operations and provided a benchmark against which its performance could be measured.

## Coping with Challenges and Setbacks: The Resilience of GTBank, 1990–2002

As already indicated above, GTBank recorded several "feats and firsts", the outcome of a combination of leadership, strategy, workforce competitiveness, resilience and adaptability of its internal processes, and prudent management. A key indicator of the bank's success is the profile of its financial operations and returns. Tables 1 and 2 contain details of its operations in the first ten years, 1991–2000. Table 1 shows that, after sustaining a loss of some N2.5 million in its first year of operation (actually seven months), the bank subsequently recorded a steady increase in its profit after taxation and earnings per share. The peak performance of 1994 was followed by a drop in 1995, which reflected a general decline in economic activities in the country.

Developments during the next quinquennium, 1996–2000, are indicated in Table 2. During this period, profit after tax and earnings per share steadily

45 Adeola, interview cited.

46 Agbaje, interview cited.

increased, with the exception of two successive trough years of 1998 and 1999, after which the bank's profitability shot up significantly.

However, as demonstrated in the following passages, the true test of GTBank's success was its ability to overcome challenges and turbulence in the national political economy on its way to achieving its celebrated successes. The major challenges are detailed below.

GTBank faced its greatest challenges during the period between 1993 and 1995, when Nigeria experienced severe political turbulence arising from the annulled presidential elections of 12 June 1993 and the Abacha dictatorship. Many banks and financial houses collapsed, and the economy shrank in the face of international sanctions and the pariah status of the country in the comity of nations. GTBank's management adopted a cautious approach coupled with innovativeness and flexibility in addressing the challenges. For example, it increased its current account holdings in the CBN from N33m in 1993 to N1.4 billion in 1994 instead of investing in Treasury Bills, which attracted a higher interest. This was because Treasury Bills were no longer accepted as part of a bank's liquid assets for bidding for foreign exchange.[47] Second, it shifted focus from financial institutions to other industries. For example, it diversified into the aviation sector and became dominant in it within two years.[48]

Managing major transitions between 1995 and 2002 was another indicator of the bank's resilience. First, the voluntary resignation of the inaugural Chairman of the Board of Directors, Chief J.K. Agbaje, months before his 80th birthday in July 1995, which could have led to a rancorous succession battle, was followed by the smooth accession of Professor Oyawoye in June 1995. Second, the sudden abdication of Adeola, the foundation MD, in 2002, followed a few months later, by the exit of two Executive Directors, Aig-Imoukhuede and Wigwe. Third, the mutation from niche banking to retail banking in the face of the harsh realities of the mid-1990s. Finally, the major restructuring, entailing a massive downsizing of the workforce, in 1998.

Personnel changes on the board were managed without overt friction, an indication of a gentlemen's agreement or an unwritten succession plan. However, there were speculations about the sudden retirement of Adeola as MD. The official position, stated in the bank's annual report for 2002, declared that "the Board would have wished that Mr. Adeola delay his retirement," but he was "very clear in his mind that it is time to leave."[49] This implied a voluntary

47 GTBL, Minutes of the Annual General Meeting (AGM), 20 April 1994.

48 GTBL, Minutes of Board Meeting, 19 October 1994, min. 4.3.

49 GTBL, *Annual Reports and Accounts, 2002*, Chairman's Statement, 8.

exit, against the preference of the bank. However, a newspaper speculated that there was more to the development than was presented to the public:

First, that the exit of Aig-Imoukhuede and Wigwe spurred Adeola's decision, though no direct relationship was established between the two events. Second, that Aderinokun and Agbaje had delivered an ultimatum, a day after the resignation of the two Executive Directors, that they too would leave if Adeola did not end his long tenure as MD. Indeed, it was alleged that his twelve-year tenure was twice what had been agreed at the outset. Third, Adeola's devotion to his Fate Foundation was considered inimical to his responsibilities as MD of GTBank. Finally, it was speculated that his political ambitions regarding the 2003 Nigerian general elections hastened his abdication (Mayowa 2002: 16). Neither Adeola, nor Aderinokun commented on these speculations and this suggests that the official line was a reflection of an unwritten agreement between them.

Unlike the exit of Agbaje and Adeola, the departure of Aig-Imoukhuede and Wigwe was a crushing blow below GTBank's belt. It bred resentment for three reasons – a reorganisation was being concluded with the two men as lynchpins of the unfolding structure; both men set up shop only a few metres away on the same street (Oyin Jolayemi) as MD and Deputy MD of Access Bank, which they had taken over; and their move was not disclosed but was uncovered by a third party, upon which GTBank compelled them to resign. This was a double blow – the loss of highly placed, experienced and expensively trained staff, and the emergence of a major competitor in the same market powered by alumni with sensitive insider information. It is to the credit of GTBank that personal relations were repaired in due course and mutual co-existence has subsisted.

An early challenge that the bank surmounted was the automation of its operations. From the start, it advertised the extensive use of technology in its operations as one of its competitive advantages. That, indeed, gave it an edge, but also posed a serious challenge when its eagerness to automate and stay ahead of competition was exploited in the abortive adoption of a banking software known as BA4SQL. The full meaning of this name is not stated in the company's records. The saga began with a presentation to a major strategic session of the Board of Directors in February 1996 and a paper on it was approved by the Board in March 1996.[50] Details of the proposal cannot be provided here, but the software appeared to be a revolutionary breakthrough in banking operations at the time. In addition, as an investor in the development of the software, GTBank would also earn a percentage of the profit from its worldwide sales. In the final analysis, the project turned out to be a hoax, which was discovered

50 GTBL, Minutes of Board Meetings, 3 February 1996, Min. 3.2-3.6; and 6 March 1996, Min.2.

when a team from Nigeria visited the offices of BankAct, the software developer, only to discover that it required a further eighteen months to deliver the product. GTBank was forced to abandon the project with a substantial loss of investment and with lessons learnt.[51] An alternative was found in the Oracle-based BASIS (Banking Automation System for Integrated Services), which subsequently served it well.

A major test for GTBank was the adversity of the 1997/98 financial year. For example, the profit before tax of N856.2 million in the last quarter of 1997/98 was 17 per cent less than for the corresponding period in 1997. It was the only year in which the bank could neither pay bonus to its staff, nor increase staff salaries.[52] The "extremely harsh" business environment produced the disequilibrium in the operations and financial returns of the bank, which, the MD conceded, "jolted [management] back to reality" from the euphoria of previous years' successes. One manifestation of this adversity was the disappointing returns from branch expansion. Specifically, the Abuja branch of the bank had been opened at high cost with much fanfare and high expectations in anticipation of a windfall arising from the transfer of public sector accounts from the CBN to commercial banks. But, the anticipated business from government parastatals did not materialise. The same fate had befallen the Aba branch, which failed to yield returns commensurate with the investment in establishing it.[53] The adversity of 1997/98 tested the resolve of the bank in various ways, a few of which are considered below.

A major restructuring took place GTBank in 1998, a consequence of a hard-headed appraisal of its performance, and the prevailing circumstances in the industry and the wider political economy. Diligent investigations revealed that the bank had 87 management staff, twice as many as those of its competitors. The huge number was retained out of loyalty to dedicated staff and to prevent loss to competition of staff that the bank had invested much in training. Aderinokun admitted that, in addition to the financial burden of a bloated workforce, it was discovered that five people were doing the work of one person and they were getting in each others' way.[54] But, getting rid of otherwise loyal and diligent staff tested the resolve of management. A three-person senior management committee was mandated to propose criteria for disengaging half of the 87 management staff. Their individual proposals were found to be remarkably

51 Talabi, interview cited. There is no reference to this saga in the literature.

52 GTBL, Minutes of Board Meeting, 29 April 1998, Min. 18 for the discussion in this paragraph.

53 GTBL, Minutes of Board Meeting, 8 July 1997.

54 Interview: Aderinokun, 21 December 2004.

similar and the criteria were cryptically described as "best-fit, competence, capacity and flexibility."[55] The affected staff were notified individually and handsomely compensated, and Adeola and Aderinokun reportedly assisted several of them in getting suitable jobs elsewhere.[56] Nonetheless, this caused some lingering resentment, as revealed in the controversy surrounding the sale of Magnum Trust Bank.

A constant threat to GTBank during the period considered in this essay was the peculiar business environment, euphemistically referred to as "the Nigerian factor". From the start, Citibank, described as "the most profitable bank with an ethical profile,"[57] was seen as the model and the bank to beat. Indeed, beating Citibank was one of the strategic imperatives of "Project Era+", GTBank's overall strategy unveiled in December 1998. When it did beat Citibank in 1999, the feat was formally celebrated in the bank.[58] The choice of Citibank was, in retrospect, a curious one, given the damning reports of its involvement in large-scale money laundering (including drug money) and other unethical practices.[59] It is possible that Citibank had not become tainted by sharp practices to the knowledge of its GTBank admirers up to 1999 or that its Nigerian branch was not involved in the global sharp practices of the head office and some branches. But this seems far-fetched given the interwoven nature of banking and the pervasiveness of corporate culture in a banking enterprise.

To be sure, sharp practices or unethical behaviour in government and business (bribery, brokerage, false declarations and influence peddling) are global phenomena, but for an enterprise dedicated to ethical business practices, GTBank faced a double jeopardy in the sharp practices by rent-seeking officials and unethical competition by industry rivals. First, it refused to meet the expectations of corrupt officials, and this cost it public sector accounts. Second, it resisted the temptation to indulge in round-tripping in foreign exchange transactions, which was the open secret behind the huge profits posted by its rivals. That the bank was not averse to legitimate foreign exchange business is indicated by a newspaper report that the bank's outstanding financial returns in the second quarter of 1999/2000 – gross earnings of N2.5 billion compared to N1.5 billion in the corresponding period of the previous year – were "largely

55 Interviews: Aig-Imoukhuede and Wigwe, 7 and 17 November 2004.

56 Wigwe, interview cited.

57 GTBL, Minutes of Board Meeting, 23 December 1998, Min. 124.1.

58 Wigwe, interview cited.

59 The disconnect between Citibank's tarnished global image and GTBank's admiration of its supposed ethical stance is intriguing.

accounted for [...] [by] the significant increase in commission earned on foreign exchange transactions."[60]

The temptation to join others in unwholesome practices was strong in the face of the crises that faced the wider economy and the banking sector in the 1990s. While acknowledging that "unscrupulous competitors" were profiting from the business environment, the Board and management constantly re-affirmed GTBank's commitment to high ethical standards.[61] The bank reportedly survived by resorting to aggressive salesmanship, which persuaded a number of bureaucrats to patronise it for enlightened self-interest. Officials under pressure to deliver results partnered the bank knowing that it would deliver without default.[62] GTBank also circumvented the corrupt system by courting and obtaining the accounts of organisations and contractors who had benefited from the system. This was an indirect way of getting a fraction of public sector accounts.[63]

Another major challenge that confronted GTBank was the choice it had to make between remaining a niche bank, catering to an upscale clientele with limited prospects in the long run, or shifting to retail banking that required massive branch expansion. This was a direct challenge to the founding vision of the bank that set out to be an ethically sound niche bank of choice. The first formal move in this direction was a major policy decision taken by the Board of Directors at its meeting on 3 February 1996, endorsing a management initiative in a detailed report by the MD, Adeola. It was decided to go into retail banking (individuals and small businesses) from which it would generate the liquidity to sustain its operations at the higher levels of banking: Upper (multinationals and blue-chip companies, that is, established, profit-making companies whose stocks and shares are the most traded and sought-after on the stock exchange) and Middle (small- and medium-sized firms).

This was what prompted the bank to acquire Magnum Trust Bank ("Magnum"), and later to embark on both branch expansion in Nigeria and offshore expansion in West Africa. Within eighteen months of the acquisition of Magnum, the branches of the latter increased from one to eleven.[64] But, in response

---

60 "GTB declares N437m profit in six months", *The Vanguard* (Lagos), 8 November 1999; see, also, "Guaranty Trust posts N642m profit in six months", *The Guardian* (Lagos), 11 November 1999. However, if the bank earned its profit from round tripping, characteristic of the age, this undermined its claim to high ethical standards.

61 GTBL, Minutes of Board Meeting, 7 January 1998, Min. 73.

62 Araoye and Talabi, interviews cited.

63 Oyawoye, interview cited.

64 GTBL, Minutes of Board Meeting, 15 October 1997, Min. 62.

to the changing circumstances in the industry, GTBank finally divested 51 per cent of its holding in Magnum at a considerable profit in 1999. The sale, however, pitted it against one of its shareholders, who claimed that shareholders were not privy to the transaction. The ensuing litigation was protracted, in spite of efforts at resolution, allegedly because the litigant was aggrieved over the downsizing exercise of 1998.[65] Finally, in 2001/2002, GTBank sold in two phases its remaining stake in Magnum, which was developing into a competitive rival, at a huge profit.[66]

That said, while the period from 1996 to 2000 was one of cautious branch expansion, the subsequent period witnessed a major shift to massive branch expansion, which, in addition to stretching the financial and managerial resources of the bank, was bound to dilute its corporate culture as many people would be injected into the workforce too quickly. As a merger or an acquisition was not preferred, branch expansion, a decisive departure from niche bank orthodoxy, was an unavoidable policy shift from the first quarter of the 2000/2001 financial year.[67] Accordingly, the Board approved thirteen new branches across the country.[68] Ten additional branches were also approved in June 2001 subject to approval by the CBN.[69] The bank's annual report for 2001 listed the Benin, Enugu, Jos, Asaba, Uyo, Akure, Yenagoa, Ilorin and Maiduguri branches as being "now in operation."[70]

Finally, in March 2002, Adeola unveiled the vision of a 50-branch bank in five years. The aim was to have a branch of GTBank in each of the 36 state capitals and in the major administrative centres. Lagos would still be an important hub as the city alone accounts for 60–70 per cent of the bank's direct and indirect income.[71] In 2002, new branches opened at Abeokuta, Calabar, and Owerri, and second branches commenced operations at Ikeja (Lagos), Abuja, and Port Harcourt.[72] Offshore expansion to the English-speaking countries of West Africa was a trail-blazing achievement of GTBank. The process was slow and tedious, but the opening of the first offshore branch in Banjul, The Gambia in 2002, was the precursor of others in Sierra Leone, Liberia and, after much official stonewalling, Ghana. It is instructive that the co-founding leaders of the

65 Interview: Aderinokun, 26 September 2004.

66 GTBL, Minutes of Board Meetings, 12 December 2001 and 15 March 2002.

67 Agbaje, interview cited, recalled how he and others who canvassed branch expansion were literally thrown out of the room for their "heretical views."

68 GTBL, Minutes of Board Meeting, 5 July 2000, Min. 186.2.

69 GTBL, Minutes of Board Meeting, 20 June 2001, Min. 239.

70 GTBL, Annual Reports and Accounts, 2001, 9.

71 GTBL, Minutes of Board Meeting, 15 March 2002, Min. 265.3.

72 GTBL, Annual Reports and Accounts, 2002, 7.

bank played a decisive role in these successful transnational forays. The Gambia was dubbed "Fola's project" while Aderinokun, who had run into somebody that facilitated it, "did Sierra Leone."[73]

## GTBank and Regulatory Bodies

The admirable record of performance of the bank faced the test of regulation with mixed results. On the one hand, some of its practices were applauded by the CBN in its oversight reports. The CBN commended GTBank's innovation of rendering quarterly returns on risk assets to its Board, which conscientiously reviewed all facilities presented to it. A CBN inspector commented in 1995 that it was "probably the only bank" that ensured such due diligence.[74] In 2002, CBN reported that the bank's "funds management was judicious," having surpassed the benchmark 40 per cent liquidity ratio.[75] It also noted that Director-related credits advanced by the bank constituted only 1.25 per cent of total disbursed credit, and those facilities were ascertained to be performing. Moreover, no Director-related account was involved in the write-off totalling N335,919,626.[76] CBN also reported that the bank "did not deal in ineligible transactions since the transfer of foreign exchange was documented and disclosed to the appropriate regulatory authorities."[77]

Nonetheless, infractions by the bank were detailed in various CBN reports. The most frequent concerned fraud by staff and deficient internal control systems. In 1997, for example, the CBN highlighted lack of requisite autonomy and authority by branch managers, fraud, insider related accounts, overinvestment in Magnum and the challenges of branch expansion, exemplified by the poor performance of the Aba branch.[78] The report for 1999 spotted negative liquidity and an inadequate Debt Recovery Unit.[79] In 2002, the CBN reported that the MD's span of control was "too large" because as many as six units reported to him.[80]

73 Aig-Imoukhuede, interview cited.

74 GTBL, Minutes of Board Meeting, 21 June 1995, Min. 5.15.

75 CBN Report, 2002, 32.

76 Ibid.: 38–39.

77 Ibid.: 58.

78 CBN Report, 1997, 7, 14, 16, 22.

79 CBN Report, 1999, 10, 23.

80 CBN Report, 2002, 18.

The bank's internal control system, said to be "weak in some respects," was identified as a major cause of the incidence of fraud.[81] The following reasons were adduced for this. First, there was collusion between some staff and outsiders. Second, there were cases of impersonation and conversion. Third, the high proportion of non-permanent staff, and deployment of contract staff and industrial interns in such sensitive areas as cashiery and note-counting created room for fraud. The wide disparity between the salary of permanent staff and the contract staff made the latter vulnerable to corruption, especially when some of them wanted to live and dress like the former.[82] During the Annual General Meeting (AGM), shareholders deplored the bank's violations of CBN guidelines and the consequent fines imposed by the regulatory body (Agbana 2003; Onwuka 2003).

The adverse reports on the operational performance of the bank were addressed through remedial action and payment of fines. GTBank thus exhibited some of the operational deficiencies rampant in the industry. It appears that the bank circumvented regulations that seemed to unduly hamper its operations. The management statutorily explained its action in its reports to the Board and the AGM.

## Conclusion

The challenge of building enduring institutions in the public sector and private organisations has been a recurring theme in the post-independence history of Africa. This paper contributes to our understanding of institution building in the modern banking sector of Nigeria through a microhistory of a new generation indigenous Nigerian bank that emerged in the uncertain conditions of SAP, military rule and the politico-economic turbulence of the 1990s. The uniqueness of the case study derives from its exemplification of two conjoined dynamics: the tenets of "gentlemanly capitalism" – personal friendship, trust and partnership – and entrepreneurial management – the high ethical and professional standards that underpinned the formation, corporate culture and business operations of the bank, the versatility of the management and workforce, and the professionalism of the Board of Directors. In terms of managerial integrity, the fortunes of GTBank under Adeola and Aderinokun, constrast sharply with those of the ICB and most other pioneer indigenous banks of the late 1920s–late 1940s (Hopkins 1966; Uche 2010).

81 Ibid.: 19.

82 CBN Report, 2002, 21.

That said, the role of personal friendship, school-boy ties and mutual trust in the success story of GTBank between 1990 and 2002 should not be overstated. First, monocausal explanation, which this implies, is ahistorical. Second, like other human relationships, tension and resentment subsist even if below the surface. In the case of the Adeola-Aderinokun duumvirate, the inevitable tensions were well managed. Thus, at his valedictory board meeting, Adeola paid glowing tributes to his partner and deputy of twelve years. He stated that they were "friends before becoming partners, and that to date, no third party had ever intervened to resolve a dispute between them." Aderinokun returned the compliment by asserting that he could serve as deputy to Adeola for so long because of the latter's personality. Adeola had given him "the right environment within which he could express himself" and had "at no time [...] treated [him] [...] as an underling."[83] Aderinokun disclosed that there was "nothing we did without effective consultation from either of us. Our roles were complementary."[84] That the paradigm of a successful business duumvirate by Adeola and Aderinokun can be replicated is exemplified by the success story of the duo of Aig-Imoukhuede and Wigwe, alumni of GTBank. Not only have the latter raised Access Bank from near-collapse to near-parity with GTBank, they too have also undertaken a change of the guard at the level of the MD, a position now occupied by Wigwe after his friend's tenure expired. It remains to be seen how GTBank (and Access Bank) would fare after the exit of the founding duumvirate, and whether those experiments can be replicated. This underscores the need for more microhistories of the internal workings – personalities, politics and policies – of indigenous financial institutions in Nigeria and other developing economies.

## References

Agbana, G. (2003). "Mixed Reactions Trail GTB Performance", *The Guardian* (Lagos), 6 June.

Baumol, W.J. (1990). "Entrepreneurship: Productive, Unproductive, and Destructive", *The Journal of Political Economy*, 98, 5, Part 1 (Oct.), 893–921.

Cain, P.J. & A.G. Hopkins (2002). *British Imperialism, 1688–2000*. Harlow, Essex: Longman.

83 GTBL, Minutes of Board Meeting, 15 March 2002, Min. 272.2.

84 Interview: Aderinokun, 26 September 2004.

Famakinwa, S. (2004). "Aderinokun: Defining a New Era at GTB", *This Day* (Lagos), 24 May.

Forrest, T. (1994). *The Advance of African Capital: The Growth of Nigerian Private Enterprise*. Edinburgh: Edinburgh University Press.

Gann, L.H. & P. Duignan (1978). *The Rulers of British Africa, 1870–1914*. London: Longman.

Hamalai, H.A. (1999). *Government-Business Relations and Economic Liberalisation in Nigeria*. Kaduna: Baraka Press.

Harneit-Sievers, A. (1996). "African Business, "Economic Nationalism," and British Colonial Policy: Southern Nigeria, 1935–1954", *African Economic History* 24, 25–68.

Hopkins, A.G. (1966). "Economic Aspects of Political Movements in Nigeria and in the Gold Coast, 1918–1939", *Journal of African History* 7, 133–152.

Knox, S.D. & S. Maklan. (2005). "Guaranty Trust Bank of Nigeria: Building a Trusted Brand in Financial Services", *Thunderbird International Business Review* 47, 737–755.

Maklan, S. & S.D. Knox. (2009). "The Guaranty Trust Bank of Nigeria (GTBank): From Niche Positioning to Mass-Market Branding", *Thunderbird International Business Review* 51, 385–401.

Maklan, S., Antonetti, P. & S.D. Knox. (2014). "Building a Sustainable Bank: The Case of GTBank of Nigeria", *Thunderbird International Business Review* 56, 461–473.

Mayowa, O. (2002). "Adeola's Exit from GTB: The Untold Story", *Daily Times* (Lagos), 28 May.

Ndekwu, E.C. (1994). *First Bank of Nigeria: A Century of Banking*. Ibadan: Spectrum Books.

Newlyn, W. & D. Rowan (1954). *Money and Banking in British Colonial Africa*. Oxford: Oxford University Press.

Ogunbiyi, Y. (2010). *Orange Chronicles: The GTBank Story*. Ibadan: Bookcraft.

Olukoshi, A. (ed.) (1994). *The Politics of Structural Adjustment in Nigeria*. London: James Currey.

Olukoju, A. (2002). "The Impact of British Colonialism on the Development of African Business in Colonial Nigeria". In: Alusine Jalloh & Toyin Falola (eds), *Black Business and Economic Power*, Rochester, NY: Rochester University Press, 176–198.

Olukoju, A. (2014). "Accumulation and Conspicuous Consumption: The Poverty of Yoruba Entrepreneurship in Western Nigeria, ca. 1890–1930". In: Emmanuel Akyeampong, Robert Bates, Nathan Nunn & James A. Robinson (eds), *Africa's Development in Historical Perspective*, Cambridge: Cambridge University Press, 208–230.

Onwuka, C. (2003). "GTB's Phenomenal Rise to Stardom", *Daily Times* (Lagos), 11 June.

Stevenson, H.H. & J.C. Jarillo (1990). "A Paradigm of Entrepreneurship: Entrepreneurial Management", *Strategic Management Journal*, 11, Special Issue: Corporate Entrepreneurship (Summer), 17–27.

Uche, C. (2010). "Indigenous Banks in Colonial Nigeria", *International Journal of African Historical Studies*, 43, 473–474.

Umoren, R. (2001). *Economic Reforms and Nigeria's Political Crisis*. Ibadan: Spectrum.

CHAPTER 17

# Indigenous Banking Enterprises: The Rise of Nigerian Multinational Banks

*Chibuike Uche*

## Introduction

A relatively recent phenomenon in the history of banking in Nigeria is the emergence of several indigenous Nigerian banks as multinational banks.[1] This was mainly a consequence of the decision of the Central Bank of Nigeria (CBN), in July 2004, to increase the minimum capital requirement for Nigerian banks from N2 billion to N25 billion (Alade 2014). The main reason for this spectacular 1,150 per cent increase in bank minimum capital requirement was the desire by the Nigerian authorities to force the consolidation of its banking system by encouraging the merger of its numerous small banks (Osinupebi 2012). This was to enable the country to produce mega banks that would compete internationally in the market for the provision of banking services. At the time, the Governor of the CBN explained:

> All over the world and given the internationalization of finance, size has become an important ingredient for success in the globalizing world. In the world of finance, no country can afford to operate in isolation [...]. Where is Nigeria – Africa's most populous country and potentially its largest economy? In Nigeria, we have 89 banks with many banks having capital base of less than $US 10 million, and about 3,300 branches. Compare this to eight banks in South Korea with about 4,500 branches or the one bank in South Africa with larger assets than all our 89 banks. The truth is that the Nigerian banking system remains very marginal relative to its potentials and in comparison to other countries – even in Africa. We have a duty to be proactive, and to strategically position Nigerian banks to be active players and not spectators in the emerging world.
>
> SOLUDO 2004: 2

---

1 For the purposes of this chapter, we have adopted Herbert Grubel's simple and generally accepted definition, which states that multinational banking involves the ownership of banking facilities in one country by the citizens of another country (1981: 349).

 | DOI 10.1163/9789004351615_018

Prior to a dramatic increase in the minimum share capital requirement in 2004, the presence of most Nigerian banks abroad was restricted. The operations of these banks abroad were therefore inconsequential and carried little risk. In 2000, for instance, the CBN Banking Supervision Annual Report asserted that "very few Nigerian banks operate offshore." This explains why the World Bank Mission at the time concluded that "issues related to cross-border supervision were not relevant to Nigerian banks as their activities were domestic to a very large extent" (Cf. CBN Banking Supervision Annual Report 2000: 62).

With the 2004 increase of the minimum share capital requirement, the Nigerian banks that survived the exercise realised that they had excess capital at their disposal. This encouraged them to aggressively expand their operations and services abroad in search of economic opportunities. While the provision of cross-border banking services by Nigerian multinational banks was welcome in several jurisdictions, especially in Africa, it raised serious regulatory concerns. In 2008, for instance, a CBN Circular asserted that the "Central Bank of Nigeria has observed with serious concern the aggressive expansion of banks, particularly cross border, in the recent past. These involve additional risks." The circular went on to argue that while the CBN appreciates the need for Deposit Money Banks (DMBs) to grow their bank and improve profitability as they seek to deliver value to stakeholders, "it is imperative to have in place guidelines that would further strengthen the system and ensure safety and soundness of the financial institutions, both at home and offshore" (CBN Circular 2008). Key areas of regulatory concern include the potential of such rapid expansion to create opportunity and incentive for regulatory arbitrage, money laundering, and financial contagion in the host countries of these Nigerian multinational banks (Cf. UCHE 2014).

The objective of this paper is to critique the rise of these Nigerian multinational banks and to explore the operational challenges and risks associated with the emergence of such banks. To achieve its aim, this chapter is divided into four parts. Part 1 critiques the various theories that explain the practice of multinational banking while Part 2 explores the structure and history of Nigerian banking up until the 2004 bank capital increase. Part 3 analyses the emergence of Nigerian multinational banks in the context of various theories of multinational banking and critiques the regulatory risks and challenges associated with the practices of such banks. Part 4 concludes the paper.

## Why Do Banks Go Abroad?

Attempts to explain why banks go abroad to provide services is entwined with the history of international banking. The practice of cross-border banking operations, which has been linked to the emergence of international trade, commenced several centuries ago. It has for instance, been noted that "Italian bankers of the late middle ages sometimes established branches in foreign countries to assist their cross-border lending and trade finance activities" (Jones 1990: 2).

It was, however, not until the nineteenth century that multinational banking became a popular concept. The United Kingdom led the way in this regard (Jones 1993). At the beginning of World War I in 1914, for instance, "banks headquartered in Great Britain had two thousand foreign branches, and banks headquartered in France and Germany together had five hundred" (Aliber 1984: 662). This has been described as the first wave of multinational banking. The magnitude of this expansion of multinational banking at the time has been explained by Mira Wilkins (1990: 221–222) thus:

> Before the First World War a large number of banks had become multinational enterprises [...] [T]wenty-eight UK-registered banks had 1,286 foreign branches and owned agencies in 1913. In addition, certain British merchant banks had interlocking partnerships outside the United Kingdom. So, too, German, French, Belgian, Dutch, Swiss and other European Banks had salaried representatives, owned agencies, branches, subsidiaries, and interlocking partnerships abroad [...]. French and German banks in 1914 had 500 foreign branches, Canadian banks had owned agencies, branches, and subsidiary banks in the United States in 1914. By the early twentieth century, the Yokohama Specie Bank had overseas branches in Asia, the United States and Europe [...]. [T]here were not many American banks with foreign operations before 1914.

This first wave of multinational banking, however, came to an end at the beginning of World War I in 1914. "From the start of World War I to the early 1960s, regulatory controls on capital flows and convertibility reduced the importance of international banking" (Goldberg and Johnson 1990: 124).

Although the US now play an important role in the promotion of multinational banking, this is a relatively recent development. By 1913, for instance, only six US banks had branches abroad while most of the US banks, including national banks had no branches at all. By 1960, very little had changed as only "eight US banks had foreign branches, and most US banks including those in New York, still could not branch freely throughout their home state, much less across the country" (Heurtas 1990: 249–250).

Domestic banking regulation therefore prevented US banks from participating in the first phase of multinational banking. This was so despite the fact that by 1872, the size of the US economy had surpassed that of UK and by 1915,

US exports had also surpassed that of the UK (Chinn and Frankel 2008, 2007). All this changed in the 1960s when the US led the second wave of multinational banking. The reason for the emergence of this second phase of international banking, which has been termed as the "golden era", has been linked to several factors, including growth in international trade, foreign direct investments, and the Eurodollar market.[2] Another important factor for the rapid increase in US multinational banks during this "golden era" period of multinational banking was because from the 1960s, the US began to change its banking laws thus encouraging such multinational banking. In 1962, for instance, US amended its banking rules to enable "foreign branches of national banks to compete more effectively in foreign markets" (Brimmer and Dahl, 1975: 343). In 1970, it also amended its Bank Holding Companies Act to provide a regulatory framework for the international activities of the US bank holding companies. Proactively promoting cross-border US banking services was grounded in the belief that "the establishment of overseas facilities by US banks would generally promote the foreign commerce of the United States" (Ibid.).

It was as a consequence of the above changes that the scope and range of products offered by multinational banks was extensively expanded during the period.[3] Based on the histories and experiences of banks and countries that played an active part across all periods of multinational banking (medieval, first wave, and second wave eras), various theories, which sometimes overlap, have emerged in an attempt to explain the main causative factors of multinational banking in the world.

The most pervasive explanation for the emergence of multinational banks is that banks normally follow their clients abroad (Williams 2002). This theory, which is also known as "customer-driven internationalization" (Engwall and Wallenstal 1988: 148) is so widespread that it has been referred to as the conventional hypothesis (Cf. Williams 2002). In the nineteenth century, the

2 The rationale for the powerful expansion in multinational banking "lay in the ability of large commercial banks of Western countries to exploit the regulatory asymmetries that developed within the international system. A strong incentive was the rapidly expanding demand for services that stemmed from the sustained growth of trade and multinational corporation's substantial foreign direct investments. The emergence of the Eurodollar (and other Eurocurrencies) market, a truly international money market for time deposits denominated in foreign currencies, laid the foundation for the ensuing explosion of international lending, either as medium term bank loans or long term bond issues" (Battilossi 2000: 158).

3 Currently, multinational banking services include: dealing in foreign currencies, derivative securities, gold and precious metals; borrowing and lending in foreign currencies; provision of trade finance; trading in foreign securities markets; and provision of corporate finance across borders (Williams 2009: 2).

assumption was that domestic banks that operated in host economies of multinational firms were poorly equipped to service the local finance needs of multinational businesses (Aliber 1984). This theory made sense especially during the colonial period when British banks, for example, followed the expansion of British trade and government across the colonies. This was at least in part because there was a dearth of institutions that provided banking services in such colonies. The fact that the foreign branches of British multinational banks were overwhelmingly concentrated in developing economies during the first wave of multinational banking further validate this point (Jones 1990).

The above theory has, however, since been modified to suggest that the main incentive why banks follow their customers abroad is to ensure that they do not lose such customers to other banks. In other words, the "modified rationale is that banks follow their domestic customers abroad to reduce the likelihood that they might lose their business to host country banks" (Aliber 1984: 664). This modification has been characterised as "defensive expansion" (Williams 2002: 127).

A second reason why banks go abroad is to exploit new market opportunities. In the US, for instance, it has been noted that the sheer size of the economy and its attendant investment opportunities constitute major attractions for foreign banks eager to expand their services abroad (Cf. Goldberg and Saunders 1981). This theory is also supported by banking developments during the colonial era. This explains why some of the banks that were established in the developing economies did not have operations in the UK although they were registered there. Adapting the concept developed by Mira Wilkins (1988), such banks can be referred to as "free standing multinational banks." The main focus of such banks was simply to explore opportunities of introducing banks in localities where such banks did not exist and thus facilitate trade in and with such jurisdictions. As early as 1879, for instance, colonial business interests had identified such opportunities in British West Africa. Along these lines, the proposal for the Bank of West Africa (which never commenced operations) noted that no country at the time offered a better opportunity for establishing a highly profitable Banking business than the British West African Colonies, "where the benefits of a Bank are wholly wanting, and the facilities of trade are restricted to a few large merchants whose interests are naturally adverse to each other, but who will gladly avail themselves of its advantages when established" (Quoted in Uche, 1999: 671).

A third reason that explains the expansion of banks abroad is home and host country regulation of the banking environment. As explained above, home country restrictive regulations prevented American banks from participating in the first wave of international banking which occurred before World

War I. Examples of countries, aside from the US, that have in the past restricted their banks' expansion abroad are Sweden and Japan (Cf. Hultman and McGee 1989). At another level, it has also been argued that "in part, the rapid growth of offshore banking results from efforts to circumvent the costs of national regulation" (Aliber 1976: 6).

Another reason why banks go abroad is to find and exploit additional financial resources. This has been referred to as "provider driven internationalization." Proponents of this theory argue that banks are likely to concentrate their foreign entries in cities that are well known for their intensive financial activity in order to gain access to capital (Hellman 1994). In other words, decisions on where banks open offices abroad are likely to be influenced by the level of financial activity in such cities (Engwall and Wallenstal 1988). The emergence of this theory has been facilitated by the popularity of major financial centers like New York and London as places for the establishment of overseas offices and affiliates of foreign multinational banks.

In general, however, the experiences of various jurisdictions with respect to the development of international banking is based on their various specificities and local histories. Historically, too, the reasoning behind the provision of banking services outside the home country of multinational banks is not static and thus it can change over time. Irrespective of whatever may have motivated a bank to establish subsidiaries abroad, such subsidiaries are always at liberty to explore the possibilities for expanding their services to host country firms and businesses. In other words, multinational banking subsidiaries established to service the interests of their home country businesses abroad may over time begin to provide banking services to host country businesses. With respect to the dynamic strategies of non-US banks operating in the US, this has been asserted that initially "these US based offices of foreign banks served primarily the credit and other banking needs of US affiliates of their home country customers." This gradually changed over time. In "recent years, many foreign banks have expanded their customer base by actively soliciting business from US companies, competing in terms of price and quality of service" (Terrell 1993: 913). In the next section, we will critique the origins and structure of the Nigerian banking system prior to the 2004 consolidation exercise.

## The Origins and Structure of the Nigerian Banking System

It is an established historical fact that British businesses played an important role in the establishment of British colonies across the world (Cf. Tignor 1998: 18, 1987: 479; Cain and Hopkins 1980: 463–465). Based on the above, it is not surprising that the conventional theory of multinational banking, which suggests that banks follow their customer abroad, can, at least to some extent, be applied to the establishment of pioneer British multinational banks in Nigeria[4] like the Bank of British West Africa (BBWA) and Barclays Bank (Dominion, Colonial, and Overseas).[5] This explains why such British multinational banks seldom established operations in territories without British commercial interests.

The international business focus of the British banks, however, led to complaints and protests of discrimination by Africans and culminated in the establishment of indigenous banks (Cf. Newlyn and Rowan 1954; Ayida 1960; Ajibola 1986; Brown 1966; Onoh 1982). These indigenous banks were, however, poorly capitalised, poorly staffed, and poorly managed and were thus no match for the foreign banks. Despite this, however, the first indigenous bank to be established in Nigeria, the Industrial and Commercial Bank Limited, which was established in 1929 became the first Nigerian international bank. It was established by some Nigerian and Gold Coast (Ghanaian) businessmen and formally opened for business in Lagos in 1929. The bank subsequently set up a branch in Accra (Hopkins 1966). It is instructive that, at the time, the 1906 Gold Coast Companies Act prevented the establishment of any local company to carry out any form of banking operations (Uche 1997). It was therefore plausible that the Industrial and Commercial Bank opened a branch in Accra, as opposed to registering a local bank, in order to circumvent existing regulations in the Gold Coast at the time, which prevented indigenous companies from establishing banks and providing banking services in the colony. The Industrial and Commercial Bank was, however, short lived and collapsed in 1931 (Azikiwe 1956).

Several indigenous banks were subsequently established. The enactment of the 1952 banking Ordinance, however, ensured that most of these indigenous banks failed. Between 1952 and 1953, for instance, 17 of such indigenous banks collapsed (Nwankwo 1986, 1990). Despite the establishment of the indigenous banks in Nigeria, foreign banks continued to dominate the Nigerian banking space (Cf. Rowan 1952). This began to change with the promulgation of the Companies Decree of 1968, which specifically required foreign companies, including banks to be incorporated and registered in Nigeria. The consequence of this was that Nigerian branches of foreign banks had to be incorporated in Nigeria as distinct legal entities. The main objective of the decree was to "bring

---

4 As already mentioned, the strategy of such multinational banks also included providing banking services to British multinationals in colonial territories where such services were limited.

5 For a detailed history of these banks, please see (Fry 1976) and Barclays Bank (1938).

under the control of the Nigerian government 'local' subsidiaries of foreign firms" (Ogbuagu 1983: 248). Prior to this requirement, the issue of foreign banks in Nigeria having branches or subsidiaries abroad did not arise. Even with the requirement for such banks to be registered in Nigeria as distinct legal entities, there was also little need for such banks to operate branches/representative offices abroad. This was because they were fully integrated in the business strategy of their parent multinational banks. This explains, as would be seen later, why the emergence of Nigerian multinational banks has been championed by locally owned and controlled banks rather than foreign banks.

In 1972, the Nigerian Government promulgated the Indigenization Decree. This enabled the Nigerian Government to acquire 40 per cent of the shareholding of foreign banks operating in the country. All the foreign banks agreed to this proposal, except for First National City Bank (USA), which decided to withdraw from the Nigerian market (Uche 2012). The government subsequently amended the Indigenisation Decree in 1977. This enabled it to increase its shareholding in such foreign banks to 60 per cent. The consequence of the above policy was that control of these foreign banks was effectively put into the hands of the Nigerian Government. This weakened the relationship between the foreign banks and their Nigerian affiliates. Some of the concerned foreign banks reacted to this loss of control by changing the names of their Nigerian operations. For example, Barclays Bank changed its name to Union Bank in 1979 (Cf. Uche 2012).

The indigenisation strategy of the Nigerian Government however began to change with the downturn in the economy, which was caused by dwindling oil prices and sub-optimal use of the country's resources. Under pressure from the International Monetary Fund, the Babangida administration in 1986 adopted the Structural Adjustment Programme (SAP). Specifically, SAP was designed to achieve balance of payment viability by altering and restructuring the production and consumption patterns of the economy, eliminating price distortions, reducing the heavy dependence on consumer goods imports and crude oil exports, enhancing the non-oil export base, rationalise the role of the public sector, accelerate the growth potential of the private sector, and achieve sustainable growth. To achieve the above objectives, the main strategies of the programme were the adoption of a market-determined exchange rate for the Naira, the deregulation of external trade and payments arrangements, reductions in price and administrative controls and more reliance on market forces as a major determinant of economic activity (CBN Briefs 95/03).

The adoption of SAP therefore meant that the government had to relinquish its controlling interest in most banks. Furthermore, the licensing process for new banks was liberalised leading to increased competition in the industry.

This new spirit of competition meant that the decision as to whether banks should fail or not was now to be determined by market forces.

Despite the laudable objectives of SAP, the government was unable to adopt a single market determined exchange rate for the Naira. This was mainly because it was unwilling to totally leave the fate of its currency to the forces of demand and supply. Most of the managed foreign exchange rate systems the government experimented with resulted in a dual exchange rates: the official rate and the parallel market (black market) rate. This positioned banks, the agents of the managed exchange rate system, to make illegal arbitrage profits simply by buying foreign exchange at the official rate and selling at black market rate. This defective government policy was mistaken by many as proof of banking profitability. This further opened the floodgate of applications for banking licences. Between 1985 and 1993, for instance, the number of licensed banks operating in Nigeria rose from 41 to 120. Most of these new banks were no more than currency exchange centres. The deregulation of the economy coupled with loopholes and, sometimes, outright evasion of the law, made it possible for some of these banks to survive simply by buying and selling foreign exchange (Uche and Ehikwe 2001).

Clearly, such banks, which were essentially focused on exploiting arbitrage opportunities that arose from government policies, had no need to expand their services to overseas territories. The government, however, subsequently removed most of the distortions in the foreign exchange market. This greatly reduced the arbitrage opportunities available to banks in currency trading. The financial well-being of these new banks was further complicated by the government decision, in 1995, to relax the investment laws for foreigners. With this development, foreigners were allowed to wholly own financial institutions in Nigeria. Some of the foreign banks that dominated the pre-indigenisation banking arena in Nigeria have now returned in full force. For instance, Barclays Bank, which used to be part of what is now Union Bank, is back in the country as a distinct bank that is 100 percent foreign owned. Standard Chartered Bank, which was part of what is now First Bank Plc, has also returned, as a distinct, wholly foreign-owned institution. Even Citi Bank, which, prior to the 1995 liberalisation, owned 40 per cent shares in the Nigerian International Bank, has since taken up majority interest in the bank and renamed it Citi Bank Nigeria. These fully owned foreign banks have little need for expanding their operations abroad. As subsidiaries of big multinational banks they are content with servicing the local interests of the multinational companies that are allied with their parent bank. In some cases, Nigerian businesses aspiring to internationalise their operations also find the services of such international banks attractive. The consequence of this increased competition from the strengthened foreign banks and the unstable macroeconomic environment sometimes coupled with poor service rendition by these indigenous banks was the collapse of several of the newly established indigenous banks. In 1998 alone, for instance, 26 banks were liquidated (Beck et al. 2005).

Although the Central Bank continuously tried to increase the minimum share capital of these banks as a way of ensuring banking stability, high levels of inflation ensured that such policies achieved limited results. The increases in the minimum share capital requirement for Nigerian banks over the years have been summarised thus:

> By 1988, the Central Bank had increased the minimum share capital base to 6 million [Naira] for merchant banks and 10 million for commercial banks. Uncontrolled inflation ensured that these new requirements were raised again within two years to 12 million and 20 million for merchant banks and commercial banks, respectively. In 1991, the Banks and Other Financial Institutions Decree [...] raised share capital to 40 million and 50 million for merchant banks and commercial banks, respectively [...]. By 1997, spiralling inflation had again forced the Central Bank to increase the minimum share capital requirement for banks. It was raised tenfold [N500 million] [...]. In 1999, the minimum share capital requirement for new banks was raised to N 1 billion [...]. Yet, by 2003, inflation, that bogeyman of the economy, had again materially diluted the real value of bank share capital and so the Central Bank [raised] [...] the minimum share capital requirement to 2 billion for new banks.
>
> OGOWEWO and UCHE 2006: 169

In July 2004, within a year of announcing that banks had to increase their share capital to N2 billion, the Central Bank again increased the minimum share capital requirement for banks to N25 billion. In the next section, we will argue that it was this singular regulation that extensively influenced the rapid emergence of Nigerian multinational banks.

## The New Era of Nigerian Multinational Banks

As already mentioned, in July 2004, the CBN announced the intention to radically increase the minimum share capital of Nigerian banks from N2 billion to N25 billion. The main essence of this increase was to encourage mergers and acquisitions in the Nigerian banking arena in order to create mega banks capable of competing in the provision of banking services in the global arena. The immediate consequence of the above policy was the shrinking in the number of Nigerian banks from 89 to 24 (Table 17.1). It was not surprising that all foreign owned banks survived this new policy without merging with other banks. This is because they "relied on capital injections from the parent company to meet the capital requirements" (Barros and Caporale 2012: 244).

Unlike the foreign banks, most of the indigenous banks were forced into mergers and acquisitions in order to meet the new capital requirement. A few of the indigenous banks like Zenith Bank and Guarantee Trust Bank were, however, able to meet the new capital requirement by raising funds internally or though the Nigerian Capital Market. These banks therefore did not need to merge with other banks (Cf. Table 17.1).

TABLE 17.1 *Post consolidation banks and the merged institutions*

| S/N | Name of post consolidation bank | Merged institutions |
|---|---|---|
| 1 | Access Bank | Access Bank, Capital Bank Int'l and Marina Bank |
| 2 | Afribank | Afribank and Afribank Int'l (Merchant) |
| 3 | Diamond Bank | Diamond Bank and Lion Bank |
| 4 | Ecobank | Ecobank |
| 5 | Equatorial Trust Bank | Equatorial Trust Bank & Devcom Bank |
| 6 | First City Monument Bank | FCMB, Cop. Development Bank & NAMB Limited |
| 7 | Fidelity Bank | Fidelity Bank, FSB International Bank & Manny Bank |
| 8 | First Bank | First Bank of Nigeria, FBN Merchant Bankers, & MBC International Bank |
| 9 | First Inland Bank | First Atlantic Bank, Inland Bank, IMB International Bank & NUB International Bank. |
| 10 | Guarantee Trust Bank | Guarantee Trust Bank |
| 11 | Stanbic IBTC Bank | IBTC, Chartered Bank & Regent Bank |
| 12 | Intercontinental Bank | Intercontinental Bank, Equity Bank, Global and Gateway Bank |
| 13 | Citi Bank | Nigerian International Bank (City Group) |
| 14 | Oceanic Bank | Oceanic Bank & International Trust Bank |
| 15 | Platinum Habib Bank | Platinum Bank & Habib Bank |
| 16 | Skye Bank | Prudent Bank, EIB International, Cooperative Bank, Bond Bank & Reliance Bank |
| 17 | Spring Bank | Citizens International Bank, Guardian Express Bank, ACB International Bank, Omegabank, Fountain Trust Bank & Trans International Bank |

TABLE 17.1 *Post consolidation banks and the merged institutions* (cont.)

| S/N | Name of post consolidation bank | Merged institutions |
|---|---|---|
| 18 | Standard Chartered Bank | Standard Chartered Bank |
| 19 | Sterling Bank | Magnum Trust Bank, NAL Bank, Indo-Nigeria Bank & Trust Bank of Africa |
| 20 | United Bank of Africa | United Bank of Africa & Standard Trust Bank |
| 21 | Union Bank | Union Bank, Union Merchant Bank, Universal Trust Bank & Broad Bank |
| 22 | Unity Bank | Intercity Bank, First Interstate Bank, Tropical Commercial Bank, Pacific Bank, Centre Point Bank, NNB International Bank, Bank of the North, Societe Bancaire & New Africa Bank |
| 23 | Wema Bank | Wema & National Bank |
| 24 | Zenith Bank | Zenith Bank |

SOURCE: OKAFOR ET AL. (2012: 82–83).

Despite the dramatic increase in share capital requirement, most foreign banks continued to focus solely on the Nigerian market. As already explained, integration into their parent bank international strategy ensured this. The scenario for Nigerian banks was however different. Prior to 2004, only five Nigerian banks had branches, representative offices or affiliates abroad. These were Afribank (Republic of Ireland 1988); Finbank (Gambia 1997); First Bank (UK 2002); Guarantee Trust Bank (Gambia 2000; Liberia 2002; and Sierra Leone 2002), United Bank for Africa (New York 1984) and Union Bank (South Africa 1996) (Cf. Table 17.2). The 2004 increase in the share capital of banks, however, encouraged such banks to aggressively seek opportunities for the expansion of their services abroad.

The result is that 11 Nigerian banks currently have 60 subsidiaries, one branch and three representative offices abroad (Cf. Table 17.2). Most of these subsidiaries are based in Africa. Only eight Nigerian banks have subsidiaries outside Africa, of which, seven are in the United Kingdom. These include: Access Bank (UK 2008); Mainstream Bank (Republic of Ireland 1988); FCMB (UK 2009); First Bank of Nigeria (UK 2002); Guaranty Trust Bank (UK 2007); UBA (UK 2008); Union Bank (UK 2004); and Zenith Bank (UK 2007). Given that London is a major global financial centre, it is not surprising that one of the main banking business focuses of these UK subsidiaries of Nigerian banks is "to

TABLE 17.2 *Nigerian bank branches/correspondence offices/ subsidiaries*

| S/N | Bank | Country presence | Year of approval/ establishment | Date of closure |
|---|---|---|---|---|
| 1 | Access Bank Plc | Côte d'Ivoire | sep-07 | feb-14 |
| | | Democratic Republic of the Congo | feb-08 | N/A |
| | | Rwanda | mar-08 | N/A |
| | | Sierra Leone | may-07 | N/A |
| | | The Gambia | aug-06 | N/A |
| | | Ghana | dec-08 | N/A |
| | | United Kingdom | aug-08 | N/A |
| | | Zambia | feb-08 | N/A |
| | | Burundi | feb-08 | mrt-14 |
| 2 | Afribank/Mainstream Bank Plc | Republic of Ireland | 1988 | N/A |
| 3 | Diamond Bank Plc | Cote D'Ivoire | mar-11 | N/A |
| | | Senegal | apr-11 | N/A |
| | | Togo | may-11 | N/A |
| | | UK | jun-13 | N/A |
| | | *Benin* | *nov-99* | N/A |
| 4 | FCMB Plc | United Kingdom | sep-09 | N/A |
| | | South Africa (Rep. Off.) | 2010 | jun-14 |
| 5 | Finbank Plc | Gambia | jan-97 | Divested in 2014 |
| 6 | First Bank of Nig. Plc | Congo DRC | oct-11 | N/A |
| | | ICB Ghana | oct-13 | N/A |
| | | ICB Gambia | oct-13 | N/A |
| | | ICB Guinea | oct-13 | N/A |
| | | ICB Sierra Leone | oct-13 | N/A |
| | | ICB Senegal | may-14 | N/A |
| | | United Kingdom | 2-nov | N/A |
| | | South Africa (Rep office) | 2004 | N/A |
| | | China Rep. Office | 2009 | N/A |
| | | Abu Dhabi Rep. Office | 2011 | N/A |
| 7 | Guaranty Trust Bank Plc | Gambia | dec-00 | N/A |
| | | Ghana | jan-05 | N/A |
| | | Kenya (Fina Bank) | dec-13 | N/A |
| | | Uganda (Fina Bank) | dec-13 | N/A |
| | | Rwanda (Fina Bank) | dec-13 | N/A |

TABLE 17.2 *Nigerian bank branches/correspondence offices/ subsidiaries*

| S/N | Bank | Country presence | Year of approval/ establishment | Date of closure |
|---|---|---|---|---|
| | | Liberia | apr-02 | N/A |
| | | Sierra Leone | feb-02 | N/A |
| | | United Kingdom | jun-07 | N/A |
| 8 | Intercontinental Bank Plc | Ghana | dec-05 | Merged with Access Bank Ghana |
| | | United Kingdom | jun-08 | jun-13 |
| 9 | Oceanic Bank Plc | China (Rep Office) | | 2009 |
| | | Cameroon | | 2009 |
| | | Gambia | jul-08 | jan-11 |
| | | Sao Tomé and Príncipe | | Divested in 2011 |
| 10 | Bank PHB/ Keystone Bank | Gambia | jan-08 | Under Administration since May 2014 |
| | | Liberia | mar-04 | N/A |
| | | Sierra Leone | jun-09 | N/A |
| | | Uganda | jan-09 | Divested in Feb 2015 |
| 11 | Skye Bank Plc | Sierra Leone | sep-08 | N/A |
| | | The Gambia | jul-09 | N/A |
| | | Republic of Guinea | mar-10 | N/A |
| 12 | United Bank for Africa Plc | United States (branch) | 1984 | N/A |
| | | United Kingdom | jan-08 | N/A |
| | | Benin | dec-08 | N/A |
| | | Burkina Faso | sep-08 | N/A |
| | | Cameroon | aug-07 | N/A |
| | | Chad | mar-08 | N/A |
| | | Congo Brazzaville | apr-08 | N/A |
| | | Congo Kinshasa (DRC) | apr-08 | N/A |
| | | Côte d'Ivoire | aug-07 | N/A |
| | | Gabon | apr-08 | N/A |
| | | Ghana | JULY 2005 | N/A |
| | | Guinea | apr-08 | N/A |
| | | Kenya | apr-08 | N/A |
| | | Liberia | aug-07 | N/A |
| | | Mozambique | apr-08 | N/A |
| | | Senegal | mar-08 | N/A |
| | | Sierra Leone | jul-08 | N/A |

| S/N | Bank | Country presence | Year of approval/ establishment | Date of closure |
|---|---|---|---|---|
| | | Tanzania | apr-08 | N/A |
| | | Uganda | may-08 | N/A |
| | | Zambia | apr-08 | N/A |
| | Union Bank Plc. | United Kingdom | sep-04 | N/A |
| | | Benin | aug-04 | Under Administration since 2012 |
| | | South Africa (Rep. Off.) | jun-96 | N/A |
| 14 | Zenith Bank Plc | Gambia | feb-09 | N/A |
| | | Ghana | sep-05 | N/A |
| | | Sierra Leone | jan-08 | N/A |
| | | South Africa (Rep. Off.) | mar-07 | N/A |
| | | United Kingdom | mar-07 | N/A |

SOURCE: CENTRAL BANK OF NIGERIA (MARCH 2015).

source international capital into Nigerian projects and businesses" (Cf. FCMB Annual Report 2009: 15).[6]

Despite the increasing numbers of Nigerian multinational banks in the UK, there is little risk that such banks can constitute a systemic threat to the UK banking system. This is because of their relatively small size in comparison to the UK banking system. Despite this, the UK authorities have been increasingly enhancing the regulatory structure around such banks. In 2004, for instance, the UK regulatory authorities required that all banks operating in the country had to be fully incorporated and regulated as UK banks. This forced all Nigerian banks that had branches in the UK to incorporate and register such branches as distinct legal entities in the UK. In the case of Union Bank Plc, the transformation of its London branch to a fully owned subsidiary has been explained thus:

> Following recent reforms in the United Kingdom banking legislations, the Financial Services Authority directed that our bank's London branch be incorporated as a fully-fledged subsidiary of the parent bank, locally incorporated in the United Kingdom [...]. The full banking status of the London Branch further strengthens Union Bank's off-shore banking capabilities by creating an excellent interface for consummating cross border banking transactions such as remittances, project financing,

6 See also Guarantee Trust Bank Annual Report (2012: 42).

> international payments and correspondent banking relationships especially between corporate and private individuals in Nigerian and their business partners in the EU countries and indeed in the rest of the world. Furthermore, subsidiarisation as part of Union Bank's growth strategy, is the beginning of the presence of Union Bank of Nigeria Plc in other strategic global financial centres in the drive to strengthen our regional and global presence on the banking scene.
>
> Union Bank Annual Report and Accounts 2005: 17

One immediate consequence of this requirement is that it brought the activities of such foreign banks fully under the regulatory purview of the UK Government and the European Commission (Cf. FBN UK Limited Annual Report and Accounts 2013).

The fact that the size of Nigerian banks is immaterial in the context of the UK banking system, coupled with the fact that they are now fully regulated by UK authorities clearly reduces the potential risks that Nigerian banks could pose to the UK economy. The same cannot be said of the subsidiary of Nigerian banks that have proliferated in smaller African countries and in some cases are prominent in the provision of banking services in such countries.

As already mentioned, most of the subsidiaries of Nigerian banks are located in Africa. By far the most popular countries for Nigerian banks looking to set up subsidiaries abroad have been the West African countries of Sierra Leone, Liberia, Ghana, and the Gambia. All the above countries are members of the West African Monetary Zone. With the exception of Liberia, all the above countries are also former British colonies. Currently, five Nigerian banks have subsidiaries in Sierra Leone and Ghana respectively while four Nigerian banks have subsidiaries in the Gambia. Also, three Nigerian banks have subsidiaries in Liberia.

For these smaller countries, the presence of Nigerian banks is more profound. A systematic study of the annual accounts of the concerned banks around the period of their establishment in other African states shows that the establishment of the African subsidiaries of Nigerian banks have been driven more by opportunities within the host country economies than by other reasons. There is little evidence that these Nigerian multinational banks have been encouraged by their Nigerian customers to expand to such countries. This point was perhaps best made in the 2008 Annual Report of UBA, which currently has subsidiaries in 19 countries, thus:

> Twelve months ago our international operations extended only to the USA and Ghana. We are now operational in eight African countries as

> well as the USA and the UK. At 30 September 2008 we had over 200 000 customers outside of Nigeria and 55 branches. Continuing our African regionalisation strategy is crucial for three principal reasons: (1). It diversifies our asset and revenue base to reduce risk. (2). Many of these countries are growing more rapidly than Nigeria and frequently with much lower levels of banking sophistication. There are real opportunities to deliver services developed in Nigeria, after suitable adaptation, to our neighbouring countries. (3). Trade between African nations is becoming more important as well and we want to ensure that we are there to facilitate growth in trade and investment flows across Africa.
>
> UBA Annual Report 2008: 28

The 2007 Annual Report of the Guarantee Trust Bank similarly noted that "Guarantee Trust Bank Ghana Limited was established to take advantage of the rapid transformation of the Ghanaian economy" (GTB Annual Report 2007: 7).

It is as a consequence of the above strategy that Nigerian multinational banks in these countries compete with local banks for the patronage of local businesses and residents. The result is that most of the subsidiaries of the Nigerian multinational banks in West Africa have established several branches in their host countries. In 2012, for instance, Guaranty Trust Bank (Ghana) Limited established 6 new branches bringing its total branch network in the country to 22. "This is consistent with the growth trend experienced by other subsidiaries such as Guaranty Trust Bank (Sierra Leone) which expanded its network to 11 branches while Guaranty Trust Bank (Gambia) Limited increased its business outlets to 16" (2012 Annual Report: 35). Similarly, UBA Ghana has 25 branches across Ghana. Nigerian banks have indeed become major players in the provision of financial services to their host businesses and citizens in West Africa. Recently, for instance, the Ghanaian High Commissioner to Nigeria, Vincent Azumah publicly acknowledged the importance of the services Nigerian banks provide to the Ghanaian economy (*Leadership Newspaper*, 9 March 2015).

The prominent position occupied by Nigerian multinational banks in the provision of banking services in Gambia, Sierra Leone, and Liberia is similar to that in Ghana. Beyond West Africa, Nigerian banks have also adopted similar strategies. When UBA established a subsidiary in Zambia in 2010, for instance, the bank made it explicit that it was in the country "as a vehicle to ensure that Africans have their own bank that can assist in empowering indigenous Africans in growing intra-African trade and trade between Africa and the rest of the world" (*Lusaka Times*, 4 March 2010).

The emergence of offshore subsidiaries of Nigerian banks however raises serious regulatory issues for the home and host countries of such multinational banks (Cf. Aliber 1975). Given the size and importance of Nigerian financial institutions in these jurisdictions, banking crises in Nigeria could easily be exported to host country jurisdictions. While this has not yet happened, bank failures in Nigeria have impacted the operations of its foreign subsidiaries. In 2009, for instance, the revocation of the licenses of some Nigerian multinational banks also led to the closure of some of their foreign subsidiaries. After losing its licence in Nigeria in 2009, for instance, Oceanic bank closed its subsidiaries in Cameroun and the Gambia. It also divested from its São Tomé and Principe operations.

Nigeria has since recognised these risks and the CBN has now signed bilateral Memoranda of Understanding (MoU) with: the Bank of Ghana; Commission Bancaire de l'Afrique Centrale (COBAC); China Banking and Regulatory Commission; Bank of Uganda; Financial Services Authority (FSA); South Africa Reserve Bank; National Bank of Rwanda; Bank of Zambia; Central Bank of Kenya; Banque Centrale des Etals de l'Afrique (BCEAO); Central Bank of the Gambia; Bank of Sierra Leone; West African Monetary Zone (Gambia, Ghana, Guinea & Sierra Leone); Bank Negara Malaysia; Central Bank of Liberia; and Central Bank of Guinea. These MoUs, however, do not cover specific aspects of crisis management and resolution (IMF 2013).

Most of the above agreements have since been operationalised (Cf. CBN Annual Report 2011). In 2013, for instance, 15 joint examinations were conducted on off-shore subsidiaries of Nigerian banks with host supervisors in The Gambia, Ghana, Guinea, Liberia, and Sierra Leone under the Harmonised Supervisory Programme in the West African Monetary Zone (WAMZ). Also, eight cross-border on-site inspections of Nigerian banks were carried out in foreign jurisdictions outside the WAMZ (CBN Draft Annual Economic Report 2013). Despite such cooperation arrangements, problems remain (Cf. IMF 2010). Subsidiaries of Nigerian banks in Africa and beyond have been known to breach host country regulations especially with respect to money laundering. On 30 April 2008, for instance, The Financial Crimes Enforcement Network (FinCEN) and the Office of the Comptroller of the Currency (OCC) fined the New York branch of UBA $US 15 million for violations of the Bank Secrecy Act (BSA). It was specifically determined that the branch failed to implement an adequate anti-money laundering programme that was designed to "identify and report transactions that exhibited indicia of money laundering or other suspicious activity involving approximately $197 million in suspicious transactions." The OCC then concluded that a "financial institution that recklessly disregards its obligations under the Bank Secrecy Act and continues to operate without an effective anti-money laundering program, despite repeated warnings and a business focus on areas of recognized high risk, should expect to be penalized" (Financial Crimes Enforcement Network 2008).

In the United Kingdom, the Financial Conduct Authority (FCA) in 2013 fined Guaranty Trust Bank (UK) Ltd £525,000 "for failings in its anti-money laundering (AML) controls for high risk customers between May 2008 and June 2010" (Financial Conduct Authority, 2013). Also, on 23 July 2012, Bank of Ghana suspended Access Bank (Ghana) from the Foreign Exchange Market for six months. This was because the bank engaged in the "externalization of various sums in favour of a company which had no account relationship with the bank and, in another instance, in favour of a company without any documentation. The transfers were made without the documentation required by the Foreign Exchange Act and Guidelines" (*Ghana Business News*, 23 July 2012).

Nigerian multinational banks have also had to contend with the increased share capital requirement in various host countries especially in Africa. Since the beginning of the current decade, several African countries, including Sierra Leone, Uganda, Kenya, Tanzania, Ghana, and Zambia have raised the minimum share capital requirement for banks operating in their jurisdictions. Initially, Nigerian banks were able to raise money at home to meet these capital requirements. In 2012, however, CBN expressed concern that given the lull in capital markets globally, including Nigeria, "these increased capital requirements have exerted pressure on the capital bases of local banks, ultimately weighing on their profitability and competitiveness" (Euromoney 2012). The CBN therefore gave "the banks three options: (1) raise fresh capital from the offshore capital markets via private placements or public offerings; (2) pursue a merger or acquisition; or (3) if external capital raisings fail, submit a strategy for exiting the relevant foreign jurisdictions not later than 30 June 2012" (Ibid.).[7] This policy has at least in part been responsible for the withdrawal of some Nigerian multinational banks from some of their subsidiaries abroad. In

7 This policy has been criticised on the grounds that it is "predicated on the assumption that banks do not understand their own commercial self-interest and would transfer capital where there is no business case to do so. Transfer of capital overseas would however already be expected to be a topic of discussion between a bank and its supervisor. Existing prudential requirements already grant the CBN discretion to refuse outflows of capital. On the other hand, enforcing this directive risks undermining the goodwill and trust of host authorities necessary to strengthen home-host cooperation and coordination, and in that regard may cause a bigger problem for Nigerian banks. In any case, this circular would not prevent the Nigerian operations of subsidiaries of foreign banks, including regional banks, from moving capital upstream to headquarters or to other subsidiaries on this foreign parent" (IMF and the World Bank 2013: 8–9).

March 2014, for instance, Access Bank closed its subsidiary in Burundi while Keystone Bank sold its interest in its Ugandan subsidiary in February 2015.

Keystone Bank's subsidiary in the Gambia has also been under administration since May 2014. At the time, the Central Bank of The Gambia (CBG) also took over the subsidiary of Access Bank in the country. According to the CBG, "the move is meant to stabilize and bring sanity to The Gambia's Nigerian dominated banking industry" (*Star Africa*, 6 May 2014). One week later, the takeover of Access Bank was rescinded. This was because investors in Access Bank's Gambian unit promptly "injected over $15 million to recapitalize and take back control of the bank after it was briefly nationalized" (*Reuters*, 13 May 2014).

Aside from the above regulatory issues, Nigeria's reputation as a bastion for fraud and corruption sometimes hinders the ability of its multinational banks to provide financial services abroad.[8] Aside from the fact that such negative reputation normally make potential customers wary, some Nigerian civil society groups have also used this as a basis for actively campaigning against the operations of some of these Nigerian multinational banks abroad. In 2008, for instance, some members of the SaveNigeria Group, demonstrated at the London subsidiaries of GTB and Zenith. They stayed in front of the bank to hand "out flyers warning customers and the public against the risk of entrusting their money to money laundering operations called Nigerian banks" (Change Nigeria 2008).

Despite these difficulties, the services provided by Nigerian multinational banks have continued to contribute positively to the economic development of their host economies especially in Africa. Although regulation was the single most important causative factor in the emergence of Nigerian international banks, many of these banks, especially those operating in Africa, have been exploiting the business and economic opportunities in their host economies. The consequence of increased competitive pressures from Nigerian banks is the emergence of more efficient local banks. In the case of Ghana, for instance, it has been explained that many of the traditional local banks "responded to the innovative products and competition brought by the foreign banks by adopting a strategic rethink, and reshaped their focus and direction in order to be attractive to customers" (*Modern Ghana*, 19 June 2008). For the cross-border activities of Nigerian multinational banks to be sustainable and mutually beneficial to their home and host countries in the long run, the home and host country regulators of such banks must continue to cooperate so as to ensure that unhealthy and unethical banking practices are punished and discouraged (Alade 2014).

8 For a recent detailed account on the depth of fraud and corruption in Nigeria, see Ellis (2016).

## Conclusion

This chapter has argued that the single most important factor that explains the emergence of Nigerian multinational banks over time has been home country regulation. It is this that facilitated the quest by Nigerian banks to expand their services to other jurisdictions. Specifically, it was the 2004 decision by the CBN to increase the minimum paid up capital requirement for Nigerian banks from N2 billion to N25 billion that necessitated the aggressive expansion of the services of compliant Nigerian banks abroad. The findings in this chapter therefore show that the conventional hypothesis which suggests that multinational banks normally follow their customer abroad is not the main reason for the emergence of Nigerian multinational banks.

Based on the above, it is not surprising that in several African countries, subsidiaries of Nigerian banks compete with host country banks for the provision of financial services to local businesses. Although the advent of these multinational banks have raised regulatory concerns in the banking arena of home and host countries, these have been mitigated by the increased cross-border regulatory cooperation by regulators in the home and host countries of such multinational banks. Continued vigilance and cooperation by the regulatory authorities in both jurisdictions is therefore a necessary condition for the continued and sustainable provision of cross border banking services by Nigerian multinational banks.

## References

Ajibola, W. (1986). "The Politics of Banking Development". In: O. Oyejide & A. Soyode (eds), *Commercial Banking in Nigeria*, Ibadan: Unibadan Publishing Consultants.

Alade, S. (2014). "Cross-border Expansion of Nigerian Banks: Has it Improved the Continent's Regulatory and Supervisory Frameworks?" *Bank for International Settlement Research Papers* Number 76 (February).

Aliber, R. (1975). "International Banking Growth and Regulation", *California Journal of World Business*, Winter 1975, 9–15.

Aliber, R. (1976). "Towards a Theory of International Banking", *Federal Reserve Bank of San Francisco Economic Review* (Spring), 5–8.

Aliber, R. (1984). "International Banking: A Survey", *Journal of Money, Credit and Banking* 16, 661–678.

Ayida, A. (1960). "A Critical Analysis of Banking Trends in Nigeria", *Nigerian Institute of Social and Economic Research Conference Proceedings*, Ibadan: Nigerian Institute of Social and Economic Research.

Azikiwe, N. (1956). *Banking Monopoly in Nigeria*: Statement made by the Hon. Premier in the Eastern House of Assembly on 8 August 1956, Enugu, Government Press.

Barros, C. & G. Caporale. (2012). "Banking Consolidation in Nigeria, 2000–2010", *Journal of African Business*, 13, 244–252.

Battilossi, S (2000). "Financial Innovation and the Golden Ages of International Banking", *Financial History Review* 7, 141–175.

Beck, T., Cull, R. & A. Jerome. (2005). "Bank Privatization and Performance: Empirical Evidence from Nigeria", *Journal of Banking and Finance* 29, 2355–2379.

Brimmer, A. & F. Dahl. (1975). "Growth of American International banking: Implications for Public Policy", *Journal of Finance* 30, 341–363.

Brown, C. (1966). *The Nigerian Banking System*, London: George Allen and Unwin.

Cain, P. & A. Hopkins. (1980). "The Political Economy of British Expansion Overseas, 1750–1914", *The Economic History Review*, 33, 4, 463–490.

Central Bank of Nigeria (Various Years), *Annual Report*.

Central Bank of Nigeria (Various Years), *Banking Supervision Annual Report*.

Central Bank of Nigeria (2013). *Draft Annual Economic Report*.

Central Bank of Nigeria (2008). Circular to all Banks on Offshore Expansion (7 October).

Change Nigeria (2008). *Why We Target Nigerian Banks Abroad* (3 December 2008), downloaded from <http:12//www.ocnus.net/artman2/publish/Africa_8/Why_We_Traget_Nigerian_Banks_Abroad.shtml> (last accessed 4 March 2015).

Chinn, M. & J. Frankel. (2007). "Will the Euro Eventually Surpass the Dollar as Leading International Reserve Currency?" In: R. Clarida (ed.) *G7 Current Account Imbalances: Sustainability and Adjustment*, Chicago, IL: University of Chicago Press.

Chinn, M. & J. Frankel. (2008). "Why the Euro Will Rival the Dollar", *International Finance* 11, 49–73.

Ellis, S. (2016). *This Present Darkness: A History of Nigerian Organised Crime*, London: Hurst and Company.

Engwall, L. & M. Wallenstal. (1988). "Tit for Tat in Small Steps: the Internationalization of Swedish Banks", *Scandinavia Journal of Management* 4, 147–155.

*Euromoney* (2012), "New Capital Rules Twart Nigerian Banks' Regional Expansion Drive", 21 June 2012, downloaded from <http://www.euromoney.com/Article/3050097/New-capital-rules-thwart-Nigerian-banks-regional-expansion-drive.html> (last accessed on 3 November 2016).

Financial Conduct Authority (2013). "FCA fines Guaranty Trust Bank (UK) Ltd £525,000 for failures in its anti-money laundering controls", 9 August 2013, downloaded from <http://www.fca.org.uk/news/fca-fines-guaranty-trust-bank-uk-ltd> (last accessed on 8 April 2015).

Financial Crimes Enforcement Network (2008). Joint release by the Financial Crimes Enforcement Network Office of the Comptroller of the Currency (USA) dated April 28, 2008, downloaded from <http://www.fincen.gov/news_room/nr/html/20080428.html> (last accessed 7 April 2015).

First Bank of Nigeria [FBN] (UK) Limited, (Various Years). *Annual Report and Accounts.*

First City Monument Bank (FCMB). *Annual Report* (Various Years).

Fry, R. (1976). *Bankers in West Africa: The Story of the Bank of British West Africa Limited,* London: Hutchinson Press.

*Ghana Business News*, (23 July 2012), downloaded from <https://www.ghanabusinessnews.com/2012/07/23/bank-of-ghana-acts-on-foreign-exchange-offences-sanctions-access-bank-five-forex-bureaux/> (last accessed 30 April 2015).

Goldberg, L. & D. Johnson. (1990). "The Determinants of US Banking Activity Abroad", *Journal of International Money and Finance* 9, 123–137.

Goldberg, G. & A. Saunders. (1981). "The Determinants of Foreign Banking Activity in the United States", *Journal of Banking and Finance* 5, 17–32.

Hellman, P. (1994). "The Internationalization of Finnish Financial Service Companies", *International Business Review* 5, 191–208.

Heurtas, T. (1990). "US Multinational Banking: History and Prospects". In: G. Jones (ed.), *Banks as Multinationals*, London: Routledge.

Hopkins, A. (1966). "Economic Aspects of Political Movement in Nigeria and in the Gold Coast, 1918–1939", *Journal of African History* 7, 133–152.

Hultman, C. & L. McGee. (1989). "Factors Affecting Foreign Banking Presence in the US", *Journal of Banking and Finance* 13, 383–396.

International Monetary Fund (IMF) (2013). Nigeria: Financial Sector Stability Assessment, *IMF Country Report* No. 13/140 (May).

International Monetary Fund (IMF) (2010). *Resolution of Cross-Border Banks—A Proposed Framework for Enhanced Coordination* (June).

International Monetary Fund and the World Bank (2013). *Financial Sector Assessment Program: Nigeria, Banking Cross-Border Issues* (Technical Note, May).

Jones, G. (1990). "Banks as Multinationals". In: G. Jones (ed.), *Banks as Multinationals*, London: Routledge.

Jones, G. (1993). *British Multinational Banking*, Oxford: Clarendon Press.

*Leadership [Nigeria] Newspaper*. (Various Issues).

*Lusaka Times*, (4 March 2010). downloaded from <http://www.lusakatimes.com/2010/03/04/nigerias-united-bank-of-africa-spreads-to-zambia/>

*Modern Ghana* (3 December 2008). "Why We Target Nigerian Banks Abroad", downloaded from <http:12//www.ocnus.net/artman2/publish/Africa_8/Why_We_Traget_Nigerian_Banks_Abroad.shtml> (last accessed 4 March 2015).

*The Nation [Nigeria] Newspaper*. (Various Issues).

Newlyn W. & D. Rowan. (1954). *Money and Banking in British Colonial Africa*, Oxford: Oxford University Press.

Nwankwo, G. (1986). "Indigenization of Nigerian Banking" In: O. Oyejide & A. Soyode (eds), *Commercial Banking in Nigeria*, Ibadan: Unibadan Publishing Consultants.

Nwankwo, G. (1990). *Prudential Regulation of Nigerian Banking*, Lagos: University of Lagos Press.

Ogbuagu, C. (1983). "The Nigerian Indigenization Policy: Nationalism or Pragmatism", *African Affairs* 82, 241–266.

Ogowewo, T. & C. Uche. (2006). "(Mis)using Bank Share Capital as a Regulatory Tool to Force Bank Consolidations in Nigeria", *Journal of African Law*, 50, 161–186.

Okafor, C., Russell, K. & L. Lawal. (2012). "Effects of the Nigerian Banking Consolidation on Competition". In: Kojo Menyah & Joshua Abor (eds) *Finance and Development in Africa (Research in Accounting in Emerging Economies, Volume 12 Part B)*, Bradford: Emerald Group Publishing Limited, 75–96.

Onoh, J. (1982). *Money and Banking in Africa*, New York: Longman.

Osinupebi, F. (2012). "The Nigerian Bank Consolidation of 2005: A Case for Scale in Banking?" *The Heinz Journal* 9, 1–11.

*Reuters* (13 May 2014). "Access Bank Resumes Control of Gambia Unit after Nationalization", downloaded from <http://in.reuters.com/article/2014/05/12/gambia-banks-access-idINL6N0NY4XP20140512> (last accessed 8 April 2015).

Rowan, D. (1952). "Banking in Nigeria: A Study in Colonial Financial Evolution", *Banca Nazionale del Lavoro Quarterly Review* 5, 158–175.

Soludo, C. (2004). "Consolidating the Nigerian Banking Industry to Meet the Development Challenges of the 21st Century", Address by Mr Charles Chukwuma Soludo, Governor of the Central Bank of Nigeria, at the Special Meeting of the Bankers' Committee (Abuja, 6 July 2004), downloaded from <http://www.bis.org/review/r040727g.pdf> (last accessed 8 April 2015).

*Star Africa* (6 May 2014). "Gambia's Central Bank Takes over Two Nigerian Banks", downloaded from <http://en.starafrica.com/news/gambias-central-bank-takes-over-two-nigerian-banks.html> (last accessed on 8 April 2015).

Terrell, H. (1993). "US Branches and Agencies of Foreign Banks: A New Look", *Federal Reserve Bulletin* (October), 913–925.

Tignor, R., (1998). *Capitalism and Nationalism at the End of Empire: State and Business in Decolonizing Egypt, Nigeria and Kenya, 1945–1963,* Princeton. NJ: Princeton University Press.

Tignor, R. (1987). "Decolonizing and Business: The Case of Egypt", *The Journal of Modern History* 59, 479–505.

Uche, C. (1997). "Banking Scandal in a British West African Colony: The Politics of the African Continental Bank Crisis", *Financial History Review* 4, 51–68.

Uche, C. (1999). "Foreign Banks, Africans and Credit in Colonial Nigeria, c.1890–1912", *Economic History Review* 52, 669–691.

Uche, C. (2012). "British Government, British Businesses, and the Indigenization Exercise in Post-Independence Nigeria", *Business History Review* 86, 746–771.

Uche, C. (2014). "Regulation and Financial System Stability in Africa", *Journal of International Banking Law and Regulation* 29, 650–653.

Uche, C. & A. Ehikwe. (2001). "Marketing of Banking Services in Nigeria", *Journal of Financial Services Marketing* 6, 133–146.

Union Bank of Nigeria Plc (Various Years). Annual Report and Accounts.

Wilkins, M (1988). "The Free-Standing Company, 1870–1914: An Important Type of British Foreign Direct Investment", *Economic History Review* XLI, 259–282.

Wilkins, M. (1990). "Banks Over Borders: Some Evidence from Their Pre-1914 History". In: G. Jones (ed.), *Banks as Multinationals*, London: Routledge.

Williams, B. (2002). "The Defensive Expansion Approach to Multinational Banking: Evidence to Date", *Financial Markets, Institutions and Instruments* 11, 127–203.

Williams, B. (2009). *Multinational Banking and Global Capital Markets, International Economics, Finance and Trade*, downloaded from <http://www.eolss.net/sample-chapters/c13/e1-23-04-00.pdf> (last accessed 9 April 2015).

www.ingramcontent.com/pod-product-compliance
Lightning Source LLC
Chambersburg PA
CBHW071411230926
51846CB00001B/58